**I BOW MY HEAD IN ALL HUMILITY TO THE ALMIGHTY WHO BLESSED ME WITH THIS KNOWLEDGE**

**I AM INDEBTED TO MY FAMILY MEMBERS AND MY PATIENTS FOR THE TRUST AND FAITH THEY PLACED IN ME TO DO THIS WORK**

## Comments on the first edition of Living as Nature Intended

Gladys Taylor McGarey is a respected doctor in American Medical community and is being given the title of "Mother of Holistic Medicine". She runs "The Gladys T. Mcgarey Medical Foundation" since 1988 in Arizona State and was honored in 2011 with "Woman of the Decade Award" as well.

Her comments after reading the book, in Feb. 2012

"You have done a masterful job with a very difficult subject explaining the various areas of medicine we are dealing with. The vast amount of scientific information you have brought out in regards to subjects like the coordination between the sympathetic and parasympathetic systems, brought the heart and spirit in to the picture and this is not easy. This book is not a quick read, it requires and demands deep study. It is however very well written and easily read. I congratulate you on a job well done and wish you great success. It should be read by every doctor who is really interested in helping their patient truly heal."

Her comments on the book launch, (15th July 2012)

"This book by Dr. Shagufta Feroz is a beautiful blending of the science of modern medicine and the art of medicine. One without the other makes the practice of medicine incomplete. The science of medicine is nurtured by roots which sustain us with knowledge and history of our past and the essence of our cultural heritage. Living people have real life issues which we as physicians deal with in our work with patients. In this book we have answers to and ways of working with our patients problems. It is not only a good read but also a text book to be studied "

## First edition review by WAPF (USA) magazine

This article appeared in Wise Traditions in Food, Farming and the Healing Arts, the quarterly magazine of the Weston A. Price Foundation, Fall2012

One common, off-the-cuff mainstream criticism of alternative medicine is that it is not evidence-based. It is not possible for anyone who works for or advocates conventional medicine to say that without dangling from one of the higher peaks of hypocrisy. Even if you don't agree, the fact that large crowds are increasingly giving the alternatives a try indicates there is a problem with the mainstream. Many people's personal experience with conventional medicine is unsatisfactory, so who cares if it is scientific? Perhaps we should not gullibly accept everything published on Medline just because it is published on Medline.

Dr. Feroz, a WAPF chapter leader in Pakistan, is obviously not suggesting that we immerse ourselves in conventional medicine in order to live as nature intended. She covers a wide range of alternative subjects. One topic briefly touched is the fascinating work of Dr. Fritz Albert Popp on the biophoton field. He has found that DNA generates very weak, coherent (laser-like) signals at frequencies of several billion hertz and uses those signals to communicate among cells. Unfortunately, cell phones also operate at those frequencies so getting too cozy with your cell phone is not going to be good for your health.

This book takes a holistic approach to health and a lot of subjects are covered over a lot of pages. The nutrition theme is pervasive and is consistent with WAPF principles. The importance of liver health is another major theme. Problems with the liver eventually cascade into problems all over the body. There are at least thirty metabolic functions performed by the liver. While filtering and detoxification functions are well-known, other lesser-known functions include storing minerals and vitamins, including fat-soluble vitamins; constructing about fifty thousand enzyme systems used throughout the body; and helping maintain blood pressure, blood sugar regulation and electrolyte balance. That is merely the very short list.

UCLA research compiled another list of behaviors associated with a healthy lifestyle. If you want to try those suggestions, they would be: sleeping seven or eight hours a night, eating breakfast, not eating between meals, maintaining normal weight, regular physical activity, engaging in moderate drinking, and not smoking. A quote from the May 2007 issue of the Journal of the American Medical Association says "Evidently, the ruse is over regarding the need for useless drugs . . . especially when simple lifestyle changes are just as effective. . . "The British Medical Journal stated that lifestyle changes are at least as effective as prescription drugs in reducing the risk of type 2 diabetes. The New England Journal of Medicine confirmed that statement.

Dr. Feroz quotes an observation to the effect that exercise is generally useless for weight loss. My personal experience is that while that opinion is controversial, it is nevertheless true. Exercise is a good thing but won't help most people much with weight loss if diet is not addressed, but not in the way it is conventionally considered. Another controversial observation along the same lines is that calorie counting is a huge scam. I would have to agree with that too. In fact, if you are a patient of Dr. Feroz, you are not allowed to count calories. That should be a no-brainer. Many people have been desperately depriving themselves of calories (or trying to) for decades now. Look around. How's that working out?

Timing is everything. That might be a slight exaggeration but timing is discussed extensively as it relates to a healthy lifestyle. It makes a difference when you sleep, how long you sleep, when you eat breakfast and other meals. The connection between lack of sleep and lack of health is pretty well known by now. It seems that eating breakfast is correlated with a smaller waist and better cognitive function. Speaking of thinking clearly, chapter fourteen gives the reader some quotes from Dr. Russell Blaylock explaining that we have an epidemic of neurological disorders that used to be rare. While neurosciences literature has no explanation (perhaps because that group of scientists doesn't't eat breakfast) there is a long list of likely causes, from MSG to aluminum, lead, mercury and pesticide exposure, to mineral deficiencies, to transfats, to lack of probiotics, to watching too much television.

The subject of women's health comes up toward the end of the book. Dr. Joan Borysenko is quoted as stating that "Women tend to be excluded from medical studies because they are too complicated to understand. That's something every man has known for the past several thousand years."

Perhaps some of the confusion is due to all the spin that occurs when the British Medical Journal reports that there are 29 percent more deaths from breast cancer among those who had mammography compared to those who didn't. The spin gets dizzying as vested interests try to explain why that doesn't mean you stop scheduling those regular mammograms. If you had breakfast this morning you may already know the thumb is UP for this book.

Reference: http://www.westonaprice.org/thumbs-up-reviews/living-as-nature-intended-by-dr-shagufta-feroz

# Table of Content

## Introduction

It is a widely acknowledged fact that almost all diseases are linked to an unhealthy lifestyle, yet no one knows exactly what the perfect lifestyle is. Do you? Some believe there is no such thing as a "one size fits all" perfect lifestyle. Everyone is unique and therefore their physical and emotional needs can be dramatically different from others. I have found medical doctors to echo some general principles of healthy living, never paying particular attention to each individual's needs. It's not their fault really, they are not taught this in medical school. It is amazing how little attention is paid to the miraculous preventive and healing powers of a healthy balanced lifestyle. I envision a world where people virtually never fall sick. Some may call it a fairy tale; I believe it to be the future. The lifestyle is a bundle of behaviors that makes sense to both others and oneself in a given time and place, including social relations, consumption patterns and entertainment. A human being's life is nurtured by multiple factors from birth to death, and these important external and internal factors make their worldly survival possible. There are also many unseen factors that work to harmonize human life with the macro rhythms of the universe. We get disease as a result of deviation from these factors and need to modify our lifestyle to get back to normal health.

The current medical definition of lifestyle modification includes mainly dietary instructions, control of smoking, avoidance of alcohol intake and regular exercise. These superficial factors cannot solve the rapidly increasing number of health problems, which are crippling humanity and burdening our healthcare infrastructure. Lifestyle modification is a highly specialized field and every medical practitioner should be trained in it. Without modifying lifestyle no one can ever claim to provide a holistic treatment. All medical treatments, if missing the rules of lifestyle modification, are incomplete and never therapeutic.

"Living as Nature Intended" is the sum of over 25 years of medical practice and research. In search of an integrated holistic approach to prevent and cure disease, I have experimented with modern medicine, acupuncture, holistic nutrition, and quantum sciences to name a few. I finally stumbled upon what I believe to be the most effective and ironically simple means of preventing and curing disease. SLP (Synchronized lifestyle modification Program) is a personalized lifestyle modification plan which induces homeostasis, balances biorhythms and rejuvenates liver. Once on this path, there is auto correction of every disease process.

What's controversial about my book is that I will challenge long standing perceptions of a healthy lifestyle, and I will prove them wrong by indisputable evidence. I will defiantly advise people to eat body compatible favorite whole foods that will make diet gurus gasp and I know I am right. An interesting part of the SLP is that there is no calorie count and no check on the quantity of food. All that is needed is dietary discipline. In reading this book, you will learn about the SLP's rule of six. According to this rule there are only six body chemistries, six groups of disease, and six combinations of natural foods to manage or reverse countless diseases. The key to SLP success is in its eight rules of diet correction, which help in prevention, treatment and reversal of a disease process.

"Living as Nature Intended" is split in to three parts, the first few chapters substantiate my claims of importance of homeostasis in biorhythms and the liver as a master organ based on scientific evidence, studies and research and their role in lifestyle modification. In this section you will also learn about lifestyle and its role in health and disease. The second part will educate you in detail about SLP, and importance of how correct eating influence health by regulating biorhythms and liver functions. Lastly, I will discuss the role of SLP for maintaining good health, preventing, and curing various acute and chronic diseases.

This book will be relevant to every human being out there that eats. It will provide equal dietary guidance for infants, toddlers, teenagers, adults and the elderly. The most encouraging sign of modern times is our concern for what we eat, but we do not know how to eat correctly. This is evident from the hundreds of books, newspaper articles, websites and blogs on food. Progressive research is opening our eyes to the miracles of food every day. I believe it to be an astronomical breakthrough in defining our eating habits and revealing the secrets of a healthy life simply based on how we eat. What people will find even more intriguing is that I will shatter common beliefs and take them in a completely new direction.

# CHAPTER NO: 1

## HOLISTIC QUANTUM SCIENCES

Today's humanity intuitively feels a deprivation, a feeling of emptiness and frustration. We all live in mega centers filled with pollution, vices, crimes and decay. The purpose of life as we know now is but a mere rat race of purposeless, materialism, greed and destruction. This secularized urbanized modern humanity is reaching its height of madness in leading all beings, human, animals and vegetation towards total and final annihilation. We are killing all species of vegetation and animal life with the tools of power, technology and modern science. We are digging our own grave by the toxic and hazardous poisons being discharged into the earth and its atmosphere. We are creating a bigger "ozone" hole in the sky each day.

The crisis of modern man begins with the acceptance of a totally wrong scientific philosophy. The basic premise of this philosophy is that man is here on this earth to dominate and exploit nature to the fullest. Modern man has secularized the natural religious philosophy by divorcing God. By redefining that "man is god", modern man blatantly proclaimed victory over nature. That nature is to be "conquered", subdued, and used to the fullest regardless of the consequences. This has become the hallmark of "success" for today's civilization. The great super powers and industrialized nations are responsible for more than 85% of the total pollution and toxic waste discharged on this planet earth. Imagine 15 major industrialized countries account for nearly 85% of the total world pollution. If this trend is followed by all 156 country members of United Nations, the planet Earth will be uninhabitable within 10 years. So intellectuals have to take emergency measures to reverse this speedy destructive process. The rediscovery of holistic sciences is one of the revolutionary steps.

## Holistic sciences

The term 'Holistic' means totally all-inclusive, all comprehensive, integrative, systematic, balanced and takes into account all factors. Should we follow this definition then Holistic Science would mean an all-encompassing science of nature and life inclusive of ecology, biology, physics, chemistry and other sciences. It would also include technology and methods of how to use it in harmony with nature and its inhabitants. The current definition of 'holistic science' merely pertains to the science of healing and nutrition. This is a very narrow definition because healing or good health and good nutrition cannot exist on its own without being nurtured in a natural and balanced environment. It also cannot exist in an immoral and vice ridden civilization. It is of paramount importance that all Holistic Practitioners work together to redefine holistic science. We should not talk of ecology per se; rather it should be "Holistic Ecology" that covers the full spectrum of nature, man, spirit and the universe in its entireness.

### *Philosophy*

Holistic science is an approach to research that emphasizes the study of complex systems. This practice is in contrast to a purely analytic tradition, called reductionism which purports to understand systems by dividing them into their smallest possible or discernible elements and understanding their elemental properties alone. Holistic in science is an approach to research that emphasizes the study of complex systems. Two central aspects are:

The way of doing science, sometimes called "whole to parts," which focuses on observation of the specimen within its ecosystem first before breaking down to study any part of the specimen.

The idea that the scientist is not a passive observer of an external universe; that there is no 'objective truth,' but that the individual is in a reciprocal, participatory relationship with nature, and that the observer's contribution to the process is valuable.

The term holistic science has been used as a category encompassing a number of scientific research fields. The term may not have a precise definition. Fields of scientific research considered potentially holistic do however certain things have in common. First, they are multidisciplinary. Second, they are concerned with the behavior of complex systems. Third, they recognize feedback within systems as a crucial element for understanding their behavior. The Santa Fe Institute, a center of holistic scientific research in the United States, expresses it like this "The two dominant characteristics of the SFI research style are commitment to a multidisciplinary approach and an emphasis on the study of problems that involve complex interactions among their constituent parts."

***Categories***

The field of cognitive science, or the study of mind and intelligence has some examples for holistic approaches. These include Unified Theory of Cognition and many others, many of which rely on the concept of emergence, i.e. the interplay of many entities make up a functioning whole. Another example is psychological nativism, the study of the innate structure of the mind. Non-holistic functionalist approaches within cognitive science include e.g. the modularity of mind paradigm. Cognitive science need not concern only human cognition. Biologist Marc Bekoff has done holistic, interdisciplinary scientific research in animal cognition and is the patron of Captive Animals Protection Society.

Quantum mechanics is another holistic science. In the standard Copenhagen Interpretation of quantum mechanics there is a holism of the measurement situation, in which there is a holism of apparatus and object. There is an "uncontrollable disturbance" of the measured object by the act of measurement according to Niels Bohr. It is impossible to separate the effect of the measuring apparatus from the object measured. The observer-measurement relation is an active area of research today like the phenomenon of Quantum DE coherence, Quantum Zeno effect and Measurement problem.

Holistic science sometimes asks different questions than a strictly analytic science -- as is exemplified by Goethe in the following passage: "We conceive of the individual animal as a small world, existing for its own sake, by its own means. Every creature is its own reason to be. All its parts have a direct effect on one another, a relationship to one another, thereby constantly renewing the circle of life; thus we are justified in considering every animal physiologically perfect. Viewed from within, no part of the animal is a useless or arbitrary product of the formative impulse (as so often thought). Externally, some parts may seem useless because the inner coherence of the animal nature has given them this form without regard to outer circumstances".

A lively debate has run since the end of the 19th century regarding the functional organization of the brain. The holistic tradition (e.g., Pierre Marie) maintained that the brain was a homogeneous organ with no specific subparts whereas the Localizationists (e.g., Paul Broca) argued that the brain was organized in functionally distinct cortical areas which were each specialized to process a given type of information or implement specific mental operations. The controversy was epitomized with the existence of a language area in the brain, nowadays known as the Broca's area. Although Broca's view has gained acceptance, the issue isn't settled insofar as the brain as a whole is a highly connected organ at every level from the individual neuron to the hemisphere stance.

## Modern Holistic Sciences

Holism as a health concept has long existed outside of academic circles, but only relatively recently has the modern medical establishment begun to integrate it into the mainstream health care system. In the United States, the first National Conference on Holistic Health was conducted by the Health Optimizing Institute and The Mandala Society with the University of California, San Diego School of Medicine in June 1975. This continued there for ten years with about three thousand health professionals participating each year. The recording of these

Conferences, that was the emerging of Holistic Health in American, is in the nine volumes of The Journal Of Holistic Health provided by the Mandala Society. Over 150 authorities in aspects of Holistic Health participated and are recorded in the Journals. The Mandala Society Conferences and work supported the creation of the Association For Holistic Health in 1976, the Holistic Medical Association in 1978 and The American Holistic Nurses Association, 1979. Many regional Holistic Health Associations followed with the American Holistic Health Association being established in 1989.

**Holistic Health**

The philosophy of holistic health is not itself a method of treatment, but is an approach to how treatment should be applied. Holistic concepts of health and fitness view achieving and maintaining good health as requiring more than just taking care of the various singular components that make up the physical body, additionally incorporating aspects such as emotional and spiritual well-being. The goal is a wellness that encompasses the entire person, rather than just the lack of physical pain or disease. This means that not feeling sick, does not necessarily mean you are well, just that you are between well and sick. When symptoms develop, it is often long after the cause of the symptoms occurred. It is often used in contrast to the medical model that focuses on treating symptoms and syndromes without attempting to address functioning beyond the absence of disease, the Holistic approach focuses on the cause. The holistic process offers individuals the opportunity to be the creators of their own reality of health, through an understanding of all levels of health and a balanced lifestyle.

## Emerging holistic sciences

### *1-Biopsychosocial model*

The biopsychosocial model (abbreviated "BPS") is a general model or approach that posits that biological, psychological (which entails thoughts, emotions, and behaviors), and social factors, all play a significant role in human functioning in the context of disease or illness. Indeed, health is best understood in terms of a combination of biological, psychological, and social factors rather than purely in biological terms. This is in contrast to the traditional, reductionist biomedical model of medicine that suggests every disease process can be explained in terms of an underlying deviation from normal function such as a pathogen, genetic or developmental abnormality, or injury.

The biopsychosocial paradigm is also a technical term for the popular concept of the mind–body connection, which addresses more philosophical arguments between the biopsychosocial and biomedical models, rather than their empirical exploration and clinical application. The model was theorized by psychiatrist George L. Engel at the University of Rochester, and putatively discussed in a 1977 article in Science, where he posited "the need for a new medical model"; however no single definitive, irreducible model has been published. However, the general BPS model has guided formulation and testing of models within each professional field. Interestingly, evidence for the application of the biopsychosocial model was found in ancient Asian (2600 B.C.) and Greek (500 B.C.) civilizations prior to Engel's introduction of the theory in 1977. The novelty, acceptance, and prevalence of the biopsychosocial model vary across cultures.

The biological component of the biopsychosocial model seeks to understand how the cause of the illness stems from the functioning of the individual's body. The psychological component of the biopsychosocial model looks for potential psychological causes for a health problem such lack of self-control, emotional turmoil, and negative thinking. The social part of the biopsychosocial model investigates how different social factors such as socioeconomic status, culture, poverty, technology, and religion can influence health. The biopsychosocial model of health is based in part on social cognitive theory. The biopsychosocial model implies that treatment of disease processes, for example type two diabetes and cancer, requires that the health care team address biological, psychological and social influences upon a patient's functioning.

In a philosophical sense, the biopsychosocial model states that the workings of the body can affect the mind, and the workings of the mind can affect the body. This means both a direct interaction between mind and body as well as indirect effects through intermediate factors. The biopsychosocial model presumes that it is important to handle the three together as a growing body of empirical literature suggests that patient perceptions of health and threat of disease, as well as barriers in a patient's social or cultural environment, appear to influence the likelihood that a patient will engage in health-promoting or treatment behaviors, such as medication taking, proper diet, and engaging in physical activity.

***2-Psychoneuroimmunology***

Psychoneuroimmunology (PNI) is the study of the interaction between psychological processes and the nervous and immune systems of the human body. PNI takes an interdisciplinary approach, incorporating psychology, neuroscience, immunology, physiology, pharmacology, molecular biology, psychiatry, behavioral medicine, infectious diseases, endocrinology, and rheumatology. PNI studies, among other things, the physiological functioning of the neuro-immune system in health and disease; disorders of the neuro-immune system (autoimmune diseases; hypersensitivities; immune deficiency); and the physical, chemical and physiological characteristics of the components of the neuro-immune system in vitro, in situ, and in vivo.

***3-Alternative medical systems***

In western culture, alternative medicine is any healing practice "that does not fall within the realm of conventional medicine", or "that which has not been shown consistently to be effective. "In practice, alternative medicine encompasses therapies with a historical or cultural, rather than a scientific basis. Commonly cited examples include naturopathy, chiropractics, herbalism, traditional Chinese medicine, Unani, Ayurveda, meditation, yoga, biofeedback, hypnosis, homeopathy, acupuncture, and diet-based therapies, in addition to a range of other practices. It is frequently grouped with complementary medicine, which generally refers to the same interventions when used in conjunction with mainstream techniques, under the umbrella term complementary and alternative medicine, or *CAM*. Some significant researchers in alternative medicine oppose this grouping, preferring to emphasize differences of approach, but nevertheless use the term CAM, which has become standard.

A 1998 systematic review of studies assessing its prevalence in 13 countries concluded that about 31% of cancer patients use some form of complementary and alternative medicine. Alternative medicine varies from country to country. Dr. Edzard Ernst believes that in Austria and Germany CAM is mainly in the hands of physicians, while some estimates suggest that at least half of American alternative practitioners are physicians. In Germany, herbs are tightly regulated, with half prescribed by doctors and covered by health insurance. The National Center for Complementary and Alternative Medicine (NCCAM) defines CAM as "a group of diverse medical and health care systems, practices, and products that are not currently part of conventional medicine." The Cochrane Complementary Medicine Field says:

"What are considered complementary or alternative practices in one country may be considered conventional medical practices in another. Therefore, our definition is broad and general: complementary medicine includes all such practices and ideas which are outside the domain of conventional medicine in several countries and defined by its users as preventing or treating illness, or promoting health and well-being. These practices complement mainstream medicine by

1) Contributing to a common whole,
2) Satisfying a demand not met by conventional practices, and
3) Diversifying the conceptual framework of medicine. "

***4-Integrated Medicine***

Integrative Medicine, or Integrated Medicine, is a form of medicine that combines conventional medical treatment with Complementary and Alternative Medicine (CAM) treatments to provide the best of both worlds to patients. The primary effect of the revitalizing effort of Integrative Medicine is the emphasis on the patient-physician relationship, which recognition by conventional care providers on the importance of lifestyle, diet, exercise, and emotional well-being for overall health. Patients are encouraged to take an active role in their health care, as well as doctors taking responsibility as role models for their patients. The Integrative Medicine focus on healing is dramatically affecting our system of health care today.

Ralph Snyderman and Andrew Weil state that "integrative medicine is not synonymous with complementary and alternative medicine. It has a far larger meaning and mission in that it calls for restoration of the focus of medicine on health and healing and emphasizes the centrality of the patient-physician relationship." The combination of orthodox and complementary medicine with an emphasis on prevention and lifestyle changes is known as integrated medicine. The Washington Post reports that a growing number of traditionally trained physicians practice integrative medicine, which it defines as "conventional medical care that incorporates strategies such as acupuncture, reiki and herbal remedies."

***5-Lifestyle Medicine***

Lifestyle Medicine is based on the recognition of the central role of lifestyle in many chronic diseases. The use of lifestyle change interventions within conventional medicine to lower the risk for chronic disease or, if disease is already present, to serve as an adjunct to the management plan. It includes exercise, eating habits, stress management, tobacco and alcohol use. Current definition by Egger 2008says, the therapeutic use of lifestyle interventions in the management of disease at all levels to help manage the growing number of cases presenting to doctors now with a lifestyle-based cause of disease such as obesity and type 2 diabetes. The application of environmental, behavioral, medical and motivational principles to the management of lifestyle related health problems in a clinical setting.

## CAM and evidence-based medicine

Some scientists reject the use of the classification of any therapy as 'alternative medicine' on the grounds that "there is only medicine that has been adequately tested and medicine that has not, medicine that works and medicine that may or may not work." These scientists advocate a classification based on scientific evidence, and state that "*w*hat most sets alternative medicine apart, in our view, is that it has not been scientifically tested and its advocates largely deny the need for such testing." The US Institute of Medicine analyzed this approach to defining alternative medicine, which it called normative, and found it problematic because some CAM is tested, and much of mainstream medicine lacks strong evidence. The IOM found that in a study of 160 Cochrane systematic of mainstream techniques, 20% were ineffective and 21% had insufficient evidence.[16] The IOM therefore defined alternative medicine broadly as the non-dominant approach in a given culture and historical period. A similar definition has been adopted by the Cochrane Collaboration, which is the leading body of evidence-based medicine, and official government bodies such as the UK Department of Health. This definition does not take into account the Off-Label use of drugs which has not been scientifically tested. Off-label use of medications is very common. Up to one-fifth of all drugs are prescribed off-label and amongst psychiatric drugs, off-label use rises to 31%.

***Conventional medicine is not evidence based***

Well-known proponents of evidence-based medicine, such as the Cochrane Collaboration and Edzard Ernst, Professor of Complementary Medicine at the University of Exeter, use the term alternative medicine but agree that all treatments, whether "mainstream" or "alternative", ought to be held to standards of the scientific method. Their view is that evidence-based medicine is an ideal state which has not yet been achieved by either current mainstream or alternative medicine. Ernst characterizes the evidence for many alternative techniques as weak, nonexistent, or negative, but states that compelling evidence exists for others, particularly certain herbs and acupuncture – although this evidence does not mean these treatments are mainstream, especially not worldwide. What is alternative varies by discipline as well and country. For example, biofeedback is commonly used within the Physical Medicine & Rehabilitation community, but is considered alternative within the medical community as a whole, and some herbal therapies are mainstream in Europe, but are alternative in the United States.[26]

***Evidence based criteria has to be modified***

M.R. Tonelli argues that CAM cannot be evidence-based unless the definition of evidence is changed. He states that "the methods of developing knowledge within CAM currently have limitations and are subject to bias and varied interpretation. CAM must develop and defend a rational and coherent method for assessing causality and efficacy, though not necessarily one based on the results of controlled clinical trials." Further, A review of Michael L. Millenson's book Demanding *Medical Excellence: Doctors and Accountability in the Information Age* described it as "a wakeup call to both medicine and nursing" due to what Millenson calls a "lack of scientific-based medical practice".

According to the review, the book states that "85% of current practice has not been scientifically validated" and that it suggests that users of the research presented by Medline should question research articles rather than assuming they are accurate simply because of where they are published. The review states that Millenson's thesis and conclusion call for all health researchers and policy makers to do a better job in assuring valid methodology and avoidance of bias in published research. Michael Dixon, the Director of the NHS Alliance stated that "People argue against complementary therapies on the basis of a lack of evidence. But I'd say only 10 per cent of what doctors do in primary care is evidence-based." Angell and Kassirer acknowledge that "many treatments used in conventional medicine have not been rigorously tested, either" but say that the scientific community is generally aware that this is a failing that needs to be remedied."

To remove clinical experience from medical care and replace it purely with objective data is at the heart of evidence based medicine. Because of the effect of the evidence-based movement, the drug industry incorporates bibliographical references to clinical trials that endorse their products in their ads, and using the pretext of objective data, drug companies are manipulating facts for their own purposes.

**CAM Classifications by NCCM**

NCCAM classifies complementary and alternative therapies into five major groups. The classification is rather loose, and there can be some overlap.

I. Whole medical systems cut across more than one of the other groups; examples include Traditional Chinese medicine and Ayurveda.

II. Mind-body medicine takes a holistic approach to health that explores the interconnection between the mind, body, and spirit. It works under the premise that the mind can affect "bodily functions and symptoms".

III. Biologically based practices use substances found in nature such as herbs, foods, vitamins, and other natural substances.

IV. Manipulative and body-based practices feature manipulation or movement of body parts, such as is done in chiropractic and osteopathic manipulation.

V. Energy medicine is a domain that deals with putative and verifiable energy fields.

## Quantum Sciences

### *Quantum Theory*

Quantum science seeks to investigate the sciences in terms of the quantum theory. This includes attempts to study biological processes and dynamic molecular structures in terms of quantum mechanics (QM). For example, investigations of dynamic molecular structure and energy transfer at the quantum level have credibility if they explain macroscopic biological observables that otherwise are inexplicable. Fundamental biological processes that involve the conversion of energy into forms that are usable for chemical transformations are quantum mechanical in nature. These processes involve chemical reactions, light absorption, formation of excited electronic states, transfer of excitation energy, and the transfer of electrons and protons in chemical processes such as photosynthesis and cellular respiration.

### *1-Quantum Biology*

Quantum biology uses mathematical computation to model biological interactions in light of QM effects. The need for a quantum theoretical study of genetic systems has been pointed out by Erwin Schrodinger in 1946, and followed up with a detailed formal approach to Quantum Genetics by Robert Rosen in 1961. Slowly, our culture is waking up from modern life's dream of individuality and dominion, into a world whose survival may depend on shared visions of connectedness and inter-dependence. It is extremely important for medicine to accept that the body is imbued with mind. Our society to realize as primitive cultures do that because mind – body co-evolved with nature, they are intimately inter-connected. If these ideas take deep root then techno-industrial medicine may learn to respect human adaptability and connectedness, and chart a more sustainable course.

***2-Role of Mind***

"The possibility of conscious playing a role in the workings of the universe is something early quantum physics considered. Their findings lead to remark that the universe is a far different place than the legacy of Descartes, Bacon, and Newton." The physicist Arthur Eddington said that the stuff of the world is mind stuff and the mind stuff is not spread in time and space. The human mind is considered to be a small part of a much greater mind. According to his view, the mind is a quantum system capable of spreading out infinitely across the universe and interacting in a participatory way with the universe.

***3-Belief of Great Chain***

The belief of a great chain of being was predicted on seeing reality as having a vision for the purpose driven by a consciousness, or a spirit, and that this drive was one continuous and interrelated manifestations of spirit. This great chain reaches in a perfectly unbroken or uninterrupted fashion from matter to life to mind to soul to spirit. The quantum view states that life emanates as infinite possibility waves from a great void, the quantum vacuum, and it is all pervasive throughout the universe. It is postulated that in the everyday world, a silent pulse connects ordinary reality with this quantum reality, and through quantum creativity, or the shifting of the mind, the two worlds can be connected. In order to achieve the status of a higher being, humans have to learn this quantum connection.

***4-Vibration Science***

We live in a matrix of oscillating fields; the tiniest fluctuations in one interlocked field carry over perturbation into others. Many times per second, pulses travel completely around the world between our planet's surface and the ionosphere sending coordinating signals to all organisms. "Since life began, the Earth has been surrounding and protecting all living things with a natural frequency pulsation known as the "Schumann Resonance". Ludwig discovered that while the earth vibration could be clearly measured in nature and on the ocean, it was almost impossible to measure the earth's pulse in the city, where man made signals drown out the natural signals that nature has created. When you're out in nature, your body tunes into the earth's frequency and can repair, rejuvenate and heal itself more efficiently.

***5-Sunlight and Live Foods***

Dr. Johanna Budwig from Germany has stated that live foods are electron-rich, and act as high-powered electron donors and "solar resonance fields" in your body. Therefore natural foods attract, store, and conduct the sun's energy in your body. The greater your store of light energy, the greater the power of your overall electromagnetic field, and consequently the more energy is available for the optimum health.

***6-Human Body Emits Light***

The human body literally glows, emitting a visible light in extremely small quantities at levels that rise and fall with the day. Past research has shown that the body emits visible light, 1,000 times less intense than the levels which can be seen with the naked eye. In fact, virtually all living creatures emit very weak light. To learn more about this faint visible light, scientists in Japan employed extraordinarily sensitive cameras capable of detecting single photons. Five healthy male volunteers in their 20's were placed bare-chested in front of the cameras in complete darkness in light-tight rooms for 20 minutes every three hours. The researchers found the body glow rose and fell over the day, with its lowest point at 10 AM and its peak at 4 PM, dropping gradually after that. These findings suggest there is light emission linked to the body clock, most likely due to how metabolic rhythms fluctuate over the course of the day.

"If you can see the glimmer from the body's surface, you could see the whole body condition," said researcher Hitoshi Okamura, a circadian biologist at Kyoto University in Japan. Others have explained the existence of light and energy around your body in terms of a "biophoton field." Dr. Dietrich Klinghardt discusses this field in The Five Levels of Healing, which is based on a healing model developed some 12,000 years ago. This energetic model for health has influenced Tibetan medicine, traditional Chinese medicine (TCM), and Ayurvedic medicine as well. The existence of the biophoton field was scientifically proven by Dr. Fritz-Albert Popp in 1974. Your physical health is dependent not only on what goes on inside of your body, but is also interconnected with and dependent on other non-physical levels of energy, such as the energy surrounding your body, called the biophoton field. In highly simplistic terms, the biophoton field can be viewed as a highly sophisticated computer that processes, stores and retrieves information that is then used to regulate your biological processes.

It is known in biology that every cell in your body has over 100,000 biochemical reactions per second, all of which must be carefully timed and sequenced with each other. Many (mostly European) scientists have investigated the organizing principle behind this sophisticated dance. Dr. Popp also proved that biophotons originate from your DNA and that they are laser-like in nature. He developed the biophoton theory to explain their biological role and the ways in which they help control your biochemical processes. The DNA inside each cell in your body vibrates at a frequency of several billion hertz (which is unfortunately the same range at which modern cell phone communication systems also work).

This vibration is created through the coil-like contraction and extension of your DNA which occurs several billion times per second and every time it contracts, it squeezes out one single biophoton; a light particle. That photon contains all the information on everything going on in your DNA at that moment. One single biophoton can carry more than four megabytes of information, and relays this information to other biophotons it crosses in the biophoton field outside your body. All the photons that are emitted from your body communicate with each other in this highly structured light field that surrounds your body. This light field also regulates the activity of your metabolic enzymes.

The information transfer on biophotons is bidirectional, which means your DNA sends information out on a photon, and on the same photon the information of all the biophotons from your body is broadcast back to your cells, and to your tubulin, which are light conductive molecules in your connective tissue. The tubulin, in turn, receives the information-carrying light impulse and conducts it at the speed of light throughout your body, where it is translated inside each cell into activating or inactivating certain metabolic enzymes. Biophoton research also puts a whole new spin on the impact of environmental toxins.

***7-Humans are energy beings***

Whether it's a grain of sand, a piece of steel, a plant, animal or an organ in your body is composed of atoms. Without getting into all the mathematical equations and specifics of the scientific discoveries of this reality, everything that exists, either physical or non-physical, contains some variation of atoms and subatomic particles. The varying amounts of each of these put together, form various shapes or energies which determine form, or rates of vibration. Depending on the specific amounts of each of these ingredients determines the structure of each object that can be seen and determines whether the thing is solid, liquid, or gas, and which also determines whether it can be sensed with the 5 human senses or not. Regardless of its form, broken down into its most basic structure, everything that exists, seen and unseen, consists of a rate of vibration as well.

A good example of this that everyone is familiar with would be the wind. Although it can be felt, at a certain vibration it cannot be seen with the human eye or heard with our ears. When the rate of vibration changes to the point that it causes the rate of the wind to increase and became strong enough to pick up dirt or debris, it would then be at a level (vibration) that would allow all 5 of the human senses to experience it. In other words absolutely everything, whether physical objects, your body, sounds, colors, feelings, oxygen, thoughts, feelings, emotions etc. exist as a result of energy or what science refers to as Quanta which are vibrating energy packets constructed of any number of sub atomic particles. A vibration is made up of energy pulsations of positive and negative polarity called frequency. Atoms act like little radio transmitters broadcasting waves.

Humans, as well as all kinds of supposedly inert matter, constantly emit rays. Everything sends out waves of different lengths. The wave lengths of the body are as individual as fingerprints. Under the laws of vibration each individual has distinctive rates of vibration or resonance harmonics. The resonance of your physical body is determined by your emotions, food, thought and external toxins. The way you take care of your body physically, emotionally and mentally determines how many negative frequencies or toxins are being built up in it. There are four general ways imbalance in the body is created. Through toxic substances we eat pollution we breathe, exposure to a negative energetic environment, and how we process information in our thinking & feeling. Raising your vibration is the only effective way to live the life you truly want to live. While you are radiating a low vibration or frequency your life will never really be in harmony and you will constantly live with an inner feeling of Dis- ease

The healthy body is a flowing interactive electro-dynamic energy field. Every cell also resonates a unique characteristic frequency. Frequencies that are rich in harmonics supply the body with a full band of frequencies that can support and strengthen the bio-system. They can if the body is healthy rapidly restore the energy state and ideal frequency to every cell in the body. The resonant cavities of the body such as the gut, lungs, trachea, throat, and nasal passages produce vibration signatures, similar to the resounding chambers of guitars, which give them each a unique personal tone even though they all use similar strings.

Enhancing the harmony or resonance of the body multiplies the number of frequencies called overtones. Plucking a guitar string sets up an ascending cascade of overtones that quickly die out as the string returns to rest. However, bowing a violin string allows these harmonics to ascend to infinity as long as the string is being drawn. This example shows that the more resonant and coherent something is the more overtones it contains. Therefore, improving the harmonic resonance of the body can result in increased coherency, which fills in any holes present in the membranes. Therefore complete balance of the actual and potential components of our mind and body in the perfect harmony and resonance would be the essence and equivalent of...Good Health.

The human body is a multidimensional, vibrational being with numerous, complex energetic interactions continually taking place. These complex energetic interactions - a bioenergetic communication network - emit vibratory information that precisely specify the activities taking place within the body, and these vibratory emissions are measurable with modern equipment. Current research hypothesizes that every part of the body - mental, physical, and emotional - forms this continuous interconnected bioenergetics communication network. Each part of the body, even the smallest constituent, is a part of this bioenergetics communication network. Vibration medicine stimulates this network, and the body's restorative systems respond without the side-effects associated with the use of pharmacological substances. Everything living vibrates at certain frequency, this is true not only for molecules, cells, tissues, and organs, but also for parasites, bacterium, viruses, etc. Imbalances, disorders and diseases alter the bioenergetics communications network, and through the use of vibrational medical devices balance can be restored. Your body can then go to work healing itself!

Every illness is an autoimmune illness. When your immune system cannot ward off a problem in your system in time, something fails. Your only defense is your immune system. By raising the oscillating frequency of every atom in your body, we are increasing the rate at which the immune system operates as well as eliminating the negative toxins your body is trying to fight off. The quantum fluctuations (vibrations) that make up the memory of the cells of our body start creating different "memories". This type of frequency reprogramming allows the body to remember the natural effectiveness of the immune system and regenerate back 100% to its original state.

## Quantum Holistic Healing

### *1-Quantum Leap*

"Research on spontaneous cures of cancer, conducted in both United States and Japan has shown that just before the cure appears, almost every patient experiences a dramatic shift in awareness. He knows that he will be healed, and he feels that the force responsible is inside him but not limited to him. It extends beyond his personal boundaries throughout all of nature. At that moment, such a patient apparently jumps to a new level of consciousness that prohibits the existence of cancer. This leap in consciousness seems to be the key. It does not have to come in a flash; however it can be cultivated deliberately, through holistic sciences techniques. The word that comes to mind when a scientist think of sudden changes is quantum. The word denotes a discrete jump from one level of functioning to a higher level the quantum leap."

### *2-Healing is Universal*

"Indeed the process of healing has a spiritual and mysterious quality that transcends scientism. In this broader perspective, the intersection between science and art and between rational thought and imagination begin to blend. As such this is the entrance into the realm of the integral thinker. To enter into this domain, logic is not denied, rather it is expanded in the broadest possible way, taking a person into a universe that operates by laws that both transcend and include the laws of scientism. This is a universe predicted on laws of quantum mechanics, complexity and nonlinear dynamics, it is also a universe that has at its core a spiritual intelligence." Healing is a universal quality and a universal process. We all possess natural powers of healing in our own body, mind, and spirit. We all have access to personal qualities which can assist healing in other people. Healing is not bestowed upon people by doctors. Doctors do not make people better; they help them to get better. And so do parents, friends, neighbors, comedians, poets, and relatives.

Dr. Deepak Chopra writes in his book 'Quantum Healing' that "at any one time, the number of activities being coordinated in our bodies is quite literally infinite. Like the Earth's ecosystems, our physiology appears to operate in separate compartments that in fact are invisibly connected: we eat, breathe, talk, think, digest our food, fight off infections, purify our blood of toxins, renew our cells, discard wastes, vote for the Republicans, and much more besides".

***3-Macro and Micro Cosmos are connected***

"Our ecology is more planet like than most people realize. Creatures roam our surface, as unmindful of our hugeness as we are of their minuteness. Colonies of mites, for example spend their entire life cycle in our eyelashes. Within the body's vast array, the functions of any single cell- such as one of the 15 billion neurons in the brain- fill a good sized medical text. The volumes devoted to any one system of the body, such as the immune system or the nervous system, take up several shelves in a medical library. The healing mechanism resides somewhere in this overall complexity, but it is elusive. There is no one organ of healing".

He further writes " any one of the processes involved in healing a superficial cut, the clotting of blood , for example is incredibly complex, so much so that if the mechanism fails, as it does with hemophiliacs, advance scientific medicine at a loss to duplicate the impaired function. A doctor can prescribe drugs that replace the missing clotting factor in the blood, but these are temporary, artificial, and have numerous undesirable side effects. The body's perfect timings will be absent, as well as the superb coordination of a dozen related processes. By comparison, a man made drug is a stranger in a land where everyone else is blood kin. It can never share the knowledge that everyone else was born with".

Same phenomenon happens when a processed food enters the body chemistry. A human body has a perfect enzyme system ready to digest the natural whole foods. A natural food contains a team of nutrients which are perfectly woven in a manner compatible with the human system. By modifying the whole food, that network breaks and now that food is an alien to the body. If processed food is strong and rejection system is weak, there is cellular damage and therefore a base of disease process starts.

Dependent on exposure to these chemical foods is the nature and intensity of disease. Current evidence shows degenerative processes have started appearing after a shorter duration i.e. at a young age. "The first thing that is killed in the laboratory is the delicate web of intelligence that binds the body together. Even if we break down its knowledge into finer and finer bits, looking for the secret in some miniature hormone or messenger enzyme, we will not find a protein strand labeled 'intelligence,' and yet there is no doubt that intelligence is at work".

"No physician in his right mind would claim that he had healed a broken bone simply because he had set it. The real job of healing is done by something else, something that we do not fully understand and cannot reproduce, and something that, for want of a better term, we vaguely call 'nature'." Similarly the battle against the infection is a collaboration process. Unless the forces of the patient's own systems are operative against infections, all the physicians' medicines will be useless.

Unfortunate fact is that medicine has become addicted to the administration of vast quantities of non-biological medications. Dr. Roger writes that the basic fault of all these medications is that they have known no connection with the disease process itself. They tend to mask the difficulty, not eliminate it. They contaminate the internal environment, create dependence on the part of the patient and complicate the physician's job by erasing valuable clues as to the real source of trouble.

***4-Listen to Your Body***

Unfortunately most of us go through the day without being aware of how we are in our bodies and what they are trying to communicate. We tune our bodies in order to get our jobs done, finish our commutes, home and run our errands before we finally lie down and go to sleep, and we hope to wake up feeling good. Even when our bodies finally get our attention with excruciating sensations that we can't ignore, do we listen as they tell us what they want, what they need? Instead of our ignoring or anesthetizing your body consider working with it in a cooperative way. Knowing yourself makes you a healthy holistic being. It's a knowing that can come only from within our bodies, from our own hearts and guts. It is inside out rather than outside in.

It's also through our bodies that we sense the rightness of a situation or detect danger. Like a radar system, our body wisdom lets us know when we are going too fast and need to slow down, or when we need to be vigorous and in motion. Our bodies know what to do as long as we don't overwrite the messages with abstract goals and ideas and the latest faddish information in the name of health, success, morality, beauty or spirituality. We are outfitted with all the apparatus we need: neurotransmitters, sensory receptors, homeostatic adjusters, detoxification units, chemical regulators, biorhythm regulators and so on. Intelligence suffuses every cell in the body- in all of its enzymes, genes, hormones, anti-bodies and nerves regulating essential functions.

The emotional and the physical being are connected, in the third week of our lives as an embryo; three sheets of cells are present. One of these primitive or germ layers, the ectoderm gradually gives rise to the skin, brain and nervous system. This means that from the same group of cells we develop the structures that allow us to feel physical sensation-sensory receptors. It means skin and brain function as a single unit. The skin is the outer layer of the brain or brain is the deepest layer of the skin. Scientific research in the PNI is proving that the brain and its functions are actually located all over the body. Candace Pert of the national institute of health and other brain researchers have found receptor sites for neuropeptides (brain chemicals), not only in the brain nervous system and immune system but also throughout the body. When we are aware of physical changes taking place in our bodies then we also know that emotions we are feeling.

### *5- Biochemical Individuality*

The book 'Biochemical Individuality', authored by the late world-renowned biochemist Roger Williams, Ph.D., first published in 1956. Dr. Williams contributed to the evolution of the understanding of the molecular origin of disease with the development of the concept of biochemical individuality. He described anatomical and physiological variations among people and how they related to their individual responses to the environment. He was the first to gain recognition for the term "biochemical individuality" and how this related to differing nutritional needs for optimal function among different people. He pointed out that even identical twins could be different in their needs for optimal function based upon the fact that they developed in different environments in uterus. Although identical twins share the same genes, their differing nutrition and developmental environments can result in different expression of the genes as they grow older. Epigenetic says that gene expression can be modified by various internal and external environmental factors.

***6-Genetic Polymorphism***

Genetic polymorphism is the term which has emerged in the past decade to describe this variation in function surrounding a specific genetic trait. The second major breakthrough in thinking made by Dr. Williams is the recognition that nutritional status can influence the expression of genetic characteristics. Once again Dr. Williams foresaw this important concept in Biochemical Individuality and set in motion research and discoveries over the past four decades that have transformed medicine. It is now well recognized that our genotype gets transformed into our phenotype as a consequence of nutritional, lifestyle and environmental factors which are important in determining our health patterns.

The concept of biochemical individuality has become part of most contemporary clinical and experimental medical and nutritional research. People are now known to fit into personally unique biochemical profiles based upon their own genetic structure, nutrition and environment. There is no such thing as a truly "normal" individual-meaning average. We are all biochemically unique and need to be dealt with as such. The Recommended Dietary Allowances (RDAs) which were developed by the Food and Nutrition Board of the National Research Council to establish the nutritional needs of "practically all healthy people" were not based upon the more recent information concerning the range of biochemical individuality among individuals. The RDAs that describe "normal" nutritional needs have questionable relevancy to the concept of optimal nutrition based upon individual needs. The contributions of Dr. Williams have opened the door for personally tailored nutritional and medical interventions that take biochemical individuality into account.

### *7- Epigenetics*

Conrad Waddington (1905-1975) is often credited with coining the term epigenetics in 1942 as "the branch of biology which studies the causal interactions between genes and their products, which bring the phenotype into being". Epigenetics appears in the literature as far back as the mid-19th century, although the conceptual origins date back to Aristotle (384-322 BC). He believed in epigenetics: the development of individual organic form from the unformed. This controversial view was the main argument against our having developed from miniscule fully-formed bodies. Even today the extent to which we are preprogrammed versus environmentally shaped awaits universal consensus. The field of epigenetics has emerged to bridge the gap between nature and nurture. In the 21st century you will most commonly find epigenetics defined as 'the study of heritable changes in genome function that occur without a change in DNA sequence'.

"The difference between genetics and epigenetics can probably be compared to the difference between writing and reading a book. Once a book is written, the text (the genes or DNA: stored information) will be the same in all the copies distributed to the interested audience. However, each individual reader of a given book may interpret the story slightly differently, with varying emotions and projections as they continue to unfold the chapters. In a very similar manner, epigenetics would allow different interpretations of a fixed template (the book or genetic code) and result in different read-outs, dependent upon the variable conditions under which this template is interrogated." Thomas Jenuwein (Vienna, Austria)

#### *Nutrition and Biochemical Individuality*

Some of the world's foremost nutrition and medical researchers are now actively involved in developing a better understanding of the field which Dr. Williams pioneered. Rucker and Tinker from the University of California at Davis, Department of Nutrition, have described the role of nutrition in gene expression and its relationship to biochemical individuality as "a fertile field for the application of molecular biology". It is now well known that significant biochemical diversity occurs in such physiological functions as the ability of the individual to detoxify exogenous and endogenous substances.

The control of blood cholesterol, the metabolism of the potentially harmful amino acid homocysteine, and the response certain cancer genes have to the diet and environment. These are all examples of how nutritional status can influence disease patterns based upon biochemical individuality. Dr. Williams coined the term "genetotrophic disease" to describe diseases which resulted from genetically determined nutritional metabolic needs not being met by the individual and which result in poor gene expression. Motulsky has recently argued that many of the common degenerative diseases are the result of the imbalanced nutritional intake with genetically determined needs for good health.

Therefore biochemical individuality refers to the unique nutritional needs each person has, based on their genetics, lifestyle, and environmental exposure to various stresses. Biochemistry is a complex web of interactions that controls the way your body uses amino acids, vitamins, minerals, carbohydrates, and fats for all your body functions. Amino acids, for example, are used to produce hormones, skin, and bone. For your biochemistry to function properly, your body requires the right amounts and proportions of nutrients. The amount of a certain nutrient the average person requires may not be the optimal amount you need for good health.

Symptoms of disease can occur in response to problems with biochemical processes. Depression provides a good example. The body requires certain nutrients in order to manufacture mood- regulating hormones (serotonin, dopamine, and epinephrine). For these hormones to be properly manufactured, your body needs the amino acids phenylalanine and tryptophan, vitamins B3 and B6, and the minerals iron and copper. Low levels of these nutrients the raw materials needed to manufacture the hormones can produce depression. People may become deficient in the required nutrients because they don't get enough of the nutrients in their diet, or their unique biochemistry may simply require additional amounts of one or more nutrients for the biochemical pathway to function properly.

***Genes are not fixed***

The genetic concept with which most nutrition and medical searchers grew up intellectually before the contribution of Dr. Williams was that of Gregor Mendel. His concept of dominant recessive genetic characteristics gave us the belief that our characteristics are "locked in stone" when the sperm meets the egg. Dr. Williams opened the eyes of the research communities that expression of genes and therefore phenotypic function was modifiable through altered diet and nutritional status. He pointed out human biochemical variation in function was much greater than nutrition and medicine recognized prior to his publications. Simopoulos has stated that "of all the recent scientific advances contributing to our understanding of the role of nutrition in disease prevention and the variability in human nutrient needs, the recognition of genetic variation as a contributing factor must rank at the highest."

## Conventional Medicine and Human Body

In medical system the human body is regarded as a machine that can be analyzed in terms of its parts. Disease is seen as the malfunctioning of biological mechanisms which are studied from the point of view of cellular and molecular biology. The doctor's role is to intervene, either physically or chemically, to correct the malfunctioning of a specific mechanism. In this approach every cause should have a predictable effect and likewise, a predictable cure. The human being is seen as a collection of organs, tissues, and other components into which it can be reduced.

The whole is considered nothing more than the sum of its parts. In this way of thinking every cause that leads to a predictable effect and has a predictable cure can be taken care of easily. There should be no post-surgical complications, nor post-surgical recurrences of the original problems. Also, all drugs should take care of the problem being treated, and all side effects of drugs should be known and easily catalogued. In this model there is no place for the effects of consciousness and the mind on the body because consciousness is seen as nothing but the result of brain process.

**Metabolic Classification**

We need to use and expand the body of research on biochemical differences, and do research on groups of people that are the most similar biochemically. Thankfully this wheel does not need to be re-invented, as metabolic classifications involving the interaction between the autonomic nervous system, the oxidative system and the endocrine system have been used with great success in the field of nutrition. Two people with the same degenerative disease can have virtually opposite biochemical imbalances and that when two opposite biochemical protocols are administered, both get well. This clearly means that it's not the diseases that should be treated but the underlying metabolic imbalances that have caused the diseases that need to be addressed. From this viewpoint, the diseases are the symptoms, the manifestations, the expressions of the underlying imbalances. This same scenario applies to every degenerative condition. Whether its cancer, diabetes, heart disease, arthritis, chronic fatigue, allergies, or headaches, the same principles apply. The reality of metabolic individuality demands that the person who has the disease, not the disease that has the person, be treated! To summarize:

I. Biochemical individuality is responsible for the fact that nutrients behave differently in different metabolic types in terms of their stimulatory/catabolic/acid or sedating/anabolic/alkaline influences

II. The variable influences of nutrients on different metabolisms along with the same condition arising from totally different biochemical imbalances make it impossible to treat conditions with a standardized treatment protocol

III. Successful, predictable, reliable therapy can only be chosen once you know the metabolic type of the patient because only then will you know how to treat.

It is true that there are tens of thousands of biochemical reactions that take place on a daily basis in human metabolism. So, it would be impractical and impossible to think in terms of treating and monitoring all of those reactions in an attempt to understand and address biochemical individuality. And, yet, this is precisely what we have been doing when we either try to treat a weak organ, address supposed vitamin or mineral deficiencies, or attempt to interpret laboratory results of blood, urine, hair, saliva or other tissue samples in terms of what we think are excesses or deficiencies.

**Homeostatic Systems**

The solution to this dilemma lies in the fact that all those tens of thousands of metabolic processes fall under the control and regulation of just a few fundamental homeostatic systems, the most significant of which are dualistic in nature. These homeostatic mechanisms function through complementary yet opposing influences. How does this relate to nutrition? Research has uncovered the fact that every nutrient and every food has a specific inhibitory or stimulatory effect on one or more of those systems and on one side or other of these homeostatic control mechanisms. Thus, another very important principle is revealed: There is no food or nutritional supplement that is right or good for everyone.

Whether any supplement is "good" or "bad" depends on the particular biochemical balance of the individual in question, meaning which fundamental homeostatic mechanism is out of balance and what the effect of the nutrient in question will be on that imbalanced system; will it improve the imbalance or worsen the imbalance? It is the strength and balance of these control mechanisms in each individual, which define metabolic individuality and determine the metabolic type. Most significantly, metabolic typing research has uncovered the fact that no adverse condition can exist that does not involve an imbalance in one or more of these fundamental homeostatic control mechanisms!

Currently, nine of these fundamental homeostatic control mechanisms have been discovered and are utilized to define one's metabolic type.

Certain nutrients stimulate and strengthen the sympathetic output, while others increase the parasympathetic output; and, certain nutrients increase the rate of glycolysis, while others slow it down. Of central importance is the discovery that each person is genetically predisposed to greater or lesser strengths in the divisions of the autonomic nervous system and to greater or lesser rates of oxidation.

These genetically based and environmentally influenced differences help define their biochemical individuality and their metabolic type. The variable influences of these homeostatic controls, that is, the variable strengths and weaknesses, manifest in individual differences that define the metabolic type, for instance in the acid/alkaline balance. They determine both the tendency of an organism towards acidity or alkalinity and they determine how an organism metabolizes any given nutrient, producing either an acid or alkaline result.

**Sympathetic / Parasympathetic predisposition**

So, first of all we have the fact that a Sympathetic predisposition or one for a Fast Oxidation (meaning: fast conversion of carbohydrates to energy) result in shifts towards acidity, while a Parasympathetic predisposition or a Slow Oxidation result in alkaline shifts. Secondly, and just as significantly, and this is very, very important, the same foods and nutrients that acidify by virtue of their stimulating influence on the autonomic system, will alkalinize through their influence in the oxidative system. There are few rules which rule homeostasis:

First within each homeostatic system, there are opposing, yet complementary influences, each of which influences oppositely the acid/alkaline balance. While the sympathetic branch causes a tendency of the metabolism towards acidity, the parasympathetic causes a leaning towards alkalinity. And while a fast oxidation makes for more acidity, a slow oxidation makes for more alkalinity.

Second, a given nutrient will have an acidifying influence on one homeostatic control system, and an alkalizing influence on the other system. For example, in one metabolic type, potassium will alkalize through acceleration of parasympathetic output, while in another type; potassium will acidify through increasing the rate of glycolysis.

Third, one more very important fact: In any given individual, one or another of the homeostatic control systems will dominate. Either the autonomic system has the stronger impact and determines the influences of nutrients in a given individual, or the oxidative system can exert its impact. Whichever system dominates will determine how nutrients behave in that person, whether they acidify or alkalinize. In other words, it is not the food or nutrient itself that determines acid or alkaline effects in the body, but it is the dominant system influenced by that food that is behind it all and ultimately determines the acid/alkaline result and other reactions to nutrients.

**Health excel System of Metabolic Typing**

The Dominance Factor was formulated in 1983 by W.L. Wolcott; in his Health excel System of Metabolic Typing. The Dominance Factor explains why for any predictable, reliably successful therapy, you must first determine the dominant system and the metabolic type before you can know how nutrients behave in a patient's metabolism and what will therefore balance body chemistry proving to be your medicine and not your poison. The application of these concepts has been formulated into a specific metabolic typing testing methodology that turned out to be very successful indeed. So the conclusion is:

I. Any nutrient and any food can have virtually opposite biochemical influences in different individuals or metabolic types.

II. Any adverse symptoms or degenerative condition can arise due to virtually opposite biochemical imbalances.

III. Biochemical Imbalances disrupt homeostasis or biorhythms. Disrupted biorhythms generate symptoms which collectively produce disease.

# CHAPTER NO: 2

# THE HARMONY WITHIN: BIORHYTHMS

The theory of biorhythms claims that one's life is affected by rhythmic biological cycles, and seeks to make predictions regarding these cycles. These inherent rhythms are said to control or initiate various biological processes and are classically composed of three cyclic rhythms that are said to govern human behavior and demonstrate innate periodicity in natural physiological change: the physical, the emotional, and the intellectual (or mental) cycles. Others claim there are additional rhythms, some of which may be combinations of the three primary cycles. Some proponents think that biorhythms may be potentially related to bioelectricity and its interactions in the body.

## Chronobiology

Chronobiology is a branch of biology that studies rhythms in living beings. Prof. Dr. G. Hildebrandt is one of the fathers of the Chrono-medicine, and is renowned worldwide as a leading medical authority in the fields of Chrono-biology, Balneology, medical climatology and physical medicine. In his work "Biological Rhythms in Humans and their counterparts in Music " Dr. Hildebrandt shows how the rhythmical processes in a healthy human organism follow the harmonic laws of nature and, in the truest sense of the word turn it into a music physiology. The classical theory originated at the turn of the 19th century, between 1897 and 1902, from observational research.

### *Chrono-medicine and various ailments*

Dr. Hermann Swoboda (Professor of Psychology, University of Vienna ), who was researching periodic variations in fevers, looked into the possibility of a rhythmic change in mood and health. He collected data on reaction to pain, outbreak of fevers, illnesses, asthma, heart attacks, and recurrent dreams. He concluded that there was a

23-day physical cycle and a 28-day emotional cycle. Dr. Wilhelm Fliess (nose and throat specialist) independently was researching the occurrences of fevers, recurrent illnesses and deaths in his patients. He also came to the conclusion that there was a 23 and a 28-day rhythm. Fliess's theories were of great interest and importance to Sigmund Freud during his early work in developing his psychoanalytic concepts.

***Homeostasis or steady state***

In 1925 the great physiologist Walter Cannon of Harvard Medical School introduced the principle of homeostasis, or steady state. Cannon drew on the work of French physiologist Claude Bernard, who suggested in 1885 that the body strives to maintain constancy in its internal environment. Cannon asserted that the body continually fine tunes itself to adapt to demands placed upon it, maintaining equilibrium. So the notion of health as equilibrium goes back to ancient times. But the problem with homeostasis is: it is incomplete, it tells the truth but not the whole truth. All bodily functions differ markedly over the twenty four hour day. These variations are not random, they occur in synchrony with our habitual daily patterns of activity and rest. These changes do not simply reflect a fine tuning process, but more than thousand rhythmic bodily functions.

***Disease disrupts biorhythms***

Leading medical centers worldwide showed that many illnesses disrupt normal body rhythms, the signs and symptoms of many illnesses vary across the 24 hours a day, over the month, and around the year. The time of the day you take diagnostic tests or undergo medical procedures alters the result. The results of the diagnostic tests vary over a period of 24 hours and on day to day basis too. The time you take medicine matters a lot. How you organize your daily life, with respect to sleep, meals, exercise, and other factors may make symptoms better or worse. These factors hasten or slow your recovery. Chrono-therapy or time treatment, aims to correct these underlying causes or reduce their adverse impact.

***Biorhythms sensors***

The human body is embedded with rhythm regulation sensors, like baro-receptors sensing fluctuation in blood pressure, appestat centre in brain regulates the appetite, thermostat is adjusting the body temperature, ph regulating sensors, SA node controlling heart rhythm, body balance apparatus in brain and ears, etc. which are regulating moment to moment this dynamic state of human chemistry. Holistic sciences describe the role of various body organs in harmonizing these sensors and their functions. In order to get optimum holistic health, our biorhythm regulatory sensors and vital organs especially liver should be in a healthy state. Our biorhythms and liver functions are interdependent.

Bio-rhythmic cycles start the day we are born and run for a lifetime, they are triggered by hormones released at birth and your birth date is day one for these cycles. These cycles are independent of environmental cycles such as day and night or the seasons. In order to have a healthy bio-rhythm, we need to have a lifestyle which is in harmony with the inner rhythms. If we are sensitive enough to receive our internal signals we will be protected from incoming ailments.

Chrono - medicine tells us that if a person is at physical or emotional comfort it indicates harmony between that individual and the environment. Living in contrast to the body's rhythms produce different diseases. My clinical experience and a retrospective study done on about 30,000 patients in the past seven years revealed that there are two major types of biorhythms, static and non-static or dynamic biorhythms.

## Classification of biorhythms

1-Static Biorhythms

2-Non-static or dynamic Biorhythms

### *1-Static Biorhythms*

Biological body type is the only type of static biorhythms which are partially static, and can change state if required by the body. Body type is determined on the basis of various biological factors like musculoskeletal frame, skin, complexion, voice characteristics, vital functions, emotional and psychological factors. The body type is flexibly fixed and is controlled by the state of the master organ – liver.

#### *Body Typing*

Body typing is the recognition of different body types. It attempts to address questions which modern medicine, in spite of the use of sophisticated medical tests, has been unable to answer. Why for instance, does one person suffer from diabetes and another from hypoglycemia? Why it is that one person can cope with an enormous amount of stress while another succumbs to a much smaller amount? Why does one person have a fast metabolism while another has a slow metabolism? Why it is that one person is a bookworm while another prefers sport or physical activity? Why it is that one person is much more sensitive than another? Why it is that one person is constantly catching colds and flu while another person rarely gets any illness, and yet both people are medically 'normal'? Why is it that some people find it almost impossible to lose weight while others find it impossible to gain weight? Why is it that some people are extroverts while others are introverts? Remember genes are not to be blamed.

Body typing is the study of these differences. It is based upon the fact that our physical, psychological, and behavioral differences, and our susceptibility to certain diseases, are related to internal physiological and biochemical differences, especially our own unique body type or glandular make up. Since body typing acknowledges the interplay of all these factors in our total wellbeing, it is essentially holistic in nature. The recognition of different body types was a central part of the holistic healing systems of ancient Greece, China and Subcontinent more than 2000 years ago. Although the Western tradition of ancient Greece has been replaced by reductionist scientific medicine over the past 200 - 300 years. Indian Ayurveda system, Pakistan's herbalists and the Chinese Five Phase system are still dependent on various body types. These traditional body typing systems were based upon unique insight into, and observation of, the various types of human physiques and behavior patterns, even though the mechanisms behind these differences could not be fully understood until more was learned of human physiology and biochemistry. Below is an account of various body types:

***I-Sheldon Body Types***

During the middle of the twentieth century it was Sheldon who categorized the physique of people and developed three basic body types, namely, endomorphs, ectomorphs, and mesomorphs. Subsequently these three basic somatotypes were analyzed from the point of view of their temperament or psychological profile. Following the work of Sheldon, the understanding of the various body types began to accelerate as science revealed the importance of the endocrine glands and the hormones they produce in determining various human characteristics, both physical and psychological. Research into glandular diseases and hormonal excesses and deficiencies eventually led to the use of glandular terminology to describe the various body types according to which glandular features are dominant.

***II-Bieler Body Types***

In the 1960's Bieler described three basic glandular types, Adrenal type, Thyroid type, and Pituitary type, each of which had definite physical and psychological characteristics. Since the description of the three basic glandular types by Bieler, two additional types have been described, namely, the Gonadal type, and the Pancreas type.

### *III-Roger and Biochemical Individuality*

Roger Williams, the brilliant American scientist who pioneered research into the various physiological and biochemical aspects of human variation which he termed biochemical individuality. Williams' extensive studies into biochemical individuality revealed numerous variations in glandular size and metabolism in people who were considered to be medically normal. Williams reported for instance, that there was a tenfold variation in the thickness of adrenal glands, and a six fold variation in the size of thyroid glands, in normal healthy persons. Williams also found a wide variation in the efficiency with which dietary nutrients were utilized in normal persons. According to Williams, these variations are responsible for many of the differences between normal people.

### *IV-Dr. George and four panels of personality*

An outstanding advance in organizing the data which relate the physical characteristics of individuals to their disease susceptibilities has been made by the Constitutional clinic of Columbia University and the Presbyterian Hospital of New York, under the direction of Dr. George Draper. He has found it necessary that in order to study man as a whole, to view him from four different angles: his form, his function, his immunity mechanism, and his psychology. These four attributes he has designated as the "four panels of personality".

### *V-SLP Body Types*

In SLP, human typology or body type classification is done on the basis of present, past medical history, childhood traumas, psychological and family history. Other parameters are details about the dietary routine, nocturnal sleep, exercise details, general physical examination, and pulse diagnosis. Above mentioned diagnostic tools help in assessing body form, function, immune system and psychology. In SLP, state of biorhythms and liver are the key factors for classifying body type or body chemistry. SLP body types are six, which are fixed but can change under various conditions. As all glandular functions are regulated by liver, therefore pituitary, thyroid, adrenal, pancreatic and gonadal body types are easily regulated by improving the health of master gland liver. It is learnt that there is no blanket rule to classify the body types, as the chemical body type changes its chemistry from one to the other depending upon the bodily requirement.

Body by structure is acidic with an alkaline blood and reflects optimally functioning liver and balanced biorhythms. This perfect chemistry in an adult would have reflected in good stamina, ideal weight, optimum digestion, pleasant mood, perfect sleep, good immunity, no disease and therefore no aging. Ideal chemistry would have converted a human into an emotion less robotic machine and that is the reason ideal chemistry is rarely seen. Human evolution and the fast pace of this technology filled world has made humans more thoughtful, intelligent, ambitious, competitive and restless. The organ and the system which is making us cope with this technology evolution is liver and biorhythms respectively. Probably liver is also at its peak of evolution. This hyperactivity has either exhausted liver or made it work hyperactively. 99% of patients coming to my clinic have various levels of dysfunctional liver.

Dysfunctional liver is not the diseased liver, but it is either sluggish or hyper-activated, and it cannot be diagnosed on routine laboratory test. Below mentioned six chemical body types are classified on the basis of liver and biorhythms. Six body types give an idea about the basic six homeostatic mechanisms regulating health and disease as well. The knowledge about these six chemical types is extremely important for a therapist because we cannot reverse a chronic degenerative disease without knowing these six chemistries. SLP chemical body types are:

1. Acidic body with hyper liver
2. Acidic body with hypo/sluggish liver
3. Hyper-acidic body with hyper- liver
4. Hyper-acidic body with hypo/sluggish liver
5. Acidic body, hyper-liver and water retention
6. Acidic body, hypo/sluggish liver and water retention

***SLP Rule of Six***

If you are living an unhealthy lifestyle, the two basic body types (acidic or alkaline) will generate six types of pathologies which are diagnosed on six types of pulse. Six pathologies lead to six group of diseases with multiple sub-diseases over a period of time. Diseases are managed by six combinations of group of natural foods organized on the principles of SLP. All acute, chronic diseases, familial diseases, psychological, metabolic and rare medical disorders are easily explained on the basis of six pathologies. Six pathologies are the result of disharmony in basic biorhythms and liver dysfunction due to incorrect eating habits, disturb sleep and subtle stress.

***2- Non static or dynamic Biorhythms***

Human life is regulated by dynamic biorhythms. Basic dynamic rhythms follow certain facets of physiological cycles. They are often represented graphically as either symmetric or asymmetric waveforms, though most theories rely on symmetric forms. The most commonly used form is the sinusoidal waveform, which is thought to be a plausible representation of a bioelectric activity cycle. The purpose of mapping the biorhythmic cycles is to enable the calculation of critical days for performing or avoiding various activities.

***i-Time regulated types of non-static biorhythms***

- Ultrafine are the biological rhythms having extremely short cycles (lasting less than 24 hours).
- Circadian are the biological rhythms having a period of about 24 hours (lasting a day).
- Infradian are biological rhythms composed of long-term cycles (lasting several days).
- Exogenous are cycles influenced by external factors.
- Endogenous are cycles not influenced by external changes.

- Circatrigintan are cycles that recur every month (around 25-35 days).
- Circavigintan are cycles that recur tri weekly (around 17-23 days).
- Circadiseptan are cycles that occur biweekly (around 12-17 days).
- Circannual are cycles that recur every year (around 365 days).

***Circadian Rhythm***

The physiological functions of virtually all organisms are governed by 24-hour circadian rhythms. Your circadian clock is an essential time-tracking system, which your body uses to anticipate environmental changes and adapt to the appropriate time of day. When your circadian rhythm is disrupted, it can have a profound influence on your physical health. Previous research has already linked disrupted sleep cycles to obesity, diabetes, insomnia, depression, coronary heart diseases and even cancer. One study shows that there's a tightly regulated codependency between your circadian clock and your metabolism and cellular performance. Says Paolo Sassone-Corsi, Distinguished Professor and Chair of Pharmacology:

"Your circadian rhythms and metabolism are closely partnered to ensure that cells function properly and remain healthy. When the balance between these two vital processes is upset, normal cellular function can be disrupted, and this can lead to illness and disease. The findings suggest that proper sleep and diet may help maintain or rebuild this balance."

Scientists have discovered that your circadian rhythms regulate the energy levels in your cells. In addition, the proteins involved with circadian rhythms and metabolism is intrinsically linked and dependent upon each other. This finding has far-reaching implications, which could include new ways to treat cancer, diabetes, obesity and a host of related diseases. 24-hour circadian rhythms govern fundamental physiological functions in almost all organisms. There are about 100 circadian rhythms, regulating the micro environment of human body and maintaining a holistic balance.

***ii-Biological Clock***

Non-static biorhythms are responsible for 24 hours routine physical, mental and spiritual activities, this changing system of biorhythms make us adjust against the changing surroundings of our body, and they are responsible for the dynamic biophysics of the human system. The body's biological clock plays an important role in the regulation of these non-static biorhythms. This clock called the supra-chiasmatic nucleus or SCN is actually a pair of pinhead-sized brain structures that together contains about 20,000 neurons. The SCN rests in a part of brain called the hypothalamus, just above the point where the optic nerve crosses. Signals from the SCN travel to several brain regions, including the pineal gland, which responds to light induced signals by switching off production of the hormone melatonin. The SCN also governs homeostatic functions that are synchronized with the sleep/wake cycle, heart rate, blood pressure, including body temperature, hormone secretion, and urine production.

The body's biological time system works like a real world company, with the SCN as chief executive officer. Nerve connections from the eyes tell the SCN what levels of light are available. The SCN interprets this message and delegates tasks to vice presidents in the hypothalamus and nearby pituitary gland. They in turn issue commands to mid-level managers elsewhere in the brain and in organs throughout the body, all the way down to the individual cells making up the round the clock work force. Reports from the field filter their way back to the SCN, which constantly processes and modifies job assignments.

Some peculiarly human behaviors, such as flying to distant spots across time zones, or working on different shifts, upset the staff. They get orders from two bosses at the same time, the day manager and the night manager. Some workers pay attention to one, and others, to the other. Their internal mix-ups appears in travelers as jet lag and shift workers as trouble adapting to new hours for waking and sleeping. The SCN straightens things out, though this job may take several days to several weeks.

***iii-Holistic non static biorhythms***

Other important non-static or dynamic rhythms which regulate metabolism, immunity, energy levels and aging process are:

1. Hormones
2. Various food cravings
3. Body ph balance
4. Body temperature
5. Nocturnal sleep rhythm

***1-Hormones***

Our health and life depends on how accurately instructions are conveyed to our cells so that they can act in harmony. It is the communication among the individual cells that will determine our health and our life. The communication takes place by hormones, therefore the most important molecules in your body that ultimately will decide your health and life are hormones. The two most important hormones that deliver messages about energy and metabolism are insulin and leptin. Insulin works mostly at the individual cell level, telling the vast majority of cells whether to burn or store fat or sugar and whether to utilize that energy for maintenance and repair or reproduction.

Leptin is a very powerful and influential hormone produced by fat cells that has totally changed the way that science looks at fat, nutrition, and metabolism in general. Prior to leptin's discovery, fat was viewed as strictly an ugly energy storage depot that everyone was trying to get rid of. After it was discovered that fat produced the hormone leptin (and subsequently it was discovered that fat produced other very significant hormones), fat became an endocrine organ like the ovaries, pancreas and pituitary, influencing the rest of the body and, in particular, the brain.

Leptin, as far as science currently knows, is the most powerful regulator that tells your brain what to do about life's two main biological goals: eating and reproduction. Your fat, by way of leptin, tells your brain whether you should be hungry, eat and make more fat, whether you should reproduce and make babies, or (partly by controlling insulin) whether to "hunker down" and work overtime to maintain and repair yourself. In short, leptin is the way that your fat stores speak to your brain to let your brain know how much energy is available and, very importantly, what to do with it. Therefore, leptin may be "on top of the food chain" in metabolic importance and relevance to disease.

If a person is getting too fat, the extra fat produces more leptin which is supposed to tell the brain that there is too much fat stored, more should not be stored, and the excess should be burned. Signals are therefore sent to an area of the brain in the hypothalamus (the arcuate nucleus) to stop being hungry, to stop eating, to stop storing fat and to start burning some extra fat off. Controlling hunger is a major way that leptin controls energy storage. Hunger is a very powerful, ancient, and deep-seated drive that, if stimulated long enough, will make you eat and store more energy. Asking somebody to not eat, to voluntarily restrict calories even though they are hungry, is asking the near impossible. The only way to eat less in the long-term is to not be hungry, and the only way to do this is to control the hormones that regulate hunger, the primary one being leptin.

More recently, it has been found that leptin not only changes brain chemistry, but can also "rewire" the very important areas of the brain that control hunger and metabolism. This has really caught the attention of the scientific community. Further studies have now shown that leptin, or more correctly the inability of the body to properly hear leptin's signals, in other words leptin resistance, plays significant if not primary roles in heart disease, obesity, diabetes, osteoporosis, autoimmune diseases, reproductive disorders, and perhaps the rate of aging itself. It helps to control the brain areas that regulate thyroid levels and the sympathetic nervous system which also has huge impacts on blood pressure, heart disease, diabetes, osteoporosis and aging. Leptin's stimulatory effect on the sympathetic nervous system also helps determine the adrenal stress response including cortisol levels.

The importance of insulin in health and disease is becoming well-known. Aside from its obvious role in diabetes, it plays a very significant role in hypertension, cardiovascular disease, and cancer. However leptin may even supersede insulin in importance, for new research is revealing that in the long run glucose and therefore insulin levels may be largely determined by leptin. It had been previously believed that the insulin sensitivity of muscle and fat tissues were the most important factor in determining whether one would become diabetic or not. Elegant new studies are showing that the brain and liver are most important in regulating a person's blood sugar levels especially in type 2 or insulin resistant diabetes.

It should be noted again that leptin plays a vital role in regulating your brain's hypothalamic activity which in turn regulates much of a person's "autonomic" functions; those functions that you don't necessarily think about but which determines much of your life (and health) such as body temperature, heart rate, hunger, the stress response, fat burning or storage, reproductive behavior, and newly discovered roles in bone growth and blood sugar levels. Another very recent study reveals leptin's importance in directly regulating how much sugar that the liver manufactures via gluconeogenesis. Many chronic diseases are now linked to excess inflammation such as heart disease and diabetes. High leptin levels are very pro-inflammatory, and leptin also helps to mediate the manufacture of other very potent inflammatory chemicals from fat cells that also play a significant role in the progression of heart disease and diabetes.

It has long been known that obesity greatly increased risk for many chronic diseases including heart disease and diabetes, but no one really knew why. Leptin appears to be the missing link. Leptin will not only determine how much fat you have, but also where that fat is put. When you are leptin resistant you put that fat mostly in your belly, your viscera, causing the so-called "apple shape" that is linked to disease. Some of that fat permeates the liver, impeding the liver's ability to listen to insulin, and further hastening diabetes. Leptin appears to play a significant role in obesity, heart disease, osteoporosis, autoimmune diseases, inflammatory diseases and cancer. These are the so-called "chronic diseases of aging". Leptin also is instrumental in regulating body temperature, partly by controlling the rate of metabolism via its regulation of the thyroid.

Metabolic rate and temperature has long been connected with longevity. Anything will dissolve faster in hot water than cold water. Extra heat will dissolve, disrupt and disorganize. It is commonly advised to "increase metabolism" and increase "thermogenesis" for health and weight loss. That will be determined at the quality of your leptin signaling. If it is poor, if you are insulin and leptin resistant, your metabolism is unhealthy and high. If you then increase its rate you will likely accelerate your demise. To increase the quality of your metabolism you must be able to properly listen to insulin and especially to leptin. If your fasting blood serum level of leptin is elevated you are likely leptin resistant and you will not be healthy unless you correct it. People become leptin-resistant by the same general mechanism that people become insulin-resistant; by overexposure to high levels of the hormone.

***2-Various Food Cravings***

By developing your awareness of the factors that create cravings, you can feel more in control of your body while acquiring an attuned sensitivity to your needs and body signals. From an acid/alkaline perspective, strong craving for certain forms of acidity during pregnancy draw minerals into the blood for neutralizing. While this acidity might adversely affect the mother, the developing fetus seems to be the probable benefactor. Food cravings are signals sent by our bodies indicating mineral deficiency, which then stimulate us to unhealthy eating. All cells in our bodies (except for fat cells) become starved for glucose and amino acids as a result of excess calcium, and this leads to increased cravings for glucose and for minerals. The foods that most people eat are frequently low in minerals because most fruits and vegetables today are grown in mineral-poor soil and few foods are vine-ripened. As a result, our metabolisms are slowed, and our cells can't obtain the essential amino acids needed for full health.

If you experience cravings for sugary foods, this could be an indication that you are becoming insulin resistant and entering a state called metabolic syndrome which results in elevated insulin levels, high blood pressure, elevated total cholesterol and triglycerides, and obesity. Cravings for salty foods reflect mineral deficiencies in the body, including a lack of sodium. To lose weight and keep it off permanently, you must treat metabolic imbalances by correcting for any mineral deficiencies. Simply reducing caloric intake and getting frequent exercise won't achieve lasting weight loss. A slow metabolism, which leads to obesity, is a result of the body's failure to get the essential amino acids and glucose our cells require.

*Categories of food cravings*

i. Nutritional
ii. Acid/ alkaline balance
iii. Blood sugar
iv. Emotional
v. Genetics
vi. Allergy response
vii. Elimination/detoxification

These are internal broadcasts the body uses to signal its different needs. It's important to give an ear to these signals, but equally important to recognize that there is a fine line between fueling dietary addictions and just following dietary intuition. Craving is a natural compensatory phenomenon; therefore you will crave only for natural foods. Many diseases disrupt important food craving biorhythm and sick people start craving for unhealthy foods. Addictive cravings can be for artificial foods, sugars, junk, drugs, cigarettes or alcohol, which will always indicate disease chemistry.

I have seen cancer patients intensely craving for unhealthy foods which will nourish cancer. Chronic disease is like a demon residing in your body, and enjoying full freedom to damage your body. It makes you helpless by demanding for the disease supporting foods by generating strong addictive cravings. Understanding the meaning behind different cravings can liberate you from feeling guilty or out of control with your eating. Self-mastery begins with awareness.

***3-Body ph balance***

Total healing of chronic illness takes place only when and if the blood is restored to a normal, slightly alkaline ph. The magnitude of meaning behind this research is of incredible importance to someone who is fighting a disease, overcoming an illness, or just desiring to feel better. Your body ph affects everything; human blood stays in a very narrow ph range right around 7.35. Below or above this range means symptoms and disease. When ph goes off, microbial looking forms in the blood can change shape, mutate, grow and initiate a disease process. When ph goes off, enzymes that are constructive can become destructive. When ph goes off, oxygen delivery to cells suffers.

Body ph is of utmost importance to the functioning of our vital organs. The brain, which can be called the central processing unit of our body, cannot store energy. It draws energy every second from the blood supplied to it by the veins. This blood has a ph level which in turn affects the level of insulin, which decides the amount of sugar that is to be absorbed by the blood. So if the body ph misbalances, the brain instantly feels the pressure. A high acidic body ph would not let the brain draw the energy that is does from the blood cells which will in themselves be low on insulin and so energy.

After the brain the next most vital part in out body is the heart. If the body ph gets more acidic then the negatively charged fatty acid in the blood cells become positively charged. As soon as that happens they get attracted like magnets to the negatively charged vein walls. Such attraction between the blood cells and the vein walls causes the arteries to get blocked over time. Thus most generations that have meats as their main diet can cause their body ph to get acidic thus causing the fatty acid to change poles making the cells stick to the veins thus causing heart diseases. William Philpott M.D. in his 'Biomagnetic Handbook'made an important body ph / electrical connection. 'As the pH of the blood goes more acid, fatty acids which are normally electro-magnetically charged on the negative side switch to positive and automatically are attracted to and begin to stick to the walls of arteries which are electro-magnetically charged on the negative side. (And as science states, opposites attract.) It should start to make sense that a society which over-emphasizes food that could push blood to be more acid will have a high rate of heart disease. And so it goes.'

ph control impacts every biochemical process in the body including, enzymes which are part of that biochemical process. There are hundreds if not thousands of enzyme processes which take place in the body. Many are so specific that they are like complex square pegs that need to "fit" into specific square holes in order to carry out their duty. If blood ph is off balance even a little, some important pegs are not "fitting" their respective slots. Enzyme function and thus life itself begins to suffer.

Mineral assimilation is affected by ph. Minerals have different ph levels at which they can be assimilated into the body. Minerals on the lower end of the atomic scale can be assimilated in a wider ph range, and minerals higher up on the scale require a narrower and narrower ph range in order to be assimilated by the body. For example sodium and magnesium have wide ph assimilation ranges. It narrows somewhat for calcium and potassium. It further narrows for manganese, iron, zinc, copper and iodine.

Iodine, which is high up on the atomic scale, requires near perfect ph for its assimilation into the body. Iodine is one of the most important minerals for proper functioning of the thyroid. But, the thyroid doesn't get access to iodine unless the body ph is near perfect. With a society in a largely ph unbalanced state, one would suspect a lot of thyroid problems. Malfunctioning thyroids have been connected to arthritis, heart attacks, diabetes, cancer, depression, overweight, fatigue and more. Due primarily to agricultural soil depletion and over-acidic food consumption, mineral deficiency is a large problem facing most people today. And mineral deficiency relates to the quantity of life energy or, more specifically, electricity, in our bodies. The speed at which the electricity flows is controlled by the body's ph balance.

Most people and clinical practitioners believe the immune system is the body's first line of defense, but in actuality it is not. It is very important, but more like a very sophisticated clean-up service. We must instead look at the importance of ph balance as the first and major line of defense against sickness and disease and for health and vitality. A state of acidosis is simply the lack of oxygen and available calcium which the body uses to maintain its alkaline balance. Calcium makes up 1.6% of our body weight. It is literally the human glue that holds the body together. Calcium is so biochemically active that it has been likened to an octopus. A calcium ion can hold onto seven other molecules while it grabs onto one molecule of water. No other ion can do this. And it is the right size to easily get in and out of the human cell. As it does this, it takes a chain of nutrients into the cell and then leaves to get more nutrients.

The biggest problem scientists have found is that over time the human body becomes depleted of calcium. A compound called mono-ortho-calcium phosphate is the chemical buffer for the blood. This buffer maintains the alkaline level (or the lack of acidity) in your blood. Without it you would die. If the acidity levels of your blood changes even slightly you die immediately. But in order to supply enough calcium for buffering we must have enough calcium being absorbed from our diet or our body will simply rob the needed calcium from our bones and teeth.

The more acidic we become, the harder it is for oxygen to be present, so our biological terrain also becomes more anaerobic. Without adequate oxygenation, unfriendly bacteria, viruses, molds, and fungus can live and prosper. Then our cells cannot carry on their life-giving functions in a very efficient manner because our biological chemical reactions need oxygen. Life and death are in the biological terrain and the battle cry here is to reclaim your biological terrain. This is so important that some practitioners working with the inner biological terrain and its implications to the health of our bodies are beginning to say "There are no specific diseases, only specific disease conditions, and there is only one disease. And that one disease is acidosis."

The human body is very intelligent. As we become more and more acidic the body starts to set up defense mechanisms to keep the damaging acid from entering our vital organs. It is known that acid gets stored in fat cells. After all, if the acid does come into contact with an organ the acid has a chance to create holes in the tissue and this may cause the cells to mutate. The oxygen level drops in this acidic environment and calcium begins to be depleted. So as a defense mechanism, your body may actually make fat to protect you from your overly-acidic self. Those fat cells and cellulite deposits may actually be packing up the acid and trying to keep it a safe distance from your organs. The fat may be saving your vital organs from damage. Many people have found that a return to a healthy inner biological terrain helps them to lose excess fat.

**Buffering systems**

There are complex biochemical processes taking place in the body constantly in an attempt to keep blood ph as near perfect as possible. These are known as the ph buffering systems. These buffering systems need a good balance of minerals to work effectively. If we are getting inadequate mineral intake from the food we eat, we are going to start having problems with our ph balancing systems. And if our ph is unbalanced, the result is cancer, arthritis, diabetes, heart disease, chronic fatigue, allergies, and obesity.

If you don't feel good, one of the basic things that stand between you and perfect health is your body's ph. Your basic metabolic body balance. Since Louis Pasteur discovered the germ theory of disease that states germs are the cause of disease, time has proven him correct. But note Dr. Pasteur's dying words: "The germ is nothing, the inner terrain is everything." The inner terrain referred to in Dr. Pasteur's statement is now being called our biological terrain and comprises our body's digestive tract, lymph system, blood, urinary tract, interstitial and interstitial fluids.

As our bodies are alkaline by design and acid by function. We live and die at the cellular level. All the cells (billions of them) that make up the human body are slightly alkaline, and must maintain alkalinity in order to function and remain healthy and alive. However their cellular activity creates acid and this acid is what gives the cell energy and function. As each alkaline cell performs its task of respiration, it secretes metabolic wastes, and these end products of cellular metabolism are acid in nature. Although these wastes are used for energy and function, they must not be allowed to build up. One example of this is the often painful lactic acid which is created through exercise. The body will go to great lengths to neutralize and detoxify these acids before they act as poisons in and around the cell, ultimately changing the environment of the cell.

***4-Body Temperature***

Warmth is one of the necessities of life. Vital activities are possible only between certain narrowly defined limits of temperature. Cold inhibits and excessive heat suspends them. Body heat is energy; it is employed not just in resisting cold but also in accelerating cellular activities. Temperature, within certain narrow limits, is so absolutely essential to life that all functions are excited by any attempt at its variation. Animals are roughly divided into two major classes: warm-blooded (endotherm) and cold-blooded (ectotherm). This is according to whether they have means of producing and maintaining their own temperature or are dependent upon the surrounding medium (water or air) to provide it.

Thermoregulation is the ability of an organism to keep its body temperature within certain boundaries, even when the surrounding temperature is very different. This process is one aspect of homeostasis: a dynamic state of stability between an animal's internal environment and its external environment. If the body is unable to maintain a normal temperature and it increases significantly above normal, a condition known as hyperthermia occurs. The opposite condition when body temperature decreases below normal levels is known as hypothermia.

As in other mammals, thermoregulation is an important aspect of human homeostasis. Most body heat is generated in the deep organs, especially the liver, brain, and heart, and in contraction of skeletal muscles. Humans have been able to adapt to a great diversity of climates, including hot humid and hot arid. High temperatures pose serious stresses for the human body, placing it in great danger of injury or even death. For humans, adaptation to varying climatic conditions includes both physiological mechanisms as a byproduct of evolution, and the conscious development of cultural adaptations.

***Skin and thermoregulation***

The skin assists in homeostasis (keeping different aspects of the body constant e.g. temperature). It does this by reacting differently to hot and cold conditions so that the inner body temperature remains more or less constant. Vasodilatation and sweating are the primary modes by which humans attempt to lose excess body heat. The brain creates much heat through the countless reactions which occur. Even the process of thought creates heat. The head has a complex system of blood vessels, which keeps the brain from overheating by bringing blood to the thin skin on the head, allowing heat to escape. The effectiveness of these methods is influenced by the character of the climate and the degree to which the individual is acclimatized.

***Hypothalamus and thermoregulation***

Thermoregulation in both cold blooded and warm blooded is controlled mainly by the preoptic area of the anterior hypothalamus. Such homeostatic control is separate from the sensation of temperature. In humans, a diurnal variation has been observed dependent on the periods of rest and activity, lowest at 11 p.m. to 3 a.m. and peaking at 10 a.m. to 6 p.m. During various studies when Organisms were presented with the problem of regulating body temperature have not only behavioral, physiological and structural adaptations, but also a feedback system to trigger these adaptations to regulate temperature accordingly.

In humans a variation of body temperature is seen like in female menstrual cycle during the follicular phase (which lasts from the first day of menstruation until the day of ovulation), the average basal body temperature in women ranges from 36.45 to 36.7 °C (97.6 to 98.1 °F). Within 24 hours of ovulation, women experience an elevation of 0.15 - 0.45 °C (0.2 - 0.9 °F) due to the increased metabolic rate caused by sharply elevated levels of progesterone. Fever is a regulated elevation of the set point of core temperature in the hypothalamus, caused by circulating pyrogens produced by the immune system.

A group of monks known as the Tummo are known to practice techniques that allow them to raise their body temperatures substantially. Meals sometimes cause a slight elevation, sometimes a slight depression—alcohol seems always to produce a fall. Exercise and variations of external temperature within ordinary limits cause very slight change, as there are many compensating influences at work.

***Human physiology and varying temperatures***

***Hot***

i. 37°C (98.6°F) - Normal body temperature (which varies between about 36.12-37.5°C (96.8-99.5°F)

ii. 38°C (100.4°F) - Sweating, feeling very uncomfortable, slightly hungry.

iii. 39°C (102.2°F) - Severe sweating, flushed and very red. Fast heart rate and breathlessness. There may be exhaustion accompanying this. Children and people with epilepsy may be very likely to get convulsions at this point.

iv. 40°C (104°F) - Fainting, dehydration, weakness, vomiting, headache and dizziness may occur as well as profuse sweating.

v. 41°C (105.8°F)- Fainting, vomiting, severe headache, dizziness, confusion, hallucinations, delirium and drowsiness can occur. There may also be palpitations and breathlessness.

vi. 42°C (107.6°F) - Subject may turn pale or remain flushed and red. They may become comatose, be in severe delirium, vomiting, and convulsions can occur. Blood pressure may be high or low and heart rate will be very fast.

vii. 43°C (109.4°F) - Normally death, or there may be serious brain damage, continuous convulsions and shock. Cardio-respiratory collapse will likely occur.

viii. 44°C (111.2°F) or more - Almost certainly death will occur; however, patients have been known to survive up to 46.5°C (115.7°F).

***Cold***

i. 37°C (98.6°F) - Normal body temperature (which varies between about 36-37.5°C (96.8-99.5°F)

ii. 36°C (96.8°F) - Mild to moderate shivering (it drops this low during sleep). May be a normal body temperature.

iii. 35°C (95.0°F) - (hypothermia) is less than 35°C (95.0°F) - Intense shivering, numbness and bluish/grayness of the skin. There is the possibility of heart irritability.

iv. 34°C (93.2°F) - Severe shivering, loss of movement of fingers, blueness and confusion. Some behavioral changes may take place.

v. 33°C (91.4°F) - Moderate to severe confusion, sleepiness, depressed reflexes, progressive loss of shivering, slow heartbeat, shallow breathing. Shivering may stop. Subject may be unresponsive to certain stimuli.

vi. 32°C (89.6°F) - (medical emergency) Hallucinations, delirium, complete confusion, extreme sleepiness that is progressively becoming comatose. Shivering is absent (subject may even think they are hot). Reflex may be absent or very slight.

vii. 31°C (87.8°F) - Comatose, very rarely conscious. No or slight reflexes. Very shallow breathing and slow heart rate. Possibility of serious heart rhythm problems.

viii. 28°C (82.4°F) - Severe heart rhythm disturbances are likely and breathing may stop at any time. Patient may appear to be dead.

ix. 24-26°C (75.2-78.8°F) or less - Death usually occurs due to irregular heart beat or respiratory arrest; however, some patients have been known to survive with body temperatures as low as 14.2°C (57.5°F).

*Stress and low temperature of body*

Persistently low temperatures typically come on or worsen after severe stress such as childbirth, divorce, death of a loved one, job or family stress, surgery or accidents. The body slows down, and the body temperature drops in response to the stress and is supposed to recover once the stress is over, but sometimes it doesn't (a condition known as Wilson's Temperature Syndrome, or WTS). When body temperatures are low people are overwhelmed, feeling at the end of their ropes, about to give up hope, they can't function normally for their children and spouses. And when their temperature normalizes, it is as though there was never anything wrong.

They get their lives back. They begin looking forward to living a normal life. They're thrilled to be well. They're mad that they were sick for so long (and lost so much of their lives) when the problem and solution were so simple.

*Core temperature*

Core temperature, also called core body temperature, is the operating temperature of an organism, specifically in deep structures of the body such as the liver, in comparison to temperatures of peripheral tissues. Core temperature is normally maintained within a narrow range so that essential enzymatic reactions can occur. Significant core temperature elevation (hyperthermia) or depression (hypothermia) that is prolonged for more than a brief period of time is incompatible with human life.

For my diagnostic procedure, I need to know history of seasonal intolerances and the temperature of extremities i.e. hands and feet. People who become cold intolerant and shiver badly during winter months are potential cases of kidney failure and other serious diseases. Body temperature is one of the important biorhythms and cold feet sensation is sufficient enough to guide about the metabolic status of the body. It takes about 2-3 months to warm the body internally and to stabilize body temperature against changing seasons. Extreme heat and cold intolerance indicates failure of the temperature regulating biorhythm.

***5-Nocturnal sleep rhythm***

Your circadian rhythm evolved over hundreds of generations to align your physiology with your environment. Your body clock assumes that like your ancestors, you sleep at night and stay awake during daylight hours. If you confuse the situation by depriving yourself of enough hours of sleep, or eating meals at odd hours (times at which your internal clock expects you to be sleeping), you send conflicting signals to your body. Based on the implications of this latest study, it's easy to see how a compromised circadian system caused by unhealthy sleep patterns can lead to so many different kinds of disease, as proper cellular function and metabolism is essential for optimal overall health. One of the worst things you can do to disrupt your body clock is to engage in regular night shift work, by doing that you are sacrificing your longevity.

Researchers looked at how lack of sleep may affect the immune system. Chronic sleeplessness may harm the immune system, since lack of sleep is linked to an increase in cytokine molecules that control immune response. The resulting inflammation and changes in blood chemistry may be behind a variety of diseases, such as heart disease, hypertension, diabetes, obesity, depression and neurological conditions. "The foundations of good health are good diet, good exercise and good sleep, but two out of three doesn't get you there," said Dr. Anne Calhoun, a neurology professor at the University of North Carolina. Sleep is important in maintaining your health, say experts. Without it, you become more susceptible to health problems, such as heart disease, stroke, diabetes, obesity and depression.

One study on more than 1,400 middle-aged adults over four years found those with sleep apnea, in which the airway becomes repeatedly blocked and sleep is interrupted, were twice as likely to develop depression. Sleep can work to activate or inhibit hormone production in the hypothalamus, which is the part of the brain that gives the body signals regarding when to adjust temperature, blood pressure, digestive secretions and immune activity. Insufficient sleep also inhibits the pancreas from producing insulin, the hormone required for the digestion of glucose.

A groundbreaking 1999 study showed that after six days on only four hours of sleep, healthy volunteers would fall into a pre-diabetic state. Sleep also gives the heart a chance to slow down, and those who less than six hours a night have as much as a 66 percent greater prevalence of hypertension. The largest study of sleep duration and mortality followed over one million participants for six years. Those who slept about seven hours had the highest survival rate, and those who slept less than 4.5 hours had the worst. Nine hours of sleep or more each night was also associated with a higher mortality risk, however.

A French study of nearly 600 people found a higher rate of sleep problems and daytime sleepiness among allergy sufferers, compared with a controlled group of people of the same age and sex who lived in the same area. "The results show a significant impact of allergic rhinitis on all dimensions of sleep quality and, consequently, a lower quality of life as reflected by more somnolence, daytime fatigue and sleepiness, and impaired memory, mood and sexuality," Dr. Damien Léger of Assistance Publique Hôpitaux de Paris and colleagues wrote. In the same issue of Archives of Internal Medicine, other studies concluded that men with diabetes and men with short or poor-quality sleep tended to have less control of their blood-sugar levels.

In 2004, researchers at the University of Chicago discovered that sleep loss could reduce the body's ability to regulate hormones that control hunger. This could lead to an increase in appetite and a preference for high-carbohydrate foods. Research subjects who slept only four hours a night for two nights had an 18 per cent decrease in leptin, a hormone that tells the brain there is no need for more food, and a 28 per cent increase in ghrelin, a hormone that triggers hunger. "It provides biochemical evidence connecting the trend toward chronic sleep curtailment to obesity and its consequences, including metabolic syndrome and diabetes," said Eve Van Cauter, professor of medicine at the University of Chicago, in a press release.

As hunger increased in the research subjects, their food choices changed. After two nights of diminished sleep, the volunteers found foods such as candy, cookies and cake far more appealing than fruit, vegetables or dairy products. "We don't yet know why food choice would shift," Van Cauter said. "Since the brain is fuelled by glucose, we suspect it seeks simple carbohydrates when distressed by lack of sleep." Modern society seems to have forgotten the importance of sleep, according to Van Cauter. "We are all under pressure to perform, in school, at work, in social and professional settings, and tempted by multiple diversions. There is a sense that you can pack in more of life by skimping on sleep. But we are finding that people tend to replace reduced sleep with added calories, and that's not a healthy trade."

Another study, presented at a conference sponsored by the American Academy of Sleep Medicine on June 11, 2007, suggested that people who don't get enough sleep are less likely to cook their own meals and more likely to rely on restaurants and fast-food outlets for some of their meals. The study suggested that that could lead to weight gain or other nutrition-related problems. A September 2006 issue of Archives of Internal Medicine looked at the link between sleep and health. "The theme that emerges throughout this issue is that sleep serves as an indicator of health and quality of life," guest editors Dr. Phyllis Zee and Fred Turek of Northwestern University Feinberg School of Medicine in Chicago wrote.

Exposure to light at night can inhibit the pineal gland's production of melatonin. The pineal gland directs your body's rhythmic activities--including sleep, appetite, and the onset of puberty--through its production of melatonin. This hormone is primarily secreted at night, and it requires darkness to be produced. Bright light suppresses melatonin secretion. The hypothalamus gland, also located in the brain, is richly supplied with melatonin receptors. This gland regulates your body's overall homeostasis, including things like blood pressure, emotions, temperature, and the endocrine (hormonal) system.

Hormones secreted by the hypothalamus stimulate the anterior pituitary gland to secrete its hormones; and these, in turn, stimulate the thyroid gland, the adrenals and the ovaries to secrete yet other hormones. The ovaries (and the testicles) are also thought to contain melatonin receptors. You can see how melatonin production and thereby sleeping in darkness or with light can affect the whole body's functioning, including the menstrual cycle, if the hypothalamus doesn't receive sufficient melatonin, its ability to regulate the hormonal system will be impaired.

Heart attacks and strokes are more common during the early morning hours. This fact may be explained by the way sleep interacts with the blood vessels. Lack of sleep has been associated with worsening of blood pressure and cholesterol, all risk factors for heart disease and stroke. Your heart will be healthier if you get between 7 and 9 hours of sleep each night. People working the late shift have a higher risk for breast and colon cancer. Researchers believe this link is caused by differing levels of melatonin in people who are exposed to light at night. Light exposure reduces the level of melatonin, a hormone that both makes us sleepy and is thought to protect against cancer. Melatonin appears to suppress the growth of tumors. Be sure that your bedroom is dark to help your body produce the melatonin it needs.

A good night's sleep makes you feel energized and alert the next day. Being engaged and active not only feels great, it increases your chances for another good night's sleep. When you wake up feeling refreshed, use that energy to get out into the daylight, do active things, and be engaged in your world. You'll sleep better the next night and increase your daily energy level. Researchers do not fully understand why we sleep and dream, but a process called memory consolidation occurs during sleep. While your body may be resting, your brain is busy processing your day, making connections between events, sensory input, feelings and memories. Your dreams and deep sleep are an important time for your brain to make memories and links. Getting more quality sleep will help you remember and process things better.

Sleep impacts many of the chemicals in your body, including serotonin. People with a deficiency in serotonin are more likely to suffer from depression. You can help to prevent depression by making sure you are getting the right amount of sleep, between 7 and 9 hours each night.
Sleep is a time for your body to repair damage caused by stress, ultraviolet rays and other harmful exposures. Your cells produce more protein while you are sleeping. These protein molecules form the building blocks for cells, allowing them to repair damage.

My clinical observation is that, in the last 10-15 years people are becoming more care less about the importance of sleep. In my society the introduction of advanced technology, social media and 24 hours transmission of T.V. channels have badly affected the health of teens. Another negative factor is the promotion of low rate night deals from burgers and pizza manufacturers which is an attraction for them. Lot of youngsters are coming to me with their problems of an early onset of hypertension, disturb lipids, polycystic ovaries, and even teen age depression. Another horrifying reality of this lifestyle is sudden death due to cardiac failures in young individuals.

The status of dynamic or Non-static biorhythms is the vital diagnostic tool of SLP. These biorhythms provide me with a window which allows me to peep into the status of liver. Peripheral body temperature is an important biorhythm for me and is an indicator of liver core temperature, therefore holistic health. For instance a person with cold extremities round the year, is having a serious chemical imbalance which can affect the heart, liver, kidney, brain functions seriously. As liver is responsible for 500 functions, therefore correction of its functions leads to optimum holistic health. If you know how to harmonize the biorhythms, you are in fact repairing various liver functions. Once the liver is in a healthy state, holistic health is attained.

## CHAPTER NO: 3

## LIVER: NATURE'S MASTER PIECE

The liver is one of the largest internal organs and the largest gland in the body, yet it gets very little respect. The brain, heart, and lungs are always described as essential to the body's health. Without the liver though, the physical body could not operate. It is mostly abused by the medical doctors because of their limited knowledge about this organ. Each and every pharmaceutical medicine passes through liver, disturbs its homeostasis and makes it dysfunctional. The largest of the internal organs, the liver, weighs at 2.5 to 5 pounds. It is suspended behind the ribs on the upper right side of the abdomen and spans almost the entire width of the upper abdomen.

The liver has four lobes: right, left, caudate and quadrate. The right is the main lobe which organizes and humanizes nutrients. It is the main chemical factory producing 50,000 enzyme systems, 13,000 chemicals and thousands of synergists that help with body functions. The left lobe regulates and maintains the body's holistic functions. People with toxic left lobes are often environmentally sensitive or pan-allergic i.e. allergic to nearly everything. The left lobe works to maintain body homeostasis or biorhythms. It generates cravings so that deficiency of a particular nutrient is fulfilled and chemical homeostasis is restored back to normal. The lower lobe is where the essential fatty acids and fat soluble vitamins A, D, E and K are stored so that the liver and other glands can produce cholesterol and hormones. This is also where the liver stores environmental toxins like radioactive substances, pesticides, herbicides, food preservatives and dyes. The liver will detoxify what it can, but if it can't break down a particular substance, it stores it there and in tissues throughout the body.

One unique feature of the liver is that it is capable of regenerating itself after a portion is removed. After a loss of up to 75% due to injury or surgery the remaining liver can grow back and restored to normal within several months. The liver filters more than a quart of blood each minute.

At any one time, as much as 10 percent of all the blood in the body is present in the liver. The liver being such a vascular tissue receives 25% of its blood from the hepatic artery, which carries fresh oxygenated blood to the liver so that it can do its work of processing the substances that arrive from the intestine. The blood from the intestine represent 75 % of the liver's blood, and it leaves the liver by the hepatic veins to a larger vein, called inferior vena cava, which goes to the heart.

The liver is so basic to health that unless its function can be improved, many patients will not experience significant and lasting improvement on a nutritional or holistic healing program. The liver is important because a person's nutritional level is not only determined by what he or she eats, but by what the liver processes. The liver is the central organ of general anabolic metabolism, in fact is "the archetypal organ of life that lives entirely in anabolism."

Yet it is extremely difficult to detect early warning symptoms specific to liver metabolic imbalances since it is quite a "forgiving" organ that can withstand a myriad of abuse before capitulating and giving-up the fight. Rudolf Steiner pointed this out in lectures early in this century, when he stated, "It is quite difficult to diagnose when the liver is not in order, and frequently one is unaware of it because the liver is the single organ that doesn't hurt when something is wrong with it. People can suffer for a long time from a liver ailment without knowing of it."

## Liver functions

Unfortunately blood testing has no real way of telling us the health of our liver or our biological age. By the time we reach the chronological age of 30 our liver is probably functioning at 75% of its ability at best. The health and vitality of all body systems depend to a large extent on the health and vitality of the liver. Every day scientists discover that the liver seems to have some type of connection to every function in the human body. The liver monitors all the vital functions performed by the heart, brain, kidney, stomach, endocrine glands and regulates blood chemistry. As we know it today the liver has well over 500 functions and these functions are growing at the rate of 25 new functions each year. The liver is the most responsive and considerate organ in the body. It clearly sends out signals to us when things are not going well or when it simply does not like something. These warning signs should not be ignored with the hope that they will just go away. The liver is not a fragile organ and will not complain unless it is totally necessary.

***1-Metabolic Liver functions***

The liver as we know it has well over 500 functions and is known as the laboratory of the human body. Many scientists believe the liver is connected or at least aware of every disease or dysfunction going on inside the body. The liver is a multitasking organ, with many functions. Nearly all the blood that leaves the stomach and intestines passes through the liver for processing. According to the American Liver Foundation (ALF), the liver is a chemical "factory," involved in these myriad body functions. Below are some metabolic functions of this amazing organ.

1. Metabolizes proteins, fats, and carbohydrates, thus providing energy and nutrients
2. Stores vitamins, minerals, and sugars
3. Filters the blood and helps remove harmful chemicals and bacteria
4. Removes damaged red blood cells
5. Manufactures bile salts which emulsify fats and the fat-soluble vitamins A, D, E, and K for proper absorption. The liver also removes some fat-soluble toxins from the body
6. Helps to assimilate and store fat soluble vitamins (A, E, D, K)
7. Stores extra blood which can be quickly released when needed
8. Creates serum proteins which maintain fluid balance and act as carriers

9. Helps maintain electrolyte and water balance
10. Creates immune substances such as gamma globulin
11. Breaks down and eliminates excess hormones
12. Vascular health care
13. Provides blood clotting factors
14. Breaks down ammonia (and other toxins) created in the colon by bacteria; thus preventing death
15. Helps to maintain blood pressure
16. Constructs cholesterol and estrogen, reconstructs hormones
17. Humanizes nutrients. Virtually every nutrient must be bio-transformed by the liver into its proper biochemical form before the nutrient can be stored, transported or used in cellular metabolism.
18. Constructs 50,000 systems of enzymes to govern metabolic activity throughout the body
19. Converts the thyroid hormone thyroxin (T4) into it more active form triiodothyronine (T3). Inadequate conversion may lead to hypothyroidism, chronic fatigue, weight gain, poor memory and other debilitating conditions.
20. Creates GTF (Glucose Tolerance Factor) from chromium, niacin and possibly glutathione. GTF is needed for the hormone insulin to properly regulate blood-sugar levels.
21. Activates B vitamins into their biologically active coenzyme forms.
22. Manufactures carnitine from lysine and other nutrients. Carnitine is the only known bio-nutrient which can escort fats into the mitochondria where they are used to generate ATP energy. The mitochondria generate 90% of the ATP energy at the cellular level.
23. Converts lactic acid from a toxic waste to an important storage fuel. Lactic acid is produced when glucose is metabolized through the energy production cycle. When excessive levels accumulate, you experience sore muscles. A healthy liver will extract lactic acid

from the bloodstream and convert it into the reserve endurance fuel, glycogen.

24. Serves as the main glucose buffer, preventing high or low extremes of blood sugar. The liver is the key regulator of blood sugar between meals due to its manufacture, storage, and release of glycogen, the starch form of glucose. When blood sugar is low, a healthy liver converts stored glycogen into glucose, releasing it into the bloodstream to raise blood sugar levels. When blood sugar is high, a healthy liver will convert the excess into stored glycogen or fat.
25. Chief regulator of protein metabolism. The liver converts different amino acids into each other as needed.
26. Produces cholesterol and converts it into the various forms needed for blood transport.
27. Converts essential fatty acids such as GLA, EPA, and DHA into the lipoprotein forms necessary to allow transport via the bloodstream to the 60 trillion cells requiring fatty acids.
28. Main poison-detoxifying organ in the body. The liver must break down every substance toxic to the body including metabolic wastes, insecticide and pesticide residues, drugs, alcohol, etc. Failure of this function will usually cause death in 12 to 24 hours.
29. Removes ammonia, a toxic by-product of animal protein metabolism, from the body.
30. Breaks down hormones after they have served their function. i.e., if the liver does not break down insulin fast enough, hypoglycemia results because the circulating insulin continues to lower blood sugar.

The liver is vital to a host of other metabolic functions, but this brief overview should serve to illustrate the central role the liver plays in maintaining good health.

***2-Liver and Biochemical individuality***

Liver determines chemical body types; in fact we inherit liver chemistry from our parents. In my opinion liver controls the genetic blue print as well. Therefore we have common physical, mental, emotional, social aspects of our personalities with our parents. This is the reason that we share diseases present in our genes as well. Different liver states are responsible for various biochemical imbalances and ultimately leading to diseases. We cannot completely change the built-in liver chemistry but we can slow down or put off disease process by modifying the life style which is specifically liver protective.

***3- Liver and biorhythms***

1. Since rhythm is the key to all healing, we must look at what rhythms operate so powerfully in the liver. The liver is most active in rebuilding the body during the night. Within the context of the daily circadian rhythm, we note that the liver has a biphasic rhythm, with the assimilatory phase beginning at 3 PM in the afternoon and reaching its maximum at 3 AM, whereupon the liver begins to enter its secretary phase for the next 12 hours. This is further confirmed in the Chinese medical system where the liver meridian is most active between 1 —3 AM.
2. Liver controls hormonal level by producing GTF factor which is controlling insulin production. Leptin and insulin functions are interconnected; therefore many vital functions are indirectly controlled by liver.
3. Left lobe generates food cravings to maintain the body chemistry.
4. Liver controls body ph by regulating electrolytes and water metabolism by manufacturing important hormones for ph balance.
5. Core body temperature is maintained by liver so that enzymatic functions are not disturbed. Core temperature regulates peripheral body temperature.
6. Being the master biorhythm regulator, it regulates sleep as well.

7. According to the Chinese philosophy of Qi circulation, In a 24 hour rhythm, the liver is rejuvenated between 1a.m. to 3a.m., and gets ready for the next day's routine. People who are awake at this time are suffering either from obesity, bloating, depression or an early onset of degenerative disease.
8. As it is a seat for the soul, a healthy liver can make us emotionally and spiritually healthy.

***4-Liver and Traditional Chinese Medicine***

The main functions of the Liver are to store blood and ensure the smooth flow and direction of Qi (energy) movement in the body. It is also said to contribute to our body's resistance to external pathogenic influences. "The Liver is the origin of courage and resoluteness if it is in a state of good health." (Maciocia). It is also believed that the Liver influences our ability to plan our lives. Other functions according to Chinese philosophy are:

Storing of blood

Ensuring the smooth flow of Qi

Controls the sinews (tendons, connective tissues, muscles strength)

Shows its health on the nails

Opens into the eyes

Houses the Ethereal Soul (Hun)

Effects dreams

***i-Storing of blood***

The liver is the most important organ for storing blood; it regulates the volume of blood in the whole body.

*I-Alters blood volume according to physical activity*

The liver stores blood when the body is at rest or sleeps (between 1-3a.m.), when it is active it allows the blood to move to the muscles. These functions have a great effect on the energy one has. If the blood flows properly to the skin the natural protection against external pathogenic factors will be strong.

*II-The storage of blood strongly influences menstruation*

Menstruation will be normal if the liver is storing blood properly. If the blood is deficient there will be amenorrhea or oligomenorrhea. If there is heat or hyper-liver blood can move recklessly and cause menorrhagia or metrorrhagia. The Liver is the main organ of healthy gynecological functioning. Liver Qi (energy) stagnation can lead to blood stagnation which can cause painful menses, PMS, and clotting of menstruation blood. Most problems associated with women reproductive systems are due to liver malfunction.

***ii-Ensuring the smooth flow of Qi***

The liver ensures the smooth flow of Qi(energy) throughout the entire body, in all organs, in all directions. Disorders of this function are the most common patterns seen in practice. Every organ Qi has a particular direction in which it is supposed to flow. The direction of movement of liver Qi is upwards and outwards in all directions to ensure the smooth flow everywhere, therefore it effects and helps regulate every organ. Smooth flow of Qi affects following body functions.

*I-Strongly effects emotions*

If liver function is normal, people will have smooth flowing emotional states favoring happiness. If the flow of Qi is stagnated, frustration, depression, irritability, anger, hypochondriac pain, stuffiness in the chest, lumps in the throat, abdominal distension can occur. Various pre-menstrual syndrome symptoms will also arise, i.e. mood swings and breast tenderness. Therefore emotions reflect the smooth flow of liver Qi, and stagnated liver QI affects the emotions adversely.

*II-Effects the digestion of food by the spleen and stomach*

If the Qi is not flowing smoothly, the spleen and stomach have trouble performing their digestive functions. If the liver Qi is stagnated it can overact on the stomach causing a reversal in the downward movement of stomach Qi causing vomiting, belching, and nausea. If it overacts on the spleen it will affect its natural upward flow of Qi and cause diarrhea.

*III-Flow of bile*

If liver Qi is stagnated the flow of bile can get obstructed resulting in bitter taste in the mouth, belching, or jaundice

***iii-Controls sinews (tendons, connective tissues, muscles strength)***

The sinews ability to contract and relax depends on the nourishment from liver blood. If liver blood is deficient it can cause spasms, stiffness, and reduced range of motion, numbness, muscle cramps, tremors, tetany, seizures, and reduced strength in the limbs.

***iv-Shows its health on the nails***

The nails are considered to be an extension of the sinews; therefore they are closely related to the state of the liver blood. If liver blood is deficient the nails will become dry, cracked, dark, indented, and generally unhealthy.

***v-Opens into eyes***

The eye is the special sensory organ which is directly connected to the liver. They require nourishment from the liver blood in order to see properly. If liver blood is deficient there can be blurred vision, myopia, floaters, colorblindness, dryness, soreness, itchiness, and other eye disorders. If liver has heat the eyes can get blood shot, painful and burning. If the liver has created internal wind the eyeballs may turn upwards or shake.

***vi-Houses the Ethereal soul (Hun)***

The liver is residence of the ethereal soul (Hun). The Ethereal soul does not die with the organic body, it is non-material therefore yang in nature. Its counterpart, the corporeal soul (po) which resides in the lungs would be the Yin, or material aspect to our being and it dies with the body. The Ethereal soul is said to influence the planning of our lives and the feeling of purpose. Lack of direction or purpose is due to a deficiency of the liver, this cause the soul to be uprooted and float resulting in confusion, lack of visionary conclusion and wandering.

***vii-Effects dreams***

When liver is in excess, one dreams of being angry and restlessness, if liver is deficient scenes of failures are seen.

***5-Anthroposophical Medicine***

Rudolf Steiner, founder of Anthroposophical medicine, theorized that the liver is the controlling organ of our fluid or life body and in fact in many languages the name for the liver is the same as the word life I like to call it the "lifer" for without a healthy functioning liver, life is simply not possible. The fluid body, or in Anthroposophical terms the etheric body, is like the plant inside of us. (According to Anthroposophical thought the plant body consist of a mineral body taken up into the living sphere, in other words a plant is a living mineral.)

Rudolf Steiner mentions this in his lectures in *Anthroposophical Medicine*, "If the liver is not properly formed, then a will-defect develops that is expressed in a person's wanting to do something, however, this desire does not pass over into carrying out of the will impulse but remains stuck in thinking. "*The Foundations of Chinese Medicine* says, "The liver is like a general from whom the strategy is derived. The liver imparts to us the capacity to plan our life smoothly and wisely. In disease, a liver disharmony can manifest with an inability to plan our life and a lack of direction.

***6-Liver and embryology***

Dr. Karel Maret writes, "The liver holds a central position in embryological life making up 10% of the volume of the embryo as compared to being only 2% of the volume of an adult. It produces the blood for the fetus up to the seventh month of embryonic life, and thereby, steers the whole incarnation process of the fetus. It doesn't require much thinking to recognize that if the liver is not formed properly during the intra-uterine period due to metabolic or environmental stresses in the mother or even an existing subclinical genetic weakness, then the incarnation process of the child will be partially compromised. This may later express itself as imbalances in the "will impulses" in the child or adult, and appears to me to be increasingly prevalent in people.

(Excerpted from *Lilipoh: Life, Liberty, and the Pursuit of Happiness Through Health*)

## Researches Discovering New Liver Functions

### *1-Thyroid and liver*

Thyroxin and tri-iodothyronine are essential for normal thyroid growth, development and function. These hormones regulate the basal metabolic rate of all cells, including hepatocytes, and thereby modulate hepatic function; the liver in turn metabolizes the thyroid hormones and regulates their systemic endocrine effects. Thyroid dysfunction may perturb liverfunction, liverdisease modulates thyroid hormone metabolism, and a variety of systemic diseases affect both organs.

### *2-Female reproductive system*

The liver initiates the menstrual cycle and the spleen controls the creation of the blood in the body. When there is any disharmony in the liver, symptoms arise such as the mood swings that we often associate with PMS, including periods of depression, sadness, irritability, crying, and anger. When the spleen is also involved, a woman can develop symptoms such as a foggy sense of clumsiness, IBS, or anemia. PMS comes about when the liver's function is impaired.

Medical therapy for endometriosis is to lower estrogen level either by suppressing estrogen production or suppressing the serum estrogen level by derivatives of testosterone. A better alternative however is to strengthen the liver so that it can more efficiently inactivate and remove estrogen. The liver regulates estrogen by inactivating it through oxidation and conjugation with sulfate or glucuronide. The conjugated estrogens are excreted mostly in the bile with a small amount excreted in the urine. The fact that hyper-estrogenism accompanies certain types of liver disorders confirms the important role of the liver in estrogen inactivation. "The hyper-estrogenism occurs as a result of failure of hepatic (liver) removal of estrogen from the circulation". As a matter of fact the symptoms often associated with endometriosis such as chronic fatigue, allergy, emaciation and poor complexion are not caused directly by endometriosis but are signs of liver disorders. During pregnancy the liver is under extra load. If it was in a healthy state prior to conception then the female has less associated complications.

### *3-The headaches*

The headaches so far described are of the congestive type, characterized by excessive blood pressure to the brain. Anything that tends to raise the blood pressure will therefore create or aggravate these ailments. A common cause is pathogenic obstruction in the capillary circulation, which results in active congestion in the internal organs and the brain. Another common type is the so-called bilious headache, which is attributed to an inactive or hypo liver state. Anything that interferes with bile formation in the liver or its discharge from the gall bladder or bile duct, not only causes surging back of the bile into the general circulation but also a deficiency of it in the intestinal tract, which in turn gives rise to acidity of the intestinal contents, indigestion, constipation, fermentation, and gas formation. This intestinal toxemia is reflected to the brain in the form of congestion and headaches.

### *4-Obesity*

Although most people know that they can't live without the liver, few are aware of the important role that this organ plays in weight loss. That's because the liver either produces or activates all of the hormones in the body that are necessary for fat-burning. Without optimal liver function, natural weight loss becomes a very difficult goal to achieve. Due to chronic abuse of the liver through things like heavy alcohol use, medications, bad eating habits especially an overconsumption of fats and heavy animal-based proteins, the liver can become overloaded and irritable. These results in an inflammatory response in the abdominal cavity, which results in an accumulation of fluid (called ascites). As the retained fluid collects in the stomach area, the stomach will often begin to protrude outward, producing the appearance that is sometimes called a "beer belly".

In women, the problem can get bad enough that the protruding belly makes them look pregnant when they are not. For people with this water weight deposition, weight loss can be frustrating because exercise will not "burn it off" - because it's not fat. Since natural weight loss approaches fail to get results in these situations, some people resort to diet and drugs, which may work at first, but ultimately harm the liver even more and create even more abdominal water retention. Ironically, with water retention weight gain associated with liver dysfunction, some diet plans and weight loss products can actually make the situation worse and lead to even more fluid retention. The Atkins's diet, because it is so high in protein and fat, tends to be hard on the liver and will often lead to even more retaining of fluid. Certain products sold to help with weight loss may have ingredients that further stress and irritate the liver and result in even more water retention in the long-run.

In addition to the water retention issue, good liver function is necessary for the proper production and/or activation of the hormones that stimulate fat burning. For instance, the liver is needed to convert the inactive form of thyroid hormone (T4) to the active form (T3). When the liver is overworked and cannot do the hormone conversions efficiently, the body cannot burn fat efficiently, no matter how much exercise you may do or what other natural weight loss steps you take.

In addition to activating fat-burning hormones as with thyroid hormone, the liver produces Insulin-like Growth Factor (IGF), which is another fat-burning hormone. IGF controls blood sugar during the relatively long-period that you go without eating during sleep. When you are asleep at night, your blood sugar levels fall and the liver generates IGF to cause the fat tissues to burn fat to boost blood sugar. Again, if liver function is not as good as it should be, this hormone is not produced efficiently and you don't burn much fat. The other thing that occurs is that your blood sugar will go lower than it should and you wake up in the morning feeling very fatigued and irritable.

***5-Metabolic disorders***

A healthy body stores fat in the form of triglycerides in specialized fatty tissue as an energy reserve. Under certain conditions the delicate balance of the lipid metabolism gets out of control and fat is accumulated in the liver, leading to the dreaded fatty liver. This increases the risk of many metabolic diseases, such as the metabolic syndrome known as "deadly quartet". The combination of fatty liver, obesity, diabetes and hypertension is regarded as the primary cause of life threatening vascular events such as myocardial infarction and stroke. Dr. Stephan Hertz, head of the junior Research Group "Molecular Metabolic Control" at the German Cancer Research Center (DKFZ), has published the mechanism by which the body's own glucocorticoid hormones contribute to the disruption of the lipid metabolism.

The researchers in Herzig's team specifically switched off the cortisol receptors in the liver of mice, thus blocking the hormone effect. As a result, the triglyceride level in the livers of the experimental animals dropped considerably. Investigations have revealed that in the absence of the cortisol receptors, large amounts of the HES1 protein are produced in the liver of these animals. HES1 activates a number of enzymes that break down fat and thus counteracts fat accumulation in the liver. If on the other hand normal mice are treated with cortisol, their HES1 levels in the liver drops, while triglyceride levels rise.

***6-Atherosclerotic changes***

Ageing liver may be responsible for gumming up blood vessels in the elderly, leading to heart attacks and strokes, says an Australian geriatrician. Unlike the linings of blood vessels elsewhere in the body, those in the liver have large pores in them. They also lack basement membrane and have other differences that enable the liver to remove large lipoproteins called chylomicron remnants from the blood. Chylomicron remnants left in the blood stream encourage plaques to form, leading to atherosclerotic changes in the body. Animal studies have shown that with aging, the number of pores halves and the thickness of the lining increases by up to five folds.

### *7-Cardiovascular problems*

Australian scientists from Sydney's ANZAC Research Institute believe it may be our livers, blocking up blood vessels which lead to cardiovascular problems in the elderly. In a young liver, the fat we eat escapes through these holes. But researchers have discovered that as we age these holes in the liver get smaller and eventually disappear. "The fat in your diet, the cholesterol in your diet instead being processed by the liver, goes into the blood vessels of the heart and brain to go on and can cause stroke and heart disease,"Professor Le Couteur said.

### *8-Hormones and liver*

Pregnenolone, like DHEA, is a steroidal hormone manufactured in the body. Pregnenolone is a precursor hormone synthesized from cholesterol, principally in the adrenal glands, but also in the liver, skin, brain, testicles, ovaries, and retina of the eyes. Indeed, pregnenolone is the grand precursor from which almost all of the other steroid hormones are made; including DHEA, progesterone, testosterone, the estrogens, and cortisol. Despite its powerful metabolites, pregnenolone is acknowledged to be without significant side effects, with minimal or no anabolic, estrogenic or androgenic activity. Many physicians and scientists believe that replacement of pregnenolone to youthful levels is an important step in the treatment of aging and symptoms of aging. It may be one of the most important hormones because it seems to have a balancing effect. It is a precursor to many other hormones and may be able to bring the levels of other hormones up or down as needed.

### *9-Natural Killer (NK) cells*

Pit cells are one type of hepatic sinusoidal cells, defined morphologically as large granular lymphocytes (LGLs) and functionally as liver-associated natural killer (NK) cells. They are situated inside the sinusoidal lumen, adhering to the endothelial cells and Kupffer cells. They contain multi-vesicular body-related dense granules and rod-cored vesicles. The number and size of granules and vesicles differ between hepatic NK cells and peripheral blood cells, suggesting possible differentiation of the latter into the former in the microenvironment of the liver. In addition to NK cells, Natural Killer T (NKT) cells are also abundant in the liver. They share several morphological properties with NK cells, and at least some are probably observed as pit cells under an electron microscope. NK cells recognize target cells with their surface receptors such as inhibitory and activating receptors. They exert antitumor functions by exocytose of perforin/granzyme-containing granules, induction of death receptor-mediated apoptosis in target cells.

### *10-Organ transplant*

The progress of medical science in the past 30 years has been so rapid that yesterday's miracles are tomorrow's common place procedures. So it has proved with heart and liver transplants, which have become almost routine in hospitals around the world. The patients of organ transplant have acquired the holistic traits of the respective organ donors. Scientists have now started claiming that our memories and characters are encoded not just in our brain, but throughout our entire body. Consciousness, they claim, is created by every living cell in the body acting in concert. They say that our hearts, livers and every single organ in the body stores our memories, drives our emotions and imbues us with our own individual characters. Our whole body, they believe, is the seat of the soul, not just the brain. There are now more than 70 documented cases, where transplant patients have taken on some of the personality traits of the organ donors.

The New England Journal of Medicine has reported a case of liver transplant from Sydney's West mead Children's Hospital. An Australian teenager girl, who received a liver transplant, has astonished medical experts by taking on her donor's immune system. The blood group of recipient was changed to the donor's blood type, and other tests revealed the stem cells from the donor liver had penetrated her bone marrow. Doctors found the girl's immune system had almost totally been replaced by that of the donor and she no longer has to take anti-rejection drugs.

***11-Stem cells and liver***

Mature liver cells in humans are generated from bone marrow derived stem cells, a team of Yale and New York University researchers has discovered, paving the way for improved treatment of liver damage and disease. "We have proven that in humans there are stem cells for the liver in the bone marrow", says Dr. Neil Theise, associate professor of pathology at New York University School of Medicine and lead author of the study. The study published in the July 09 issue of Hepatology, analyzed liver samples from female leukemia patients who had undergone bone marrow transplantation from a male donor, and from male liver disease patients who had received a liver transplant from a female donor. Bone marrow derived cells were identified by the presence of a Y- chromosome found only in males.

***12-Liver regeneration***

The way the liver renews itself may be simpler than scientists had been assuming. A new study, appearing in *The Journal of Biological Chemistry,* provides new information on the inner workings of cells from regenerating livers that could significantly affect the way physicians make livers re-grow in patients with liver diseases such as cirrhosis, hepatitis, or cancer. "The human liver is one of the few organs in the body that can regenerate from as little as 25 percent of its tissue," says Seth Karp, assistant professor of surgery at Harvard Medical School, Boston, and main author of the study. "It is not known how the liver does it, but our results provide some details of what makes the liver so unique." Although organ regeneration has been observed in many animals, the details of how it happens at the cellular level are still not completely understood. So far, scientists have shown that cells that participate in tissue regeneration behave as if they were part of a growing organ in an embryo. In other words, the cells act as if the liver is growing, as do other organs in a developing embryo.

Re-growing livers this way would be especially useful for patients whose liver are so damaged - say, by a tumor that has spread to most of the liver - that a large part would be removed. Unless such patients receive the right amount of liver transplant from an organ donor, they do not always survive. Quickly stimulating the growth of the remaining portion of their liver could be their only chance of survival. To investigate how the liver regenerates, Karp and his colleagues set out to determine which proteins are involved in the regenerating cells. The scientists were also interested in testing whether regenerating cells behave like embryonic ones, as is commonly assumed for other organs and various findings showed that a regenerating liver does not behave as a developing embryo.

Instead, regeneration could actually be only due to an increase in cells that multiply through regular cell divisions, a process called hyperplasia.

The next step will be for scientists to understand whether the regenerating cells are stem cells. Studies have shown that adult stem cells are involved in the repair of many organs, but in the case of the liver, the cells repairing it through regeneration may simply be regular cells, not stem cells. "We think that the liver re-grows through a relatively simple process, which could explain its prodigious ability to repair itself," Karp says.

### *13-The phenomenon of openness*

A Russian scientist Ilija Prigogine said "The main character of any living system is openness." He connected biological knowledge with chaos research and brought deep insights into the mysteries of life. Openness means a continuous balanced flow of absorbing energy, processing inside the system and discharging. That is the main pattern of every life structure and precondition to be able to evolve. Whether concerning a person or a termite state, bacteria cultures, a company, the structure of a state, the biosphere of our planet or a galaxy: all evolving systems are open and continuously balancing the absorption, processing and the discharge of energy. The human liver shows the same dynamic, being a living system, our liver is working openly. It absorbs substances, and processes them according to purpose and then passes on the results of its work on to multiple systems of the human body.

### *14-Soul and liver*

Extending our concept of energy in the body, we can now look at one of the high frequency energies. The Wei chi is a superficial energy that runs over the surface of the body just inside and above the skin. Some people can see it in certain light as an etheric whitish glow that can extend perhaps half an inch out from the body (This should not be confused with the human aura that is an even higher frequency and extends much further). It is classically referred to as our protective energy. It is really a mixture of frequencies, each controlling different aspects of protection physical, climatic, emotional, psychic, etc. One can have strong physical Wei chi but weak emotional wei chi.

When we are injured, the Wei chi is the first energy to arrive in force and plan our defense and repair. It encourages the flow of meridian energy, nerve impulses and eventually the biochemical agents necessary for repair. Wei chi protects us from our environment. A person with strong Wei chi can withstand sudden changes in climate and temperature. A person with weak Wei chi suffers from sudden climatic change even to the point of serious health problems. Wei chi depends on its ability to flow smoothly through the skin and over the body in order to function optimally. As mentioned earlier, Wei chi is not like the aura. It appears as a thin film or envelope of glowing energy around the body of a healthy person. In some people it is only just above the skin. In others, it can radiate from half an inch to an inch. (In extreme cases - three inches.)

Wei chi has very strong metaphysical connections and implications. In natural (Chinese, Indian, Sharmanic etc.) medicine, if the wei chi needs to be strengthened, the organ that we have to treat is the liver and its associated energy systems. In metaphysics the liver is the organ associated with the soul. There are many interpretations of the soul. Simply put, the soul is the part of our body, or energy presence that helps us to process life and records the processes of our life (Whether it is just this life, and/or past lives). The soul processes life, sorts out our karma, and is constantly synthesizing all the events that are happening. It is also involved with the process of planning and making decisions. In Chinese medicine, each organ has a yin and a yang component. This is seen in other systems as well.

The yang aspect of the soul is the Wei chi that is found on the surface of the body. Our Wei chi is not only there to protect us from life but it is also our first contact with the world around us. All the inputs coming from our environment, people and events make contact with the Wei chi first. Although some of it penetrates directly into the body through the five senses, most of the input is processed by the wei chi Healthy wei chi determines how well we can process and digest our life on a psychological, physical and energy level. This processing in the Wei chi builds up during the day.

When we go to bed at night a procedure occurs between 1am and 3am whereby the wei chi withdraws from the surface and travels internally to the liver and other major organs to synthesize and 'pass on' this processed information (This time relates to the Chinese clock that demonstrates the internal concentrations of body energy according to the time of day). That is why when we lie in bed at night (even on a warm night), our wei chi withdraws, and we feel more vulnerable, and often feel colder and need to cover up for protection. This also explains why shift workers who work through the night can often have many problems processing their lives and making plans and decisions. It also accounts for many of the negative effects of jet lag where the Chinese clock is disturbed, and the Wei chi travels inside at the wrong times. Healthy Wei chi means healthy processing of life and as stated before, that Wei chi is best treated through the liver.

**Risk Factors for liver disease**

These risk factors have been time tested individually and studied for over 20 years and are clearly damaging and destructive to the daily functions of the liver. These risk factors are part of our routine life style, and in order to get consistent health one has to modify the life style permanently. Many of these risks have been proven to cause cancer in humans. The common risk factors are:

1. Junk foods: such as French fries, donuts, fried chicken and processed snack. These foods are cooked in overheated, overused, hydrogenated fats. Fried foods are a major source of liver-toxic lipid peroxides (rancid fats) and trans-fatty acids. Lipid peroxides are immune suppressive and damage liver cell membranes. Trans-fatty acids suppress production of PGE1, an important liver-protecting anti-inflammatory prostaglandin. The results of animal experiments announced at the annual meeting of the American Association for the Study of Liver Diseases has

lent credence to the belief that sugary soft drinks play a role in the development of liver disease. There is an increasing prevalence of liver disease in the United States, and the increased consumption of high fructose corn syrup in soft drinks may partly be to blame.

2. Alcohol: The liver converts alcohol into toxic acetaldehyde during its alcohol detoxification process. Acetaldehyde inhibits PGE1 production. It is a powerful free radical inducer, and is largely responsible for the liver, brain, heart, kidney, skin, and blood vessel lining damage associated with chronic alcoholism.
3. Coffee: Coffee crops are sprayed with pesticides. Carcinogenic hydrocarbons are produced during roasting and the highest levels are found in dark roasts.
4. Smoking: Tobacco smoke contains toxic benzopyrene, polycyclic aromatic hydrocarbons, cyanide, acetaldehyde, tars, etc. As the body's main detoxifying organ, the liver must work overtime to remove this stew of toxins.
5. Fuel exhaust: Auto and diesel exhaust contain dozens of liver damaging poisons such as lead, sulfur and nitrogen oxides, acetaldehyde, cadmium, and peroxyacetylnitrile.
6. Birth-control pills: There have been some cases where as little as two to three weeks of use have been documented to severely reduces the ability of the liver to detoxify naturally produced estrogen. The livers of women on B-vitamins / protein deficient diets may have difficulty metabolizing estrogen to nontoxic estriol, leaving it instead in the form of liver-toxic estradiol.
7. Candida: Candida yeast ferments dietary sugars into liver-toxic acetaldehyde in the process of turning sugar into energy. Candida also appears to increase gut and urinary levels of ammonia, another liver toxin.
8. Pesticides: such as PDT, Aldrin, chlordane, lindane, 2, 4, 5-T dioxin, and toxaphene can cause chronic liver damage even at levels measured in parts per billion because they tend to accumulate in body fat over a lifetime.

9. Long-term drug use, whether prescribed or illegal are potentially liver-toxic. Potential liver damage is a common warning found in prescription drug descriptions. Liver damage is a major side effect of chronic steroid abuse by athletes.

10. Acetaminophen: People should be careful not to take too many drugs containing acetaminophen at the same time. Taking more than 15 grams can lead to irreversible liver disease. Whether smaller doses over long periods of time (such as those recommended for relieving arthritis symptoms) harm the liver has not been determined, but prolonged use increases the risk of kidney damage. Additional research is needed, but some reports indicate that fasting, i.e., you stop eating because of a bad cold or influenza while taking acetaminophen may contribute to liver damage. People who consume large amounts of alcohol are at highest risk of developing liver damage from overuse of acetaminophen.

**Liver Toxicity and warning signs**

There are many pre-disease warning signs and symptoms the body clearly relays to you that the liver needs help. The sign and symptoms vary according to the duration and intensity of exposure of liver to un-natural lifestyle factors and environmental toxins. These two major factors affect the optimum functioning of liver result in hypo-liver or hyper- liver dysfunctional states. These two liver chemistries are not into the category of disease and mostly not detectable by the routine laboratory tests. If dysfunction of liver persists then it leads to fatty liver, NAFLD, hepatitis, cirrhosis or hepatic tumors etc. The Liver normally takes a very long period to be converted from a dysfunctional state to a disease state. If we recognize the warning signs of a dysfunctional liver, we can be protected from in-coming liver diseases. Following is a list of various signs and symptoms associated with a dysfunctional liver:

1. One important sign of an ailing liver is the dirty complexion of the owner, because liver cannot cope with excess of melanin brought

on by the sun, patchy areas of pigmentation appear on the body and freckles on the face.

2. Depression, anger, frustration, impatience, melancholy, irritability, physical fatigue, getting quite and becomes introvert.
3. Loss of interest in life, lack of motivation, disbelief and missing religious obligations.
4. Poor digestion, stomach pain, gas, bloating, bitter taste in mouth, nausea, loss of appetite, constipation or diarrhea
5. Eye complaints, red or flushed face, ringing in the ears, burning palms and soles
6. Weak tendons and ligaments, muscle and joint pains, and suffer from restless leg syndrome
7. Chronic menstrual problems, scanty menstruation, poly cystic ovaries, varicose veins, and habitual abortions. Engorgement of breasts and lumps in the breast.
8. Males have hormonal imbalance resulting in early receding of hair line, and various levels of sexual disorders
9. Difficulty in breathing, respiratory distress and poor oxygenation of blood leads to feeling of suffocation and claustrophobia.
10. Vertigo, extreme dizziness, convulsions, spasms, tremors, and episodes of eye twitching.
11. Blood disorders which lead to anemia, skin problems, allergies
12. Migraines and other types of headaches, severe body pain, insomnia and impaired higher brain function leading to impaired judgment and cloudiness of mind.
13. Disturbed lipid profile and formation of fatty lumps or lipomas all over the body.
14. Resistant weight loss or an underweight body.

## Liver Profile Tests

Different cells have different enzymes inside them, depending on the function of the cell. When cells die or are damaged, the enzymes leak out, causing the blood level of these enzymes to rise. The most important thing to remember about liver function tests or "LFTs" is that they do not in fact measure liver function. They have meaning, but they generally cannot be interpreted without clinical information. Also, the numbers do not always detect liver disease. Some patients with severe advanced liver disease will have nearly normal enzyme levels.

## Non Alcoholic Fatty Liver Disease (NAFLD)

NAFLD is commonly seen, and young people are worst affected, resulting in obesity especially central obesity, hormonal disorders, dyslipidemia, and poor immunity.

***How common is NAFLD?***

NAFLD is now the most common cause of chronic liver disease in the United States. NAFLD refers to a spectrum of liver disease that begins with liver cells abnormally storing fat, in the absence of chronic alcohol use. NAFLD can be mild in some people, but in a progressive form (steatoehepatitis or NASH) there is risk for cirrhosis, liver cancer, and liver-related death.

The Medical Observer Journal of Australia in July 2004 published an article titled "Non-alcoholic fatty liver disease is the new epidemic of liver disease facing the Western world". Back in the 1980's fatty liver was mainly seen in alcoholics; but rarely in children. Today, fatty liver is now recognized as the most common cause of abnormal liver function tests in the USA, UK and Australia.

***The consequences of a NAFLD***

The healthy liver regulates fat metabolism and is the major fat-burning organ in the body. Indeed the healthy liver not only burns fat, it can pump excessive fat out of your body through the bile into the gut. Thus, if your liver is healthy you will not have much difficulty in controlling your weight. Conversely, a liver that is fatty is doing the opposite of what it should be doing. A fatty liver is storing fat when it should be burning fat and removing excess fat from your body. Indeed a fatty liver becomes a warehouse for fat and if it is allowed to progress for many years, the liver may finally become just a "bag of fat" with dire consequences for your health and longevity.
A liver biopsy confirms excessive fat in the liver. These liver function tests support this diagnosis: It is best to avoid the biopsy and use blood test or diet history of the patient.

Albumin: somewhat low
Globulin: usually elevated
Cholesterol: usually elevated
Total bilirubin: elevated
alkaline phosphatase: elevated
Transaminase: usually low (less than 300 U)
Prothrombin time: possibly prolonged.

Other findings may include anemia, leukocytosis, elevated white blood cell count, albuminuria, hyperglycemia or hypoglycemia, and iron, folic acid, and vitamin B12 deficiencies.

***Reversal of a fatty liver***

Yes you can, by cleansing the liver consistently and improving your lifestyle eliminating the bombardment of liver toxic substances. Conventional or orthodox medicine has no specific therapy or drug treatment to reverse a fatty liver. In fact, many drugs such as cholesterol lowering drugs can exert toxic effects on the liver cells. If you follow a liver specific lifestyle modification program, it can reverse a fatty liver in three to six months.

# CHAPTER NO: 4

# HARMONIZE WITH NATURE: A NATURAL LIFESTYLE

## What is a lifestyle

The definition of lifestyle is a bundle of behaviors that makes sense to both others and oneself in a given time and place, including social relations, consumption patterns and entertainment. A human being's life is nurtured by multiple factors from birth to death, and these important external and internal factors make their worldly survival possible. There are also many unseen factors that work to harmonize human life with the macro rhythms of the universe. I label these as the SLP Natural lifestyle factors (NLF), they work at the individual, collective and universal levels. I believe we live three parallel lives but are ignorant or in a phase of denial about two of them, focusing only on the physical aspects of our life. Biophysics would also define NLF as those factors which work on the individual, collective and universal conscious of a human being. The ultimate objective of these factors is to drive us to our death through the most successful, secure and safest route.

Universal laws have pre-programmed humans with a partially fixed genome and destiny. This destiny program is flexible with multiple paths available, some are destructive and some beneficial. We have to use our intelligence, intuition, wisdom and religious training to select the right path. Anything un-natural in our life puts us in confrontation with Nature, and we suffer badly because we are a tiny creature in the huge macro-cosmos. If we observe and try to apply all the aspects of the natural lifestyle factors in our life, we will be correctly aligned with nature and are going to enjoy life to its maximum. NLF is always holistic in effect, whether it is the individual, collective or universal aspect of a human's life.

## SLP Natural lifestyle factors (NLF)

SLP classifies NLF into three categories

1. Individual factors
2. Collective factors
3. Universal factors

***Individual factors*** are those which are directly affecting the physical state of a human body. These are;

I. Dietary routine
II. Physical activity or exercise
III. Nature of work
IV. Amount and quality of nocturnal sleep

If we eat natural foods with a dietary discipline we enjoy holistic health. All natural foods contain high "life energy" and these foods can talk to body cells because they are made for each other. Food discipline gradually introduces intuitional eating i.e. finally the soul takes control of the physical body and body enjoys optimum health. The human body is designed for various movements like walking and running; so natural exercises are open air walking, running, sports or yoga.
Nature wants us to live in the moment, long term planning, worries, insecurities and stresses are not part of our pre-programmed nature. Therefore routine life's stress becomes a killer. Sleep at night is the nature's healing time for the human body. Do not expect holistic health if you are not getting 6-8 hours of night sleep. Nothing is superior to nature's healing. Give sufficient time to your soul at night so that it can rejuvenate itself from heavenly energy.

***Collective factors*** are those which are generated as a result of interaction between two individuals or with a team of people in the surroundings. These factors are initially operative in the home environment and are reflected in various relationships. School, college and university environment strongly affect human chemistry because the first twenty years are spent mainly under the influence of teachers and friends. Work place, nature of work and work load contribute to lifestyle factors as well. Prevailing political situation, electronic and print media are other strong collective factors. Disrupted collective lifestyle factors lead to indulgence in various addictions like caffeine, smoking, drugs, alcohol and other social issues in the society.

***Universal factors*** are intrinsic in nature and are, responsible for motivating us to play an important role in the macro-cosmos by becoming more humane. This gives us happiness and an inner peace. Great scientists, researchers, healers, leaders, revolutionists, social workers and environmentalists are the people who are using this innate potential for the healing of humanity and planet as well. Every human being goes through a process of evolution, which requires an average duration of 40 –60 years. If one is connected to a natural lifestyle then optimum holistic health, prevention from degenerative diseases, longevity and enlightenment is the outcome. Disconnection from the universal factors leads to chronic degenerative disease, speedy aging, fear of death, disbelief, stressful and unhappy life.

***NLF and biorhythms***

SLP Natural Lifestyle Factors (NLF) directly affects the biorhythms at individual, collective and universal levels. The human brain acts as a bridge between the human quantum body and the chemical body. Brain acts as a step down transformer between an energy body and physical body or between mind and cell. Brain is absolutely dependent on the liver for its uninterrupted supply of nutrient rich alkaline blood, sugar and oxygen. If the liver is dysfunctional, it will not be catering right nutrients in right ratio to the brain, outcome is behavioral disorder. A healthy liver has to synchronize the effects of electro-magnetic activity, cosmic energies, changing seasons, variable external temperature and existing lifestyle through its 500 functions. NLF connects macro cosmos with micro cosmos to maintain the homeostasis while keeping biochemical individuality intact.

**Benefits of a healthy lifestyle**

With the increased understanding of our bodies that we have gained from science over the past few decades, the benefits of a healthy lifestyle are becoming more apparent. For people of all ages, weights, and abilities the benefits of a healthy lifestyle are endless. Good Health is not something that you buy from a drug store or a department store, but can be achieved by practicing collective patterns of health-related behavior, based on choices made from available options. Following this logic, if you wish to realize the benefits of a healthy lifestyle, you have to repeat some healthy pattern as a part of your daily or weekly activities, some patterns like eating right and exercising. Other routine benefits include: reduced health care costs, reduced illness and injuries, reduced doctors visit, keeps you employed and improved employee/employer relations.

Our eating habits are more important than our genes, because through wrong combinations of food, we trigger hidden diseases in our genes. So forget about genetic factor, if you are following a natural healthy dietary pattern. Wrong food combinations, incorrect timings, wrong type of foods and extreme temperatures of foods produce unhealthy chemicals which badly influence the ph of blood and ph of other body fluids. This minor shift in blood ph leads to a chain of chemical reactions at the cellular level, resulting in fluctuations in the insulin levels, body temperature, and hormonal levels which affect tissues, organs and finally systems, depending on the duration of exposure to your bad eating habits. Remember the most food sensitive organ is the liver and the most food sensitive system is the digestive system, both are absolutely depend on your dietary habits.

Wellness is about being comfortable in your space: your body, your attitude, and your environment. A healthy lifestyle can greatly increase a person's longevity. The issue with a lot of people nowadays is that they are so busy working and/or taking care of everyone around them, that they neglect their own health and wellness. The best way to ensure good health is by taking care of you. The care stakes are high but the potential rewards are great, preventing premature death, unnecessary illness and disability, controlling health care cost and maintaining a high quality of life into old age. With a healthy lifestyle, you are who you are and you don't have to be self-conscious about those things that you otherwise would be if you didn't care about your lifestyle.

With a healthy lifestyle, you have control over your sleep patterns so that you feel generally well rested throughout the day. Everything works together to help other aspects of your lifestyle, make sense and benefit you. Science has proven that healthy weight loss, healthy eating and fitness routines make dramatic improvements in health, and help control common chronic illnesses like high cholesterol, high blood pressure, diabetes, stress, and general lack of stamina.

Another benefit of a healthy lifestyle is a steady flow of stamina and strength; you can perform activities and exercises that will enhance your flexibility. With a healthy lifestyle, you have a balanced and varied diet that provides your body its needed nutrients and energy as well. You have strength to train to help build the muscle that supports the bones and joints; therefore decreasing the risk of falls and fractures.

As we age, our bones biologically begin to lose mass and strength. Weight-bearing exercise such as walking and strength training helps slow the onset of and/or prevent osteoporosis and some research shows that participating in such activities can actually build bone density and begin to reverse the disease. The good news is you don't have to train like an Olympic athlete to enjoy the benefits of a healthy lifestyle. The secret and logic are repeating a chosen healthy pattern as a part of your daily or weekly activities. I hope that this will get you to a healthy lifestyle if you are not there already. A healthy lifestyle is a way of life.

## Lifestyle factors and various researches

### *1- Negative / Positive factors*

Studies have proven that there are negative life style factors and positive life style factors. Negative life style factors are bad habits like smoking, alcohol, drugs, lack of exercise, sleepless nights etc. Other injurious life style factors are guilt, fear, envy, jealousy, insecurity, faith disorders and lack of religious rituals. Positive life style factors are healthy dietary habits, sound nocturnal sleep, regular outdoor physical activity caring nature and healthy stress management. Indulgence into some charity work and social projects, positive approach towards failure and success and a very strong faith in Creator are other positive lifestyle factors.

Studies have shown that the way a person lives his or her life, in the later years can make those years exciting for the person. These lifestyle factors have more influence on the quality of life than genetics. There are numerous benefits from living a healthy lifestyle in the later years. Mid- and late-adulthood can be an exciting and active time of life, a renaissance. Somewhere around the age of fifty, a rebirth occurs followed by a "coalescence of all that has been lived and learned and a period of grace and generosity" (Sheehy, 1995, p.139). In her book 'New Passages', author Gail Sheehy writes that life after 45 is a stage of life radically altered from what previous generations have experienced. She calls it Second Adulthood, a time to open to new and more meaningful ways to be alive (Sheehy, 1995). Sheehy says "An American woman who today reaches age 50 free of cancer and heart disease can expect to see her 92nd birthday. The average man who is 65 today - an age now reached by more than 70 percent of the U.S. population - can expect to live until 81. This amounts to a second adult lifetime (pp. 5-6)."

***2-Lifestyle is important than Genes***

Lifestyle factors have a greater impact than genetics, which account for about one third of the problems associated with aging (Johns Hopkins, 1998). According to the Johns Hopkins Medical Letter 'Health after 50', there are significant factors, which increase longevity, prevent or delay disabling illness, and improve the quality of life. They are:

1. Exercise. This by itself is the most important factor. Physical activity aids cardiovascular and respiratory functions, slows the loss of muscular strength, increases bone mass, aids digestion and bowel functions, promotes sound sleep, and prevents depression.
2. Nutrition. This area encompasses a healthy diet, use of supplements, and drinking plenty of water. The experts advocate a low fat diet with a minimum of 5 servings of fruits and vegetables, and 2 to 4 servings of low-fat dairy products each day. A multivitamin is recommended to fill in gaps from the diet, as well as 6 to 8 glasses of water or clear fluids to promote optimal organ function.
3. Not smoking. Cessation of smoking reduces the risk of heart disease, stroke, some cancers, bronchitis, and emphysema.
4. Avoidance of excessive alcohol. Limiting alcohol to one glass of wine or spirits per day reduces the risk of liver disease and certain cancers. However, the older you get, the more cautious you should be, even about drinking small amounts.
5. Stress reduction. Reduction of stress and anxiety helps to strengthen the immune system and decreases susceptibility to disease.
6. Cultivating satisfying relationships. Social interaction and support have been found to reduce stress, help cognitive functioning, and prevent depression.
7. Challenging the mind. Learning new skills and regular mental activity promote healthy mental functioning.

### *3-Cognitive capacity and life style*

From a psychological perspective, studies are showing that cognitive capacity "most often determines whether people can attain extreme old age while remaining active" (Volz, 2000). The good news is that research by psychologists at Princeton University demonstrated that new brain cells, which enable learning and memory, grow continuously throughout a person's lifetime. Memory enhancement and mental functioning are supported by good diet, mental activity, and connectedness with other people. Again, these are all part of the John Hopkins recommendations and emphasize the importance of a healthy lifestyle.

### *4-Periodontal or oral health*

A study in the May issue of the *Journal of Periodontology* identifies lifestyle factors that have the most impact on periodontal health. The study followed a group of 219 factory workers in Japan from 1999 to 2003 in an attempt to evaluate the effect of different lifestyle factors on the progression of periodontal diseases. Each worker was evaluated on a list of the following lifestyle factors: physical exercise, alcohol consumption, tobacco use, duration of sleep, nutritional balance, and mental stress, hours worked and eating breakfast. The study found that the number one lifestyle factor that independently impacted the progression of periodontal disease was smoking; hours of sleep closely followed.

Over 41% of study participants who showed periodontal disease progression from 1999 to 2003 were current smokers. In addition, lack of sleep was identified as a significant lifestyle factor that may play a role in the progression of periodontal disease. The participants who received seven to eight hours of sleep exhibited less periodontal disease progression than those who received six hours of sleep or less. High stress levels and daily alcohol consumption also demonstrated a significant impact on periodontal disease progression.

"This study points out to patients that there are lifestyle factors other than brushing and flossing that may affect their oral health. Simple lifestyle changes, such as getting more sleep, may help patients improve or protect their oral health," explained Dr. Preston D. Miller, DDS, and AAP president. "It is also important to keep these in mind as the body of evidence linking oral disease with systemic diseases continues to grow because ultimately these lifestyle factors might impact a patient's overall health."

***5-Chronic degenerative diseases***

Cancer, diabetes, heart attack and stroke account for the majority of chronic illnesses that cost Americans millions of dollars and countless lives each year. Yet just four lifestyle factors that are well within most individuals' control may reduce diabetes by 93%, heart attack by 81%, stroke by 50% and cancer by 36%, according to a new study conducted by Earl S. Ford, M.D., M.o.H. of the Centre for Disease Control and Prevention in Atlanta, Georgia. The study was published in the August 10/24 issue of Archives of Internal Medicine, a journal of the American Medical Association. After the data was collected, researchers looked at how well they conformed to the four major lifestyle factors that appear to prevent chronic diseases such as cancer, heart disease and diabetes. These factors include:

1. Never smoking
2. Having a Body Mass Index (BMI) below 30 (thin, normal or slightly overweight but not obese)
3. Exercising at least three and a half hours a week
4. Following a healthy diet, which the researchers defined as high fruit and vegetable consumption combined with limited meat intake.

   Nearly all of 23,513 study participants had at least one of the four factors. Nine percent boasted all four factors.

***6-Biorhythms and a Natural lifestyle***

The human biological clock completes a cycle of about 25 hours when it is oblivious to the passage of time. However, the earth rotates in a cycle of 24 hours, repeating light and darkness. Many social activities are based on a 24-hour cycle. Therefore, we are unconsciously adjusting our biological clock from a 25-hour cycle to a 24-hour cycle. Living environments play a significant role in this adjustment of the biological clock and are called synchronizers. The synchronizer with the largest impact on the clock is light. Other than that work, meals and other social activities act as a synchronizer to some extent. This adjustment mechanism of human biological rhythm would be acquired through a history of evolution.

Dr. Shigekazu says humans living in modern societies are surrounded by factors that make it difficult to adapt our biological rhythms to a 24-hour cycle. These factors include loss of difference between day and night, exposure to bright lights at night, shift working, the service industry open at midnight and the spread of the Internet. While sleep disorders and other undesirable affects due to these factors have been reported, humans in fact live or propagate in such living environments. Surely, humans have acquired a certain level of biological adaptability to 24-hour active societies. However, it should also be noted that there are individual differences in the adaptability and that these changes in lifestyles might have negative effects on children in a growth period, and can lead to multiple adult health issues.

**Lifestyle diseases**

Lifestyle diseases (also sometimes called diseases of longevity or diseases of civilization interchangeably) are diseases that appear to increase in frequency as countries become more industrialized and people live longer. They can include Alzheimer's disease, atherosclerosis, asthma, cancer, chronic liver disease or cirrhosis, Chronic Obstructive Pulmonary Disease, Type 2 diabetes, heart disease, metabolic syndrome, nephritis or chronic renal failure, osteoporosis, acne, stroke, depression and obesity.

In the Paleolithic era, the diet was healthy, but infectious disease and natural causes tended to shorten lifespan. As agriculture developed, the lifespan initially increased as famine receded, and advances in technology and hygiene eventually greatly reduced infectious disease. But the modern diet has led to new diseases and increased disability. In 1900, the top three causes of death in the United States were pneumonia/influenza, tuberculosis, and diarrhea/enteritis. Communicable diseases accounted for about 60 percent of all deaths.

In 1900, heart disease and cancer were ranked number four and eight respectively. Since the 1940s, the majority of deaths in the United States have resulted from heart disease, cancer, and other degenerative diseases. And, by the late 1990s, degenerative diseases accounted for more than 60 percent of all deaths. It should be noted, however, that lifestyle diseases have their onset later in an individual's life and need a longer lifespan in order to become the cause of death. This suggests that the life expectancy at birth of 49.24 years in 1900 was too short for degenerative diseases to occur, compared to a life expectancy at birth of 77.8 years in 2004. Also, survivorship to the age of 50 was 58.5% in 1900, and 93.7% in 2007.

Seven key shifts in dietary habits in last 100 years

Healthy eating habits have a major role in our lifestyle, so we have to take care of our foods very seriously. Verne Verona in his book "Nature's cancer fighting foods" (pg. 1) writes, over the last 150 years our eating patterns, food quality, and nutrition ratios have dramatically shifted to a packaged, mass produced, adulterated and refined fare that has sacrificed wholesome nutrition for consumer convenience and corporate profit. Here are seven key shifts that have occurred in the last 100 years;

1. Refined sugar increase / Whole grain decrease
2. Animal source protein increase / Vegetable protein decrease
3. Saturated fat increase / Unsaturated fat decrease

4. Increase of fiber-absent foods / Decrease of Whole fibrous foods
5. Increase of artificial additives / Decrease of foods naturally containing them
6. Increase of synthetic chemicals / Decrease of natural quality
7. Increase of fast- paced lifestyle / Decrease of meal- time rituals

## Benefits of a healthy lifestyle proven by researches

### *1-UCLA research*

The overall benefit of a balanced lifestyle emerged in 1965, when a Southern California research team headed by Nadia Belloc and Lester Breslow, who was dean of public health at UCLA, decided to follow the aging patterns of people in Alameda Country. A twenty three page lifestyle questionnaire was handed out to almost seven thousand subjects asking them in great detail about their health status and lifestyle. After five and a half years, 371 subjects died. By looking back at the original response to these questionnaires, researchers discovered that the most important distinguishing feature of those who survived was not their income, physical condition, or genetic inheritance, but a handful of extremely simple lifestyle habits:

1. Sleeping seven or eight hours a night
2. Eating breakfast almost every day
3. Not eating between meals
4. Normal weight for their age
5. Regular physical activity i.e. engaging often in active sports, long walks, gardening, or other exercise
6. Moderate drinking
7. Never smoking cigarettes

***2-Dr. Weston A. Price research***

Weston A. Price was an American dentist who practiced in the 1920s to 1940s, in Cleveland, Ohio. He was well known and well respected in his day, widely published in peer-reviewed journals. He was the author of a textbook on dentistry used by the US Navy. He served as head of research for the National Dental Association. He had a laboratory in his home office where he evaluated different foods for nutrient content. He wrote prolifically and did a lot of research on root canals. Dr. Price became more and more concerned about the increasing amount of dental caries he was seeing in his patients. He noted that tooth decay and dental deformities not only caused a lot of suffering but also that the people who had these problems invariably had other health problems. He concluded that the teeth were a visual indicator of the health status in the rest of the body. Now this was a time when the world was opening up; adventurers were going to areas where there had never been any contact with modern civilization before. Their observations and photographs appeared in such magazines as the National Geographic. A frequent observation was that isolated peoples had beautiful teeth. In fact, the first settlers in America described the teeth of the Native Americans as "white and straight as piano keys".

These reports intrigued Dr. Price very much and he decided to start out on a series of travels to find these people with beautiful teeth. These investigations lasted ten years. Dr Price sought the answers to two questions. Were these reports of populations that did not suffer from dental caries and dental deformities (and by inference had good overall health) actually true? And if the answer to the first question was yes, then he sought the answer to the second question: what were the people eating? He was not interested in what unhealthy people were eating. He knew what unhealthy people were eating. He wanted to know what the diets of healthy people contained.

His investigations took him to isolated Swiss villages and a windswept island off the coast of Scotland. He studied traditional Inuit peoples (Eskimos), Native American tribes in Canada, Florida Everglades, South Sea islanders, Aborigines in Australia, Maoris (Mow-ree) in New Zealand, Peruvian and Amazonian Indians and tribesmen in Africa. In Switzerland

Dr. Price observed that the children never brushed their teeth – they had never seen a tooth brush. Many of the children's teeth were covered with green slime, but they had virtually no cavities. Price observed that the children were very hardy. They played in frigid streams barefoot during weather in which he and his wife had to put on heavy overcoats. The men in the villages were noted for their strength – they routinely won the athletic contests throughout Switzerland and the women were noted for their beauty.

The villages produced all of their own food right in the valley. The number one food in the diet was the very food that was blamed for causing the epidemic of tuberculosis throughout the rest of Switzerland and the world: raw milk. These people kept cattle and goats that grazed on the rich, lush pastures beneath the melting glaciers, and the diet consisted of raw milk, raw cheese, and raw cream and raw butter. One theory about why we have so many health problems today is that they are caused by foods new to human evolution milk products and grains. But here was a healthy population living principally on these two foods. It is important to note that the milk products were raw, not pasteurized, and the bread was made with grains that were prepared very carefully by sourdough techniques and fermentation.

Dr. Price also visited Swiss villages that had connection by road to so-called civilization, and in these villages he found stores selling sugar, white flour, jams and jellies, canned condensed milk, canned foods and vegetables oils. He also counted cavities and took photographs in these villages. If the store had already been there for a few years, he found one tooth in three was decayed, and if the store had been there long enough for a new generation to come along, the children born to the parents who had changed their diet had dental deformities. Their teeth were coming in overlapping, crowded and crooked. Their faces were narrower than those of the children he had seen in the Loetschental Valley. Most tragically, tuberculosis became a huge problem in these communities. Weston Price's research indicates that these conditions are in fact not genetic but, rather caused by a lack of vital nutrients during the formative period of the body.

While dentists do correlate cavities to nutrition, their focus tends to be on sugar or acid-generating foods. The typical solution for decay is to fill the cavities, encourage the patients to increase their level of dental hygiene while decreasing their consumption of sweets. According to Price, when given enough specific nutrients, the body will re-mineralize the tooth naturally so that no decay arises. Dr. Price discovered that there were no processed foods in any of the diets of the healthy people he studied. There were animal foods in every diet, and the food was all nutrient dense - meaning it contained high levels of vitamins and minerals. Nutrient dense foods are seafood, organ meats, raw dairy, eggs and meat.

Like Price, Dr. Frances Pottenger was also a researcher. His research revealed that predictable changes in health can occur when you change diet. In his study, cats that were fed an all-raw diet lived generation after generation in good health. When the raw food was replaced by pasteurized milk and partially cooked meat, allergies and skeletal deformities occurred in the first generation. The offspring of these poorly fed cats developed glandular problems (such as thyroid, adrenal and pancreatic). The next generation experienced a whole host of degenerative diseases, and the fourth generation exhibited mental disorders and was infertile, meaning they did not reproduce. It means when the human diet produces "facial deformities," as we are seeing these days, extinction will occur if that diet is followed for several generations.

***3-Stanford University research***

According to Stanford university of school of Medicine(2000) in California, " not only do persons with better health habit survive longer but in such persons, disability is postponed and compressed into fewer years at the end of life". Based on the study over a period of 55 years on life style, including life time smoking, obesity and exercise of 1741 males and females, the scientists have concluded that healthy habits can extend life span while lending off disability.

### *4-Morbidity / Mortality weekly*

Morbidity and mortality weekly report (2001) writes maintaining a normal weight, eating a nutritious diet, exercising and not smoking are all crucial to staying healthy, but only about 3% of people manage to achieve all four of these healthy habits.

### *5-Michigan Department of Community Health*

The Michigan Department of Community Health and the Centers for Disease Control and Prevention conducted a telephone survey of more than 4,000 Michigan residents in 1998 and 2000. The investigators found that about 38% of adults maintained a healthy body weight, while just over 20% ate the recommended amount of fruits and vegetables. Only about one quarter engaged in regular physical activity, and roughly the same number smoked. Women were more likely to engage in all four healthy behaviors than men. Fewer than 2% of men achieved all four behaviors, whereas 4.5% of women did. In addition, the number of college graduates achieving all four behaviors was three times higher than the number of those with a high school education or less. The researchers also note that those who reported being unhealthy were less likely to practice the behaviors than those who reported excellent health.

### *6-Canadian Medical Association*

Canadian Medical Association journal,(2002) has published that in Nova Scotia 58000 people die every year from either cardiovascular disease or cancer. Fortunately people are becoming conscious of unhealthy lifestyle and are trying to find ways to increase their quality of life as well as their life span by living healthier. Researchers discovered that a healthy lifestyle and exercise routine could be the key to reducing the risk of cardiovascular disease among menopausal women. The strong relationship between healthy eating and good cardiovascular health could be seen in the slowing of plaque buildup among menopausal women who participated in the diet and exercise control group of a study.

***7-Yahoo News***

Yahoo news (August10, 2004) quotes a study consisted of 353 women between the ages of 44 and 50 years. Over a four-year period ultrasounds were used to measure the thickness of their carotid artery walls. The participants were divided into two groups, a lifestyle intervention group and an assessment-only "control" group. The women in the control group exhibited an accelerated thickening of the arteries, which increased from 0.003 millimeters per year before they reached menopause and shot up to 0.008 mm during and after menopause. The thickening of the arteries of the women in the lifestyle intervention group were reduced to 0.004 mm per year. The women in the intervention group also didn't experience any rise in their LDL cholesterol levels over a 4.5-year period. Based on the results of these studies, experts concluded that menopause represents a unique opportunity for women to work at reducing their risks of cardiovascular condition.

Yahoo news (Dec. 15, 2005) explains a four-pronged lifestyle program that works to improve memory and brain efficiency in older adults in as little as two weeks, University of California researchers found. The study involved 34 adults with normal memory who either made no lifestyle modifications or made the following changes as part of a "memory improvement plan" for 14 days: Eating five small meals per day. This was done to prevent dips in blood sugar that can occur when three larger meals are eaten. The meals consisted of healthy foods including omega-3 fats, whole-grain carbohydrates antioxidants and regular physical exercise.

Participants took brisk walks daily and performed other physical conditioning to improve brain circulation. Participants performed brainteasers, crossword puzzles and other memory exercises to help improve their memory skills. The participants underwent positron emission tomography (PET) scans to measure brain activity before and after the study. PET scans of those who followed the memory improvement plan had a significant decrease in brain metabolism in the brain area linked to working memory and cognitive functions. This means they were essentially using less brain power, or, in other words, were using their brains more efficiently. Study participants ranged in age from 35 to 70, with an average age of 53 years.

***8-WHO warning***

A senior World Health Organization official (2006) warned that governments must take urgent action against obesity or it will soon be too late. WHO suggested that we don't have to wait for a new government agenda if you or your child is overweight or obese, you can take the steps to getting healthy on your own, starting with some basic life style changes. '75 Percent of Our Population Will be Overweight by 2015,' was the finding by a research team at John Hopkins University (Yahoo news July 18, 2007) who examined 20 different published studies and national surveys about weight and eating behavior. Their conclusion is far from encouraging. Americans across all age groups, genders and races are getting fatter, and if the trend continues, 75 percent of U.S. Adults will be overweight by the year 2015.

***9-AMA Journal***

The Journal of the American Medical Association (May 2007) writes "Evidently, the ruse is over regarding the need for useless drugs or any other potential procedures for heart disease devised by conventional medicine to separate you from your hard-earned dollars, especially when simple lifestyle changes are just as effective, according to a recent clinical trial."

Scientists compared the effectiveness of stents a crude tool that's become a standard part of a heart doctor's tool kit over the past quarter-century to safer lifestyle alterations, including more exercise, better eating habits ideally based on your body's unique nutritional type and smoking cessation, in a clinical trial involving nearly 2,300 patients with a minimum of one blocked artery. Patients relying on lifestyle changes alone lived just as long as those who received stents, and they enjoyed a better quality of life too! All the more reason, you have to take responsibility for your own health issues, so you can become better informed about the range of safer, cheaper and healthier alternatives, none of which have a thing to do with the obviously unnecessary step of implanting a stent.

***10-BMJ Study***

Making simple lifestyle changes is at least as effective as taking prescription drugs in reducing the risk of developing type 2 diabetes, According to a British Medical Journal study (Jan. 2007). Changes such as switching to a healthier diet and increasing exercise helped to reduce the risk of diabetes by about 50 percent. The lifestyle changes were just as effective, or more so, than taking an anti-obesity drug or a diabetes drug among people at high risk of developing type 2 diabetes. The prestigious New England Journal of Medicine also found all the way back in 2002 that lifestyle changes work better than drugs in treating diabetes. Rates of type 2 diabetes are expected to double by 2030, so it is critical that you protect yourself from this pervasive disease. Diabetes is close to 90 percent preventable, as it is often a direct result of dietary and lifestyle factors. The sooner you begin to treat the diabetes, the easier it will be to control, so it is important to take action as soon as possible.

***11-University of California***

Some of us may find the constant reminder that one should eat healthily, exercise regularly and maintain a normal BMI annoying. The attitude is born out of either a sense of denial or belief: denying that the ill effects of having an unhealthy lifestyle will ever affect one's health or believing that destiny, and not lifestyle will determine if one gets seriously ill or not. Perhaps a recent report from the University of California might make these individuals reconsider. Researchers studied changes in the prostate gene expression in men, with low-grade prostate cancer, who underwent intensive lifestyle and nutrition intervention over a period of 3 months (PAS 2008; 105: 8369 –8374).

Thirty one men with low-grade prostate cancer, who declined immediate surgery, hormonal therapy or radiation, participated in the study. They agreed to a comprehensive lifestyle change instead. A prostate biopsy was performed prior to initiation of the lifestyle change program. The 3 month lifestyle modification comprised of a 3-day intensive residential retreat followed by weekly outpatient follow-up by a study nurse. The modifications included a low fat (10% of calories from fat), whole foods, plant-based diet; stress management 60 minutes / day (gentle yoga-based stretching, breathing, meditation, imagery and progressive relaxation), moderate aerobic exercise (walking 30 minutes / day for 6 days / week) and a one hour group support session per week.

The diet was supplemented with soy (one daily serving of tofu plus 58 gm of a fortified soy protein powdered beverage), fish oil (3 gm daily), vitamin E (100 units daily) selenium (200 mg daily) and vitamin C (2 gm daily). Another prostate biopsy was performed at the end of the 3 months intervention. The gene expression from the normal prostate tissue obtained before and after the lifestyle changes was compared. At the end of 3 months, they found 48 genes up-regulated and 453 genes down-regulated (simplistically, up-regulation means switched on and down-regulation means switched off) in the prostate tissue.)

***12-Archives of Internal Medicine***

Published in Archives of Internal Medicine, a study drew diet and lifestyle data from approximately 25,000 Germans aged 35 to 65, who completed their responses at the start of the study in the mid-1990s. The authors then examined their responses in relation to four healthy lifestyle factors: never smoking, having a BMI lower than 30, exercising at least 3.5 hours per week, and following a healthy diet, such as consuming relatively high amounts of fruits and vegetables and low amounts of meat. After an average of 7.8 years, the study found that four lifestyle factors were linked to a 93 percent reduced risk of diabetes, 81 percent reduced risk of heart attack, 50 percent reduced risk of stroke and 36 percent reduced risk of cancer. Each lifestyle factor by itself was also associated with reducing the risk of each of the chronic diseases, with a BMI under 30 exerting the largest reduction in risk.

***13-Japanese research***

Dietary habits are the habitual decisions an individual or culture makes when choosing what foods to eat. Japanese research group led by Professor Yasuhiko Minokoshi and Dr. Tetsuya Shiuchi, scientists at the National Institute for Physiological Sciences, NIPS, and Japan, found that meals stimulated with sweet taste and motivated with its anticipation regularly activates "orexin" in the brain and it stimulates muscle glucose metabolism via the sympathetic nervous system, thereby reducing blood glucose level in mice. They report their finding in *Cell Metabolism* published on Dec 2, 2009.

It is known that orexin plays an important role in the regulation of sleep/wakefulness and autonomic nervous system in human as well as experimental animals. Therefore, this finding implies the strong relationship between habits of diet and our health. Pleasant meal with tasty foods and with family and friends may prevent hyperglycemia by activating orexin neurons. In contrast, irregular dietary habits, especially eating fast food just before sleeping, may cause hyperglycemia and possibly obesity. "Orexin neurons have been shown to decrease the activity at night. Thus, eating just before sleeping may not be able to activate orexin neurons effectively, and then resulting in hyperglycemia", said Prof Minokoshi. With the increased understanding of our bodies that we have gained from science over the past few decades, the benefits of a healthy lifestyle are becoming more apparent. For people of all ages, weights, and abilities the benefits of a healthy lifestyle are endless.

Good Health is not something that you buy from a drug store or a department store, but can be achieved by practicing collective patterns of health-related behavior, based on choices made from available options. Following this logic, if you wish to realize the benefits of a healthy lifestyle, you have to repeat some healthy pattern as a part of your daily or weekly activities, some patterns like eating right and exercising. Other benefits includes: Reduced health care costs, reduced illness and injuries, reduced doctors visit, keeps you employed and improved employee/employer relations. Dietary habits are the habitual decisions an individual or culture makes when choosing what foods to eat.

Our eating habits are more important than our genes, because through wrong combinations of food, we trigger hidden diseases in our genes. So forget about genetic factor, if you are following a natural healthy dietary pattern. Wrong food combinations, incorrect timings, poor selection of type of foods and extreme temperatures of foods produce unhealthy chemicals which badly influence the ph of blood and ph of other body fluids. This minor shift in blood ph leads to a chain of chemical reactions at the cellular level, resulting in fluctuations in the insulin levels, body temperature, and hormonal levels which affect tissues, organs and finally systems, depending on the duration of exposure to your bad eating habits. Remember the most food sensitive organ is the liver and the most food sensitive system is the digestive system, both are absolutely depend on your dietary habits.

***Lifestyle Modification***

Wellness is about being comfortable in your space: your body, your attitude, and your environment. A healthy lifestyle can greatly increase a person's longevity. The issue with a lot of people nowadays is that they are so busy working and/or taking care of everyone around them, that they neglect their own health and wellness. Make sure your heart is healthy and your bones are strong and Keep it that way to see the benefits of a healthy lifestyle. The best way to ensure good health is by taking care of you. The care stakes are high but the potential rewards are great-preventing premature death, unnecessary illness and disability, controlling health care cost and maintaining a high quality of life into old age. With a healthy lifestyle, you are who you are and you don't have to be self-conscious about those things that you otherwise would be if you didn't care about your lifestyle.

With a healthy lifestyle, you have more control of your life as you work with your body against those aspects of living which may work to hold you back if you would let them. With a healthy lifestyle, you have control over your sleep patterns so that you feel generally well rested throughout the day. Everything works together to help other aspects of your lifestyle make sense and benefit you. Science has proven that healthy weight loss, healthy eating and fitness routines make dramatic improvements in health, and help control common chronic illnesses like high cholesterol, high blood pressure, diabetes, stress, and general lack of stamina.

Another benefit of a healthy lifestyle is a steady flow of stamina and strength; you can perform activities and exercises that will enhance your flexibility. With a healthy lifestyle, you have a balanced and varied diet that provides your body its needed nutrients and energy as well. You have strength to train to help build the muscle that supports the bones and joints; therefore decreasing the risk of falls and fractures.

Cardiovascular exercise, also known as aerobic exercise, strengthens the heart muscle, therefore increases the heart's efficiency. As we age, our bones biologically begin to lose mass and strength.

Weight-bearing exercise such as walking and strength training helps slow the onset of and/or prevent osteoporosis and some research shows that participating in such activities can actually build bone density and begin to reverse the disease. The good news is you don't have to train like an Olympic athlete to enjoy the benefits of a healthy lifestyle. The secret and logic are repeating a chosen healthy pattern as a part of your daily or weekly activities. We hope that this will get you to a healthy lifestyle if you are not there already. A healthy lifestyle is a way of life.

The medical system, now widely acknowledged as lacking key healing components, has recently introduced the concept of lifestyle modification. The current definition of lifestyle modification includes mainly correction of dietary habits, control of smoking, avoidance of alcohol intake and regular exercise; there is no concept of natural lifestyle factors. These superficial factors cannot solve the rapidly increasing number of health problems, which are crippling humanity and burdening our healthcare infrastructure. Lifestyle modification is a highly specialized field and every medical practitioner should be trained in it. Without modifying lifestyle no one can ever claim to provide a holistic treatment. All medical treatments, if missing the rules of lifestyle modification, are incomplete and never therapeutic.

## SYNCHRONIZED LIFESTYLE MODIFICATION PROGRAM (SLP)

Synchronized lifestyle modification was initially called Shagufta Liver Program, but name is changed for better global understanding. Since the past twenty seven years I was applying the rules of a natural lifestyle in my family medicine practice because my gut feeling told me that these are the rules of nature and I can't heal medical disorders without incorporating them into my practice. Very recently I realized that I was right on the scientific tract, and in fact I was modifying their individual lifestyle. From the same duration, I started analyzing the relationship between the individual components of a lifestyle and their impact on various human systems. My clinical experience on the few thousand patients in the past ten years is that, the Liver is the master organ controlling all physical, emotional, mental and spiritual functions. It is the organ which is neglected and abused quite often. All the advanced medical health care systems, pharmaceutical drugs, environmental pollutants and electromagnetic radiations damage liver, and suppress its immunity. During this process I have learnt that we can't heal it without an integrated scientific approach.

Therefore SLP focuses on the restoration of the liver health by harmonizing the external routine of that person with the ongoing internal biorhythms through an individualized food plan based on diet correction rules. The major components of SLP are eight rules of diet correction, which gradually help an individual to attain holistic harmony. In personalized lifestyle modification, besides diet correction, sleep is regulated, stress is managed, and correct exercise is advised. SLP generates harmony in biorhythms and liver which are interdependent for giving us holistic health. A personalized lifestyle modification heals disorders like obesity, diabetes, hypertension, arthritis, allergies, depression, autoimmune disorders, chronic liver disease, kidney failure, or cancer. Restoration of liver health leads to a restoration of major biorhythms like blood ph, blood oxygen levels, body temperature, food cravings, insulin, leptin levels which balance biochemistry, and disease starts reversing.

## CHAPTER NO: 5

## SYNCHRONIZED LIFESTYLE MODIFICATION PROGRAM : SLP

Before going into SLP details, we must understand the definition of positive health as defined by Patrick Holford in his book "The Optimum Bible". He writes "positive health is characterized by a consistent, clear, high level of energy, emotional balance, a sharp mind, a desire to maintain physical fitness and a direct awareness of what suits our bodies, what enhances our health, and what our needs are in any given moment. This state of health includes resilience to infectious diseases and protection from the major killer diseases such as heart disease and cancer. As a result the aging process is slowed down and we can live long and healthy life. At its most profound level, health is not merely the absence of pain or tension, but a joy in living, a real appreciation of what it is to have a healthy body with which to taste the many pleasures of this world".

Dr. Deepak Chopra writes in his book 'Ageless Body, Timeless Mind' that a healthy diet must have two components: 1- it has to be psychologically satisfying 2-it has to provide a balanced supply of nutrients several times a day. He writes "my own feeling is that if a patient exhausted by effort and distress has his life invaded by doctors and other do-gooders wanting to constrain his eating and other behaviors, the hassle factor and loss of autonomy could prove the last straw. A strong sense of personal freedom, coupled with personal happiness, is critical to surviving in good health to a ripe old age. Fear is not a good motivator because it creates its own stress. Yet millions of people have been indoctrinated about cholesterol, on the assumption that the price of fear is small compared to the price of high cholesterol".

I absolutely agree to the above mentioned philosophies, and in fact these are the key factors in SLP. It is a freedom program which gives you the choice to select between health and disease and also between nature and anti-nature. Nature has provided us with an amazing immune system, which comprises one third of the human body's cells. God intended to fuel our inner healing force with the right natural substances to enable the body to function up to its natural potential. The body is a complex organism that has the ability to heal itself, if only you listen to it and respond with proper nourishment and care. In spite of all the abuse our bodies endure, they still usually serve us well for many years before signs of illness may start to appear.

Our modern lifestyles have gotten us off the track, with fast foods, alcohol abuse, drug dependencies, a polluted environment and high-tech stress. The definition of a balanced diet varies from person to person because everyone has biochemical individuality and their own sets of food likes and dislikes. The balanced diet varies throughout life as individual chemistry changes. It is dependent on age, gender, level of physical activity, stress, nature of work, changing seasons, weather conditions, emotional and spiritual states.

Lifestyle modification has become an important component of every healing science. It helps in keeping one healthy and slows down the process of aging. A general lifestyle modification plan cannot treat, manage or reverse a disease process. If you align one's lifestyle with nature it helps in the prevention and reversal of a disease process. SLP introduces holistic health by making changes in the existing lifestyle in such a manner that the body attains harmony with its natural biorhythms. The primary focus is to restore biochemical individuality by harmonizing biorhythms and liver health. The most important component of SLP is correct diagnosis and one has to understand the patient, not the disease for management and reversal of a disease process. I will cover the details of SLP in the following sections:

1. *AIMS AND OBJECTIVES OF SLP*
2. *COMPONENTS OF SLP*
3. *SLP DIAGNOSTIC TOOLS*
4. *SLP METHODOLOGY*

5. *SLP FOLLOW UPS*

## Aims and objectives of SLP

***1-To introduce holistic health.***

Holistic health or holistic medical practice refers to maintenance of the entire health of the person (physical, mental and spiritual system) rather than just one aspect of health. Thus, an asymptomatic or symptomatic individual is best served by a health maintenance approach that includes assessment and treatment of the whole person rather than one specific part.

***2-Liver reserve restoration***

More than ever before in the history of mankind, human beings need to have healthy livers to break down the chemicals that have crept into our environment. Radiologists can tell us that the condition of "fatty liver" is spreading like an epidemic, and unfortunately now seen at a very young age as well. When a Body compatible food plan is prescribed it always become biorhythm and liver specific for that particular individual. Within the first two weeks of SLP, the liver starts detoxifying and later improvement in liver health is seen. The recovery of disease is reciprocated by the level of improvement in the liver health.

***3-Reversal of chronic degenerative diseases***

SLP treats all chronic diseases, inclusive of cancer, as a chronic biochemical disorder and not impressed at all by the musical medical terminologies. All chronic diseases start responding when body compatible whole foods are organized to match, with the internal body clock routine, an important biorhythm. If the disease is at an advanced stage the progression of a disease slows down with less systemic complications.

***4-To activate intuitional eating***

The human body is fitted with a perfect set of apparatus needed for survival and well-being. The instinct for self-preservation guides through body wisdom and wants us to be one with nature. Environmental pollution, chemical foods, unnatural dietary patterns and emotional traumas block the inner voice. Once physical, mental and emotional cleansing is done, intuition gets activated and it never allows self-abuse.

***5-Restoration of the connection of micro with macro-rhythms***

Once the body is aligned with micro-biorhythms, holistic health and solace is the outcome. This internal peace compels an individual to think on the higher objectives and only then the higher human universal role starts to manifest.

**SLP Components are:**

I-Eight rules of correct eating
II-Sleep regulation
III-Stress management
IV-Exercise
V-Food supplements

**I-Eight rules of correct eating**

Correct eating stands for the selection of natural whole foods and correction of dietary habits in order to harmonize the dietary routine with the ongoing biological rhythms in the body. When we eat natural whole foods correctly it is absorbed optimally, works holistically and works on biochemical individuality. Here are the key diet correction rules of SLP:

1-Selection of natural foods

2-Correct food timings

3-Favorite foods should be selected

4-How much to eat

5-Correct food combinations

6-Food rotation

7-Food temperature

8-Correct water intake

***1-Selection of natural foods***

The fuel for our body's engine comes directly from the things we consume. The foods we eat contain nutrients in the form of vitamins, minerals, coenzymes, enzymes, water, amino acids, carbohydrates, and lipids. Natural foods are foods that are minimally processed. Natural foods do not include ingredients such as refined sugars, refined flours, milled grains, hydrogenated oils, sweeteners, food colors, or flavorings. Another definition is that a food that has been not been processed in any way that alters covalent bonds, and to which no artificial substance has been added. Natural foods are also called whole foods or organic foods. Whole foods are those that are unprocessed and unrefined, or processed and refined as little as possible before being consumed.

**Organic foods** are made according to certain production standards. Under organic production, the use of conventional non-organic pesticides, insecticides and herbicides is greatly restricted and saved as a last resort. If livestock are involved, they must be reared without the routine use of antibiotics and without the use of growth hormones, and generally fed a healthy diet. According to Dr. Price, the best natural foods are foods rich in vitamins and minerals; he labeled them as nutrient dense foods. Nutrient dense foods are sea foods, eggs, raw dairy, organ meat and meat. In Pakistan natural foods are called Desi foods which include locally grown wheat, naturally grown vegetables, fruits, raw milk, raw butter, raw sugar, ghee and desi poultry. We are fortunate that natural foods are still part of our culture, because Pakistan is an agricultural country and with little effort we can eliminate all un-natural and processed foods from our society. Therefore for good health we have to select natural and locally grown foods.

In order to enhance the absorption and assimilation of natural foods we have to consider two important factors i.e. seasonality of food and body compatibility. Seasonality of food refers to the times of year when a given type of food is at its peak, either in terms of harvest or its flavor or nutritional value. Seasonal food was practiced since ancient civilizations as people ate what Mother Nature produced which varied according to seasons. Body compatible food is that natural food which matches biochemical individuality, and therefore is optimally absorbed, assimilated, excreted; becoming a remedy for that particular biochemistry. However, eating only natural foods is not going to solve health issues. So it is an art to organize the food in such a manner that it becomes a medicine acting therapeutically and on a preventive level as well. With experience of how foods act in the body and the ability to self-evaluate, one can learn which foods are compatible to his or her particular body type or constitution and physical condition. Looking at the individual properties of food and varying body chemistries it is safe to conclude that a universal diet does not exist.

***Classification of natural foods***

Thousands of years ago, master healers in China perceived a way to classify natural food and disease according to simple, easily observed patterns: one eats cooling foods for overheated conditions, warming foods are best for people who feel too cold. Detoxifying foods are for those who carry excess toxins; building foods are good for deficient people. Alkaline foods for hyper-acidic chemistry or acidic foods for hyper- alkaline states. Various traditions in the East focus on other dimensions of food like the ability to moisten/dryness, relieve pain/cause pain, increase energy/deplete energy, calm mind/ agitate mind or retain water/ excrete water and others. Natural whole foods can regulate bowel habits, increase beneficial intestinal flora, regulate blood sugar, enhance immune system and can even minimize or control tumor growth. Ayurveda classifies natural foods into five categories depending upon their taste, property, heating or cooling effect, post-digestion effect and special properties.

***Industrial /Scientific / GMO foods***

Foods which should be strictly avoided are: all scientific foods like low fat, high fiber, low calorie, bran based, foods with added nutrients, processed and refined foods are toxic to a human system. GMO foods are genetically modified foods and are an advanced version of scientific foods. In 2009, the American Academy of Environmental Medicine (AAEM) stated that, "Several animal studies indicate serious health risks associated with genetically modified (GM) food," including infertility, immune problems, accelerated aging, faulty insulin regulation, and changes in major organs and the gastrointestinal system. The AAEM has asked physicians to advise all patients to avoid GM foods.

The Institute for Responsible Technology is a world leader in educating policy makers and the public about genetically modified (GM) foods and crops. Founded in 2003 by international bestselling author and GMO expert Jeffrey Smith, IRT has worked in more than 30 countries on 6 continents, and is credited with improving government policies and influencing consumer-buying habits. The genetic engineering process creates massive collateral damage, causing mutations in hundreds or thousands of locations throughout the plant's DNA. Natural genes can be deleted or permanently turned on or off, and hundreds may change their behavior. Even the inserted gene can be damaged or rearranged, and may create proteins that can trigger allergies or promote disease. There are eight GM food crops. The five major varietiessoy, corn, canola, cotton, and sugar beets have bacterial genes inserted, which allow the plants to survive an otherwise deadly dose of weed killer. Farmers use considerably more herbicides on these GM crops and so the food has higher herbicide residues. About 68% of GM crops are herbicide tolerant.

***2-Correct food timings***

A natural, favorite food taken in the correct amount still can’t become a remedy if the timing of intake is wrong. Body is regulated by a 24-hours clock, which is controlled by our autonomic system. The biological action of a single food varies with its time of intake. It can be a stimulant, or relaxant depending upon its time of intake. Single food act timings are important because the body handles many other biological processes besides digesting food. Eating, digesting and assimilating food is a multi-organ function and there are various pre-meal, peri-meal and post-meal biological settings, which the body has to manage. If we are not disciplined about food timings, we will be eating food at the cost of some other vital function. Proper meal timing leads to increased energy levels, decreased risk of obesity and fewer food cravings. Effective meal timing provides a consistent source of energy throughout the day by keeping blood sugar levels stable. Achieving the right balance of portion control and proper timing of meals will help keep your metabolism revved up and allow your body to use calories more efficiently.

***Breakfast***

Globally healthy meal timing starts with breakfast. While it may be the hardest meal to fit into a hectic schedule, it is critical in terms of kick-starting your metabolism for the day. While there is no official time to eat breakfast, it is best eaten shortly after waking up, usually before your daily activities begin. Often, people skimp on breakfast or skip it completely because they simply don't have time in the morning. Others think skipping the morning meal will help them shed pounds. A study from the University of Massachusetts, published in the American Journal of Epidemiology in 2003, found that people who skipped breakfast were at a greater risk of being obese than people who ate the morning meal. Another study, published in the Journal of the American Dietetic Association in September 2005, found breakfast eaters had lower body mass index levels (a measure of body fat based on height and weight), higher intakes of nutrients including calcium and fiber, and lower intakes of fat and cholesterol than non-breakfast eaters.

Meanwhile, numerous studies have shown that people who eat breakfast are better able to pay attention and concentrate throughout the day, due to increased energy levels. In fact, a review of 47 studies published in the Journal of the American Dietetic Association in May 2005 found that breakfast consumption improved cognitive function related to memory, test grades and school attendance in students. Furthermore, a January 2005 study published in the American Journal of

Clinical Nutrition found that regular eating habits resulted in a lower energy intake and lower total levels of cholesterol, including the so-called "bad" cholesterol LDL or low-density lipoprotein, which gets deposited in the walls of arteries and can lead to heart attacks and strokes.

Perhaps the most common result of poor meal timing is overeating at dinner because you're tired and famished after a long day. If you haven't eaten since lunch, by the time dinner rolls around your energy levels will be sagging, and you will be more likely to eat more than your body needs and make unhealthy food choices. If you get home from work late and make a habit of sitting down to a full dinner before you go to bed, it may have an impact on your weight. The pitfall with eating the majority of your daily calories in the evening is that the body isn't as efficient at burning these late-night calories. A person's metabolism naturally slows as the day wears on. Secondly, late-night impulsive food choices tend to be high in fat and calories.

While there is no scientific evidence to prove that eating large meals late at night will lead to weight gain, researchers from the University of Texas published findings in the Journal of Nutrition in January 2004 that found meals consumed in the early parts of the day are more satiating provide more of a sense of fullness than meals consumed later in the day. As a result, during the evening, people are less satisfied by meals and are more vulnerable to overeating. Furthermore, research published in the American Journal of Clinical Nutrition in 1993 found that significantly more calories are burned digesting the same meal in the morning, compared to the afternoon or evening. Finally, keep in mind that your daily eating patterns form a cycle. There is a ripple effect from eating late at night and delaying or avoiding breakfast. If you are not hungry in the morning and go without breakfast, you run the risk of starting the cycle of poor meal timing and not spreading your caloric intake properly throughout the day. Also keep it in mind that overeating at any time of the day whether it is morning, noon or night will lead to weight gain.

***Chinese body clock***

SLP dietary timings are organized on the basis of body clock timings explained by Acupuncture and Chrono-medicine. The Chinese clock is a 24 hours clock based on the circulation of Qi in the human body. The Chinese Meridian Circulation reflects "a real clock" in our body. Ancient Chinese practitioners used this timetable to prescribe medicine for their patients. It also represents how efficiently our organs function in certain periods. Hence, it is a good guideline for humans to achieve optimum health. Anton Jayasuriya in his book 'Clinical Acupuncture'has described the organs peak performance periods and time of the Qi circulation.

I. Lung: 3a.m. –5a.m.
II. Large intestine 5a.m.-7a.m.
III. Stomach 7a.m.-9a.m.
IV. Spleen 9a.m.11a.m.
V. Heart 11a.m.-1p.m.
VI. Small intestine 1p.m-3p.m.
VII. Urinary bladder 3p.m.-5p.m.
VIII. Kidney 5p.m.-7p.m.
IX. Pericardium 7p.m.-9p.m.
X. Sanjiao 9p.m.-11p.m.
XI. Gall bladder 11p.m.-1a.m.
XII. Liver 1a.m.-3a.m.

Between 7 to 9a.m., a large amount of blood flows into the stomach to help enhance the digestion of food. Also, the blood is concentrated in the pancreas to assist the breakdown of complex food into small molecules so that they can be absorbed easily into the bloodstream through the small intestine and transported to the entire body. That is why 7a.m to 9a.m. will be an ideal time to have our breakfast as this is the best time for the stomach to digest food efficiently. At the same time blood is concentrated in the large intestine, and large intestine works efficiently to secrete the feces.

According to the Qi timetable, blood is concentrated in the lungs at 3 to 5 a.m. This is a good time to rest and to "recharge" the power of the lungs. Thus, the lungs should have enough rest to enhance its efficiency. The fact explains why at this time the blood circulation is the slowest and the rate and frequency of breathing is minimal. Otherwise, the ability of the lungs will decrease when they do not have enough rest. Qi circulates through liver between 1am-3a.m. therefore natural detoxification is done at this time. When the liver is detoxified properly only then can it handle fat metabolism perfectly. Therefore people who are awake habitually between 1a.m. to 3a.m. are obese, psychologically disturb, have hormonal imbalance, metabolic imbalances and low immunity. So, make sure you avoid doing any activities at this time. In short, do not do things that conflict with your body's natural instinct; otherwise your body may collapse one day.

I have learnt that statistically, only a small number of people are on correct food intake timings. Majority are on a late breakfast routine, few taking breakfast while going to office or taking their breakfast after reaching their work places. Only few were serious about breakfast quality, timing and enjoying their food. The quick pace of modern life style has eliminated the food ritual of celebrating breakfast. I have seen that a person who was never in a habit of taking breakfast almost always ends up with a chronic degenerative disorder. People missing their breakfast were taking a heavy lunch and suffering from abdominal obesity or stomach disorders.

***Pre-breakfast***

While following SLP, one has to take breakfast before 9a.m. or within half an hour of waking up. Most people are unable to follow this. I found that food results were not satisfying with late breakfast. I kept on looking for the breakfast solution, and finally an idea of pre-breakfast came into my mind. Pre-breakfast has to be taken within first few minutes of waking up. While doing regular pulse analysis I have learnt that, on waking up first pulse to appear is of liver. In my imagination, the liver resembles a computer. When we switch on the computer, it takes few minutes before showing you the details on the desktop. When we wake up, and from a lying down position go to a sitting posture, the liver activates. The liver has over 500 functions to perform but the priority changes every day. So every morning, the first few minutes after waking up are extremely important, as the liver is prioritizing functions from the long list of its functions.

An unhealthy liver can't take healthy decisions about your life. I found foods rich in antioxidants and omega 3 & 6 fatty acids are liver supportive and help it in taking healthy decisions about your health. One study shows that the adrenal gland pours its secretions into blood streams within the first few minutes of waking up. To my astonishment pre-breakfast became the most important component of SLP. While selecting foods for the pre-breakfast I have to be extremely careful about body type, food choice, quantity, weather, presence of disease and pulse type. This is a person specific section of SLP based and is therapeutic. For pre-breakfast type, time, and dose of food is extremely important, and only section where I have to quantify the food.

If I find water retention in the pulse analysis, I have to select foods with diuretic properties; if I find post meal sugar cravings, then sugary foods for pre-breakfast are chosen. Individuals with high stress levels are given nuts; people with cold intolerance are given warm honey water. Foods given at pre-breakfast help in stimulating metabolism, induce satiety, overcome allergies, control mood swings, bring a glow on the face, control weight which bounces back and enhance immunity. If someone loses 50kg with SLP and is very careful about the intake of pre-breakfast, the weight will never bounce back. So the diet plan starts with a pre-breakfast which is within the first few minutes of waking up, ideally without leaving the bed and rinsing of mouth. First morning saliva is important in healing and a lot of researches are currently ongoing on the diagnostic role of morning saliva. It kills Helicobacter pylori and has a unique composition which never forms during the day. Un-stimulated whole saliva showed significant circadian rhythms in flow rate and in the concentrations of sodium and chloride but not in protein, potassium, calcium, phosphate or urea.

After pre-breakfast and breakfast, one has to take mid-morning and evening snacks. By default body is not allowed to have heavy lunch and makes you drowsy. Light snacks at three hour intervals between 9a.m. to 4p.m. are helpful in maintaining good energy, clarity of mind, less anger and weight management.

***Post dinner snack (PDS)***

Dinner time is between 7p.m. to 9p.m. with a gap of 2 to 3 hours required between dinner and sleep time. A post dinner snack (PDS) comes in, if the interval between dinner and sleep is of more than three hours. PDS induces sound sleep, switches off hyperactive mind, controls appetite, mood swings, energy and peak work performance on the next day. Any food intake before three hours interferes with the digestion process of the previous meal and unhealthy metabolites are produced.

***3-Favorite foods should be selected***

Food preferences are influenced by a number of factors such as biochemical individuality, personal experiences, cultural adaptations and perceived health benefits. Taste, however, is the most important determinant of how much a food is liked or disliked. In order to convert a natural food into a remedy, one has to consider individual food likings or preferences. Preferences help me decide a body compatible food program. Humans are biochemically unique therefore their food choices vary, though they may be on a natural lifestyle. My clinical experience has taught me that food likings or choices vary with varying body chemistry, liver status and homeostasis affected by the day to day happenings in one's life.

While selecting foods, the nutritionist has to consider the difference between food preference, cravings and food addictions. Food preference reflects a particular constitution, body type or biochemistry. Cravings indicate deficiency of a specific nutrient and food addiction tells of the presence of an abnormal biochemistry. Food preferences also reflect genetically determined food choices for that particular body type. Gut is most receptive to the food in the morning and its absorption is optimum before 9 a.m., therefore, the favorite foods should be selected for the breakfast. High food compatibility leads to best healing is expected. So besides selecting natural foods one has to consider his/her likes or dislikes. A very healthy food rich in healthy nutrients can become toxic to a person if he dislikes it or it is non-body compatible.

***Intuitive eating***

Intuitive eating is a nutrition philosophy based on the premise that becoming more attuned to the body's natural hunger signals is a more effective way to attain a healthy weight; rather than keeping track of the amounts of energy and fats in foods or satiety levels. It's a process that is intended to create a healthy relationship with food, mind and body. Intuitive eating is the opposite of dieting, the latter of which is externally driven. It is a key component of the "Health at Every Size movement". Supporters argue that eating in response to internal cues of hunger and fullness, while allowing all foods to be a part of the diet; will help maintain one's "natural" weight. Natural weight is the weight range predetermined by genetics. When someone is disconnected to his or her internal cues of satiety, it is easier to be trigged by external factors to eat.

If someone has rigid rules for so-called healthy eating, he or she is more likely to succumb to overeating. Scientifically, this all-or-none type of eating, built around eating rules rather than internal hunger/satiety cues, is referred to as restraint eating or Restraint Theory. Every single individual is born with this intrinsic mechanism of intuitive eating but in my experience, it takes a minimum of about four weeks to transform non-structured eating or addictive eating to intuitive eating. The chemical chaos has to be corrected by modifying eating habits and by a gradual introduction of favorite natural foods in their lifestyle.

The earliest proponents of the intuitive eating approach include Gwen Shamblin, author of *The Weigh down Diet*, and Evelyn Tribole and Elyse Resch, authors of the book, *Intuitive Eating*. Although this approach has been used mainly for weight loss, it's also a general philosophy for eating. Proponents believe that factors like being caught up with diet fads, making weight loss the sole objective or chronic stress mask intuitive eating. Some important principles mentioned in the book '*intuitive eating*' are:

- **i.** Reject the Diet Mentality: Throw out the diet books and magazine articles that offer you false hope of losing weight quickly, easily, and permanently.
- **ii.** Honor Your Hunger: Keep your body biologically fed with adequate energy and carbohydrates. Otherwise you can trigger a primal drive to overeat. Once you reach the moment of excessive hunger, all intentions of moderate, conscious eating are fleeting and irrelevant. Learning to honor this first biological signal sets the stage for re-building trust with yourself and food.
- **iii.** Make Peace with Food: Call a truce, stop the food fight! Give yourself unconditional permission to eat. If you tell yourself that you can't or shouldn't have a particular food, it can lead to intense feelings of deprivation that build into uncontrollable cravings and, often bingeing. When you finally "give-in" to your forbidden food, eating will be experienced with such intensity, it usually results in last supper overeating, and overwhelming guilt.
- **iv.** Challenge the Food Police: Scream a loud "NO" to thoughts in your head that declare you're "good" for eating under 1000 calories or "bad" because you ate a piece of chocolate cake. The Food Police monitor the unreasonable rules that dieting has created. The police station is housed deep in your psyche, and its loud speaker shouts negative barbs, hopeless phrases, and guilt-provoking indictments. Chasing the Food Police away is a critical step in returning to Intuitive Eating.

v. Discover the Satisfaction Factor: The Japanese have the wisdom to promote pleasure as one of their goals of healthy living. When you eat what you really want, in an environment that is inviting and conducive, the pleasure you derive will be a powerful force in helping you feel satisfied and content. By providing this experience for yourself, you will find that it takes much less food to decide you've had "enough".

***Food restriction***

The theory of food restriction holds that people desire those foods that they or their doctor's feel should be avoided. According to the dietitian Debra Waterhouse, food cravings do not cause weight gain, but denying the cravings do. This creates a vicious cycle. For example, a person may feel guilty for wanting a freshly baked croissant that he or she smells upon entering a shopping mall. The urge is avoided, but a couple of hours later, the person may want it more than ever, give in to the craving, and quickly eat the entire croissant. This leads to even stronger feelings of guilt, along with the resolve not to eat anything remotely similar for some period of time. Soon, however, the craving strikes again and it is more intense.

The cycle becomes one of denial leading to deprivation, then to overindulgence, and then back to denial. This denial-deprivation-overindulgence pattern confirms the negative view of all food as either good or bad. It would be better, however, to imagine a world where foods are not designated as bad and not allowed, but where reasonable portions of any food can be part of a healthful diet. Favorite natural food combinations give pleasure, help in control of appetite, weight management, control mood swings and help in recovery from a disease process.

A study done at Quartermaster food and Container Institute for the Armed forces Chicago, suggested that experiences in the early years of life, prior to age 16 are among the strongest controlling factors in food preferences. Researchers speculate that preference differences among men and women may relate to the notion that the upbringing of men may have conditioned them to prefer hot or labor intensive meals, while women seek convenient comfort foods that require less preparation. "It's important to realize that comfort foods can actually be healthy for you," said Dr. Brian Wansink, lead author and Director of the Food and Brand Lab. "We are seemingly conditioned to prefer certain comfort foods." A study conducted at the Department of Epidemiology and Public Health, University College London.

The basic physiology and morphology of *Homo sapiens* sets boundaries to our eating habits, but within these boundaries human food preferences are remarkably varied, both within and between populations. This does not mean that variation is entirely cultural or learned, because genes and culture may co-evolve to determine variation in dietary habits. Our evolutionary heritage of food preferences and eating habits leaves us mismatched with the food environments we have created, which leads to problems such as obesity and type 2 diabetes.

Babies recognize the smell of their own amniotic fluids immediately after birth. Given the choice, newborns prefer breasts that have been dabbed with fluids from their amniotic sac (Varendi et al 1996). Interestingly, taste preference often changes in conjunction with body needs. Similarly animals often develop food aversions, particularly if they become ill soon after eating a certain food, even though that food was not the cause of the illness - surely you have experienced this yourself. Food preferences and aversions involve the sense of taste, but these phenomena are almost certainly mediated through the central nervous system rather than directly through taste cells.

My experience is that favorite food choices may vary with varying biochemistry, age, sex, work routine, stress or with changing season as well. One disturbing observation is if the body is badly affected by a chronic disease process, then a harmony is created between the body and the disease. The wicked disease first disrupts the biorhythms, adjusts them according to its requirement and creates an environment which helps disease growth. Now the body craves for those nutrients which are going to nourish the disease, a patient with a terminal stage of cancer craves for cancer nourishing foods. So one has to be extremely cautious while learning about their own food preferences and selection of foods.

I would like to mention about one of my patients who was suffering from diabetes, hypertension, cardiac disease and his weight was 140 kg. When he came to me he requested me to include a local dessert called halwa (made of semolina) in his food plan. He had very intense and irresistible craving for that dessert but was not permitted by the family and doctors. The craving was so strong that he use to get up quietly at night, make halwa for himself and, only after eating it, he could sleep. He was not bothered about his weight and illnesses, but wanted to have halwa in the diet. I advised 500 grams of halwa on every alternate day for his breakfast with a very careful arrangement of a body compatible diet plan during the rest of the day. After two weeks when he came back, he had lost 3 kg of weight, sugar levels were normal and no more craving for that dessert. In three months he lost 20 kg and his Hba1c came within normal range. While handling the particular patient I kept aside my knowledge of conventional medicine and was surprised at the amazing healing power of body wisdom.

***4-How much to eat***

The control of food intake is a physiologically complex, motivated behavioral system. Hormones such as cholecystokinin, bombesin, neurotensin, anorectin, calcitonin, enterostatin, leptin and corticotropin-releasing hormone have all been shown to suppress food intake. The body is in a continual state of hunger, which is intermittently relieved by eating. This perpetual drive to eat is periodically suppressed by inhibitory impulses generated by such things as the presence of food in the gastrointestinal tract, the flow of nutrients into blood and other factors. After these "satiety factors" have dissipated, the desire to eat returns. Metabolic demands of people and animals increase with sickness or trauma, often in conjunction with anorexia. Sickness combined with anorexia leads to accelerated starvation. When it's cold, animals and people eat more than when it's hot. Children maintain energy balance with wildly varying intakes of food per meal. These kinds of observations suggest that a very complex system is in-charge of regulating hunger, energy balance and body weight.

***Role of the Central Nervous System***

For many years, the hypothalamus was thought to be the key to control of food intake. This view derived from classic experiments in which food intake was studied in rats with lesions in various areas of the brain. Such studies clearly identified two regions in the hypothalamus that dramatically influence feeding behavior. Lateral hypothalamus (hunger center), animals with lesions in this area become anorectic and lose weight. Ventromedial hypothalamus (satiety center), animals with lesions in this area overeat and become obese. Subsequent studies showed that, although these hypothalamic centers are clearly very important in controlling hunger and satiety, they don't explain the whole story.

***Pre-gastric Factors***

We all know of "environmental" conditions that can dramatically affect food intake. These include appearance of food, taste and/or odor of food, learned preferences and aversions. Almost everyone has an aversion to one or more types of foods. Psychological factors like fear, depression and social interactions often affect food intake. Understanding these factors is of particular importance to clinicians because they can be manipulated to manage anorectic patients.

***Gastrointestinal and Post-absorptive Factors***

The degree of gastrointestinal fill is the most important signal from the digestive tract. A full stomach and intestine induce satiety, probably via the vagus nerve relaying that fact back to the hypothalamus. Additionally, the enteric hormone cholecystokinin is well documented to induce satiety in experimental settings. As nutrients such as glucose and amino acids are absorbed, their concentrations in blood rise, as do the concentration of several hormones like cholecystokinin, but also insulin and glucagon. These changes also have been linked to the sensation of hunger or satiety.

***Appetite / hunger***

Appetite is a complicated phenomenon, linking biology with environment. It is a bio psychological system, meaning it is the result of both our biology (hunger) and psychology (desires and feelings). Hunger, on the other hand, is purely biological. It is that nagging, irritating feeling that makes one think about food and the need to eat. It gets stronger the longer one goes without food, and it weakens after eating. Although the physiological reasons people feel hunger have not been clearly identified, the feeling of hunger rises and falls based on the activation of neural circuitry related to eating.

Unfortunately for some people, eating behavior is not governed by hunger and satiety (feeling of fullness), but by a variety of other factors. For example, some people eat in response to their feelings of anxiety, depression or stress. Eating temporarily helps lessen these feelings and thus tends to become a coping response whenever they have these bad feelings. Weight gain may occur if people eat for reasons other than hunger. One strategy to help people manage their weight is for them to learn to differentiate between appetite and hunger, to learn to "listen to their bodies," and to eat only when they are hungry and to stop when they are full. Hunger-control medications can help reduce the biological need to eat, but people still need to manage their psychological feelings about eating.

SLP never quantifies the food, it allows organized but quantity free intake of foods in the prescribed timings of meal intake. The objective is to first satisfy the appetite and saturate the body with the missing nutrients. After about two weeks appetite starts reducing and only hunger is left, and body is satisfied with small portions of food. Majority of food cravings in the program start settling in the first two weeks, worst cases take four to eight weeks to re-adjust their malfunctioning appetite control systems. Degree of reversal of cravings or normal hunger or appetite is directly proportional to the duration and degree of self-abuse due to erratic dietary habits.

### *5-Correct food combinations*

#### *Incompatible foods produce alcohol in intestines*

If you have to combine several types of foods in a single meal, it is ideal to combine compatible foods i.e. those which require approximately the same conditions for digestion—including length of time, type of enzymes, digestive juices, and degrees of alkalinity or acidity. When foods are consumed in incompatible combinations, fermentation results and alcohol is produced in the digestive tract with the potential liver damage. Complicated mixtures of food interfere with this process of digestion, make it less efficient and may cause digestive problems. When we compound the problem by adding seasonings, the true taste of individual foods is further disguised. This makes it extremely difficult for the digestive system to supply secretions that can cope with such meals and digestion is inhibited and impaired.

The digestive glands react to the foods to the best of their ability. They interpret the signals they receive and supply the best secretions they can muster to preserve the health and the integrity of the organism. When a saturation point is reached, due to continuous bombardment from intolerable food combinations, the ability of the overworked digestive system to make the necessary adaptations is reduced or destroyed, and disease is the result. Optimal digestion requires that we eat in such a way as to offer the least hindrance to the work of digestion by making the best use of our knowledge of the chemistry and physiology of digestion and of the limitations of the human digestive system. Food combinations are not just wild ideas out of someone's head, but actually have scientific reasoning based on how the human digestive system processes food. Proper food combinations also help many people alleviate their digestive problems and eliminate the need for any digestive medication. Compatible foods has also helped people with IBS, acid reflux, acid indigestion, etc.

***Dr. Hay's food combination***

Dr. William Howard Hay introduced food combinations in the early 1900s and his basic premise is that excess acidity from the products of digestion results in a lowering of the body's vital alkaline reserve, and this depletion causes toxemia or autointoxication. Modern medicine has also come to recognize in recent years that it takes acidity to support sickness - a slightly alkaline person will not contract degenerative disease. Food combining refers to the combination of foods which are compatible with each other in terms of the ingredients needed to digest each type of food. Because food combining dramatically reduces the amount of energy used in processing food, it is something that athletes should carefully consider, although it will improve energy and digestion for everyone.

***SLP food combination***

Keeping in mind the magnificent system of biorhythms going on in a human body, food should harmonize with the body to increase its performance. In SLP foods are combined on the basis of their chemical properties, ph, and length of digestion period. Two important Rules of Food Combination are: Simple carbohydrates can't be mixed with complex carbohydrates, fats and proteins. Simple carbohydrates are digested within half an hour, whereas complex carbohydrates, fats and proteins take three to four hours to digest. Therefore all fruits, desserts, juices or soft drinks should be taken either half an hour before a meal or three and half hours after the meal. The very common practice of taking fizzy drinks or juices with meals is responsible for indigestion by causing blood sugar fluctuations. Wide swings in blood sugar create the release of stress hormones and can initiate the buildup of arterial plaques. The repeated release of stress hormones leads to the development of diabetes, cardiac problems, obesity, chronic indigestion, arthritis and other serious degenerative disorders like cancers.

In 1966-1967, the U.S. Department of Health, Education, and Welfare found that 49.2 percent of the people interviewed had hypoglycemic symptoms, as cited by William Dufty in his book, "Sugar Blues." Some experts suspect that the figures are still the same, if not higher, with about half of all Americans suffering from low blood sugar. Ideal time to take fruits, desserts or fizzy drinks is during the day. 9a.m. to 4p.m. is the time when the body is busy with the intellectual functions and needs simple carbohydrates to maintain sugar levels. Brain survives on the regular supply of oxygen and glucose; therefore sugary foods during the day are metabolized completely and will never make you obese. If simple carbohydrates are eaten in the day time they help in the control of appetite and help in weight loss as well. Combinations of simple and complex carbohydrates lead to fermentation and the formation of alcohol like compounds which are liver toxic.

Second rule of food combination is that by chemistry, foods are either acidic or alkaline or close to neutral. As we know that blood's ph is 7.35 which is close to neutral on the scale of 1 – 14. So whatever we eat should be close to neutral ph. Change in blood ph affects vital processes in a life threatening manner and blood ph below 6 or above 8 is fatal. If foods are chosen only from the acidic group, it will lead to acidic ph disorders and cancer is one of those. Excess of acidic foods cause anxiety, palpitations, stomach disorders, body aches, insomnia and excess of alkaline foods can cause bloating, generalized swelling, lethargy, drowsiness and vertigo. Alkaline foods have minerals like calcium, magnesium, high water content, and fats. Whereas acidic foods have sodium, chloride, sulphur, proteins and complex carbohydrates.

Excess of alkaline foods lead to other group of diseases like water retention, crying spells, depression, swollen joints, and difficulty in breathing are commonly observed imbalances. Nature has provided us with vegetables, fruits, nuts and grains classified in acidic, alkaline and neutral categories. Ideally while taking foods we should balance grains, nuts, vegetables and fruits from the three chemical food groups each. Red meat is acidic, but when we combine vegetables, meat becomes less acidic. The acidity of meat is decreased by cooking it in white butter or ghee, therefore avoid fat free cooking of meat. Neutral foods are rich in antioxidants, vitamins and minerals, are liver supportive and balance the other two chemical food groups too.

***Food groups***

***i-Alkaline foods***

Vegetables: carrots, turnips, zuccini, capsicum, cabbage, radish, pumpkin, cucumber, lettuce, broccoli, celery, parsley, green beans, iceberg

Fruits: banana, guava, water melon, melon, pear, custard apple, leechi, garma, lime, kiwi,

Nuts: almonds, cashew nuts, seeds

***ii-Neutral foods***

Vegetables: ginger, garlic, mustard leaves, olives

Fruits: mango, grapes, apricots, papaya, dates, figs, chikoo, mulberry,

***iii-Acidic foods***

Vegetables: Potato, cauliflower, brinjal, sweet potato, peas, onion, spinach, mushroom, lemon, chestnut, bitter gourd

Fruits: Orange, apple, plums, peach, coconut, cherry, grapefruit, falsa, Japanese fruit or parmesan, pineapple, strawberry,

Nuts: Peanuts, walnuts, pine seeds, pistachio, hazel nuts

According to Ayurveda, every food has its own taste (rasa), a heating or cooling energy (virya) and post-digestive effect (vipaka). When two or three different food substances of different taste, energy and post-digestive effect are combined together, the digestive process (agni) can become overloaded inhibiting the enzyme system and resulting in production of toxins in the system. Thus, according to Ayurveda, one should eat according to one's constitution and take fruits, starches, proteins and fats separately at different times of the day. Combining foods improperly can produce indigestion, fermentation, putrefaction and gas formation. This condition, if prolonged, can lead to toxemia and disease. According to Ayurveda eating bananas with milk can diminish agni, change the intestinal flora to produce toxins and may cause sinus congestion, cold, cough and allergies.

### *6-Food rotation*

#### *The Rotation Diet*

The Rotation Diet plan was developed in 1986 by psychologist and obesity expert Martin Katahn, the Director of the Vanderbilt University Weight Management program; he designed an eating plan in which followers rotate their daily calorie intake for a one-month period to achieve their desired weight loss. Daily exercise is also recommended on the plan. Diet plans that do not restrict people from their favorite food and yet give them a solution to lose weight are sure to find many takers. Lose weight without forgoing your favorite food - this is the basis of the rotation diet plan. Reducing weight without bringing down the metabolic rate of the body is the secret behind rotation diet.

Allergy rotation diet plans are useful for people with multiple allergies in preventing new allergies and identifying hidden allergies in common foods. Rotation diets are sometimes used along with elimination diets to treat existing food allergies and prevent new ones from developing. Rotation diets involve eating biologically related foods on one day, and then avoiding those foods for a period of time. Rotation diets work by limiting exposure to potential allergens, and providing the body and immune system with a rest period following ingestion of high-risk foods. High-risk foods include all of the "big eight" allergens (egg, wheat, soy, cow's milk, peanut, tree nuts, fish and shellfish), along with any suspected allergens. Typically, if a high-risk food is eaten one day, you must avoid that food for the following three to five days. Members of the same food family also must be avoided during that time. For example, if you eat yogurt on day one, you cannot eat any dairy products, or foods containing dairy, for the following several days.

"By limiting exposure to potential allergens and high-risk foods, your immune system is less likely to respond defensively to those items. This makes it less likely you will develop a new allergy, and actually increases the number of foods you can tolerate. Health benefits are noticeable within a few weeks. Follow a strict four-day rotation schedule. This is a schedule that will alternate permissible foods every day, preventing your body from developing an allergy to any particular food, or preventing your body from becoming excessively irritated to foods to which you are already allergic. Keeping your body guessing by constantly changing your food sources is a natural way to keep your body healthy and alleviate the symptoms of allergies without resorting to prescription medication".

***SLP food rotation***

The reason for rotating foods in SLP is different from the above mentioned philosophies. My clinical experimentation has told me that if one food is repeated on two consecutive days, multiple side effects of that particular food start appearing after approximately 36 hours. Healing rate starts declining, a boredom factor comes in, bloating appears, chemistry of that particular food starts affecting the blood ph and metabolism stagnates. These are key factors which forced me to prescribe a four day food rotation plan; one food can be repeated after three days. This rotational pattern is helping me to handle multiple food allergies and other ailments as well.

SLP is a holistic diet plan and therefore the pleasure factor is a primary area of focus. While prescribing the four day meal plan, I have to carefully focus on food preferences. My aim is to select those foods which are body compatible for that particular individual. My favorite clients are children, I ask them to give me a list of twenty of their most favorite foods. Interestingly the therapeutic foods are always present in their list which reflects a subtle control of food choices. I enjoy this process of food selection for food rotation. Before asking this question, I have analyzed the client's pulse and already have an idea about the list of their body compatible foods. By giving them the choice to select the foods for their plan, I give them mental freedom and try to break the existing myths of food restriction.

In the four days food rotation plan, the most important section is the pre-breakfast. Whatever food is prescribed, it becomes a potent medicine, because of the significance of the arousal state. I see many patients with multiple food allergies. In the first few minutes after waking up, the body can be deceived to accept foods it is normally allergic to. This trick along with food rotation helps gradually overcome food allergies. If we keep on repeating the same food, the end metabolites of that food can cause allergies. By rotating, end metabolites of different chemistries are formed, which help in cleansing and detoxifying each other. As a result there is less toxin overload on the liver and kidneys. By rotating food we supply the body with a variety of nutrients. I have learnt that a natural food has healing and disease causing effects simultaneously. By repeating the same food for 3-5 days, disease causing affects are activated and pre-disease symptoms start appearing.

***7-Food temperature***

Temperature regulatory Centre is responsible for keeping body temperature in a narrow range. The vital core temperature is maintained by liver. The human body's stomach temperature is the same as the human body's core temperature which is approximately 37 degrees Celsius, or 98.6 degrees Fahrenheit. However, if you eat something colder, or something warmer, and measure the temperature of your stomach immediately afterward, it can show dramatically different temperatures. Meal temperature may be considered as a component of dietary therapy for patients with functional dyspepsia. Foods or drinks with cold temperature will slow down the stomach motility. Similarly foods with temperature higher than the core temperature will increase the stomach motility. For optimum absorption food has to be at a temperature which is close to the body temperature.

The temperature of food is also related to the external temperature or season. During intense summer slightly cold water, cold liquids and cold foods can be taken, to prevent over heating of the body. Whereas cold weather forces us to take warm soups or hot meals, which is a compensatory requirement of the body to maintain the low inner body temperature. Cold temperature decreases stomach motility and it holds food for a longer period. This health risk factor is promoted for weight loss, because cold foods and drinks make you burn more calories. Acute Cardiac arrest is reported when extreme food or drink temperature shocks are given in a short span to your cardiovascular system. Therefore you cannot take hot and spicy foods with ice cold water. SLP advises foods and drinks to be consumed at temperatures which are close to the body's temperature.

***8-Correct water intake***

Dr. Howard Flaks, a bariatric (obesity) specialist in Beverly Hills, California, says, "By not drinking enough water, many people incur excess body fat, poor muscle tone and size, decreased digestive efficiency and organ function, increased toxicity in the body, joint and muscle soreness and water retention." If you're not drinking enough, your body may retain water to compensate. Paradoxically, fluid retention can sometimes be eliminated by drinking more water, not less. "Proper water intake is a key to weight loss," says Dr. Donald Robertson, medical director of the Southwest Bariatric Nutrition Center in Scottsdale, Arizona. "If people who are trying to lose weight don't drink enough water, the body can't metabolize the fat adequately. Retaining fluid also keeps weight up."

Dr Ben kim has posted on his website http://drbenkim.com/drink-too-much-water-dangerous.html aa terrifying incidence that On January 12, 2007, a 28-year old Californian wife and mother of three children died from drinking too much water. Her body was found in her home shortly after she took part in a water-drinking contest that was sponsored by a local radio show. Entitled "Hold Your Wee for a Wii," the contest promoters promised a free Wii video game machine to the contestant who drank the most water without urinating. It is estimated that the woman who died drank approximately 2 gallons of water during the contest. This tragic news story highlights the importance of understanding why drinking too much water can be dangerous to your health.

Whenever you disregard your sense of thirst and strive to ingest several glasses of water a day just because you have been told that doing so is good for your health, you actually put unnecessary strain on your body in two major ways: Ingesting more water than you need can increase your total blood volume. And since your blood volume exists within a closed system - your circulatory system - needlessly increasing your blood volume on a regular basis puts unnecessary burden on your heart and blood vessels.

Your kidneys must work overtime to filter excess water out of your circulatory system. Your kidneys are not the equivalent of a pair of plumbing pipes whereby the more water you flush through your kidneys, the cleaner they become; rather, the filtration system that exists in your kidneys is composed in part by a series of specialized capillary beds called glomeruli. Your glomeruli can get damaged by unnecessary wear and tear over time, and drowning your system with large amounts of water is one of many potential causes of said damage. For the average person, it is virtually impossible to know that this burden exists, as there are usually no obvious symptoms on a moment-to-moment basis. But make no mistake about it: this burden is real and can hurt your health over the long term.

As your circulatory system becomes diluted with excess water, the concentration of electrolytes in your blood will drop relative to the concentration of electrolytes in your cells. In an effort to maintain an equal balance of electrolytes between your blood and your cells, water will seep into your cells from your blood, causing your cells to swell. If this swelling occurs in your brain, you'll experience increased intracranial pressure i.e. your brain will get squeezed because the flat bones that make up your skull don't provide much give. Depending on how much water your drink in a short period of time, you could experience a wide variety of symptoms, ranging from a mild headache to impaired breathing. And as occurred recently in the tragic water-drinking contest, it is quite possible to die if you drink enough water in a short enough period of time.

***Quantity of water intake***

"Most people know they should drink about eight cups of water (About 2000cc) per day. This amount of water provides your body with enough moisture clears the gut and stomach as well as speeds up blood circulation. But what they overlook is the correct drinking method. The best way to drink water is to drink one cup in a series of small swallows or mouthfuls in a sitting position. You shouldn't drink only when you are thirsty". Water requirement varies with weather, physical activity, disease state, medications, body type and type of food intake. The time of water intake is extremely important as untimely intake leads to water retention. In hot climate water intake may vary between 18-24 glasses per 24 hours. Water has to be taken half an hour before or one and half hour after a meal. It's a good idea to hold off on a meal until the water is absorbed by every cell in your body, so try not to eat for half an hour after drinking water. The stomach completes its digestive role after 90 minutes and becomes empty. Water one and half hour after food rinses the stomach and gets it ready for the next meal.

***Timings of water intake***

"The commute to the office in the morning can be stressful, and this dehydrates your body. Drink at least 250cc of water when you get to work to refresh yourself from the commute. After working several hours in a closed office, the heat may dry out your skin. Drink some water to help moisturize your body and decrease work-related stress. In the afternoon many people may feel sleepy and cannot concentrate on their work. If this sounds like you that means you should drink some water to give yourself a lift. Before you leave the office, drinking water can make you feel full. It especially works for people on diets. Drink a cup of water half an hour to an hour before you sleep, which can help prevent blood clots".

***Temperature of water intake***

The temperature of water is very important and you should always try to take water at room temperature during summers. In winters, lukewarm water protects us from the severity of external temperature. According to Ayurveda, life is based on the five primary elements of space, air, fire, water and earth. Each element giving rise to the next: space creates air, air creates fire, fire creates water and water creates earth. Therefore, water contains not only its own unique intelligence but also the intelligence of space, air and fire. By boiling drinking water for five minutes the intelligence of the element of fire is magnified, which enhances the properties of the water. Sipping boiled water cleans the fine inner channels of the body and burns ama (undigested food toxins). Ayurveda prescribes three different temperatures for drinking boiled water, depending on the body type and climate.

***Water therapy***

According to alternative medicine advocates, one form of water therapy is the consuming of a gutful of water upon waking up in order to "cleanse the bowel". A liter or more is the common amount ingested. This water therapy, also known as Indian or Chinese Water Therapy, is claimed to have a wide range of health benefits; or at least no adverse effects. Ingesting about one and a half liter of water in the morning is usually harmless but this is approaching the level which can lead to water intoxication, an urgent and dangerous medical condition. I have seen many people following this practice and all of them had excessive water retention. There was no improvement in their general health or ailments. I found this therapy to be a total failure and recommend that it should never be given a trial and water intake should be carefully monitored.

**II-Sleep regulation**

In routine getting too little night sleep may increase a person's visceral fat, fat that accumulates around the body's internal organs. Kristen G. Hairston, from Wake Forest University School of Medicine (North Carolina, USA), and colleagues studied the five-year change in visceral adipose tissue and subcutaneous adipose tissue associated with sleep duration in a group of African Americans and a group of Hispanic Americans, ages 18-81 years, enrolled in the IRAS Family Study. In participants under age 40, the team found a clear association between averaging five hours or less of sleep each night and large increases in visceral fat. In sleep the body handles all those processes which cannot be handled during the active biological state.

The Liver, our most vital organ, can rest only at night in the lying down posture and there is maximum storage of blood at that time. If someone is in resting mode at night and is sitting and watching movies or reading books, the liver cannot rejuvenate. If the liver has not taken a rest between 1a.m. to 3a.m., it will not be rejuvenating the body and you cannot get holistic health. Besides the physical and mental components of liver functions, there is a spiritual aspect as well. According to universal law, the soul only gets a chance at night to re-energize itself. If this spiritual phenomenon does not happen at night, the spiritual body falls sick and the resulting symptoms are chronic diseases, depression, fear, insecurity and disbelieve.

SLP recommends and induces 6-8 hours of a natural night sleep as an important healing tool. People who are not managing nocturnal sleep suffer from obesity, bloating, mood swings, poor healing ability and accelerated skin and mental aging. I have not seen improvement in chronic degenerative diseases if there is poor quality of night sleep. The control of diabetes mellitus is directly related to the intake of a body compatible pre-breakfast, breakfast and 6-8 hours of nocturnal sleep. High fasting blood sugar is an indicator that diabetes is not under control and is adversely affecting other systems. As we know Diabetes is a lifestyle disease, but I would say high fasting blood sugar is absolutely a lifestyle disease. High fasting sugar poorly responds to oral hypoglycemic or insulin injections. Once lifestyle is modified with timely meals with food rotation and 8 hours of night sleep, fasting sugar starts decreasing after four weeks. Dr. Deepak Chopra writes that by regularly taking a healthy breakfast and a good night's sleep, you may add eleven years to your life.

## III-Stress management

### *No blanket rule for stress management*

Hundreds of stress management techniques are available, but these are of no use for you, because these can't give you permanent relaxation. As human beings carry a biochemical individuality every one carries a specific built-in stress management program for his/her life. If you don't follow body type specific stress management, you will not be relaxed. For one type of chemistry yoga is relaxing but the other type gets relaxed by playing golf. That built-in stress management character can be observed at a young age in the form of that person's hobby. Nature wants us to manage our stress by physical or sporty activity, creative activity or spiritual practices. Creative activities include writing, reading healthy literature, listening music of choice, singing, playing musical instruments, painting, designing and all other inspirational activities. One has to discover that built-in stress management tool and apply it in their routine life.

### *Cellular chemical stress*

Unhealthy lifestyle leads to a disturb blood chemistry, which leads to cellular chemical stress. This chemical stress creates a mineral imbalance. The body has an intricate system of checks and balances which operate through mineral levels and ratios. There is a constant and complex dance of minerals going on in the body, and the body very specifically retains and releases minerals in order to control certain body functions. If this mineral imbalance persists, it leads to a hyperactive mind syndrome which later converts into a fully blown mental disease.

***Hyperactive mind syndrome***

Hyperactive mind syndrome has a set of symptoms which are due to a chemical imbalance in cells. This state triggers an aimless ongoing thought process which badly affects physical health and induces insomnia. A hyperactive mind is the result of an imbalance in minerals with raised levels of copper and decreased zinc levels. The increase in the copper level is stimulating, and it does not give time to switch the mind off. Depending on the severity of the toxicity and the susceptibility of the person, copper can affect the mind very strongly. Initially copper toxicity may make a person active, productive and creative. But eventually such feelings will be undermined by lack of energy and results in dissociation of body and mind. People with hyperactive mind have millions of ideas and are always making lists, but who do not have the energy to follow through. This leads to irritability, anger and frustration followed by depression.

Hyperactive mind syndrome indicates important mineral imbalance especially between copper and zinc and the root cause for this imbalance is intake of lot of nutrient deficient processed foods. Whenever there is an excess of stimulating copper, it becomes very hard to go to sleep and the mind sets in a race mode. The body will begin storing the excess copper in the brain as the liver becomes overloaded. Copper stimulates the diencephalon, which is the emotional brain and zinc stimulates the cortex, the new brain, the rational mind, and is calming to the emotions. Thus, copper-toxic people often keep themselves in a state of high drama, and their symptoms can even mimic bi-polar syndrome. Carl Pfeiffer, PhD, MD, has found that one-half to two-thirds of schizophrenics have high levels of copper and low levels of zinc and magnesium, especially during acute phases. Copper has an adverse effect on methylation, a metabolic pathway that is essential for detoxification and for controlling free-radical activity. Poor methylation can be an important factor in cases of autism and schizophrenia.

The copper toxicity reduces the ability to cope with normal everyday stress because it impairs adrenal function. A lot of adrenal activity requires zinc, which high level of copper impairs. The result is weakening of body metabolism. Another important combination is of calcium and magnesium, which is part of the body's brake system. They stabilize the body and prevent excessive metabolism as a defense against stress. Slowing down metabolism can slow down the rate of collapse and allow the buildup of protective minerals such as calcium, magnesium and zinc. In essence, since the body can no longer handle stress, it builds a calcium shell and the calcium shell numbs and dulls your sensations and your emotions so you will not over-react. A high level of calcium is a sign that calcium is building up in the soft tissues and this calcium is being taken from the bones. This stress is pathological in nature and responsible for the causation of multiple degenerative disorders. Raised levels of triglyceride, uric acid and fasting blood sugar are biochemical signs that the liver is under chemical stress. Hypertension, cardiac ailments, chronic stomach disorders, IBS, arthritis, autoimmune disorders, allergies, asthma, neurological disorders, cancer etc. are the outcome of this type of stress.

An interesting phenomenon about this stress chemistry is that this personality also carries a built-in stress defusing ability in the form of high creative and spiritual energies. No external treatment can permanently relieve their stress. With medications it is only suppressed temporarily and these suppressed emotions accumulate and emerge in the form of a serious physical ailment. Built-in stress defusing remedy is the presence of a passion for a creative activity. Usually they carry a passion for reading, writing, and singing, playing musical instruments, painting, acting or many other creative activities. If these people follow a nature based healthy lifestyle and allocates only 30 minutes to their passion they will never suffer from type two stresses.

***SLP stress types***

In my routine practice I observe three categories of stress during pulse analysis and pulse reveals pre-disease psychological state too. Out of three one is environmental stress which generates from home, educational institute, work place, society or media. Environmental stress is not detrimental to holistic health and simply produces anxiety. The second type of stress found in pulse analysis is deep emotional stress, and reflects a caring, hypersensitive, perfectionist, logical and competitive nature. This reflects childhood emotional traumas, repeated ailments, over medications, poor relationships, broken family history, and parental conflicts. This stress also reflects a trauma resulting from the death of a near and dear one. Type two stress is always preceded or associated with a hyperactive mind syndrome. The third type of stress reflects an unhealthy lifestyle and the genetic predisposition of carrying a negative approach towards life. Out of the three, the worst is type two stress which always leads to psychosomatic and chronic degenerative disorders.

Emotional memories of traumatic life events are stored in a particularly robust way by your brain, making effectiveness of a treatment very difficult. Researchers have now successfully tracked down the molecular bases of these strong, persistent memories. It has long been known that emotional memories of both a positive and a negative kind make strong impressions on your brain, and consequently have a very large effect on your behavior. A research group has shown that the enzyme calcineurin and the gene regulation factor Zif268 decisively determine the intensity of emotional memories. For the first time, this has enabled the regulatory processes at the synapse, which are important for emotional memories, to be linked to the processes in the cell nucleus. Researchers found that although traumatic memories can be overcome slowly through intensive training, they are not replaced. Negative memories, they say, need to be actively replaced by positive memories. While the research has no clinical applications at present, it could eventually lead to an understanding of the mechanisms underlying psychological traumas or brain diseases related to memory problem

***Childhood traumas***

A study published in the American Journal of Preventive Medicine also supported this view when it found a strong relationship between the number of childhood traumas and the number of health risk factors for leading causes of death in adults. In particular, they found a significant relationship between the number of childhood trauma exposures and the following disease conditions:

I. Ischemic heart disease
II. Cancer
III. Chronic bronchitis or emphysema
IV. History of hepatitis or jaundice
V. Skeletal fractures
VI. Poor self-rated health

Dr. Hamer actually takes this finding a step further. He found that most disease originates from an unexpected shock experience. This could run the gamut from witnessing a murder to being abused as a child or losing your home to a fire. It could also stem from infidelity, divorce, or any situation that causes you trauma and shock. Now if you ignore this trauma, it will fester in your body and it will most likely lead to disease. The longer you let something like this linger, the more severe, and harder to overcome, the physical illness becomes.

***Skin aging and stress***

Stress can cause your face to have more wrinkles or it can accelerate skin aging. Archives of Dermatology (Jan.2001) writes "Are anxiety, dejection and confusion written all over your face"? Researchers now say that this figure of speech may prove to be true. A new study has found that stress appears to decrease the skin's ability to function properly, heal wounds and fight disease. Researchers looked at 27 medical, dental and pharmacy students at the University of California, San Francisco who all had healthy skin. The researchers measured levels of anger, confusion, anxiety, depression, fatigue, and tension on three separate occasions over 8 weeks in 1999, a time period that included two vacations and a week of examinations.

In that time, the investigators repeatedly applied and stripped sticky tape from the students' forearms. The researchers then measured how quickly the participants' skin recovered its ability to essentially "breathe" properly. The research team found that skin recovery seemed to be directly linked to stress levels with high stress during exams associated with the decreased ability of the aggravated skin to return to normal function. The authors conclude that they have found the first direct link between stress and a decline in the ability of the skin to resume normal functioning after disruption. Aside from recovering from having sticky tape applied and removed from the skin, this link may place a stressed out individual at greater risk of common skin disease, such as psoriasis or dermatitis, the report indicates.

Mental hyperactivity is the result of emotional stress, chemical foods, bad dietary habits, and poor sleep. All of this accumulates to create a hyper-liver or toxin overloaded liver state which leads to the start of a disease process. As all the components of SLP focus on detoxification and rejuvenation of liver, mental hyperactivity starts settling within 6-8 weeks. I have noticed that in this mental state, food preferences are for proteins and healthy fats. 50-60% of this chemistry is modified by following eight rules of diet correction. Initiation of the any hobby gives additional 20% support and patient is out of this state within 3-6 months. For normal clients 30 minutes of stress management of their own choice is recommended. This type of stress management has to be adopted as a lifestyle and only then it slows mental aging. Remember there is no general rule for stress management and it has to be individualized. You are the one to learn about your specific stress handling with the help of your therapist.

## IV-Correct exercise

### *Over exercise*

Too much exercise can actually be harmful to your health. Excessive exercising is defined as working out for more than 3 hours a day and/or being so obsessed with exercise that it interferes with other parts of a person's life. People who over-exercise do it even when they are sick. The physical risks are numerous. A very real risk with this disorder is dehydration if the sufferer is not drinking enough fluids. Over-exercise can also lead to insomnia, depression, and fatigue. Additional physical side effects include muscular and skeletal injuries, like shin splits, bone fractures, arthritis, or damage to cartilage and ligaments. Too much exercise can lead to the release of excessive free radicals, which have been linked to cellular mutations and cancer. Females may no longer menstruate as a result of a regular and heavy exercise.

Over-exercise is linked with eating disorders, such as bulimia and anorexia. A person who over-exercises may have unrealistic expectations of what their body should look like. Over-exercise can lead to injuries and long-lasting infections. Thirty minutes of moderate exercise three times a week is the minimum you should aim for. About sixty minutes a day of moderate or vigorous exercise is the most you should do. So do not over-exercise, enjoy your daily routine and reap the benefits. Your heart is only good for so many beats, and that's it...don't waste them on exercise. Everything wears out eventually. Speeding up your heart will not make you live longer; that's like saying you can extend the life of your car by driving it faster. Too much overload and/or too little recovery may result in both physical and psychology symptoms of overtraining syndrome. Common warning signs of overtraining include:

I. Washed-out feeling, tired, drained, lack of energy
II. Mild leg soreness, general aches and pains
III. Pain in muscles and joints
IV. Sudden drop in performance
V. Insomnia
VI. Headache
VII. Decreased immunity (increased number of colds, and sore throats)
VIII. Decrease in training capacity / intensity
IX. Moodiness and irritability
X. Depression
XI. Loss of enthusiasm for the sport
XII. Decreased appetite
XIII. Increased incidence of injuries.
XIV. A compulsive need to exercise

More than 45 million Americans now belong to a health club, up from 23 million in 1993. And yet obesity figures have risen dramatically in the same period. "In general, for weight loss, exercise is pretty useless," says Eric Ravussin, chair in diabetes and metabolism at Louisiana State University and a prominent exercise researcher. Many recent studies have found that exercise isn't as important in helping people lose weight as you hear so regularly in gymnasium advertisements. The basic problem is that while it's true that exercise burns calories and that you must burn calories to lose weight, exercise has another effect: it can stimulate hunger. That causes us to eat more, which in turn can negate the weight-loss benefits we just accrued. Exercise, in other words, isn't necessarily helping us lose weight. It may even be making it harder.

***SLP and exercise***

When the patient starts SLP, exercise is not recommended for the first 4-8 weeks. I don't want them to waste their reserve energy in burning fats, making the heart beat faster or induce sweating. As the human body is meant for movement, in normal routine we need to walk. 20 to 40 minutes of daily walk helps in improving blood circulation, lymphatic circulation and keeps muscles in a toned state. Nature only demands simple rhythmic movement of the muscles. Besides walking, the next best natural exercise is yoga. With yoga postures a human being gets all the benefits of walking. Yoga makes muscles flexible and works on endocrine glands. The phenomenon of flexibility is anti-aging; yoga works on the mind, is anti-aging and it makes your face glow. Out of the 150,000 yoga postures, you can form your own sets of postures for individual problem areas. So walk and yoga are natural type of exercises which can be individualized as well.

**V-Food supplements**

Most soil is depleted of many important minerals, which means that our food even organic food doesn't always have optimum nutritional value. One of the best ways to overcome this deficiency is to take supplements on a regular basis. Nutritional deficiency is almost impossible to avoid in these modern times. With our busy lifestyle, the ever-tempting convenience of fast food, it is now very difficult to enjoy excellent daily nutrition. This is not to say, though, that health supplements should replace proper nutrition. Besides, nutritional supplements are still supplements. They work by complementing your diet to make sure you get the right nutrients that you need. We need all the nutrients in their proper amounts for optimum health.

The science of Orthomolecular medicine helps the patient reach an optimal level of health with right amount of nutrients or supplements. Eventually, it was determined that malnutrition and consumption of refined, empty-calorie foods such as white bread, pastries and overconsumption of sugar could yield multiple nutritional deficiency. Biochemical individuality is a main principle of orthomolecular medicine. Thus, RDA values are not perfect guidelines for everyone. Several studies have proven the existence of biochemical individuality regarding supplements requirements. For example, studies of guinea pigs showed a twentyfold variation in their requirement for vitamin C. A study conducted with human subjects revealed that children have varying needs for vitamin B6. Orthomolecular medicine is sometimes referred to as megavitamin therapy because so many vitamins are prescribed by orthomolecular nutritionists to fulfill the need of their patients.

The types and amounts of the nutrients are determined by blood tests, urine analysis, and other tests for nutrient levels. At my Centre we do NES and QRMA to evaluate vitamin levels. Generally, patients get their vitamin needs by taking several dosages of vitamin pills a day, although they are sometimes given injections of vitamins to speed up the process. These nutritional supplements also help boost our immune system. The stronger your immune system, the more resistant your body can be against disease. Nutritional supplements are also useful in getting rid of the toxins which we horrendously take in every day. The environmental stresses we go through, chemicals we are in touch with, as well as our lifestyle - these all subject us to harmful toxins which can lead to serious health problems. Supplements, especially anti-oxidants, can help our body keep toxins to a minimum. To take full advantage of what dietary supplements can offer, you must choose the right supplement to take. I prescribe food supplements which are holistic and liver supportive. All conventional medicine vitamin based supplements are synthetic and liver toxic, therefore avoid these chemicals. Here is a list of supplements which are helpful to our holistic being.

### *I-Antioxidants*

Many of these antioxidants are phytochemicals (plant products) that are obtained by a diet rich in fruits and vegetables. However, there are animal antioxidants, such as Co-Q10, and minerals such as selenium, that act as antioxidants. The main objective of antioxidants is to neutralize free radicals, which are created when cells are under attack from various toxins, viruses, germs or fungi. They are caused by tobacco smoke, pollution, stress, and hydrogenated, overheated or rancid oils; and they are almost always produced by fried foods. If left unchecked, free radicals damage cells, leading to a suppressed immune system and, subsequently, to degenerative disease. They are a primary cause of wrinkles and sagging skin. Combat them with the high concentration of antioxidants found in wheat grass juice, barley grass, sprouts and dark green vegetables.

For added protection, you may want to take a daily supplement. Three popular antioxidants found in natural foods stores are: coenzyme Q10 (Co-Q10), grape seed extract and pycnogenol. The latter two are oligomeric proanthocyanidins (OPCs), substances that are related to tannins and have benefits in addition to their antioxidant properties. Pycnogenol is a trade name for OPCs derived from a pine tree. Other supplements with antioxidant properties include the herbs bilberry and Ginkgo biloba, and green tea. And don't forget vitamins A, C, and E, all of which have important antioxidant functions.

***II-Healthy holistic fats (essential fatty acids)***

Omega fatty acids are polyunsaturated fats. They are healthier than saturated fats and have many metabolic functions. There are many benefits of omega 3, 6, 9, supplementation. Omega 3 and omega 6 fatty acids are essential fatty acids (EFA's). Our bodies cannot manufacture them, and we must consume them in our diets. Omega 9 fatty acids are not essential. Our bodies need omega 9 fats, but we can manufacture them from other sources. Omega 3 fatty acids prevent heart disease and the complications of heart attack. People who take omega 3 fatty acids have a lower mortality rate after heart attack than those who do not. Omega 3 EFA's improve cardiac risk factors, and help prevent CHD. They normalize lipid levels, lower blood pressure and improve glucose metabolism.

Omega 3's may be helpful in a number of other conditions, too. Rheumatoid arthritis, depression, autism, and many other conditions may be improved by taking omega 3 EFA's. They are necessary for growth and development, especially in the development of nervous tissue, and may improve cognitive function and emotional health. Omega 6 fatty acids compete for enzymes with omega 3 EFA's, so the amounts of the two need to be properly balanced. Less research has been done on omega 6 EFA's than on omega 3's. Most omega 6 fatty acids produce an inflammatory response that may be necessary for healthy immune system function.

Omega 9, as mentioned, is not an essential fatty acid. Omega 9 oils are monounsaturated, and are found in olive oil. Olive oil is known to have beneficial health effects, and omega 9 oils may be necessary for healthy immune system functioning. The benefits of omega 3, 6, 9, include all of the benefits of all three types of fatty acid. The amounts and ratios of each fatty acid are balanced to optimal levels of each. Taking an omega 3, 6, 9, supplement is a good way to ensure that you are getting essential nutrients for your good health.

Research has shown that diets high in omega-3 fatty acids help prevent heart attacks, lower blood pressure, reduce allergies and inflammation, relieve or reverse symptoms of multiple sclerosis, offer anti-cancer properties, and may help combat a host of degenerative diseases. This is because the essential fatty acids 3 and 6 are also transformed into regulatory compounds known as prostaglandins. Prostaglandins regulate steroid production and hormone synthesis; they also regulate pressure in the eye, joints and blood vessels. Additionally, they mediate immune response, regulate bodily secretions and their viscosity, dilate or constrict blood vessels, regulate the rate at which cells divide and regulate the flow of substances in and out of cells. There's still more the busy prostaglandins do: they transport oxygen from red blood cells to bodily tissues, regulate nerve transmission and assist in other vital functions. Omega-6 fatty acids can be found in raw nuts, seeds, and legumes, and in unsaturated (cold-pressed) vegetable oils such as flaxseed, borage, grape seed, primrose, sesame and soybean. Omega-3 fatty acids can be found in deep-water fish, fish oil and cold pressed vegetable oils such as canola, walnut and flaxseed.

***III-Enzymes***

Enzymes are considered the "sparks of life." Even with appropriate levels of minerals, vitamins, amino acids, water and other nutrients, without enzymes, life ceases to exist. For this reason, they are said to possess life force energy. These energized protein molecules play a necessary role in virtually all biochemical activities. They are required to digest food and to repair cells, tissues and organs. In fact, they regulate and govern all living cells in plants and animals, and are responsible for providing the energy for all biochemical reactions that occur in nature. Fruit ripening, seeds sprouting, flowers blooming and people healing are all examples of enzymatic activity. Enzymes cannot be made from synthetic (non-plant) sources, as many vitamins and minerals are made.

Enzymes and coenzymes (molecules that help enzymes do their job) work together to either join molecules together or split them apart by making or breaking chemical bonds. Most enzymes are composed of a protein coupled with an essential mineral, and sometimes a vitamin, which act as the co-enzyme. There are three major enzymatic classifications: metabolic, digestive and those obtained from food. Metabolic and digestive enzymes are produced in the body, but food enzymes are not—they only come from food. Processing or cooking food above 112 degrees destroys food enzymes.

"Metabolic enzymes" build the body from proteins, carbohydrates and fats, and break them apart when they are old. All our cells, tissues and organs function because of these enzymes. They are responsible for chemical reactions within cells, such as energy production and detoxification. Each body tissue/system produces its own specific set of metabolic enzymes. Metabolic enzymes cannot be supplied through supplementation. "Digestive enzymes" are secreted along the gastrointestinal tract and help break down foods, enabling nutrients to be absorbed into the bloodstream. Our bodies manufacture and secrete about 24 different digestive enzymes depending on the type of food we eat. Digestive enzymes break down food particles for storage in the liver or in muscles. This stored energy is later converted by other enzymes for use by the body when needed.

"Food enzymes "come from plants, and are vulnerable to processing and temperatures above 112 degrees. These vital helpers predigest our food and aid greatly in the absorption of nutrients. Without them (either from food or supplementation), the natural process of full digestion is lost, which puts an undue strain on the digestive system. The three major food enzymes are: amylase, which breaks down starches into sugars; lipase, which breaks down fats into fatty acids, and protease, which breaks down proteins into amino acids. Protease is also used therapeutically for digesting viruses and bacteria, and for eliminating allergies.

Enzymes can be found in many different plant foods, but the plant must be fresh and whole in order to contain live enzymes (unless it's been specifically processed to retain the enzymes). Some foods that contain lots of enzymes include avocados, papayas, pineapples, bananas and mangos. Sprouts are one of the richest sources of enzymes. Many companies process these foods into enzyme supplements. Many pickled (or fermented) foods, as well as miso paste, also contain enzymes. Unless at least 50% of your diet consists of organic, whole, raw plant foods that contain naturally occurring food enzymes, you may want to take a daily enzyme supplement for better absorption of the food you eat.

### *IV-Probiotics (friendly microflora)*

"Probiotic," literally meaning "for life," is a term used to describe the friendly bacteria and fungi which inhabit both the large and small intestines. There are at least 400 different species of micro-flora that live in the human gastrointestinal tract. There are billions of these microbes, amounting to approximately three pounds per adult! Some of the most important of these bacteria are acidophilus (*Lactobacillus acidophilus)*, which inhabit the small intestine and bifidus (*Bifidobacterium bifidum*), which inhabit the large intestine. Large intestine plays an important role in the detoxification process the colon, when it doesn't function properly; it affects the ability of all other organs to function optimally. Probiotic is recommended because friendly intestinal flora are easily destroyed by factors such as antibiotics, stress, alcohol, high meat/fat diets, drugs and poor diet in general.

The small intestine is involved in the digestion, absorption, and transport of food. After passing through the stomach, food is further broken down in the small intestine; and vitamins, minerals, carbohydrates, proteins, and fats are absorbed. Microvilli hair-like projections along the wall of the small intestine perform two important functions: they provide necessary surface area for the absorption of nutrients and they help move food through the small intestine. Acidophilus helps to keep the spaces between the microvilli clear so they can function efficiently. Thus, acidophilus helps to promote normal peristalsis (movement of food) through the small intestine.

Acidophilus plays a role in the prevention of and defense against disease, especially of the gastrointestinal tract and vagina. As part of the "normal flora," they inhibit the growth of harmful organisms by competing for nutrients, altering the ph to a more acidic level, and shifting oxygen levels to the detriment of pathogens (disease- causing organisms). They also attach to sites otherwise preyed upon by pathogens. Other benefits of acidophilus include: production of vitamins (which are absorbed into the blood); the synthesis of many B vitamins, including biotin and folic acid; an increase in the absorption of calcium, phosphorus and magnesium; normalization of cholesterol levels in the blood and production of digestive enzymes. Acidophilus also helps maintain bowel regularity. Bifidus helps repopulate the large intestine with friendly bacteria, creating a favorable environment for large intestine health. Bifidus lowers the pH of the intestines, manufactures specific B vitamins, ensures regular bowel movements, and can help stop gas and bloating while promoting proper immune function and overall health. Finally, eating a diet rich in plant foods will help to naturally cultivate a healthy balance of probiotic organisms.

# CHAPTER NO: 6

# SLP DIAGNOSTIC TOOLS

SLP has its eleven diagnostic tools, nine of them are modified by Dr. Shagufta Feroz after 25years of observational research under guidance of Hutchison's Clinical Methods. SLP tools are developed to help analyze the individual body type, biochemistry and finally disease chemistry. A doctor has to be a keen and a sincere observer to reach initially at a diagnosis without the technical diagnostic help.

**The SLP diagnostic tools are:**

1-Body language
2-Presenting complaints
3-Past medical history
4-Family medical history
5-Treatment history
6-Dietary routine
7-General physical examination
8-Pulse analysis (sphygmology)
9-Body mapping
10-Nutri-energetic Scan (NES)
11-Laboratory tests

***1-Body language***

Body language is a form of non-verbal communication, consisting of body pose, gestures and eye movements. Humans send and interpret such signals subconsciously. "Research has suggested that between 60 and 70 percent of all meaning is derived from nonverbal behavior." Body language may provide clues as to the attitude or state of mind of a person. For example, it may indicate aggression, attentiveness, boredom, relaxed state, pleasure and amusement besides many other cues.

There is a whole host of research studies on this subject with results on both ends of the spectrum; some showing that facial communication is believed 4.3 times more often than verbal meaning, and another finding that verbal communication in a flat tone is 4 times more likely to be understood than pure facial expression. Albert Mehrabian is noted for finding a 7%-38%-55% rule, supposedly denoting how much communication was conferred by words, tone, and body language respectively. However he was only referring to cases of expressing feelings or attitudes.

On the basis of my clinical experience I agree with the findings of Albert Mehrabian. Body type classification begins as the person enters the room and sits in front of the doctor. A person with an acidic body and with hyper-liver chemistry enters the room carefully, closes the door gently and sits in a careful manner. They are usually very quiet, calm, composed and not descriptive about their health issues. They mostly have an introvert nature and don't usually care much for holistic aspects of their health. Voice is low and tone is uniform. All of these are signs of a chemical chaos within them.

People with an acidic body and hypo-liver state are expressive and careless about their body language. They enter the room in a hurry and every movement creates noise. As they are extroverts, they are very descriptive about their ailments and irrelevant details as well. Voice is loud and tone is clear, finger tapping or change of posture frequently is observed. A careful therapist has already done the broader classification of the body type and body chemistry which lays the foundation of further diagnosis.

***2-Presenting complains***

This is the most important part of every clinical session. As a doctor, we have to listen and make a note of each and every symptom which reflects a particular chemistry. "A symptom is a phenomenon, caused by an illness and observable directly in experience. We may speak of it as a manifestation of illness. When the observer reflects on that phenomenon and uses it as a base for further inferences, then that symptom is transformed into a sign. As a sign it points beyond itself perhaps to the present illness, or to the past or to the future. In medicine then a sign is thus a phenomenon from which we may get a message, a message that tells us something about the patient or the disease. The distinction between signs and symptom rests on the meaning, and this is not perceived but inferred."

***SLP Pre-disease syndrome PDS***

According to Ayurveda science there are six chemical stages of a disease: development, accumulation, aggravation, overflow, moving and localization at a distant site, manifestation with chronic complications. Conventional medical system and its diagnostic tools start the diagnosis from forth stage onwards. All patients with signs and symptoms of first four stages of disease are declared psychological or functional patients by conventional medicine. For me each and every symptom is like a part of a jigsaw puzzle, by connecting various signs and symptoms I try to complete the puzzle. A symptom is a true indicator of the blood's chemistry. Listening carefully to all symptoms is a guiding tool. No one can generate a symptom psychologically, symptom always reflect a chemical change.

I have put all pre- signs and symptoms of a disease into one heading called "SLP Pre- Disease Syndrome". The first four stages of an Ayurveda disease development fall into the category of a Pre-disease syndrome. A doctor has to learn about this syndrome and should try to intercept, before a fully develop disease. Pre-disease syndrome is a group of symptoms which indicate an imbalance in body chemistry, homeostasis, biorhythms and liver. This syndrome indicates that after a few months to a few years, a major disease is going to invade the body. It is the result of an unhealthy lifestyle, stress and accumulation of those toxins which we take in from air, food, water and poor living conditions.

The symptoms of SLP Pre-disease syndrome are: Indigestion, constipation, abdominal distention, bloating, obesity, muscle cramps, painful joints, allergies, headaches, mood swings, irritability, disturb sleep, hyperactive mind, failing vision, ringing in the ears, tremors, acne, early skin aging, cracked heels, irritability, shortness of breath, bad body or mouth odor, tartar, dandruff, falling of hair, pigmentation on face or body, vertical ridges on nails, swollen legs or feet, Puffy face, dark circles, constant fatigue, and frequent attacks of infections.

***3-Past medical history***

Past medical history is significant in confirming the medical diagnosis. I have learnt that past medical ailments and emotional traumas are reflected in the various patterns of pulse analysis. My experience tells me that emotional traumas are the root cause of a physical disease in as many as 80% of cases. The current ailment is the continuation of the past biochemistry, resulted from emotional traumas. I also have found a strong relationship between past history of jaundice, typhoid, tuberculosis, repeated infections, chronic constipation, allergies, surgeries and the existing health problem. Existing chronic ailment is the continuation of the past ailments. Exposure to an anesthesia and frequent intake of medicines also result in chronic ailments by making liver dysfunctional. Past medical history also helps to classify the body type. Past history of diseases, traumas and drugs develop an acidic body with hyper-liver. History of chronic nasal allergies, sinusitis, headaches, fainting attacks, cardiac arrhythmias, eczemas, cold intolerance and anxiety give an indication to a low body temperature and an acidic body with hypo-liver state.

### *4-Family medical history*

Gathering a complete and accurate family medical history is becoming more important because you learn about their lifestyle, eating habits, environment and body types as well. As a patient realizes the connection within their family, he or she undoubtedly seeks to gather, perhaps informally - perhaps not, more personal information regarding risk to develop particular diseases. A family medical history or medical family tree is a record of important medical information about your relatives, including illnesses and diseases, along with the relationships among the members of your family. A family health or medical history is begun by talking with your immediate family members -- parents, grandparents and siblings -- as they provide the most important links to genetic risk.

#### *Nature versus Nurture*

It has been reported that the use of the terms "nature" and "nurture" as a convenient catch-phrase for the roles of heredity and environment in human development can be traced back to 13th century France. Some scientists think that people behave as they do according to genetic predispositions or even "animal instincts." This is known as the "nature" theory of human behavior. Other scientists believe that people think and behave in certain ways because they are taught to do so. This is known as the "nurture" theory of human behavior. Fast-growing understanding of the human genome has recently made it clear that both sides are partly right. Nature endows us with inborn abilities and traits; nurture takes these genetic tendencies and molds them as we learn and mature.

Scientists have known for years that traits such as eye color and hair color are determined by specific genes encoded in each human cell. The Nature Theory takes things a step further to say those more abstract traits such as intelligence; personality, aggression, and sexual orientation are also encoded in an individual's DNA. While not discounting genetic tendencies may exist, supporters of the nurture theory believe they ultimately don't matter - that our behavioral aspects originate only from the environmental factors of our upbringing. Studies on infant and child temperament have revealed the most crucial evidence for nurture theories.

American psychologist John Watson, best known for his controversial experiments with a young orphan named Albert, demonstrated that the acquisition of a phobia could be explained by classical conditioning. A strong proponent of environmental learning, he said: Give me a dozen healthy infants, well-formed, and my own specified world to bring them up in and I'll guarantee to take any one at random and train him to become any type of specialist I might select. Regardless of his talents, penchants, tendencies, abilities, vocations and race of his ancestors. Harvard psychologist B. F. Skinner's early experiments produced pigeons that could dance, do figure eights, and play tennis. Today known as the father of behavioral science, he eventually went on to prove that human behavior could be conditioned in much the same way as animals.

A study in New Scientist suggests that sense of humor is a learned trait, influenced by family and cultural environment, and not genetically determined. If environment didn't play a part in determining an individual's traits and behaviors, then identical twins should, theoretically, be exactly the same in all respects, even if reared apart. But a number of studies show that they are never exactly alike, even though they are remarkably similar in most respects. Researchers on all sides of the nature versus nurture debate agree that the link between a gene and a behavior is not the same as cause and effect. While a gene may increase the likelihood that you'll behave in a particular way, it does not make people do things. This means that we still get to choose who we'll be when we grow up.

Epigenetic supports the nurture theory and SLP also strongly supports the ideas of nurture theory. I believe God is very kind to us but only if we live as God intended us to live. We carry genomes for inherited diseases, but dormant genes wait for their activation to initiate the disease process. Remember disease carrying genes are activated by environmental pollutants, processed foods, erratic dietary habits, lack of nocturnal sleep and hyperactive mental activity. So you can keep your genes in sleep mode by following a natural lifestyle. Therefore family history is the least important tool of the SLP diagnostics. Once an individual starts following a body compatible diet; liver rejuvenation and harmonization of biorhythms gives holistic health. So genes are not as important as your lifestyle is.

***5-Treatment history***

Most of the pharmaceutical products metabolize through the liver. The history of current and previous medicine intake gives an idea about the liver's health. In the past repeated intake of antibiotics, steroids, herbal products, anti-tuberculosis, antidepressants and anticancer treatments alter the liver's chemistry. The most damaging are steroids, antibiotics, cytotoxic drugs and anti-tuberculosis medications. All these medications overload the liver creating hyper-active liver chemistry. If the person was originally of an acidic body type with hyper-active liver, these medications cause serious liver disorders. So the past and current treatment history also helps me in reaching the correct chemistry and is an important SLP diagnostic tool.

***6-Dietary routine***

Dietary routine means meal details and meal timings which you follow at least five days a week. While asking about the food routine, I get information about other lifestyle factors as well. Knowing details about the diet routine is a very important guiding tool for the analysis of the chemistry. It starts with questions about wake up timings, then breakfast time and food details. Mid-morning snack, lunch, evening snack and food details about the dinner have to be noted. Food timings and types of food taken in routine are directly related to existing chemistry. A history of food nibbling, quantity of food intake and intake of caffeinated drinks is important. After having an idea about the dietary

routine, we get an idea about the functioning of the hunger control Centre, satiety Centre, food cravings, insulin resistance, state of temperature regulatory Centre, mental state and body ph as well.
Lot of myths exists about water intake, and 90% of people coming to my clinic are following inappropriate intake regimes. So it is important that I ask in detail about the water intake. Food cravings, and amount of junk foods consumed in a week and change of food preferences are other important component of this routine. While asking about the diet routine I learn about the sleep time, duration and quality of sleep as well. Here indirectly I get an idea about the stress level or the presence of a hyperactive mind. We also ask about the nature, time and duration of exercise. For maximum patient compliance while prescribing a food program I have to keep in mind individual dietary routine, other lifestyle factors and traveling schedule. A patient profile form is filled to keep a record as well. Below is a copy of a patient profile form.

# Dr. Shagufta Feroz

Correct Eating Activist

M.B.B.S., M.C.P.S., D.Ac., Phd (Holistic Nutrition ) CNW (ANCB)
Author of "Living as Nature Intended"
Founder of SLP & HHAM

No.______ Date__________ Name ____________________________ Age ____ Sex ____ M/F S/M

Weight __________ Measurements __________________

Address: _____________________________________________________ Tel: ____________

| | | | |
|---|---|---|---|
| 1. Objective of Consultation<br>a. Other complains:<br>M / H:<br>b. Current T/M: | ❑ Holistic Health | ❑ Chronic Degenerative Dis. | ❑ Obesity |
| 2. Past Medical History | ❑ Liver Dis./typhoid/ | ❑ Allergic Dis. | ❑ Surgery |
| 3. Wake up time | ❑ 4 a.m - 6 a.m. | ❑ 6:00 - 9 a.m. | ❑ 9:00 - 12 noon |
| 4. Breakfast time<br>Breakfast Details | ❑ No Breakfast | ❑ Within 30 Mins of waking up | ❑ After 1-2 Hours |
| 5. M. Snack & Time | | | |
| 6. Lunch | ❑ No Lunch | ❑ Full Meal | ❑ Snacks |
| 7. E. Snack & Time | | | |
| 8. Dinner Time | ❑ No Dinner | ❑ 7:00 to 9:00PM | ❑ 9:00 TO 11:00PM |
| 9. Sleep Time | ❑ 11 p.m - 12.00 | ❑ 12 p.m - 2.00 a.m | ❑ later than 2 a.m |
| 10. Water Intake in summers | ❑ Less than 8 glasses | ❑ 8 - 10 glasses | ❑ 15 - 25 glasses |
| a. Water Temp. | ❑ Plain | ❑ Mixed | ❑ Chilled |
| b. Water Timing | ❑ 30min. Before meals | ❑ During Meals | ❑ 1.5 hr. After Meals |
| 11. Junk Food | ❑ 1-2 x/week | ❑ 2-4 x/week | ❑ 5-7 x/week |
| 12. Cravings | Sugary YES/NO | Salty YES/NO | Clay or ice YES/NO |
| 13. Heat / Cold intolerance | ❑ Normal | ❑ Cold | ❑ warm / both |
| 14. Exercise / Walk | Yes / No | | |
| 15. Pulse Diagnosis | | | |

**I HEREBY AUTHORIZE DR. SHAGUFTA FEROZ TO USE ABOVE MENTIONED PROFILE FOR MEDICAL RESEARCH.**

Integrated Holistic Care Centre, Zainab Memorial Hospital, Near Kalma Chowk Lahore.
Cell: 0321-8439362, 0334-4239530, E-mail: drsferoz@gmail.com, Web: www.picchls.com

***7-General physical examination***

The following has to be noted during the general physical examination:

I. Face color and expressions, pigmentation, dark circles, puffiness of the face, eye bags and eye health. A pale, pigmented, puffy face with dull sunken eyes is an indicator of level three hyper-active liver. Holistically a healthy individual has a pleasant face with a flawless skin, glow and sparkling eyes.

II. Scalp hair and body hair (acupuncture relates scalp hair to the kidney and body hair to the lungs).

III. Skin type, coarse or smooth. As skin is the largest organ, it reflects the health of the stomach, liver and lungs. Toxin overload and nutrient deficiencies are visible on the skin. Dehydration and water intoxication is also reflected on the skin's health.

IV. The general physical examination of skin of hands and feet is important. Early wrinkling, darkening of the knuckles and pigmented spots indicate various physical or emotional traumas. Cracked heels indicate stomach disorder, internal dryness, poor nutrition and serve as a warning for an incoming disease. Nail health is important to observe. Temperature of hands and feet tell us about the body temperature regulating biorhythm. While holding the hand, tone of hand muscles is assessed and gives an idea about body Chi.

V. I measure belly at three levels which are independent of BMI (body mass index) criteria. These three abdominal measurements are; two inches above the umbilicus (belly button), at the belly button and two inches below the belly button. In a healthy adult female ideal size is of 32:34:36. This ratio reflects ideal hormonal level, good digestive ability, and ideal metabolism. The upper reading gives an idea about the stomach's function while the second reading reflects small intestine's function of food absorption. The third reading gives information about hormonal levels, metabolic state, water retention and presence of a chronic deep stress. State of hyper-active mind results in large lower abdominal size, a typical pear shape. Very interestingly these measurements always correspond with the pulse analysis. The normal gap between first and third readings is of 4-6 inches. If it exceeds six inches body is in a pre-disease state and if the gap is of 10 or more inches, a fully developed pear shapes which reflects a hyper-liver and a hyperactive mind. In a healthy male adult, the measurements are more or less the same around 38:38:38. Chemical imbalance results in an apple shape body. After starting SLP, I assess the prognosis by repeating the size measurements. These measurements are independent of the amount of weight loss, one of my patients lost 10 inches with no weight loss. It is a very useful tool to assess health, pre-disease, disease, chronic stress and disease prognosis.

***8-Pulse analysis***

Pulse analysis is a diagnostic technique used in several healing systems to determine the health conditions and course of treatment for patients. It is used in Ayurveda medicine, Eastern medicine and traditional Chinese medicine (TCM). The techniques of pulse analysis have been developed over thousands of years, as these three systems of medicine are the world's oldest. Acupuncture, a branch of TCM, has long relied on pulse diagnosis as a main tool to determine the course of treatment. In Western medicine, every time a doctor checks the pulse of a patient and listens to the heartbeat with a stethoscope, the doctor is practicing a form of pulse diagnosis. Pulse analysis is a quick, inexpensive, and non-invasive diagnostic tool. When performed by trained professionals, it can be an effective means for determining the health conditions of patients. Claudius Galen (129AD) was perhaps the first physiologist to describe the pulse.

***Aim of pulse analysis***

The aim of pulse analysis, like the other methods of diagnosis, has always been to obtain useful information about what goes on inside the body, what has caused disease, what might be done to rectify the problem, and what are the chances of success. According to Chinese understanding, the pulse can reveal whether a syndrome is of hot or cold nature, whether it is of excess or deficiency type, which of the humors (qi, moisture, blood) are affected and which organ systems suffer from dysfunction. In order to make these determinations, the physician must feel the pulse under the proper conditions - following the established procedures - and must then translate the unique pulse that is felt into one or more of the categories of pulse form.

Pulse analysis is an endlessly fascinating and challenging subject. In taking a pulse, we are literally 'putting our finger on the pulse'--the life force--of our patient. This is a great privilege. It is a moment in treatment that can facilitate a deep connection between patient and practitioner. How to teach this to students is another challenge. It is very hard to learn to understand and discuss the meaning of something as limitless as connecting to someone's pulse unless we have something explicit to measure it against, and this is where Chinese medicine can help the healer. Just as the eight principles and the five elements give us an organizing principle that helps us understand ourselves as human beings, so the twenty eight pulses of Chinese medicine provide us with a measure for understanding variations in the pulse.

By taking a pulse examination, humoral imbalances such as the three Doshas - Vata, Pitta, and Kaphha - of Ayurveda can be diagnosed. In homeopathy, pulse diagnosis is used to guide the selection of medicine. In modern medicine, certain kinds of heart attacks, such as ventricular fibrillation, may be identified by feeling the pulse and characterizing its speed, strength, and rhythm. A fast, weak, thready pulse might indicate certain kinds of heart failure or shock from blood loss. A pulse present in the upper arm, but not at the wrist, is indicative of unusually low blood pressure. Certain kinds of cardiac dysrhythmias (irregular rhythms), such as ventricular tachycardia or atrial fibrillation, may be diagnosed by overt patient symptoms and feeling of the pulse, and characterizing its speed, strength, and rhythm.

**Pulse analysis system**

Pulse Analysis System offers a particularly comprehensive and holistic approach to analysis and therapy. It is based on the premise that illness does not appear 'out of the blue', but first shows as energetic functional disturbance, followed by chemical change and finally tissue change - a process that may take some years. During the past 20 years three major software products were developed by team of researchers to analyze and interpret the pulse registration.

Pulse Metabolic Analysis
Pulse Functional Analysis
Ionic Balance Analysis

Metabolic Analysis software is a comprehensive approach to analyze ten main functional systems in the body and their interrelation. Analysis could be interpreted form western or oriental (TCM) point of view. After interpreting results, the software gives recommendations for acupuncture, nutrition, Ayurveda and Chinese herbs. Functional Analysis software gives the opportunity to express analysis of the ten major human body systems (gall bladder, liver, small Intestine, heart, stomach, spleen, large intestine, lungs, urinary bladder, kidneys) and their stability. Ionic Balance Analysis software allows us to find a proportion of essential minerals (potassium, sodium, magnesium, and calcium) in the blood and compare the balance of the same minerals distributed in sea water, which according to the research are almost at the same proportions.

## SLP Pulse analysis

Pulse analysis always fascinated me, but it became extremely difficult for me to learn and relate clinically the many types of Chinese pulses. I eventually stopped using the Chinese pulse diagnosis method but continued analyzing pulse and its relationship with health and in various disease states. Gradually I started learning about a simple method of pulse diagnosis. This was the result of fifteen years of experience of feeling pulses of a few hundred thousand people and pulse analysis became an obsession for me. In the beginning, I started connecting body language and external appearances with the pulse. I would request people even on the roads, trains, or public places to kindly allow me to check their pulses. In medical camps, seminars, health carnivals and social gatherings I got a chance to analyze a huge number of pulses.

Over a period of time a blurred picture started getting clear and a connection between a disease and a specific pulse type became clear. Later I started conducting experiments with various foods and their effects on various type of pulses. Most of these experiments I have conducted on myself and my family members. While relating pulse with food intake I learnt that food is a remedy if used correctly and the same food can become a poison too. Simultaneously I was learning about the importance of how to eat correctly. Finally an interdependent healing program started taking shape, based on a simple pulse diagnosis as a tool and healing through eight rules of diet correction.

SLP pulse analysis helps in the diagnosis of following factors:

I. Body types
II. Blood chemistry: gives an idea about ionic level, acidity, wind, toxins, phlegm, allergens, water retention and temperature of blood
III. Functional analysis: of organ health, especially of liver, heart, and kidney
IV. Psychoanalysis / hyperactive mind syndrome

V. Prognosis of a disease
VI. Past medical ailments, medical treatments and emotional traumas
VII. Aging status, both mental and biological

***How to do SLP pulse analysis***

Bilateral radial pulse is analyzed in a relaxed sitting posture. First four fingers of the right hand are used to palpate the pulse of the patient. The following characteristics have to be noticed bilaterally:

I. Pulse levels - superficial, intermediate and deep. These are felt by applying mild, moderate and deep pressure respectively. A normal pulse is felt at two levels superficial and intermediate and is labeled acidic body with normal healthy liver.

II. Side of the pulse - the right hand pulse indicates the status of important organs and the left hand pulse indicates ionic status and blood chemistry. In the right hand, the superficial pulse is of stomach, the middle of liver and the deep pulse indicates nervous system. The superficial level of the left hand pulse indicates acidity and wind, the middle level indicates bile pigments, toxins, heat and the deeper level indicates phlegm or water levels in blood. While doing pulse analysis both the pulses are examined. Normally both side pulses complement each other. In order to make the diagnosis and food plan, the right pulse is more informative, accurate, constant and reliable.

III. Type of the pulse - is the most important element in the diagnosis. While palpating a normal pulse, only two levels are felt, superficial and intermediate. A bilateral pulse at these two levels with normal strength indicates a normal pulse. A normal pulse means optimum liver health and peak digestive wellness along with controlled emotional health. But under unhealthy states there are various combinations of the three levels observed. To confirm the pulse diagnosis, I have to relate the patient's past and present medical history as well. A history of exposure to drugs, alcohol, and general anesthesia is very important. General physical examination, pulse diagnosis and body mapping should match and complement each other. There are about six types of pulses which explain six body chemistries and these six bio-chemistries lead to six groups of medical diseases. I rarely pay attention to conventional medical diagnosis and try to work with the person as a whole. My therapy is purely focused on restoring body chemistry to normal. This reversal occurs first at the chemical level then in cell renewal, tissues regeneration, restoration of organ health and finally the system.

Our modern fast paced lifestyle with its infinite social pressures, competitive work environments and takeaway foods places immense pressure on our liver. A result of this is that I have rarely seen an individual with a healthy pulse. Mostly people come with a pulse indicating an acidic body with a hyper-liver state. As mentioned earlier, a human body because of the muscular structure is acidic by function and alkaline by chemistry. Therefore we carry a constant acidic body type with varying chemistry due to our lifestyle. Various body chemistries result in different metabolic states. These chemical imbalances are linked with a group of specific signs and symptoms. In order to categorize the body chemistry, a minimum of ten signs or symptoms must be present. Here is a list of six different body chemistries, six pulses and their symbols:

***Six body chemistries and their pulses***

Following are the SLP symbols of six pulses, which reveal six chemistries and two body types. There are only two major body types: acidic body with hyper-liver and acidic body with hypo or sluggish liver. These two body types have six interchanging chemistries which if persist for a long duration convert into six pathologies. Below is an account of six body chemistries, and their pulses with their symbols.

Acidic body type with hyper liver has three presentations:

***I-Acidic body with grade 1, 2, 3 hyper liver states***

AD+L1,2,3

P

AD+L1,2,3

***2-Hyper acidic body with hyper-liver***

AD2+L2

P

AD2+L2

***3-Acidic body, hyper-liver and water retention***

AD+L+WR

P

AD+L+WR

Acidic body with hypo-liver has three chemistry presentations

***4-Acidic body with hypo or sluggish liver***

AD-L

P

AD-L

***5-Hyper acidic body with hypo-liver***

AD2-L

P

AD2-L

***6-Acidic body, hypo-liver and water retention***

AD-L+WR

P

AD-L+WR

***1-Acidic body with grade 1,2,3 hyper-liver***

Body type is acidic body with hyper-liver. On pulse diagnosis bilaterally intermediate pulses are dominant with superficial mild pulse. Degree of strength, length and volume of intermediate pulse indicates the level of a hyper-liver state. Grades of hyper-liver state are dependent on the factors of age, gender, past medical history, drug / alcohol intake, dietary habits, lifestyle, emotional traumas and various environmental toxins. All these factors are responsible for increasing work load on the liver to supply more energy and simultaneously increase toxin load as well.

Grade 1 hyper-liver state - ideally is indicated by a prominent intermediate pulse on the right side. Its chemistry is associated with a set of signs and symptoms which include:

i. mild digestive disorder
ii. disturbed lipid profile
iii. weight gaining mode or difficulty in weight loss
iv. disturbed hormonal level
v. menstrual problems
vi. polycystic ovaries
vii. pre-hypertensive or mild hypertensive state
viii. high uric acid
ix. migraines
x. irritability
xi. border line fasting sugar
xii. mostly dislike sweet foods as the blood ph is acidic
xiii. heat intolerance
xiv. warm extremities
xv. mood swings
xvi. an introvert personality

Similarly, a prominent intermediate pulse on the left side is observed. This pulse describes:

I. raised but subclinical level of bile pigments
II. toxins
III. allergens

IV. heat in the blood

Grade II hyper- liver state - is where the right intermediate pulse is long, forceful and full. This state is associated with:

i. gastritis
ii. polyphagia
iii. high triglyceride
iv. obesity
v. pear shape of abdomen in females and apple shape obesity in males
vi. menstrual disorders
vii. female hormonal imbalances
viii. infertility
ix. impotency
x. moderate hypertension
xi. cardiac arrhythmias or palpitation episodes
xii. pre-diabetic
xiii. osteoporosis and pre-arthritis
xiv. depression
xv. insomnia
xvi. fatigue
xvii. skin allergies
xviii. asthma
xix. dizziness
xx. Vertigo

Grade III hyper- liver state - is where the right intermediate pulse is long, full, powerful, bounding and can be rolled under fingers. This chemistry indicates a chemical chaos as a result of an advanced pace of liver functions. Some signs and symptoms are at extremes showing loss of biorhythms and therefore loss of auto regulatory mechanisms. Symptoms include:

i. gastric ulcers
ii. IBS
iii. excess of wind
iv. bad burps
v. polyphagia or anorexia
vi. a disturbed lipid profile
vii. grade II or III fatty liver
viii. high fasting sugar or fluctuating sugar
ix. fainting episodes
x. headaches
xi. morbid obesity
xii. underweight
xiii. abdominal obesity
xiv. hormonal imbalance
xv. uncontrolled hypertension
xvi. osteoporosis
xvii. nonspecific arthritis
xviii. cardiac disease

xix. serious allergies and asthma

xx. repeated infections

xxi. shortness of breath

xxii. claustrophobia

xxiii. Fears and various other phobias

***2-Hyper-acidic body with hyper- liver state***

It is a body type where the first two pulses are bilaterally strong, long and bounding in nature. The left blood pulse explains acidity, wind, heat, allergens, and toxins and raised levels of bile pigments in the blood. The right organ pulse describes hyperactivity in the stomach and various grades of hyper-liver. The body suffers from gastric disorders, constipation, multiple allergies, auto-immune disorders, moderate to high blood pressure, dizziness, IBS, headaches, anxiety, body pains, arthritis, hyper-pigmentations, disturb sugar levels and metabolically resistant obesity.

***3-Acidic body, hyper-liver and water retention***

All three levels of pulses are found bilaterally which are of different strengths. It indicates serious derangement of the body chemistry leading to disease development. Symptoms are dependent on the strength of pulse at each of the three levels. If the superficial is strongest, then stomach, joint disease or cardiac ailments are dominant. If the second pulse is dominant, then autoimmune disorders, liver diseases, depressions or cancers are seen. If the third pulse is dominant bilaterally, then generalized swelling, morbid obesity, severe allergic disorders and breathing problems are observed due to water retention. This explains a dysfunctional stomach, liver and kidney. If three levels are observed but not of a very strong intensity then it is a pre-disease pulse. This type of pulse explains a chemistry which leads to:

**i.** A bloated body

ii. Circulatory imbalance

iii. Numbness of limbs and swelling on the dependent parts

iv. chronic disorders in a progressive state

v. Increased frequency of urination

vi. increased salivation

vii. increased sweating and intolerance to extreme temperatures

viii. sweaty palms or soles

ix. bad body odor

x. obesity with disfigured body shape

xi. Skin allergies

xii. food allergies causing diarrhea

xiii. vertigo

xiv. tinnitus

xv. dizziness

xvi. Uncontrolled hypertension

***4-Acidic body with hypo/sluggish liver***

This pulse is felt only at the superficial levels bilaterally and no intermediate pulse. The right organ pulse describes a liver which is weak and unable to handle normal functions. The patient history for this pulse can be traced back as early as intrauterine life through to neonatal age and childhood. Dietary habits, exposure to infections, treatment history and emotional traumas are also key influencers. The Left side pulse indicates acidic ph, low body temperature and wind retention in the body. Common complaints are of gastritis, constipation, upper respiratory tract infections like tonsillitis, adenoids, sinusitis, shifting joint pains, cervical pain and lower back pain. The person has a lean and petite structure, general weakness and is prone to fungal infections. A tendency for bleeding from gums, stomach and hemorrhoids are other symptoms. A hormonal imbalance is present in both genders. Cold extremities, cold intolerance, restlessness and anxiety are also observed.

***5-Hyper-acidic body with hypo/sluggish liver***

Only superficial pulses are felt bilaterally. The organ pulse reflects a hyper acidic stomach and all other symptoms are directly related to it. The blood pulse describes acidity, wind and heat in the blood. IBS, constipation, Polyphagia, cervical spasm, lumbago, right sided sciatica, right sided migraine, insomnia, panic attacks, forgetfulness and poor concentration are various presentations of this chemistry.

***6-Acidic body, hypo-liver and water retention***

This body type is assessed by superficial and deep pulses bilaterally and no intermediate pulse. Symptoms include:

- **i.** Gastritis
- **ii.** constipation
- **iii.** upper respiratory tract infections like tonsillitis
- **iv.** adenoids
- **v.** sinusitis
- **vi.** shifting joint pains
- **vii.** weak cervical and lower back
- **viii.** obesity with highest lower abdominal measurements
- **ix.** general weakness
- **x.** hormonal imbalance
- **xi.** prone to fungal infections

**xii.** tendency for bleeding from gums

**xiii.** hemorrhoids

**xiv.** hormonal imbalance in both genders

**xv.** cold extremities

**xvi.** cold intolerance

**xvii.** restlessness

**xviii.** anxiety

**xix.** allergies (especially nasal)

**xx.** asthma

**xxi.** eczema

**xxii.** Psoriasis

***Factors affecting SLP pulse***

There are multiple factors which influence pulse and change the basic body type and psychology. Therefore other diagnostics tools of SLP are also taken into account to establish an accurate diagnosis. Pulse affecting factors are:

i. Ageing process

ii. Emotional traumas

iii. Past disease history

iv. Treatment history

v. Nature of work

vi. Environmental factors which include social factors, politics, calamities, media etc.

vii. Seasonal factors

**9-SLP Body mapping**

Body mapping is the study of the configuration of the surface of the body especially in relation to its internal parts. It facilitates useful insight into the relationship of the Mind and Body and the effect of that relationship on disease and the healing process. I found this tool consistent with my pulse diagnosis. I got basic guidance from the rules defined by "Tib-e-Mashriq"( traditional eastern herbal science) and modified the rules on the bases of my clinical experience. Therefore SLP body segments integrate with pulse and clinical presentations. My observations revealed that according to this science an adult body is divided into three horizontal segments which are, supra (above) clavicle, supra diaphragm and an infra (below) diaphragm segment. These three horizontal sections are further divided into two vertical sections making six segments in total. These six segments are labeled as right supra clavicle, left supra clavicle, right supra diaphragm, left supra diaphragm, right infra diaphragm and left infra diaphragm and they cover back and front of the body.

The supra clavicle extends from the centre of the scalp to the clavicle, the supra diaphragm is from the clavicle to the superior surface of the diaphragm and infra diaphragm is from the inferior surface of the diaphragm to the feet. These six segments reflect six chemistries of the body and the six groups of diseases as well. For example left shoulder falls into left supra diaphragm and its pain indicates an acidic body with a hyper- liver chemistry. This can be treated by food which is relevant to this pulse. The heart sits in the left supra diaphragm segment which is the segment of an acidic body with a hyper-liver. When I find problem in this segment, I don't go into cardiac disease detail; I try to reverse the existing chemistry by harmonizing liver functions. Another example is

Osteoarthritis of right knee which is in the segment indicative of a hyper acidic body with hyper liver. Therefore six segments coincide with six body chemistries and six groups of disorders.

1. Right supra clavicle = Acidic body, hypo-liver and water retention
2. Left supra clavicle = Acidic body, hyper-liver and water retention
3. Right supra diaphragm = Acidic body with hypo-liver
4. Left supra diaphragm = Acidic body with hyper-liver
5. Right infra diaphragm= Hyper-acidic body with hyper-liver
6. Left infra diaphragm= Hyper acidic body with hypo liver

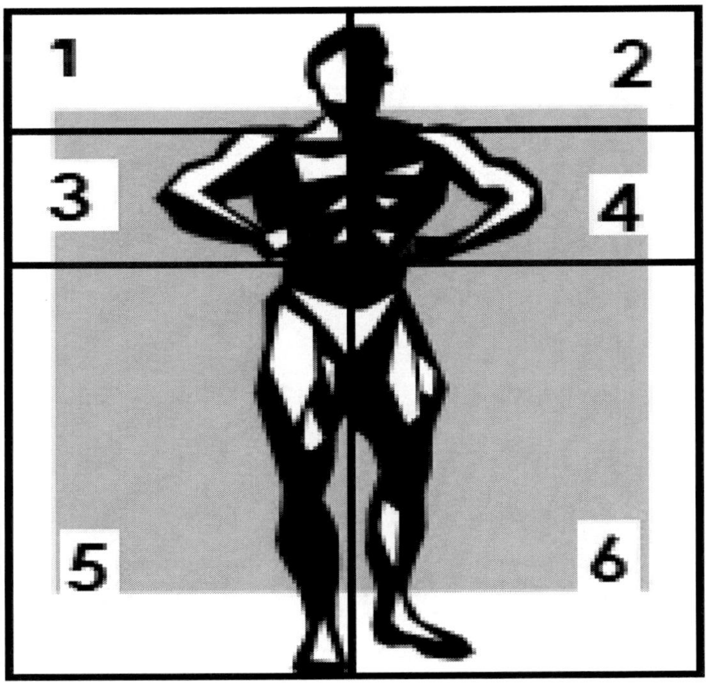


**10-Nutrienergetic scan (NES)**

Harry Massey, Founder and Chief Executive Officer, started NES Health as he was fortunate enough to have a dramatic health Journey after being diagnosed with Chronic Fatigue Syndrome when he was just 21. Having experienced the many hardships in his own healing journey, nothing seemed to work and he didn't get better until he took control of his own health. This led to meeting Peter Fraser a once-in-a-century genius who looked at biology from a completely different perspective.

Peter discovered that Information and Energy control Biology not Genes and Biochemistry. Harry, with his desire to participate in every experience to the full, followed Peter's recommendations to the letter and had a full recovery. In 2004, Harry joined forces with Peter Fraser and together they made the world's first body information reading and correction system - The NES Professional System. Since that time, Visionary and Entrepreneur Harry and the whole team at NES Health are working towards revolutionizing healthcare.

The new biology tells us that there is more to the physical body and how it functions than DNA and cells. Information and energy are crucial to health as well. The concept is simple. Imagine the body as a computer. The body's cells and organs are its hardware. This has been very well studied by Western Medicine over the last 100 years with little current understanding over what actually controls the body. How does the hardware know what to do? What is the body's software-the operating instructions that it needs to run the hardware? The new biology says that information and energy fields underlie the body and serve as its master operating system - as its software. Correct the body's control system and enhance its energy systems and it can do what nature intended it to do - work properly and maintain a state of robust health.

NES detects abnormalities in the HBF (Human Bioenergy Field), which is the body's master energy control system, ultimately determining our chemistry, and metabolism. NES integrates researches in the fields of Physics, Biophotonism, Quantum biology, Quantum chemistry, Resonance phenomenon, advanced mathematics, Information technology, Homeopathy, Western and Chinese medicine and Holistic nutrition. NES is an important component of my diagnostic tools, because it provides a detailed energy body scan which gives me an idea about the root cause of a disease. Biophysics states that disease originates in the Human Bioenergy Field (HBF). A disturbed HBF causes a disturbance in the chemical levels which later can initiate the disease process. I use the NES scan as a pre-disease tool as well. The NES System is the first and only computerized instrument capable of providing detailed information about the location and causes of ill health, and it helps in assessing the prognosis of the disease as well. It will find various disease causing factors that even the most sophisticated and expensive laboratory and imaging tests cannot detect; all this is instant and noninvasive.

The NES scan detects the health of a specific vital organ by checking its anatomical or tissue structure, nerve connection status and detecting the presence of various types of colonies of bacteria, viruses and fungus. It also tests metabolism along with functions of that particular organ as disease can originate from a single cause or combinations of the above mentioned various systems of an organ. The musculoskeletal structure is also checked in detail. Red to green bars indicates levels of disturbance in the energy body field. A red bar in a specific section is then related to laboratory test results. It tells about a disease which can invade the body within the next five years. Scans also reveal levels of environmental toxins, minerals, vitamins, antioxidants, blood oxygenation, allergies and the effect of 14 emotions on human health. The NES scan reveals pre-disease states of Diabetes, Arthritis, Allergies, Cancers, Mental disorders and other Chronic debilitating diseases.

Below is a sample NES scan.

| Scan Item | Wednesday, November 03, 2010 |
|---|---|
| Equatorial Axis | |
| Vertical Axis | |
| Magnetic Polar Axis | |
| Big Field Aligner | |
| Polarity | |
| ED 1 - Source Driver | |
| ED 2 - Imprinter Driver | |
| ED 3 - Cell Driver | |
| ED 4 - Nerve Driver | |
| ED 5 - Circulation Driver | |
| ED 6 - Heart Driver | |
| ED 7 - Lung Driver | |
| ED 8 - Stomach Driver | |
| ED 9 - Muscle Driver | |
| ED 10 - Skin Driver | |
| ED 11 - Liver Driver | |
| ED 12 - Kidney Driver | |
| ED 13 - Immunity Driver | |
| ED 14 - Spleen Driver | |
| ED 15 - Pancreas Driver | |
| ED 16 - Bone Driver | |
| EI 1 | |
| EI 2 | |
| EI 3 | |
| EI 4 | |
| EI 5 | |
| EI 6 | |
| EI 7 | |
| EI 8 | |
| EI 9 | |
| EI 10 | |
| EI 11 | |
| EI 12 | |

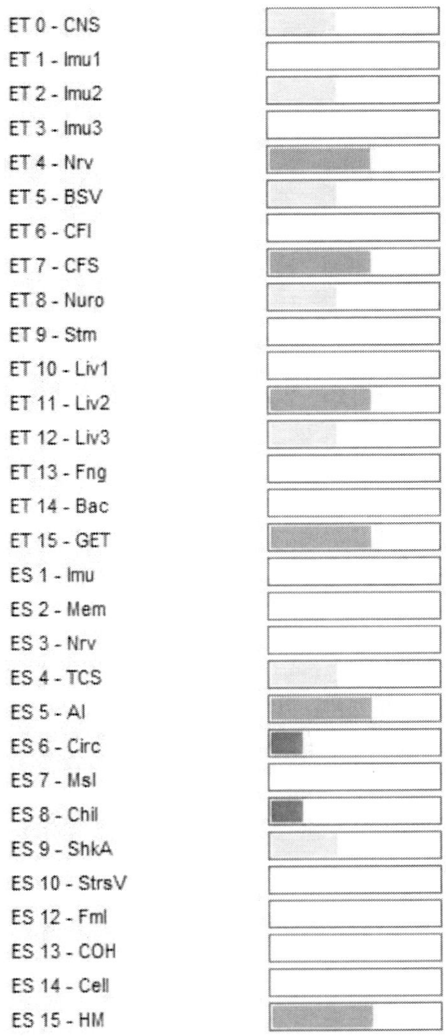
ET 0 - CNS
ET 1 - Imu1
ET 2 - Imu2
ET 3 - Imu3
ET 4 - Nrv
ET 5 - BSV
ET 6 - CFI
ET 7 - CFS
ET 8 - Nuro
ET 9 - Stm
ET 10 - Liv1
ET 11 - Liv2
ET 12 - Liv3
ET 13 - Fng
ET 14 - Bac
ET 15 - GET
ES 1 - Imu
ES 2 - Mem
ES 3 - Nrv
ES 4 - TCS
ES 5 - AI
ES 6 - Circ
ES 7 - Msl
ES 8 - Chil
ES 9 - ShkA
ES 10 - StrsV
ES 12 - Fml
ES 13 - COH
ES 14 - Cell
ES 15 - HM

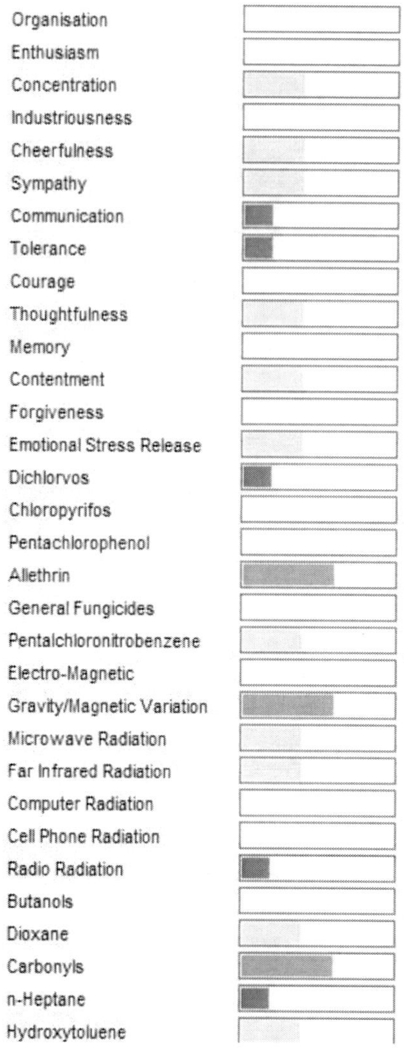
Organisation
Enthusiasm
Concentration
Industriousness
Cheerfulness
Sympathy
Communication
Tolerance
Courage
Thoughtfulness
Memory
Contentment
Forgiveness
Emotional Stress Release
Dichlorvos
Chloropyrifos
Pentachlorophenol
Allethrin
General Fungicides
Pentalchloronitrobenzene
Electro-Magnetic
Gravity/Magnetic Variation
Microwave Radiation
Far Infrared Radiation
Computer Radiation
Cell Phone Radiation
Radio Radiation
Butanols
Dioxane
Carbonyls
n-Heptane
Hydroxytoluene

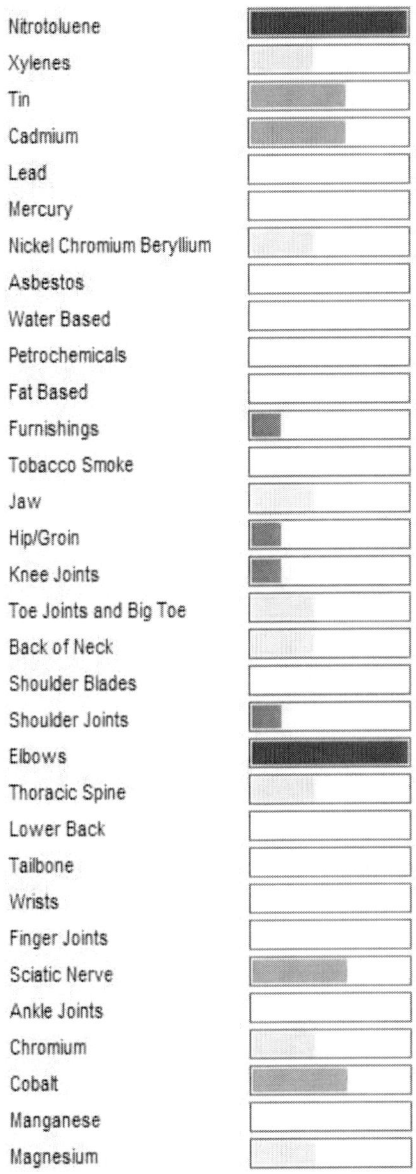
Nitrotoluene
Xylenes
Tin
Cadmium
Lead
Mercury
Nickel Chromium Beryllium
Asbestos
Water Based
Petrochemicals
Fat Based
Furnishings
Tobacco Smoke
Jaw
Hip/Groin
Knee Joints
Toe Joints and Big Toe
Back of Neck
Shoulder Blades
Shoulder Joints
Elbows
Thoracic Spine
Lower Back
Tailbone
Wrists
Finger Joints
Sciatic Nerve
Ankle Joints
Chromium
Cobalt
Manganese
Magnesium

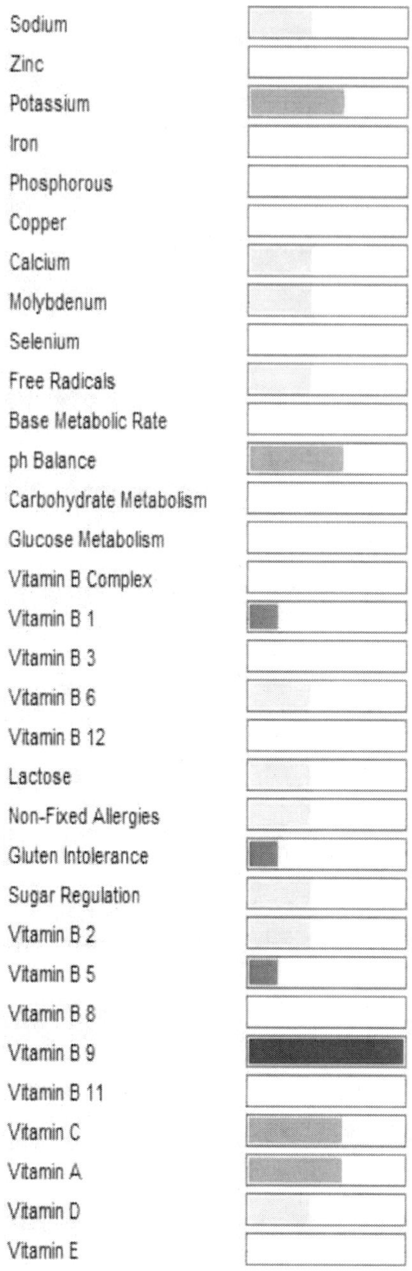


## 11-Laboratory tests

Routine laboratory tests are of least importance for my practice, because they cannot diagnose sub-disease. For prognosis sake I do recommend routine blood and urine analysis, LFTs, lipid profile, Hba1c, CRP, homocytsein levels and ultrasound.

## CHAPTER NO 7

## SLP METHOLOGY

This chapter is going to explain in detail methods of SLP practice and how it works in the reversal of a disease process. This program works at the blood chemistry and at the cellular level, healing starts from deep within and manifests itself in the physical body after 10 to 20 days. This change is permanent if lifestyle is modified permanently on the principles of the SLP.

### Scientific rules which govern SLP

A human body is not so simple to understand and cannot be fixed with a single scientific theory. Following are the various scientific principles which work collectively on this program and make it effective. These principles start fixing multiple body imbalances simultaneously, and we can observe gradual reversal of a disease process. Below is the list of scientific rules working on SLP:

1-Lifestyle modification
2- Biochemical individuality, therefore a body compatible diet plan
3-Liver rejuvenation
4-Restoration of body homeostasis
5-Rules of Psychoneuroimmunology PNI
6-Correction of biorhythms which include:

i. Restoration of blood ph
ii. Normalization of body temperature
iii. Water balance
iv. Hormonal balance
v. Satisfaction of food cravings
vi. Stabilization of blood pressure and blood sugar

vii. Sleep regulation

viii. Smooth blood and lymph circulation

7-Chrono-therapy or time treatment by harmonizing external clock with internal clock
8-Low glycemic index based foods
9-Food rotation
10-Alkaline / acidic food combinations
11-Body and mind science
12-Quantum medicine, which covers the role of spirit in health
13-Faith healing
14- Breathing exercises and Yoga

**Components of SLP clinical practice are:**

**1.** History taking

**2.** General Physical examination

**3.** Diagnosis

**4.** Personalized food plan based on Eight rules of correct eating

**5.** Sleep regulation

**6.** Stress management

**7.** Exercise

***8.*** Food supplements

***1-History taking***

While taking history, presenting complaints along with past medical history, psychological, family and treatment history are also required. Most important factor of a lifestyle is the history of dietary routine, which is taken in detail.

***2-General physical examination***

General appearance, body language, muscle tone, skin health, body and scalp hair, facial expressions and eyes are observed during a general physical examination. Other parameters are blood pressure readings, weight and abdominal measurements. The temperature of body extremities is also an important diagnostic parameter.

***3- Diagnostic tools***

There are about eleven SLP diagnostic tools, with their own clinical significance. For me the most quick, and easy tool is the pulse analysis followed by the rules of body mapping. While doing online consultations, I use rest of the ten tools for the diagnosis.

***4-Eight rules of correct eating***

The most important therapeutic SLP component is diet correction. The objective of diet correction is initially detoxification, then liver rejuvenation and finally restoration of its role as a master biorhythm regulator. Once the liver is rejuvenated, it automatically works on the rejuvenation of the immune system triggering a chain of auto-corrective processes. Remember immune cells are one third of all cells in your body. The process of diet correction includes the selection of natural whole foods and correction of dietary habits in order to harmonize dietary routine with biological rhythms in the body. When we eat natural whole foods correctly, they are absorbed optimally, become a remedy and work holistically. The same food taken in an incorrect manner is poorly digested, becomes a toxic agent and starts a disease process in the body. Therefore natural foods in themselves are not the answer for good health, instead it's the way you take them that matters the most.

So the very first rule to begin with the SLP is to have awareness about natural foods and gradually start eliminating artificial and processed foods from the dietary routine. This change requires motivation on the individual's part and also relies on the therapist's ability to demonstrate and convince the individual of the program's benefits. In some instances, this increases the kitchen budget as natural whole foods usually cost more. Shifting from processed to natural foods create resistance from other family members, friends and colleagues who in many cases are not supportive of the individual's new dietary plan. Therefore, the first four weeks are critical in terms of compliance, I have to work very closely with the individual to ensure that I can deliver a minimum of 30% improvement in their health or existing disease process through this program. The individual observes improvement after the first two to four weeks, only then they tend to stay loyal to the program.

The eight rules of diet correction are critical to changing the biochemistry gradually by aligning everyday routine with the internal biorhythm. It takes about four weeks to break partially previous food addictions, to curb un-healthy food cravings and for developing faith on a new method of food intake. First two weeks are of auto-detoxification, which are observed in the form of offensive urine, diarrhea or skin eruptions. Simultaneously, from the second week onwards a feeling of well-being starts setting in. This feeling of well-being helps the patient in developing confidence in lifestyle modification and it comes from the rejuvenation of the mind and immune system.

The intensity of stress and its duration starts decreasing automatically. Gradually I realized that when I start working on the rejuvenation of liver health, I unconsciously touch the 'auto-pilot' control system of the body triggering a chain of auto corrective processes which ultimately take the body into the land of wellness. This auto pilot is the liver waiting for the right initial instructions. Diet correction with well-organized whole foods delivers precise instructions to liver for its auto correction. I deeply enjoy this process of auto correction, and in follow up visits I try to keep the patient on the same pattern of lifestyle modification. This auto-healing process takes approximately 12 weeks to complete, resulting in good holistic health.

Various medical ailments, weight issues, mental or emotional disorders show a remarkable change in 12 weeks. The impact on advanced diseases is dependent on the level of self-abuse inflicted by the patient, duration of disease and the grade of illness. Chronic degenerative disorders take about six months to one year for 60 -80 % reversal. This whole interactive process of liver rejuvenation, biorhythms re-alignment, natural food miracles, and healing of disease process requires my active involvement with the patient. This auto corrective process has given me the confidence to say that there is no disease which is beyond the domain of SLP, because it treats individuals carrying disease and not the disease, body wisdom is fully aware how to eradicate the disease.

The SLP eight diet correction rules are:

***i-Natural foods should be selected***

The molecules of a natural food can communicate and work in synchrony with a human cell. As we are a mass of about 50 trillion cells and holistic health is dependent on the health of each and every cell and how well they communicate with each other. It has a natural ability to repair itself through its memory of wholeness, or in other words cell can revert back to its original state of health by the intake of

***ii-Correct food timings***

It is an extremely important component of the SLP. The objective of correcting food timings is to harmonize your external clock with the internal clock which regulates ongoing internal rhythm. We get optimum healing when our food timing match with the food timing of our body clock. In the entire program, timing of pre-breakfast is the most important section therapeutically. I have learnt on my clinical experience that the interval between waking up and first food intake plays a vital role in determining health or disease. People skipping breakfast or taking late breakfasts suffer from weight management disorders, chronic degenerative diseases especially uncontrolled diabetes, psychological disorders and speedy aging. SLP initially focuses on the correction of morning food timings and about 70% of healing comes from the morning holistic foods.

Plan starts with a pre-breakfast which is within first few minutes of waking up without leaving the bed. Pre-breakfast foods include dates, figs, prunes, raisins, berries, dried apricots, honey water and nuts etc. The time of food intake, type of foods, quantity, and rotation converts these small quantity foods into potent remedies. The ideal gap between prebreakfast and breakfast is of 30 -60 minutes, if this interval cannot be followed then a second PBF is given half an hour after the first PBF. In the second PBF small quantity of mix fruits, yogurt, milk, milk based desserts or mix nuts can be taken on rotation and breakfast comes about one to two hours later.

Ideal breakfast time is before 9am. At this time digestive system is functioning optimum and food absorption is maximum. The body needs nutrient dense foods in the morning especially protein and complex carbohydrates based. Food taken before 9a.m metabolizes and transforms into blood optimally and there is no weight gain even with a calorie free, quantity free and nutrient rich breakfast. An early breakfast with poor quality food does not have any healing effect and body remains in a starvation mode. Food timing is totally dependent on the individual's routine and has to be personalized. I try to persuade the client to follow only two main meal pattern during the day, which they rarely follow in the first month. Lunch is replaced with small meals like high proteins, compound salads, yogurt, soups, beans or chickpeas. The second ideal time for good digestion is between 4 pm to 9 pm; therefore snacks or dinner has to be taken during this duration. Snacks in the form of desserts, mix fruits, mix nuts, corn or coffee can be taken around 5p.m. and then dinner between 8-9 p.m.

A sweet food in the evening gives a boost to the declining mental energy and maintains a stable sugar level. If small quantity of sweet food is taken in PBF or in the evening, they help in controlling intense sugar cravings and diabetes as well. After PBF and BF the other important meal is dinner. Ideally it has to be taken before 9p.m. and the individual should sleep within two hours. If a person remains awake 3-4 hours after the dinner, then a post dinner snack (PDS) has to be taken. Post dinner snack has four food options, warm whole milk, mix fruits, mix nuts or desserts. These four foods facilitate the rejuvenation process at night, and also act as a sedative. PDS controls bloating, facial puffiness, appetite and behavior in next day. So PDS is another important component of SLP. During the day, avoid nibbling and leave at least 3 hour intervals between meals and snacks. During the day 2-3 cups of tea or coffee are good for health.

***iii- Favorite foods should be selected***

I always give choice to my patients to select their favorite foods from a natural food list. By giving them the option I learn about their genetically determined food preference for their body type. By checking the pulse and doing other examinations I already have an idea about their built-in food preferences. But the interesting part is, whatever ailment patient is suffering from, they are always aware of their food preferences and I can see a smile on their face while describing that favorite food. So the selection of food becomes easier, and all patients enjoy this interactive food selection process. This session helps me in developing their trust on me and my food plan for them as well.

My patients think that I am being considerate, but they are unaware of the highly scientific reasons behind the food selection. This is a process of fine tuning the body chemistry with the food chemistry. Once one of my patients sitting in the waiting room said “doctor, all the patients coming out of your room are smiling and they look happy. What do you do to them, are you cracking jokes with them?” In fact, this is the very first step to initiate the process of healing. Patients feel happy because baseless myths are broken; a calorie and quantity free food plan makes them feel lighter and liberates from the crushing schedules and controls of the various diets. So the mental component of pleasure and holistic health is already added to the plan.

### *iv-How much to eat*

Most of the people have malfunctioning hunger and appetite Centre due to intake of the processed foods, unhealthy dietary habits, poor sleep quality and bad stress management. Other important factors altering natural appetite are high or fluctuating insulin levels and water retention in tissues and blood. Most of the people ask about the quantity of food they should eat and very few are aware of their satisfying food levels. My theory of there being no limit on the quantity of food intake gives them freedom. My target is not to quantify their food intake, instead to fine tune the hunger control Centre, so that food quantity is regulated automatically.

When I prescribe a body compatible diet plan, I work on the correction of biochemical individuality, insulin level, re-setting of appetite Centre and induction of deep sleep as well. Biochemical individuality is restored by correction of a dysfunctional liver and biorhythms. Low glycemic index based foods normalize insulin levels and control hunger. Quantity free food intake and a selection of favorite foods satisfies psychological appetite. Induction of night sleep gives proper time for liver rejuvenation resulting in optimum food absorption leading to satiety. A collective improvement in these factors is experienced in the form of satiety within two to three weeks. Everyone has their own built-in optimum appetite level and it takes approximately 4 – 8 weeks to normalize. People who are unable to control their appetite within this duration are badly suffering from insulin resistance, are pre-diabetics, have underlying infections, bad stress or hidden cancers as well. They need to focus more seriously on their lifestyle modification.

### *v-Correct food combination*

Selection of a natural and favorite food, with correct food intake timings become a total failure if foods combined are not compatible. Combination of various food groups result in production of end metabolites which effect blood ph, body temperature, neurotransmitters and release of various hormones especially insulin. Incompatible food combinations result in disruption of biorhythms which lead to toxin overload, free radicals and even cell death. A consistent intake of wrong food combination leads to a gradual development of diseases like liver and kidney disorder over a period of 15-20 years. While combining foods, their chemical groups have to be considered i.e. alkaline, neutral and acidic. Ideally one meal should have a combination of vegetables, meat, pulses and/or wheat or rice. Intake of enzyme rich fermented vegetables pickles or yogurt enhance food absorption. Intake of soups prior to meals enhance stomach activity and helps in digestion of meals.

All starters in the form of salads, crackers or soups are usually helpful in promoting the digestion of food. Combination of simple carbohydrates and complex carbohydrates in a single meal form a lethal chemical combination. This combination leads to a 'sugar shock' or 'reactive hypoglycemia' resulting in a bad fluctuation in insulin and blood sugar levels during the digestive process of a single meal. A fluctuating blood insulin level always declares a chemical emergency leading to the release of cortisol hormone. For compensation cortisol hormone induces sympathetic over activity leading to increased metabolic activity, palpitation, bloating, indigestion etc.The side effects of this sugar shock remain there for 3-5 days and put extra burden on heart, metabolism especially of fats, appetite control, joints and immune system. People who habitually take fruits, fizzy drinks, juices or desserts along with the food or after the meal suffer from various chronic diseases, metabolic disorders, obesity, and psychological disorders.

This dietary habit takes about 15-20 years to convert a healthy chemistry into diabetes, resistant obesity, cardiac ailments, autoimmune disorders, serious arthritis or cancers. Avoiding this combination leads initially to a feeling of well-being and after 4-6 weeks, halts ongoing disease processes. Simple sugars which include juices, fizzy drinks, fruits, or desserts has to be taken a minimum of thirty minutes before or three and half hours after the meals. Their Digestive time is only half an hour and complex carbohydrates need about three hours to digest. It proves combination of foods with different lengths of digestion period is not compatible.

Other important incompatible combinations are milk, tea or coffee with foods, which leads to stomach hyperacidity, digestive disorders, flatulence and bloating. Take these drinks either one hour before or three hours after the major meals. Try to take caffeinated drinks like tea, coffee or green tea with a little bit of raw sugar. Without adding raw sugar these drinks are very acidic, raw sugar makes them mild. Caffeinated drinks without sugar cause anxiety, bloating, and hyper pigmentation. Smoking and chewing betel nut or betel leaf after meals will toxify healthy nutrients in your foods, the toxic chemical adheres to food molecules and reaches deep into the cell and blood stream. Consumption of these addictive chemicals should be delayed for at least one and half hour after the food intake.

***vi-Food rotation***

Food rotation is required to make a natural food function more effectively. Repetition of the same food results in a chemical saturation of one group of nutrients. Raised level of one group of nutrients can upset blood ph and cause over production of one type of enzymes and body secretions. Food repetition can result in various side effects like excess of internal heat, dryness, coolness, dampness, disturb body temperature, and abnormal insulin levels. Repetition of same food activates the intrinsic homeostatic system for creating chemical balance and a phenomenon of mental rejection for that particular food or for a group of foods starts setting in. It forces that individual to stop eating that food and an automatic chemical re-adjustment is done by inducing cravings for other food group. By following a rotational pattern we can avoid chemical saturation and resulting blood imbalance.

My experience has taught me that repetition of the same type of food for even two consecutive days can result in a chemical imbalance. The body starts giving warning symptoms of excess of one type of nutrient after 48 hours. SLP does not allow repetition of the same food, I advise a food plan for four days and rotation has to be followed. Rotational diet is already established in various allergic disorders but it is an important component of diet correction and the rate of healing drastically declines with the consistent intake of the one type of food. People are doing this dietary blunder especially at their breakfast meal and therefore getting sick.

***vii-Food temperature***

The temperature of food is important for the optimum absorption of food. All components of a meal should be close to the body temperature. Boiling soups or fuming meals can damage the epithelial lining of gastrointestinal tract and lead to various gut related problems. Consistent intake of hot and spicy food creates restlessness and mental aggression. People are in the habit of combining hot foods with chilled water or chilled drinks. This is a commonly observed phenomenon globally and I can relate obesity to this unhealthy dietary habit as well. Chinese people are in a habit of drinking warm water which protects them from obesity and speedy aging. So taking care of food temperature is also an important part of diet correction rules. Patients who do not take food at body temperature show relatively slow recovery from their ailments.

***viii-Correct water intake***

Water intake on an average is 4 - 6 glasses in winter and 8-10 glasses in summers. SLP specifically mentions about the correct intake of plain water. Water is not recommended with meals and should be consumed either half an hour before meal or one and a half hour after a meal. Water taken with food dilutes stomach juices, slows emptying of the stomach, changes stomach ph and drops the stomach's temperature. Water with food causes abdominal swelling and makes abdominal muscles saggy as well. Incorrect water consumption disrupts several biorhythms. Water should ideally be taken in a sitting position and you should drink it slowly. Correct water intake can save us from stomach disorders, bloating, abdominal obesity and water retention. Only water can hydrate cells; therefore all other forms of liquids cannot replace the healing effects of plain water. Follow this saying ‘drink your food and chew your water’.

**5-Sleep regulation**

Restful sleep is an expression of holistic health which is a perfect integration of body, mind and soul. In real sleep, the body is deeply at rest, the metabolism is lowered and the mind becomes unconscious of the outside world. The process of rejuvenation and detoxification is activated at night while one is sleeping. The liver only gets rest in a deep sleep state especially if you sleep on right side and is recharged for the next day’s hectic bodily routine. In my practice I have seen many people who carry a sleep debt, which means they don’t get rejuvenating sleep. Hyper-active mind is the major factor causing sleep deprivation and therefore leads to chronic degenerative disorders.

Unfortunate part is people do not realize this sleep deprivation disorder. SLP pre-breakfast, breakfast and post-dinner snacks are important for inducing a sound sleep. 6-8 hours of nocturnal sleep is required for the reversal of a disease process, weight loss, stress management, and for the slowing of the mental aging process. Interestingly a person following the 8-rules of diet correction starts observing an improvement in sleep quality, its duration and starts getting sleep at night as well. Disturbed sleep pattern is related to a dysfunctional liver and vice versa, therefore both are interdependent. Sleep regulation is an important objective, and I have seen SLP gives poor results if the individual doesn’t’t get healthy night sleep.

## 6-Stress management

SLP diagnostic tools have made me learn about various types of stress generating chemistries. Type one stress is a manifestation of an acidic body with hypo-liver or a hyper-acidic body with hypo-liver body type. This pulse reflects an anxious person who is always in a competitive mode and sets difficult life goals for himself. The state of mental race mode gives him sense of achievement, ego and mental satisfaction. This constant state of stress ultimately leads to adrenal fatigue. This stress type is easily affected by environmental factors which include new assignments, examination, work stress, family issues, political unrest and other disturbances in society. This is not a permanent and deep stress and can be handled easily with SLP. Change of work environment also helps to settle this stress. SLP works by changing chemistry to an acidic body with normal liver chemistry, through eight rules of diet correction. By harmonizing the body chemistry, the same individual becomes more tolerant to the same stress triggering factors.

Type two stress is observed in patients of body type, acidic body with hyper-liver and in people with hyper-acidic body with hyper liver chemistry. This is a chronic stress, is deep seated and usually starts at the age of 10-12 years. It keeps on accumulating due to unhealthy lifestyle factors, repeated ailments, over medications, repeated intake of antibiotics and emotional traumas. This stress later results in serious mental disorders like schizophrenia, OCD, Alzheimer's etc. Dysfunctional liver is the root cause of this type of stress. Poor detoxification, toxic metabolites, improper assimilation of foods, and multiple nutritional deficiencies further aggravate this type of stress. Type two stress is subconscious, chemistry starts with a hyperactive mind syndrome and later develops into a fully blown mental disease.

This stress is the most common stress which I encounter in my daily practice. Whenever I find this chemistry I try to inquire about their hobbies, and make sure that they start practicing their hobbies for at least half an hour along with SLP. Few people themselves realize that this type of stress invaded their system since they have stopped allocating time for their hobbies, passions or sports. There is no blanket rule regarding healing with stress management techniques. The holistic therapist has to discover the individual's unique internal stress relieving tool. Reversal of the disease process is very much dependent on the level of stress management along with a change in the dietary habits. SLP can gradually eliminate this stress by rejuvenating the liver. Over a period of 3-6 months a remarkable change in the personality is observed and stress never gets stagnant and is managed easily.

Type three stresses found in acidic body with hyper-liver and water retention and acidic body with hypo-liver and water retention. People with this chemistry suffer from a very negative attitude, they always see the darker side of a situation, and want to remain aloof and easy crying is part of their personality. Self-talk is also part of above mentioned chemistry. Lethargy, and poor motivation, is part of their temperament. This stress shows the quickest response to diet correction and after only 4-6 weeks the patient shows a drastic change in their mental approach towards life.

**7-Exercise**

Human beings are designed for movement, because it activates musculoskeletal system, nerves, blood circulation and the lymphatic system. But one has to know the type of exercise, time of exercise and amount of exercise for his or her body type. Exercise process is highly individualized and should be carefully regulated. While exercising we burn extra oxygen and produce lot of free radicals and metabolites. Exercise should always be in an open and airy space and water intake before and after has to be monitored. In my practice I rarely see an individual whom I can advise a full set of exercise on the first visit. It takes about 2-4 weeks to fill their energy stores and build up their stamina to sustain exercise.

All human beings shift between six chemistry and none of the chemistry allows strenuous exercise. Acidic body with hyper liver indicates low oxygenation, high level of toxins and low level of antioxidants in the body. In this chemistry calcium is not absorbed properly and tissue levels of calcium are high, therefore ideal conditions for the osteoporosis. Exercise worsens this chemistry, as they are already vulnerable to joint problems, muscle cramps, and cardiac ailments. All cardio exercises worsen their cardiac status and set in an early heart disease. By speeding up heart rate a cardio exercise can't strengthen heart muscle rather it weakens heart muscle and accelerates cardiac aging. According to the rules of acupuncture excessive sweating is a sign of cardiac overload, and it is not at all a sign that fat is being burnt.

Acidic body with sluggish liver indicates slow metabolism, low sugar, low blood pressure, poor stamina and therefore body is not able to sustain exercise. Calcium absorption is poor and blood levels of calcium are very low. These individuals get temporally a boost of energy and toning of muscles but it lasts only for a few weeks and then the muscles start sagging. Worst affected are females because they develop cellulites on their body which cannot be reversed. Wrong exercise mobilizes fat from upper body to lower body and cellulites are formed. Pelvic joints of females get loosen and a pear shape is the outcome of wrong selection of set of exercises and later this body becomes resistant to all types of workouts. Another adverse effect of exercise in this chemistry is early wrinkling of facial skin and a drained face. Weight loss or size loss is short lived and it de-shapes permanently the natural body musculature.

People with water retention are also badly affected by wrongly prescribed exercise, they lose and gain weight quickly but there is no size loss. Due to the strain from exercise, fluid shifts from one body area to another and abnormal body shapes emerge. Non-compatible body exercise causes irreversible damage to the bone structure, muscles, face and enhance organ aging especially of heart and liver. Other side effects of wrong exercise are irritability, mood swings, depression, and insomnia. My suggestion to all exercise experts is that, they should learn about various body chemistry and then suggest the exercises accordingly.

In a holistic health care program exercise has a 20% role in maintaining health. A holistic natural diet should be started 4-6 weeks before starting an exercise regimen, only then exercise can play its role. Exercise in a weak body can cause various levels of oxidative damage.

Exercise is part of my lifestyle modification program and is recommended at least after two weeks of starting the SLP. It has to be done for at least 30 minutes and five times a week. For men I advise open air walks, jogging and gym exercises; however the healthiest option is sporty activities. As the female body is a tender body and is less muscular, my recommendation for them is open air walk, yoga, aerobics and sports. Yoga is the only exercise which is holistic because it can work on chakras and endocrine glands along with the physical body. Yoga is rejuvenating, anti-aging and allowed in almost all disease conditions and all age groups. I am a great fan of yoga and have practiced it for the past thirty years. Breathing exercises in routine are helpful for mental rejuvenation and can cure a hyperactive mind too.

**8-Food supplements**

SLP recommends food supplements at an appropriate time in the lifestyle modification program. Many patients coming to me bring with them big jars of food supplements that have been suggested by friends, family, colleagues and health magazines. You have to use supplements only according to the individual need. On their first visit I normally stop all supplements, because these are of no use in their problems. Only supplements which help the liver in recovering are enzymes or probiotics. Once the process of natural detoxification completes, then after 4-8 weeks food supplements like antioxidants and essential fatty acids are added. NES guides me about the level of various vitamins and minerals and they are added if required. Supplements are ideally recommended for three months followed by an interval of four weeks for detoxification and then can be started again. One of the Harvard University research says incorrect or excessive intake of vitamins can reduce your life span.

Following is a SLP sample holistic food plan:

**SLP Holistic food Plan**

SLP is a freedom based food program, free from all bonding and it never restricts quantity or calorie value of a food. The natural or organic foods should be taken in a fulfilling quantity. Select four options and take them in rotational pattern at their correct timings.

***Pre-breakfast:*** within first few minutes of waking up

1. 2-3 dates
2. 2-3 figs
3. 2-3 prunes
4. 2-3 dried apricots
5. Honey water
6. 8-10 raisins
7. 8-10 blue berries or gogi berries
8. 5-7 almonds
9. 2-3 walnuts
10. 5-7 cashews
11. Organic seeds
12. 8-10 peanuts
13. 6-7 pistachio
14. 8-10 pine nuts
15. fruit

30 minutes later take breakfast or a second PBF

***Second Pre-breakfast:***

1. Yogurt+ cane sugar
2. Raw warm milk+ raw sugar
3. Mix fruits
4. Mix nuts
5. Milk coffee + sugar

Breakfast should be taken within one to two hours of second PBF

***Breakfast:*** select one option/day and take it in a fulfilling quantity.

Whole grain bread/Roti/whole grain pita with following options

1. omelet/fried egg/scrambled egg
2. potato (with skin)
3. kabab/meat
5. fish/prawns
6. organ meat
7. organic jam
8. cheese

9-hummus

Other options are

1. Organic cereal+ raw milk+ raw sugar
2. French toast
3. Stuffed prathas
4. Organic desserts

Green tea + raw sugar in small quantity

***Lunch / snacks:*** Avoid breads, chapatti, rice, pita, nan and raw salads

1. Noodles /pasta
2. Chana chat / dahibarey
3. Beans/ chick peas/ hommus

4. Mix fruits
5. Fruit yogurt / smoothies/ shakes/cold coffee
6. Fish/ kababs/ steaks
7. Compound salads
8. Soups
9. French fries/ baked / mashed potato
10. Corn
11. Mix nuts and seeds
12. Natural energy bar
13. Desserts
14. Coffee+ desserts

***Evening snack:*** three to four hours after lunch

1. Mix fruits
2. Mix nuts
3. Dessert
4. Coffee
5. Nimko

***Dinner:***

Routine meal

Green tea + raw sugar

***Post dinner snack-PDS*:** Take only if the gap between meal and sleep is of 3 hours or more.

1. Raw warm milk + little raw sugar
2. Mix fruits
3. Mix nuts
4. Dessert

## CHAPTER NO: 8

## SLP FOLLOW UPS

SLP food plan is recommended for 4-6 weeks and then first follow up is being done. Prognosis is assessed by listening to the complaints again, pulse analysis, weight check, and abdominal measurements. After four weeks an improvement is observed which is between 30 to 50% if about 90% of the recommended food plan has been adhered to. Rest of the improvement comes within the next two months only if SLP eight rules of diet correction are followed correctly. Rate of recovery is also dependent on other factors which are level of motivation for self care, age, duration of illness and mental state. I have observed various types of clinical responses to SLP:

I. It depends how soon you start pampering and loving yourself.

II. A person suffering from a serious ailment but having a positive and humorous nature responds better than a person having minor ailment but with a negative / sad personality.

III. People involved in social projects normally have good mental and physical resistance, therefore quick recovery. Their holistic projects and their healthy soul assist them in quick recovery.

IV. People who practice religion with conviction recover faster.

V. Good response is observed in people who practice yoga, breathing exercise and go for an open air walk regularly. People who have drained their body by strenuous indoor exercises have poor immunity.

VI. Family collectively following the SLP responds better than individuals as they develop an internal support and competition amongst themselves for good health.

VII. Patients on antidepressants, steroids or other medications show poor response.

VIII. Politicians and business executives with their low priority to health respond poorly.

IX. Response in children is best but dependent on the dietary modification of their mother and family as well.

X. Patients of acidic body with hyper-liver grade 3 chemistry have delayed response. They need family support to recover from their ailment and motivation as well. It takes longer period to erase chronic emotional traumas from their cell memory. Acidic body type with hypo liver is a chemistry which always responds better.

XI. An interesting observation is that people who eat various types of healthy sweet foods have positive approach towards life. Therefore they might recover completely from serious ailments which include advanced cancer as well.

A follow up of the biochemical profile, NES, and ultrasound is done after 10-12 week. Prognosis depends upon the type and stage of the disease, regarding medicine intake there is a gradual decline in the dosage and later there is no need for medicines. Diabetes and high blood pressure are two easily manageable disorders and both start responding positively within 3-4 weeks. Arthritis, allergies or autoimmune disorders show improvement after 4-5 weeks. Other chronic disorders like heart disease, cancer, hepatitis, hormonal disorders usually respond after 6-8 weeks and reversal observed in 1-2 years.

After 4-6 weeks basic dietary modification, I decide to add food supplements like antioxidants, probiotics, or digestive enzymes, if needed by the body. If the diet plan is followed up to 90% and the clinical prognosis is less than 30% then a short emergency diet plan of 5-7 days with quick results is prescribed. After this short diet plan the patient is supposed to come again after one week, if pulse shows improvement, the patient is on the healing path but will get delayed healing. Some hidden ailments like cancer or autoimmune disorders also delay the response and the patient needs thorough investigation.

Following are the details of a retrospective study conducted at my clinic, to see how lifestyle, dietary routine and disease are interrelated.

**A retrospective study conducted at Lahore Medical Spa**

**(21-5-08 to 31-5-10)**

***Abstract***

A general decline in health status, uncontrolled obesity and early age onset of all degenerative disorders has forced the medical community to look for other causes of health deterioration. Unnatural lifestyle factors are the major contributors in depleting organ reserves and leading to systemic diseases. This study examines the effects of poor dietary discipline; disturb nocturnal sleep and effects of routine exercise on liver and biorhythms. The author has conducted this retrospective study on a sample of 2542 patients coming to her general clinic for their chronic ailments like stomach disorders, allergies, various stages of diabetes, hypertension, arthritis, obesity and cancer.

Evaluation of the lifestyle included presenting complains, personal profile, past medical history, psychological and family history. General physical examination, and work routine, which included wake up time, major meals and snack timings, type of food and food combinations, frequency of junk food intake, amount and time of water intake, amount of night sleep, stress management and time allocated for the exercise.

Over the past two years during routine consultation a "patient profile"form was filled, which provided the author with the required details. Out of 2542 patients 1664 were having chronic medical disorders and were having various levels of dysfunctional liver due to an unhealthy lifestyle. Only 214 were living on a partially natural and healthy lifestyle, and they were keen to have more awareness about the holistic health.

The majority was on a "Diet Control"type of regimen, but most of them were unable to maintain their weight and the disease prognosis was bad, because their liver was dysfunctional. After coming to the author's clinic, a liver specific lifestyle modification plan was given and follow up was done for two years. The results of the study confirmed the direct relationship between the unhealthy lifestyle and liver health, which leads to obesity, psychological disorders, aging and poor prognosis of a degenerative disorder. The author intends to use this study to provide a basis for an awareness campaign of a healthy dietary routine to preserve liver and improve its health.

Key Words: un-natural life style, lifestyle, liver, dysfunctional liver, dietary routine, obesity, biorhythm, degenerative disorders, cancer, night sleep, holistic health

Presenter:Dr.ShaguftaFeroz

Investigators: Ayesha, Neelum, Henna

***Method of conducting study***

A random sample of volunteer patients were selected, who had come for their routine consultations. The results of this study was evaluated on 2542 patients over the past two years ( 21-5-08—31-5-10 ). The objective of this study was to find a relationship between their lifestyle and medical problems.

***Total number of patients***

Table 1

| Total patients | Females | Males |
|---|---|---|
| 2542 | 1900 | 642 |

***Objective of consultation***

After knowing the patient's personal details, the objective of coming to the Centre was investigated.1664 patients came for their weight management, 664 came with various chronic degenerative disorders(CDD) and only 214 were interested in their holistic well-being. This result proves that people are more interested in their physical appearance as compare to holistic health, and they only consult a doctor when they are sick. A very small number of people were interested in the preventative aspect of their health.

Table 2

| Holistic health | Degenerative disease-CDD | Weight management |
|---|---|---|
| 214 | 664 | 1664 |

664 patients were suffering from arthritis, diabetes, cardiac ailment, respiratory disorder, various allergies, hypertension, cancer and depression. Out of 1664 obese patients, 980 came only for their weight loss and 684 were suffering from obesity and chronic degenerative diseases as well. Most of the females with obesity were having pear shape body, which is related to hyper-liver chemistry.

***Past medical history***

Table 3

| Liver disease | Typhoid | Allergic dis. | Surgery/med.intake |
|---|---|---|---|
| 288 | 368 | 318 | 515/297 |

Out of 2542 patients 1786 had gone through various types of biochemical traumas to their liver. 288 had different types of hepatitis; liver disturbing history of typhoid was present in 368. Over exposure to medications and surgery was done on 812 patients. As majority was female, therefore history of minor surgeries and caesarian section was there. Exposure to general anesthesia adds to the problem of dysfunctional liver.

***Breakfast routine***

Table 4

| No breakfast | Within 30-60 min. | After 2 – 3hours |
|---|---|---|
| 758 | 628 | 1156 |

People were not at all serious about the intake of breakfast, and they were not aware of the correct food types and breakfast timings. The breakfast was always done in great hurry or few were trying to manage a very late breakfast at their workplace.

*Breakfast details*

Table 3

| Bran / Packaged cereal / Toast | Natural food |
|---|---|
| 1922 | 620 |

Poor time management in the morning forced them to select those foods which were ready to eat, like packaged cereals, bran products, or biscuits. Very small percentage was on healthy food options, but was taking late breakfast and there was repetition of the same foods as well.

***Lunch timings***

Table 4

| No lunch | Lunch | Snacks |
|---|---|---|
| 634 | 1634 | 274 |

According to the study the most important meal was lunch, and few were trying to skip their dinner as well. Because of the poor quality breakfast or no breakfast people were taking tea, coffee, juices or biscuits throughout the day. People who were taking a full meal at lunch time were obese, with pot bellies and were suffering from digestive disorders and other diseases too.

***Dinner time***

Table 5

| No dinner | Bet. 7 – 9 p.m. | Bet. 9 – 11 p.m. |
|---|---|---|
| None | 1212 | 1330 |

Most of the people were disciplined regarding taking dinner but in most cases it was late night. They were having bigger meals with many incompatible food combinations and the interval between sleep and meal was either less than 2 hours or more than 3-4 hours.

***Water intake***

Number of glasses in summers

Table 6

| Less than 8 | Between. 8-10 | Between. 11– 25 |
|---|---|---|
| 1234 | 868 | 440 |

*Temperature of water*

Table 7

| Plain | Cold | Chilled |
| --- | --- | --- |
| 381 | 1967 | 194 |

***Timings of water intake***

Table 8

| 30 min. before meals | During meals | 1.5hrs. after meals |
| --- | --- | --- |
| 190 | 2086 | 266 |

Table 8,9,10 shows that incorrect water intake is another very important contributory factor in unhealthy eating pattern. Summer season intake of water is estimated, because excess intake of water in summer leads to water retention related diseases of winter. 1234 patients were taking less than eight glasses, 868 were on 8-10 glasses, and 440 were on 11-25 glasses of water. Majority was in a habit of taking water with food therefore most of them had abdominal distention, water retention and digestive disorders.

***Junk food***

Frequency of junk food / week

Table 9

| 1-2x / week | 3-4x / week | 4-6 x / week |
|---|---|---|
| 1684 | 670 | 188 |

The culture of routine junk food intake has badly affected our society in last ten years. All fried or baked food products made with white flour, sugar and hydrogenated cooking oils fall into the category of junk food.

***Sugar / salt preference***

Table 10

| Sugar | Salt |
|---|---|
| 1068 | 1474 |

Food preference gives an idea about the body type; this factor reveals that majority were acidic with hyper liver, because their preference was for salty foods. People, who were fond of sugary foods, were taking sugary foods at the wrong timing which was further adding to their chemical imbalance. They were taking drinks, desserts, or fruits with food or right after the meal.

***Heat / cold intolerance***

Table 13

| Normal | Heat | Cold |
|---|---|---|
| 522 | 1374 | 646 |

Above values again give an idea about the body chemistry. A hyper-liver mostly generates heat, and person suffers from burning hands and feet. Summer makes them uncomfortable and sick.

***Exercise / walk***

Table 14

| Yes | No |
|---|---|
| 1507 | 1035 |

Many people think that workout has got a solution to their obesity; therefore they were doing various vigorous exercises. Whereas wrong selection of set of exercises and an unhealthy lifestyle further aggravates their chemistry and metabolism.

***Sleep time***

Table 15

| 11 p.m.—12 mn | 12.00---2 a.m. | Later than 2 a.m. |
|---|---|---|

| 870 | 1060 | 612 |
|---|---|---|

Majority were not having 6-8 hours of nocturnal sleep. People sleeping later than 1a.m. were having various health issues and early mental aging signs like impaired memory or lack of concentration.

***Pulse analysis***

Table 16

| AD+L 1,2,3 | AD—L | AD2+L | AD2--L | AD+L+WR | AD—L+WR |
|---|---|---|---|---|---|
| 971 | 411 | 167 | 154 | 590 | 249 |

971 were having acidic body with various grades of hyper-liver, and 590 were acidic with hyper-liver and different levels of water retention. 167 were hyper-acidic with hyper-liver. So 1728 out of 2542 were having hyper-liver.

Only 814 out of 2542 were with sluggish liver. This study supports the basis of SLP, by proving that unhealthy dietary pattern leads to a hyper-liver state. This chemistry is the root cause of most of the pathologies.

Summarizing above, people think that processed foods are healthy options because these are scientifically controlled. Approximately 90% were confused by the food caloric values and they imposed low calorie foods in their dietary routine which was making them further unhealthy. Unfortunately they have introduced processed and low calorie foods in the life of their children too, which is a leading factor to childhood obesity and their other health disorders.

Obesity was the most common complaint of patients, and despite following many crash diet plans and strenuous exercise plan many were suffering from weight gain/loss syndrome. Half of the obese patients were having various medical disorders as well.

**Relationship between unhealthy lifestyle and obesity**

Following is an account of various unhealthy lifestyle factors and their role in weight gain

I. Unhealthy meal timings = 100%

II. Unhealthy food choices = 100%

III. Low calorie foods = 100%

IV. Less or no exercise = 25%

V. Poor night sleep = 50%

VI. Poor stress management = 66%

**Relationship between an unhealthy lifestyle and chronic disease**

I. Unhealthy meal timings = 100%

II. Unhealthy food choices = 100%

III. Skipping of breakfast = 100%

IV. Poor night sleep = 60%

V. Poor stress management = 70%

**Results of SLP follow up**

1987 patients came back for multiple follow up visits during the last two years. 90 % of them tried to modify their existing life style. The most important awareness which was successfully created was the habit of taking a healthy breakfast. They were religiously following the intake of pre-breakfast and learnt the importance of PBF. Approximately 85% have corrected their meal timings, meal combinations and food type. Most of them tried to follow the eight rules of diet correction. All of them gradually started reducing intake of lunch, initially by reducing the quantity of food and after one to three months they stopped intake of lunch and were satisfied with snacks and were feeling good after skipping lunch.

Majority of them had corrected their water intake, number of glasses were carefully counted and they started avoiding intake of water with their meals. Only 30% shifted to plain water and rest were taking cold water. 90% of those who came back for follow up were also avoiding the lethal combination of simple and complex carbohydrates. They avoided intake of cold drinks, fruits, desserts or juices with their meals and were experiencing improvement in post meal distention, gas and indigestion. Most of them avoided repetition of same foods on consecutive days and tried to take foods which were organic or naturally grown. Incorporation of natural foods was gradual, especially organic chicken and eggs, whole wheat breads, cane sugar, natural milk and natural butter.

Out of these 1987 patients 1598 tried to sleep before the mid night. 1150 tried to add 15 -30 minutes of relaxation in the form of more family interaction, reading, listening to good music or some religious therapy. One common experience which everybody mentioned was a feeling of well-being after two weeks of SLP. As I mentioned earlier after the initial process of detoxification, liver works on the repair of immune system. Feeling of well-being is an expression of two third of your total body cells which are, immune cells. This good feeling helps in developing trust on this new way of lifestyle.

Table 17 explains in detail individual response to the diet correction rules, and response to other components of SLP.

Table 17

| Correction of meal timing | 1950 |
|---|---|
| Correction of food type | 1456 |
| Correct water intake | 1490 |
| Correction of food combination | 1887 |
| No repetition of food | 1901 |
| No mixing of simple/complex carb. | 1975 |
| Correction of sleep pattern | 1598 |
| Stress management | 150 |

This study proves that Liver Specific Life Style Modification helps in giving holistic health, improves psycho social behavior and if adopted permanently helps in the reversal of a disease over a period of time.

**SLP Wellness tips**

I would like to summarize SLP here, try to adopt these simple tips, and you will experience holistic wellness. Remember this is not a direct weight shedding program; weight loss is a bye product, in fact SLP works on the root causes of obesity.

1. Now onwards select only natural foods like whole grain breads or chapati, raw dairy, organic poultry, raw sugar and natural Pakistani kwera salt called Himalayan salt in the international market.
2. Harmonize your lifestyle with nature by following correct meal and sleep timings.
3. Body clock timings are applicable to all humans of different ages, therefore correct your children food timings as well.
4. Try to take a body compatible meal by listening to your food preferences. Your body compatible food can vary with your changing chemistry therefore adjusts natural favorite foods accordingly.
5. Be careful about food combinations; don't give frequent sugar shocks to your body by combining sweet and salty foods together.
6. Water is not as gentle as you think; it can kill a person as well, so its intake should be carefully regulated.
7. Don't forget to rotate your foods; otherwise repetition of same food is going to make you sick.
8. Food temperatures matter a lot for the proper functioning of the liver, so avoid taking very cold or hot foods. The temperature of food should be close to your body temperature.
9. Don't forget to pamper your mind every day, by deputing little time for your hobby or passion every day.
10. Energize your universal being by doing something positive for the humanity.

## Food myths

Rectify your following food myths, which I have proven clinically.

1. Calorie myth: there is no calorie control Centre in the human body, so please stop counting food calories.
2. Sugar is fattening: healthy sugar is not fattening. Moderate intake of raw sugar or dessert keeps you happy, stimulates your creativity and protects you from depression. Remember sugar is a brain fuel.
3. Excess of water intake: over hydration of body is not good for skin or kidneys therefore do not intoxicate your body with water.
4. Fat free diet: It will never make you slim. Enjoy healthy fat, they will control your weight.
5. Cholesterol is a killer: cholesterol is the mother of all hormones, therefore ignore high cholesterol, handle your stress and adopt SLP eight rules of diet correction to keep lipids at normal level.
6. Fresh fruits, raw foods and salad are very healthy: they are not because have high water content and they fall in a weak nutritional category. You need nutrient dense foods for optimum health. So be moderate about the intake of fruits and especially raw vegetables.
7. Potatoes are fattening: Potatoes satisfy your hunger and are happy food. Their skin contains GTF factor, which helps in maintaining the insulin level, therefore indirectly help in the weight loss and diabetes control. Potato pulp is acidic and peel is alkaline.
8. One big meal eaten at an erratic time would never givehealth therefore respectyour body clock rhythm.
9. Food portion control is absolutely not under your control, forced portion control of food leads to rebound obesity.
10. Biggest myth is food makes you obese, truth is erratic food intake makes you obese.

**My recent clinical experience**

In September –October 2010 and 2011 we had an outbreak of dengue in Lahore and other cities of Pakistan. Medical community was helpless in terms of controlling this disease. This was my first clinical experience to such a huge number of dengue patients. Besides symptomatic management doctors were advising them to take a nutritious diet therefore I got an opportunity to see patients with their acute disease state. On pulse analysis of dengue patients, I found mostly acidic body with hyper-liver chemistry and few were with acidic body and sluggish liver chemistry. In my opinion these two chemistries were indicating various grades of dengue fever. A careful organization of a body compatible diet led to the increase in the number of platelets from few thousands to hundred thousand in three to five days.

I remember one female dengue patient having about 20-25 blood stained stools was having only 36000 platelets in CBC report. With SLP it increased to 145,000 in five days and associated symptoms start settling. In my opinion all serious diseases deplete body proteins which they use as their messengers. Dengue patients have shown remarkable recovery to repeated intake of two proteins rich foods bone broth and half boiled organic eggs. The main focus of treatment was immunity enhancement and reassurance to overcome their fear. My experience on few hundred patients taught me that dengue is a disease of unhealthy dietary habits, weak immune system, and weak mind. Whereas conventional system labels it a disease of mosquito, virus and man. Unfortunately during this epidemic government healthcare system has exposed people to more serious future diseases by consuming loads of insecticides spray in cities.

In November 2010, I got a chance to perform pilgrimage (Haj) in the holy city of Mecca, Saudi Arabia. It is the world's largest religious gathering, and when the pilgrimage is over, most of the participants suffer from an allergic cough which last for about 2-3 months. Besides my religious obligations, I was trying to find cause of this cough as well. I observed that foods served were mainly rice, chicken and bakery food. I got a chance to do pulse analysis of people coming from different countries. As Haj program is for 20 or 40 days, after about two weeks of stay high fatigue, pollution and poor selection of food types lead to hyper-liver chemistry. This hyper-liver is unable to detoxify the blood and people start having allergic cough. People were on heavy dosage of antibiotics but cough was resistant to all medication. For such a huge gathering government cannot control pollution, but I learnt that by introducing healthy foods cough intensity and duration can be controlled. On coming back I took only one week to recover from this cough because of detoxification sessions and intake of natural foods.

In April 2011 I got a chance to attend an integrated medicine IMOSAIC conference in Minneapolis MN, USA. The conference speakers had an updated and advanced knowledge about their fields. With great pain I realized that medical science is going into unnecessary physical body details which do not play any role in healing. Conventional system is spending huge amount of funds on mega researches focusing on highly advanced diagnostic equipment. The outcome of the medical researches is never holistic, because humans are considered individual physical entity. Conventional medicine is totally ignorant about the importance of a missing key to health which is liver and biorhythms. By learning about biorhythms, conventional science will realize about the energy system of mind and soul as well.

In October 2011 I got a chance to attend a conference on Quantum medicine in Honolulu Hawaii, it was an amazing experience. The collaboration of Physicists and doctors have led to the emergence of quantum medicine which explains the relationship between body, mind, and spirit. They concluded that subtle energy or life force belongs to 96% of the universal energy and human mind is capable of directing subatomic subtle energy. They talked about the role of epigenetic, quantum leap and quantum healing in health and disease management, which are extremely simple to understand. I hope these upcoming sciences will soon update the conventional medicine and will lessen the misery of the ailing humanity.

## CHAPTER NO: 9

## CHAOS BEFORE HARMONY: LIFESTYLE DISEASES

Lifestyle diseases or diseases of longevity or diseases of civilization are diseases that appear to increase in frequency as countries become more industrialized and people live longer. Lifestyle diseases are diseases that appear to become ever more widespread as countries become more industrialized. Lifestyle diseases are different from other diseases because they are potentially preventable, and can be lowered with changes in diet and lifestyle. Lifestyle diseases are a result of an inappropriate relationship of people with their environment which includes internal and external both. The onset of these lifestyle diseases is insidious, they take years to develop, and once encountered do not lend themselves easily to cure.

Conditions that slowly develop over many years as we age cause more deaths. These insidious diseases do not lend themselves to a quick fix by allopathic medicine. A recent research paper published in the prestigious Lancet, beautifully articulated the international variation in cancer rates. It proves the relationship of dietary habits and lifestyle diseases. "In many [western] countries, peoples' diet changed substantially in the second half of the twentieth century, generally with increases in consumption of meat, dairy products, vegetable oils, fruit juice, and alcoholic beverages, and decreases in consumption of starchy staple foods such as bread, potatoes, rice, and maize flour. Other aspects of lifestyle also changed, notably, large reductions in physical activity and large increases in the prevalence of obesity."

"It was noted in the 1970s that people in many western countries had diets high in animal products, fat, and sugar, and high rates of cancers of the colorectal, breast, prostate, endometrium, and lung by contrast, individuals in developing countries usually had diets that were based on one or two starchy staple foods, with low intakes of animal products, fat, and sugar, and low rates of these cancers." "These observations suggest that the diets [or lifestyle] of different populations might partly determine their rates of cancer, and the basis for this hypothesis was strengthened by results of studies showing that people who migrate from one country to another generally acquire the cancer rates of the new host country, suggesting that environmental [or lifestyle factors] rather than genetic factors are the key determinants of the international variation in cancer rates."

**Common Lifestyle Diseases are:**

***1-Alzheimer's disease***

No one knows the exact cause, but a real breakdown of the cells of the brain does occur. There is no treatment, but good nutrition may slow the progress of this lifestyle disease, which lasts about seven years in most people who have it.

***2-Arteriosclerosis***

A generic term for several diseases in which the arterial wall becomes thicken and loses elasticity. Atherosclerosis is the most common and serious vascular disease. Plaques (atheromas) deposited in the walls of arteries are major causes of heart disease and other disorders of the circulation. In atherosclerosis yellowish plaques of cholesterol, fats, and other remains are deposited in the walls of large and medium-sized arteries. Atherosclerosis usually occurs with aging. It is linked to overweight, high blood pressure, and diabetes.

***3-Cancer***

Diseases characterized by uncontrolled, abnormal growth of cells. Cancer is definitely considered the number one disease of civilization. There are more than 150 different kinds of cancer and many different lifestyle causes.

***4-Chronic Liver Disease/Cirrhosis***

My experience has revealed that 100% of patients coming to my clinic have some level of dysfunctional liver. Dysfunctional liver indicates unhealthy dietary pattern. This dysfunctional liver leads to chronic liver disease and other lifestyle diseases over a period of about 10-20 years.

***5-Chronic Obstructive Pulmonary Disease (COPD)***

A disease characterized by slowly progressing, irreversible airway obstruction. The condition may result from chronic bronchitis, emphysema, asthma, or chronic bronchiolitis. Lot of un-natural foods, environmental pollution is important contributory factors. Cigarette smoking, improper breathing, air conditioned rooms and air pollution make it worse.

***6-Diabetes Mellitus***

Diabetes is a lifestyle disease results from stress, erratic dietary pattern and lack of physical rest. There are four main types of diabetes mellitus. Type I diabetes or insulin-dependent diabetes, type II diabetes or non-insulin-dependent diabetes, adult-onset diabetes. Type III, or gestational diabetes, occurs in some women during pregnancy. Type IV includes other types of diabetes which are linked to disease of the pancreas, hormonal changes, side effects of drugs, or genetic defects.

***7-Cardiovascular disease***

An unhealthy lifestyle factor affecting the heart muscle or the blood vessels of the heart leads to cardiac disease.

***8-Nephritis / Chronic renal parenchyma disease***

Kidney disorders are result of a diet rich in artificial and processed foods, incorrect intake of water and over usage of pharmaceutical medicines.

### *9-Stroke*

A condition due to the lack of oxygen to the brain that may lead to reversible or irreversible paralysis. Stroke is linked to advanced age, high blood pressure, previous attacks of poor circulation, cigarette smoking, heart disorders, embolism, and family history of strokes, use of birth-control pills, diabetes mellitus, lack of exercise, overweight, high cholesterol, and hyperlipidemia.

### *10-Obesity*

Obesity has reached epidemic proportions in the United States. One in three Americans is obese. The prevalence of obesity in children has increased markedly, with approximately 20%-25 % of children either overweight or obese. Obesity is also increasing rapidly throughout the world, and the incidence of obesity nearly doubled from 1991 to 1998.

### *11-Polycystic ovary syndrome (PCOS)*

It affects about 5% to 10% of reproductive age women in the United States and is considered the most common endocrine abnormality among them. In recent years, it has become evident that beyond a reproductive or cosmetic problem, PCOS represents a metabolic risk. Many women with PCOS have hypertension, impaired glucose tolerance, lipid abnormalities, obesity, or any combination of these. Even those patients who are seen for infertility "only" need to be screened for these metabolic risk factors, and they require counseling regarding this risk and its management.

Studies have shown that lifestyle changes (in this case, intensive exercise with a goal of ≥150 min/week of activity) resulting in weight loss reduced the risk Of type 2 diabetes. The same studies found lifestyle changes to be superior to metformin. Thus, all women with PCOS should be encouraged to follow a healthy diet and to engage in regular exercise. Their chance to achieve a pregnancy will improve and the risks during pregnancy will be reduced. A healthier lifestyle will also reduce their long-term risks for diabetes, hypertension, dyslipidemia, and cardiovascular disease. It is important for all primary care providers to identify patients who may have PCOS. These patients need to undergo the appropriate screening tests and should be counseled about diet and exercise. Pharmacologic intervention could be combined with this approach as appropriate, but the above-mentioned studies suggest that lifestyle modification is the first-line of treatment.

### *11-Male Infertility*

Food nutrients are used to form healthy male hormones with the assistance of a healthy liver. High stress jobs, busy lifestyle and poor quality foods have affected male reproductive health as well. Physical signs like early onset of baldness, gynaecomastia, and fats on lower body indicate bad hormonal balance.

### *12-Metabolic syndrome*

It is a combination of medical disorders that increase the risk of developing cardiovascular disease and diabetes. It affects one in five people, and prevalence increases with age. Some studies estimate the prevalence in the USA to be up to 25% of the population.

### *13- Hormone Replacement Therapy (HRT)*

Though not technically a disease, HRT is a lifestyle fad, which leads to many health complications. Hormone replacement therapy, as a term, first came up in the 1960's in the book called "Forever Feminine" by Dr. Robert Wilson. The book had the theory that menopause was a disease that could be treated by simply replacing the estrogen their bodies had stopped producing, in order to hold back the aging process. But in the last four decades, women have been prescribed HRT for all sorts of reasons not just to stop menopausal hot flushes and night sweats but to improve sex life, their hair and skin and even the morale. The crucial difference between HRT and other hormonal treatment is that HRT is prescribed to counter act the natural reduction of estrogen in the body but studies have now shown that it is actually the opposite. A study in the UK called Million Women Study has shown that HRT has caused 1000 deaths from ovarian cancer in the last decade and a half. It has been linked with invasive breast cancer, womb cancer, stroke, blood clot and coronary heart diseases. In a bid to look young, women are using HRT as a preventive measure to look young but legally and worldwide, work on Hormone replacement therapy has been discontinued since the mid 90's.

***14-Multiple Sclerosis***

Multiple Sclerosis (MS) is said to be a degenerative disease of the nervous system. It affects the brain and spinal cord, destroys the myelin sheath, the material that surrounds and protects the nerve cells. This damages, slows down and blocks messages between the brain and the body leading to the symptoms of MS. These include visual disturbances, muscle weakness, trouble with co-ordination and balance, sensations such as numbness and severe memory problems. While no one knows what causes MS, It is said to be an auto immune disease, which happens when the body attacks itself. It affects more women than men and starts between the ages of 20 and 24. Its incidence is increasing because of the change in lifestyle and bad food habits in people. These diseases remain indicators of the changing times and the overwhelming problems that we need to deal with on a daily basis.

## *15-Modern technology and lifestyle diseases*

### *I-Computer related diseases*

i-Carpal Tunnel Syndrome

A painful progressive condition caused by the compression of a key nerve in the wrist, this syndrome is the result of working on the computer endlessly. The median nerve, which runs from the forearm into the hand, becomes pressed or squeezed at the wrist. The carpal tunnel, a narrow, rigid passageway of ligaments and bones at the base of the hand, houses the median nerve and tendons. Symptoms usually start gradually with frequent burning, tingling or an itching numbness in the palm of the hand and the fingers, especially the thumb, index and middle fingers. As symptoms worsen, people might experience a tingling sensation during the day. Decreased grip strength may make it difficult to form a fist, grasp small objects or perform small tasks. In chronic or untreated cases, the muscles at the base of the thumb may waste away. Some people are unable to differentiate between hot and cold by touch. Persons with diabetes or other metabolic disorders that directly affect the body's nerves and make them more susceptible to compression are also at high risk.

ii-Thoracic outlet syndrome

One of the computer related diseases that is caused by repetitive activities. You should make short and long pauses and have rest during your workday to prevent thoracic outlet syndrome. Moreover you should do exercises for your neck, back, and hands during long pauses.

iii-Computer Vision Syndrome

Computer vision syndrome (CVS) is a temporary condition resulting from focusing the eyes on a computer display for protracted, uninterrupted periods of time. Some symptoms of CVS include headaches, blurred vision, neck pain, fatigue, eye strain, dry, irritated eyes, and difficulty refocusing the eyes. These symptoms can be further aggravated by improper lighting conditions or air moving past the eyes (e.g. overhead vents, direct air from a fan). CVS has not been proven to cause any permanent damage to the eye.

iv-Back pain

Microsoft revealed that 68% of workers suffer from aches and pains, which include back ache, and shoulder pain and pains in hands and wrists. One of the methods of prevention or reduction back pains is taking breaks, having a rest and doing exercises and stretches for your back, neck during your workday.

v-DeQuervain's syndrome

DeQuervain's Syndrome is an inflammation of the sheath or tunnel that surrounds two tendons that control movement of the thumb. It is caused by the repetitive motion of the thumb constantly being required to move up and down (usually associated with using a computer keyboard or typewriter).

***II-Cell phones and their hazards***

More than 1,000 peer-reviewed, published studies form the basis for establishing the link between mobile phone use and a variety of health problems like:

i. Brain, eye and salivary gland tumors;
ii. Neurological diseases including Autism and Alzheimer's;
iii. Debilitating illnesses including electro-hypersensitivity, anxiety syndromes, sleep disorders, and depression;
iv. Exacerbation of immune, endocrine, gastrointestinal and reproductive system symptoms

Early Warning Symptoms are fatigue, shortness of breath, lethargy, difficulty in sleep, short term memory lapses, daydreaming, loss of appetite or persistent diarrhea, sensitivity to sunlight and noise, impotence and sexual dysfunction, Ineffectiveness of prescription remedies

***III-Electromagnetic pollution***

Electro-magnetic fields have always been part of the earth's environment. Resonances occur between the earth's molten iron-nickel core and the charged gases of the ionosphere. These pulse at definite frequencies (between 0.1 and 25Hz; mostly at about 10Hz), and act as regulators for the biological time clocks of all living creatures. If man, or any live animal or plant is totally shielded from these fields for any length of time the result is discomfort, disorientation, and even death. It has recently been shown that even each cell-division is timed according to these pulses. When the first astronauts were sent into space they returned suffering from the effects of being deprived of these fields; all subsequent spacecraft have had artificial field generators built in. These fields are generally called Schumann waves, and are a normal healthy phenomenon of our planet. Man evolved in electro-magnetic field should be quite capable of handling them, which remained true until this century.

In the 20th century alone, man has changed his electro-magnetic environment to its maximum. Strong electromagnetic fields (EMFs) of about 50 to 60 cycles per second (hertz, or Hz) and the related electromagnetic radiation (EMR) are harmful to us. EMR exists around power lines, power tools, electric stoves, heaters, boilers, microwaves, cell phones, freezers and television sets when in use, extending several feet or yards around the appliance. Stay away from them if possible. Using an electric iron or an electric keyboard or working with handheld power tools can quickly drain our energies. When working with electric equipment we can reduce harmful effects by holding our hands under running water from time to time in addition to having a shower in the evening or doing grounding by walking barefoot on grass early morning.

Long-term exposure may aggravate any existing health problems or diseases and may cause or intensify especially lack of energy or fatigue, irritability, aggression, hyperactivity, sleep disorders and emotional instability. Increasing numbers of individuals are becoming hypersensitive to EMR; many can feel the electricity going through the body and may experience disabling symptoms such as convulsions, memory problems and depression. Chronic exposure to high levels of

EMR, especially while asleep, is a constant drain on our vitality. It creates chronic stress, which interferes with the regeneration and healing that normally takes place during a good night's sleep.

Try to minimize electromagnetic pollution, especially while sleeping when the pineal gland is most susceptible. Also sleep in the dark or at least cover your eyes to produce the immune-stimulating hormone melatonin. Preferably switch off all power points in the bedroom and unplug all electric leads with 2-prong plugs before going to sleep but definitely any power points or leads close to the bed. This applies also to waterbeds which need to be unplugged overnight. If the head faces a wall with power-points or other electric wiring inside the wall close to the bed then move the bed towards the middle of the room so that you can walk around the bed. The best sleeping position is with the head towards north or otherwise somewhere between north and east.

***III-Hazards of Microwave***

According to Powerwatch, a non-profit independent organization with a central role in the microwave radiation debate: "Even when the microwave oven is working correctly, the microwave levels within the kitchen are likely to be significantly higher than those from any nearby cellular phone base-stations. Remember also that microwaves will travel through walls if the microwave oven is against an inside wall."

But even if there's nothing wrong with your microwave, standing a foot away from it while it's running can expose you to radiation of 400 milliGauss, and a mere 4 milliGauss has been firmly linked to leukemia. It would certainly be wise to avoid letting your children stand near the microwave when it's running, and avoid it yourself as much as possible—especially if you're pregnant. A recent study examining the effects 2.4 GHz radiation (which is the frequency of radiation emitted by Wifi routers and microwave ovens) on the heart was just completed. The study found "unequivocal evidence" that microwave frequency radiation affects the heart at non-thermal levels that are well below federal safety guidelines, according to Dr. Magda Havas of Trent University. Dr. Havas says:

"This is the first study that documents immediate and dramatic changes in both heart rate and heart rate variability caused by an approved device that generates microwaves at levels well below (0.3 percent) federal guidelines in both Canada and the United States."

Nevertheless, some excellent scientific data has been gathered regarding the detrimental effects of microwaves on the nutrients in your food: A study published in the November 2003 issue of *The Journal of the Science of Food and Agriculture*[5] found that broccoli "zapped" in the microwave with a little water lost up to 97 percent of its beneficial antioxidants. By comparison, steamed broccoli lost 11 percent or fewer of its antioxidants. There were also reductions in phenolic compounds and glucosinolates, but mineral levels remained intact. A 1999 Scandinavian study of the cooking of asparagus spears found that microwaving caused a reduction in vitamin C. In a study of garlic, as little as 60 seconds of microwave heating was enough to inactivate its allinase, garlic's principle active ingredient against cancer. A Japanese study by Watanabe showed that just 6 minutes of microwave heating turned 30-40 percent of the B12 in milk into an inert (dead) form. This study has been cited by Dr. Andrew Weil as evidence supporting his concerns about the effects of microwaving. Dr. Weil wrote: "There may be dangers associated with microwaving food... there is a question as to whether microwaving alters protein chemistry in ways that might be harmful." A recent Australian study showed that microwaves cause a higher degree of "protein unfolding" than conventional heating.

According to Professor Franz Adelkofer, a leading scientist in the area of biological effects of EMF fields:

"There is real evidence that hyper-frequency electromagnetic fields can have geno-toxic effects. And this damaged DNA is always the cause of cancer. We've found these damaging effects on the genes at levels well below the safety limits. That's why we think it's urgent to base our safety limits on the biological effects, not the thermic ones. They should be based on biology, not on physics."

The Powerwatch article cited above summarizes the Russian research and says; “Russian investigators found that carcinogens were formed from the microwaving of nearly all foods tested. The microwaving of milk and grains converted some of the amino acids into carcinogenic substances. Microwaving prepared meats caused the formation of the cancer-causing agents d-Nitrosodienthanolamines. Thawing frozen fruits by microwave converted their glucoside and galactoside fractions into carcinogenic substances. Extremely short exposure of raw, cooked or frozen vegetables converted their plant alkaloids into carcinogens. Carcinogenic free radicals were formed in microwaved plants especially root vegetables. Structural degradation leading to decreased food value was found to be 60 to 90 percent overall for all foods tested, with significant decreases in bioavailability of B complex vitamins, vitamins C and E, essential minerals, and lipotropics (substances that prevent abnormal accumulation of fat)."

Biophotons are the smallest physical units of light that are stored in and used by all biological organisms including you. Vital sun energy finds its way into your cells via the food you eat, in the form of these biophotons which contain important bio-information and are very important to many vital processes in your body. They are partly responsible for your feeling of vitality and well-being. You gain biophotons by eating foods rich in them, such as naturally grown fresh vegetables and sun-ripened fruits, which are rich in light energy. If the "microwave effect" exists then microwaves can potentially destroy biophotons in the same way that it alters other structures, rendering your food dead and lifeless. Swiss food scientist Hans Hertel wrote: "There are no atoms, molecules, or cells of any organic system able to withstand such a violent, destructive power for any period of time. This will happen even given the microwave oven's low power range of milliwatts."

### *IV- Few more lifestyle hazards*

#### *Toxic mattresses*

Some 30 or more years ago, mattresses were made of untreated, natural materials, but now most come to the store bearing a host of petrochemicals, flame retardants and other additives. The Consumer Products Safety Commission lists the following chemicals as the primary ones used in mattresses to meet current laws: boric acid, formaldehyde, antimony trioxide, decabromodiphenyl oxide, vinylidiene chloride, zinc borate, and melamine. The initial reason for adding fire retardants to mattresses was commendable -- fire marshals reported that more individuals died or were injured from mattresses or upholstered furniture catching fire than from any other type of fire. But we're now finding from growing reports of illnesses seemingly linked to mattress purchases that this solution may also have its serious drawbacks.

But there is another potential group of troublemakers in your mattress that you should be aware of and that is pesticide residue. And organophosphates are one pesticide type known to have serious, long-term effects on human health. But pesticide residues may not be limited to your mattress. Sheets and bed toppers -- made from various man-made and natural components -- can also be laden with it. And the residue of this "chemical stew" is being breathed in nightly by countless numbers of unsuspecting sleepers. For those with impaired immune systems a problem more and more common there can be serious health ramifications. Symptoms may range from a common headache or joint ache, to unexplained rashes, eczema, nosebleeds, dizziness even severe migraines, arthritis, ringing in the ears, nausea and more.

One South Dakota family reported the following after they bought a memory foam mattress pad and pillows from a popular discount store: "We went through problems for seven months. It started with minor problems and got worse - hives, kidneys hurting, swollen lips, flu feelings, cough, sore joints, etc. My wife was going to the doctor in an attempt to figure it out. We never suspected the pad and pillows. I finally ran across a Web site while considering what type of new bed to buy, in an attempt to resolve our problems. We removed the two memory foam pillows and the memory foam mattress pad, and within two days all problems were gone. Two months later, all is well." So conventional mattresses are pretty much full of nasty, toxic chemicals and made of materials that are linked to a huge list of serious health complications including SIDS, asthma, allergies, reproductive toxicity, respiratory problems, skin irritations, cancer, and more.

***Baby Pampers***

Numerous chemicals are emitted from commercial disposables pampers, such as those from the polypropylene liner and polyethylene backing. In fact, scientists have discovered that the chemicals in disposables, when inhaled, are toxic to the respiratory system. Although studied on mice, the response was clear and the researchers concluded that diapers should be considered as one of the factors that might cause or exacerbate asthmatic conditions. Disposable diapers contain bleached materials. Although the U.S. paper mill industry has made improvements to reduce toxic waste output over the last few years, concerns remain surrounding this process. Ultimately the manufacture of diapers with bleached products puts all humans and animal at higher risk for health damages.

Even more worrisome are the super-absorbent diapers, which often contain cross-linked sodium polyacrylate, a powder that turns to a gel in contact with liquid. This is the same substance associated with toxic shock syndrome from ultra-absorbent feminine hygiene tampons. Although negative health symptoms have not been directly linked in the case of diapers, these types of chemicals are just better to avoid, especially when they are in products in close contact with such sensitive areas of the body.

There is an often-cited study by Andersen Laboratories in 1999, published in the Archives of Environmental Health. In the study conducted on mice, scientists found that "diaper emissions were found to include several chemicals with documented respiratory toxicity," according to lead author Rosalind Anderson, a physiologist. She found that the mice suffered asthma-like symptoms when exposed to a variety of diaper brands. It was noted that xylene and ethyl benzene were emitted by the diapers, chemicals that are suspected endocrine, neurological and respiratory toxins; along with styrene, a chemical linked to cancer and isopropylene, a neurotoxin. Diapers contain a variety of plastics, adhesives, glues, elastics and lubricants, some of which can cause irritation.

**Lifestyle diseases and death**

It said about 17 million people die prematurely each year as a result of global epidemic of largely preventable chronic diseases or lifestyle diseases. According to WHO, World deaths from "lifestyle" diseases will double by 2015 unless all-out efforts are taken to combat them? From the 1940's to the late 1990's, heart disease, cancer, and degenerative diseases accounted for the maximum number of deaths. Degenerative diseases, which are on the list of lifestyle diseases, accounted for 60 percent of all deaths since the late 1990s.

Death statistics for the United States can be used to determine how lifestyle diseases have been affecting people. In 1900 pneumonia/influenza, tuberculosis, and diarrhea/enteritis were the top three causes of death in the U.S, with 60 percent of all deaths attributed to infectious diseases. Heart disease was the 4th leading cause of death; cancer was way down in eighth position.

**SLP and Lifestyle diseases**

My recent observation is that lifestyle diseases are now affecting young generation as well. In the last few years of my clinical practice I have seen many patients below the age of thirty years who were suffering from advanced stage of various chronic degenerative disorders. The diseases observed were liver cirrhosis, multiple sclerosis, arthritis and serious heart disorders. Hormonal imbalances are reflected in polycystic ovarian disease, early age male baldness and infertility. A very common presentation of high lipids, high uric acid and fatty liver is seen in youth in daily clinical practice. I have seen reports of high cholesterol as early as the age of ten years. Depression is becoming very common in teens and unfortunately lifestyle diseases are affecting our younger generation earlier than the older generation. The common unhealthy lifestyle factors which I have found in patients of lifestyle diseases are:

I. Majority were on carefully regulated scientific diets prescribed by the doctors, or learnt through televisions, internet, or friends. Lot of artificial and processed foods, like white flour, broiler chicken, bran products, low fat, low calorie, fat free foods, and packaged cereals were taken in routine. Transfats laden packaged high fiber cereal were considered the safest food.

II. 80 –90% were not taking breakfasts or were taking late breakfast or it was taken in the car on their way to their workplace

III. Fizzy drinks and juices were amongst the favorites. Cold drinks were taken during the meals, and desserts were eaten after the meals.

IV. Food nibbling was observed and most of them were eating small meals two hourly.

V. Water intake was always with foods and regular intake of cold water was enough to disrupt important biorhythms.

VI. Sleeps was not important for them and were hardly getting 3-4 hours of night sleep. The quality of sleep was not good and majority was suffering from hyperactive mind.

VII. People with hypersensitive nature were carrying loads of memories of past emotional traumas. Apparently they were very social and outgoing but were suffering from insecurities, unknown fears, phobias, and were claustrophobic. All signs and symptoms of poor oxygenation of their system was present.

VIII. High radiation exposure by watching television, sitting on computers for long hours, chatting, messaging, playing computer or video games was also observed. Microwave usage was very common, even young mothers were preparing their infant's formula milk by heating water in microwave oven.

IX. The common body types observed on pulse analysis were acidic body with hyper-liver, hyper-acidic body with sluggish liver and hyper-liver with water retention. Common factor was a fatigued or dysfunctional liver which was creating imbalances by disturbing its 500 functions.

X. NES scan revealed three common causative factors, deranged big fields, environmental toxins and disturb

**SLP management of lifestyle diseases**

According to Chinese philosophy human health is affected 50% by food intake, 20% by stress, 20% by environment and 10% by genetic factors. Therefore you can understand the vital role of food in holistic health. Lifestyle diseases need integrated lifestyle modification with a major focus on a body compatible food plan taken correctly. SLP is a personalized lifestyle modification program which gives healing by inducing homeostasis in biorhythms and by rejuvenating liver. It incorporates following lifestyle factors for prevention, management, regeneration and reversal of a disease process. If no medical issues, do follow SLP to get positive health. So SLP key lifestyle factors are:

1. Follow eight rules of diet correction to rejuvenate liver and harmonize biorhythms.
2. Have six to eight hours of nocturnal sleep.
3. It manages 50-60% of stress through a favorite, quantity free, and body compatible diet.
4. Try to revive your hobby or passion and allocate at least 30 minutes for it.
5. Choose activities that you enjoy and can do regularly. Even a brisk 10 minute walk to the market or office or around office does the trick. Recruit a partner for support and encouragement. Clean the house or wash the car. Do gardening for health, it gives multiple benefits. At work, replace a coffee break with a brisk 10-minute walk. Ask a friend or colleague to join you.
6. Apply laughter therapy
7. A body compatible exercise program has to be followed.
8. Food supplements like probiotic, antioxidants, omega oils, vitamins, minerals and enzymes are required in correct dosage to complement healing along with healthy diet.
9. Specific CAM therapies are recommended, they go a long way in helping alleviate the symptoms of lifestyle diseases. For considering any CAM therapy one has to be careful enough to follow the recommendations of NCCAM. Otherwise you might land into the hands of an alternative therapy quack. Following are list of CAM therapies recommended by NCCM:
    - Alternative Medical System
    - Mind /Body Intervention
    - Biologically based therapies
    - Manipulative Methods
    - Energy Therapy

Eight rules of diet correction are the key components of SLP, without them rest of the program is not going to help you. Natural foods form the basis of the diet correction rules. So be careful about the selection of foods, only natural and body compatible foods can reverse a lifestyle disease.

## Role of natural foods in prevention of lifestyle diseases

Nature has provided us with natural foods with many bioactive compounds besides routine nutrients. The American journal of medicine (Pages 71-88 (30 December 2002) has published a study, "Bioactive compounds in foods: their role in the prevention of cardiovascular disease and cancer." "Bioactive compounds" are extra-nutritional constituents that typically occur in small quantities in foods. They are being intensively studied to evaluate their effects on health. The impetus sparking this scientific inquiry was the result of many epidemiologic studies that have shown protective effects of plant-based diets on cardiovascular disease (CVD) and cancer. Many bioactive compounds have been discovered.

These compounds vary widely in chemical structure and function and are grouped accordingly. Phenolic compounds, including their subcategory, flavonoids, are present in all plants and have been studied extensively in cereals, legumes, nuts, olive oil, vegetables, fruits, tea, and red wine. Many phenolic compounds have antioxidant properties, and some studies have demonstrated favorable effects on thrombosis and tumor genesis and promotion. Although some epidemiologic studies have reported protective associations between phenolic compounds and diseases like CVD and cancer. Other studies have not found these associations. Various phytoestrogens are present in soy, but also in flaxseed oil, whole grains, fruits, and vegetables. They have antioxidant properties, and some studies demonstrated favorable effects on other CVD risk factors, and in animal and cell culture models of cancer.

Resveratrol, found in nuts and red wine, has antioxidant, antithrombotic, and anti-inflammatory properties, and inhibits carcinogenesis. Lycopene, a potent antioxidant carotenoid in tomatoes and other fruits, is thought to protect against prostate and other cancers, and inhibits tumor cell growth in animals. Organosulfur compounds in garlic and onions, isothiocyanates in cruciferous vegetables, and monoterpenes in citrus fruits, cherries, and herbs have ant carcinogenic actions in experimental models, as well as cardio protective effects.

In summary, numerous bioactive compounds appear to have beneficial health effects. The nutrient dense foods are rich in vitamins and minerals and act therapeutically. These are raw dairy, meat, organ meat, sea food and whole eggs. Raw butter and real raw milk are two very important foods which are missing from a modern man's life, and their deficiency is responsible for multiple lifestyle diseases. Below is a reference taken from Weston A. Price Foundation website, explaining the therapeutics of raw butter and real milk.

The Weston A. Price Foundation is a nutrition education foundation with the mission of disseminating accurate, science-based information on diet and health. The Washington, DC-based Foundation publishes a quarterly journal for its 13,000 members, supports 450 local chapters worldwide and hosts a yearly International conference. The Weston A. Price Foundation is a non-profit nutrition education foundation with no ties to the government or food processing industries. Named for Dr. Weston A. Price, whose pioneering research discovered the vital importance of animal fats in human diets, the Foundation has warned against the dangers of low fat and plant-based diets. The Foundation is aggressively working to spread awareness about natural foods and their role in control of lifestyle diseases. Following reference is taken from the Foundation awareness literature.

***Raw butter:***

It has following important nutrients and important bioactive compounds.

i. Vitamins: Butter is a rich source of easily absorbed vitamin A, needed for a wide range of functions, from maintaining good vision to keeping the endocrine system in top shape. Butter also contains all the other fat-soluble vitamins (D, E and $K_2$), which are often lacking in the modern industrial diet.

ii. Minerals: Butter is rich in important trace minerals, including manganese, chromium, zinc, copper and selenium (a powerful antioxidant). Butter provides more selenium per gram than wheat germ or herring. Butter is also an excellent source of iodine.

iii. Fatty Acids: Butter provides appreciable amounts of short- and medium-chain fatty acids, which support immune function, boost metabolism and have anti-microbial properties; that is, they fight against pathogenic microorganisms in the intestinal tract. Butter also provides the perfect balance of omega-3 and omega-6 essential fatty acids. Arachidonic acid in butter is important for brain function and prostaglandin balance.

iv. CLA: When butter comes from cows eating green grass, it contains high levels of conjugated linoleic acid (CLA), a compound that gives excellent protection against cancer and also helps the body builds muscle rather than store fat.

v. Glycospingolipids: These are a special category of fatty acids that protect against gastro-intestinal infections, especially in the very young and the elderly. Children given reduced fat milks have higher rates of diarrhea than those who drink whole milk.

vi. Cholesterol: Despite all of the misinformation you may have heard, cholesterol is needed to maintain intestinal health and for brain and nervous system development in the young.

vii. Wulzen factor: A hormone-like substance that prevents arthritis and joint stiffness, ensuring that calcium in the body is put into the bones rather than the joints and other tissues. The Wulzen factor is present only in raw butter and cream; it is destroyed by pasteurization.

Transfats: These unnatural fats in margarine, shortenings and spreads are formed during the process of partial hydrogenation, which turns liquid vegetable oil into a solid fat. Trans fats contribute to heart disease, cancer, bone problems, hormonal imbalance, infertility, difficulties in pregnancy, problems with lactation, growth problems and learning disabilities in children. Recently a US government panel of scientists determined that man-made transfats are unsafe at any level.

***Raw milk:***

Galen, Hippocrates, Pliny, Varro, Marcellus Empiricus, Bacchis and Anthimus, leading physicians of their day, all used raw milk in the treatment of disease. During the 1920s, Dr. J. E. Crewe of the Mayo Foundation used an exclusive diet of raw milk to cure TB, edema, heart failure, high blood pressure, prostate disease, urinary tract infections, diabetes, kidney disease, chronic fatigue and obesity. Today, in Germany, successful raw milk therapy is provided in many hospitals. Studies show that children fed raw milk have more resistance to TB than children fed pasteurized milk (*Lancet*, p 1142, 5/8/37); that raw milk is very effective in preventing scurvy and protecting against flu, diphtheria and pneumonia (*Am J Dis Child*, Nov 1917); that raw milk prevents tooth decay, even in children who eat a lot of sugar (*Lancet*, p 1142, 5/8/37); that raw milk is better than pasteurized milk in promoting growth and calcium absorption.

*Ohio Agricultural Experiment Station Bulletin* (518, p 8, 1/33 )says that a substance present in raw cream (but not in pasteurized cream) prevents joint stiffness and the pain of arthritis (*Annual Review of Biochemistry*, 18:435, 1944); and that children who drink raw milk have fewer allergic skin problems and far less asthma than children who drink pasteurized milk (*Clinical & Experimental Allergy.* 2007 May; 35(5) 627-630). Many parents report an improvement in their children's behavior when they switch from pasteurized to raw milk. Raw milk contains numerous components that kill pathogenic bacteria in the milk, strengthen the immune system, protect the intestinal tract, prevent the absorption of toxins and ensure full assimilation of all the nutrients in the milk. These components are largely destroyed by pasteurization

## CHAPTER NO: 10

## A LOVE AFFAIR WITH YOURSELF: WEIGHT MANAGEMENT

Obesity means a person weighs more than 20 percent above his or her ideal weight. It is usually assessed with the help of BMI or body mass index, which is measured by comparing the height and weight of an individual. If the body mass index of an individual is 30 or above, then he or she can be declared as obese. On the other hand, if it exceeds 40, it is termed as morbid obesity. Health economist Eric Finkelstein told AFP "Obesity is a natural extension of an advancing economy. As you become a first world economy and you get all these labor-saving devices. Low-cost, easily accessible foods, people are going to eat more and exercise less," In the book "The Fattening of America", published June 2010, Finkelstein says that adult obesity more than doubled in the United States between 1960 and 2004, rising from 13 percent to around 33 percent. Globally, only Saudi Arabia is worse than the United States in terms of the percentage of adults with a severe weight problem. Thirty five percent of people in the oil-rich desert kingdom are classified as obese, the book says, citing data from the World Health Organization and Organization for Economic Cooperation and Development.

Obesity has become one of the top medical issues over the past decade, becoming a worldwide health epidemic with an estimated 35 percent of adults over the age of 20 overweight and 11 percent obese in 2008, according to the World Health Organization. As obesity rates continuing to rise, the American Medical Association recently labeled obesity as a disease. With the rising tide of obesity come health problems and an increased burden on the healthcare system and industry. Overweight is overtaking smoking as the main trigger of preventable deaths, accounting for increasing rates of heart disease, stroke, cancers, dementia, and diabetes. If you are overweight at 20 years of age, the lifestyle expectancy is 13 years less than people with normal body weight. Morbid Obesity technically is when a person is 100 lbs over the ideal body weight and has a BMI (or body Mass Index) of over 40. If there are at least two other serious health problems and the person is not able to achieve weight loss in under any circumstance, then a BMI of over 35 is also a qualification for weight loss surgery. Surgery for morbid obesity, as with other surgeries, has its risks, but the benefits can be totally amazing. A new body, a new social life, and much improved physical health are just a few of the benefits of morbid obesity surgery. Even with $50 million plus invested on weight reduction, just about every 12 months in America, there is no wonder diet plan, capsule, or exercise program which is guaranteed to get rid of weight. Most diet programs malfunction because of their focus solely on weight loss and none of them take obesity as a disease.

## Obesity and various age groups

### *Obesity in youth*

Robert Lustig, a Pediatrician at the Children's Hospital of the University of California in San Francisco, said: "Childhood obesity has become epidemic over the past 30 years... We are in the midst of an unprecedented rise in prevalence and severity of obesity, especially in children... Our current western food environment has become highly insulinogenic, as demonstrated by its increased energy density, high-fat content, high glycemic index, increased fructose composition, decreased fiber, and decreased dairy content. “He said the changes in the food manufacturing process, where in sugars are now added to foods that never used to contain sugar and fibers being removed, have made the food toxic and addictive leading to obesity. He has pointed out that this upsets the balance of two hormones leptin and insulin, which regulate how much we eat. High-sugar, low-fiber diet causes leptin to be suppressed by the effects of insulin leading to decreased activity and increased appetite.

It has been alarmingly found that one out of every 5 kids in developed nations is overweight. As seen in adults, it is found that if the body weight of a child is 15% to 20% higher than his normal body weight, then the child is considered is obese. According to childhood obesity statistics and facts, it is found that the percentage of obesity in teens is greater than that in children below 9 years of age. Apart from the above mentioned health problems, obesity in children can cause several psychological problems. An obese child can be subjected to ridicule in his peer group which may unknowingly lead to low self-esteem and a complete lack of confidence even in later life. Therefore obesity in children should be avoided. But it is very essential to know child obesity causes if you are thinking of preventing them.

***Causes***

The following are some of the factors that influence obesity in children.

***i-Diet***

As we know, diet plays an important role in the overall well-being of the person. There are higher chances of obesity if a child has improper eating habits and frequent intake of fast foods. Excessive eating while watching television is also one of the most common causes of obesity in children. Early age food addictions are very important contributory factors. High sugar content and presence of MSG in commercial foods lead to early age obesity.

***ii-Exercise***

Lack of exercise or any physical activity also results in obesity. Youth is more into net surfing, video games, chatting, text messaging and other indoor activities. As the fats in the body do not get burned off, they start getting deposited in the body. On the other hand, if a child has a sedentary lifestyle and no control on his diet, he is more likely to gain excess fats and suffer from the health problems at an early age. Excess or lack of sleep can also cause obesity in children.

***iii-Genetics***

Sometimes, if both the parents of the child are overweight, there are higher chances of the child being overweight. But this does not mean that obesity is inherited. In these cases, the parents should be more cautious and try to improve the eating habits of the child to prevent obesity. The eating habits of the entire family also play an important role in contributing to the risk of obesity in children.

These are the prominent causes of obesity in children. One should be aware of the results of obesity and try to avoid it. Improving the diet helps in controlling obesity up to a great extent. On the other hand, regular exercise or any sports activity also helps in burning all the excess fat in the body and helps in enjoying a healthy and normal life! A study presented in $10^{TH}$ International congress on obesity in Sydney in September 2006 says;

***Obesity in adults***

***Causes***

***i-Processed foods***

The life force in foods gives us vitality. Once a plant is picked or an animal killed, a grain spilt or milk homogenized, it begins to lose its essential life force. Simply stated, our food supply has changed along with the changes in our lives brought about by the demands of our fast-paced society. We are depending more and more on processed foods, and with each year, the FDA approves more and more chemicals for use in foods. With each year, the food industry is using more and more chemicals in their products. In fact, use of pesticides and herbicides to limit crop loss has skyrocketed over the past thirty years. The average person consumes 1 pound of pesticides, herbicides and 14 pounds of additives each year. These chemicals increase shelf life, kill bacteria, improve taste, replace fats, replace carbohydrates, even replace meat in some vegetarian preparations, and one of those lethal chemicals is MSG (aginomoto).

In 1968, John W. Olney, M.D., a respected researcher at Washington University Medical School and member of the National Academy of Science, found that mice in his laboratory that were being used to replicate a 1957 study by Lucas and Newhouse, in which the administration of MSG had resulted in retinal damage,[5] had become obese. Dr. Olney decided to sacrifice some of the mice and found lesions in the hypothalamus portion of the brain, the portion of the brain, as defined in Stedman's Online Medical Dictionary, that is "...prominently involved in the functions of the autonomic (visceral motor) nervous system and, through its vascular link with the anterior lobe of the hypophysis, in endocrine mechanisms; it also appears to play a role in neural mechanisms underlying moods and motivational states."

Dr. Olney published a paper on his findings in 1969, in which he described the hypothalamic lesions, stunted skeletal development, and obesity in maturing mice which had been given the food ingredient "monosodium glutamate" as neonates. Olney also commented on observed pathological changes found in several brain regions associated with endocrine function in maturing mice.[7] Since 1969, many scientists have confirmed Dr. Olney's findings of damage to the hypothalamus from MSG with resulting obesity.

More research has been done on the effects of MSG on the hypothalamus leading to obesity than on the effects of aspartic acid. Neuroscientists have known that MSG and aspartic acid cause lesions in the hypothalamus since 1969, but only recently has a possible explanation for the mechanism by which this occurs has come to light.

Research says that certain regions of the brain, known as the circumventricular organs, lack a blood brain barrier.[22-24]The blood brain barrier can be damaged from, among other things like high fever, stroke, trauma to the head, seizures, repeated ingestion of MSG, and the normal process of aging. The developing fetus is at particular risk since the placental barrier is not impervious to MSG; and we can assume the same is true for the aspartic acid contained in aspartame. Since most of the processed foods we eat contain MSG, as do many personal care items, supplements, and pharmaceuticals, it is almost impossible for an expectant mother to avoid it. She may also be using aspartame in diet soda or as a sweetener in coffee and/or ingesting free glutamic acid or free aspartic acid as a chelating agent in the minerals included in her multi-vitamin preparation.

Few studies have noticed rising of fetal cholesterol in intrauterine life, which can be related to the maternal intake of MSG and aspartic acid. Following birth, an infant is exposed to MSG in most, if not all of the vaccines it is given, and in most cases, is also exposed to free aspartic acid in vaccines.[30] The effect of the glutamic acid in vaccines is intensified by any mercury that is also present.[31] All infant milk formulas contain some free glutamic acid and free aspartic acid. An infant on a hypoallergenic soy-based formula will take more excitotoxic amino acids (glutamic acid, aspartic acid, and L-cysteine) per day than is contained in any serving of food. If an infant is breast fed, it appears likely that the MSG and/or aspartame ingested by the mother will pass into her milk. If the infant becomes ill, he/she may receive a medication sweetened with aspartame.

As soon as the infant begins to eat table foods, the infant will be ingesting free glutamic acid, and, in many cases, free aspartic acid. So now you can well imagine that how an early exposure to chemical laden food starts in a modern man'life. Some people really are addicted to foods in a similar way others might be dependent on certain substances, like addictive illegal or prescriptions drugs, or alcohol, researchers from Yale University revealed in Archives of General Psychiatry. Those with an addictive-like behavior seem to have more neural activity in specific parts of the brain in the same way substance-dependent people appear to have, the authors explained.

***ii-Calorie myth***

Food calorie counting has become a global phenomenon and despite a check and control on the calorie intake, people are unable to lose weight. A human body has many biorhythm regulatory centers but there is no calorie control Centre. Therefore the biggest food myth of this era is keeping a check on calorie. The human calorie requirement varies with age, sex, nature of work, stress, weather and amount of nocturnal sleep, so it varies day to day. The number of calories in a food varies with size, weight, and amount of exposure to heat to that particular food. In my practice I have seen worst results with a calorie restricted diet. If someone loses a good amount of weight with a calorie control diet, the original weight with added weight bounces back soon. With calorie control diets incidence of arthritis, liver disease, cardiac disease, cancers, autoimmune disorders and depression rises.

The calorie value of an average SLP diet plan stands between 5000-8000 calories. The most stable and permanent weight loss is with a high calorie diet plan. The book, *Good Calories, Bad Calories* by Gary Taube'sis detailed re-examination of numerous medical studies and trials, many of which are iconic in the gospel of conventional medicine, and which played key roles in influencing the way we understand diet and disease today. When examined together, the historic parade of studies, theories and treatments for obesity range from the merely silly to the downright cruel. Starvation studies with healthy, male volunteers in the first quarter of the last century showed over and over again that very low-calorie, low fat diets did not, in fact, promote significant weight loss, but did make volunteers miserable with constant, gnawing hunger, depression, loss of energy and libido, and even provoked homicidal and suicidal tendencies.

Other studies showed that increased exercise did not lead to weight loss in the corpulent, but instead, to an increase in appetite and subsequent increase in calories eaten. Still more trials that fed healthy, normal volunteers enormous meals of up to 10,000 calories a day exclusively from protein and fat sources found that only very modest weight gain occurred. The same protein and fat diet, in more moderate proportions, fed to the overweight caused significant and relatively easy weight loss with no discomfort of hunger, and in fact a feeling of wellbeing.Taube's in the same book describes alternative hypotheses to the etiology of obesity that early intake of refined carbohydrate foods as part of the puzzle to the deranged metabolism of the obese.

The subsequent discovery of the effects of the endocrine system, and especially of the hormone insulin, provided more clues to this disruption of homeostasis. Insulin causes fat to enter fat cells and adipose tissue, and also converts carbohydrates into fat. Chronically high blood levels of insulin prevent the fat from exiting the storage depots and for burning as fuel in cellular metabolism, however, and in effect the obese person is starving on a cellular level and naturally wants to eat more. Because his cells are actually malnourished, he feels lethargic and literally does not have the energy to exercise. "It's the effects of these carbohydrates on insulin that would explain the dietary observations the futility of calorie restriction, the relative ease of weight loss when carbohydrates are restricted, and perhaps two centuries of anecdotal observations that sweets, starches, bread, and beer are uniquely fattening," writes Taube's.

***iii-Lifestyle factors***

Processed foods intake, erratic dietary habits and skipping of the breakfast are the amongst the worst lifestyle factors causing obesity. The evening meal is when the majority of overweight, consume extra calories. According to A recent research by the US Department of Agriculture (USDA), overweight adults generally consume around 100 more calories a day than their normal-weight counterparts. The study found that even though some adults skipped breakfast, they compensated for the energy shortfall by eating foods high in fat and sugar, and low in micronutrients, throughout the rest of the day, and particularly at supper. "Skipping breakfast did not decrease calorie intake; it was instead linked with high odds of being overweight," said the ARS. Although at first sight it might seem that this is simply the result of changes to our diet and a dramatic drop in the level of physical activity for many Americans in recent years.

Poor stress management, job stress and sleep debt are other contributory factors. In the largest sample of healthy adults studied to date, researchers at the Perelman School of Medicine at the University of Pennsylvania have discovered that adults who routinely hit the bed later at night and are restricted to number of hours slept may be more susceptible to weight gain due to an increased amount of calories often being consumed during night-time hours. The study, published in the July issue of the journal SLEEP, looked at healthy adults who generally do not go to bed until the early a.m. hours and typically sleep less than five hours. “Although previous epidemiological studies have suggested an association between short sleep duration and weight gain/obesity, we were surprised to observe significant weight gain during an in-laboratory study,” said lead author Andrea Spaeth, a doctoral candidate in the psychology department at the University of Pennsylvania. In the sleep-restricted study group, the researchers further found that males gained more weight than females, and African-Americans gained more weight than Caucasians. “In our study, we found that when adults restrict their sleep by delaying their bedtime and staying up late, they are at increased risk for weight gain because they consume a substantial amount of food and drink late at night which is higher in fat than food and drink consumed during morning, afternoon or evening,” said Spaeth. “This late-night eating contributes to weight gain by not only increasing overall daily intake but also by disrupting the timing of caloric intake.”

***iv-Role of calcium***

Excess calcium in the body is an important contributing factor which leads to obesity. In fact, obese individuals are "starving" for other essential minerals and nutrients. Dr. Robert Thompson and Kathleen Barnes have explained the relationship between obesity and calcium in their book “The Calcium Lie”. Excess calcium and mineral-deficiency in our bodies not only leads to obesity but also to diseases and conditions including Type 2 diabetes, metabolic syndrome, Type 2 hypothyroidism, depression, anxiety, insomnia, migraines, circulatory diseases, hypertension, immune compromise and more.

There are increased cravings for glucose and for minerals. Until we address the excess calcium and mineral deficiencies in our bodies, any weight loss is almost always temporary. The foods that most people eat are frequently low in minerals because most fruits and vegetables today are grown in mineral-poor soil and few foods are vine-ripened. As a result, our metabolisms are slowed, and our cells can't obtain the essential minerals needed for full health.

Theresa Vernon writes in the article "Metals and Mind "that Calcium and magnesium are part of the body's breaking system. These minerals help you get control and slow down, to avoid burning yourself out. By contrast, sodium and potassium accelerate the metabolism, partly by increasing adrenal cortical hormones. Newborns have a very high rate of metabolism and relatively low calcium levels. As we age the body begins to apply the calcium brake; as copper builds up, the calcium and magnesium levels rise while the sodium and potassium decline. Rising calcium in the tissues is a defense against the chronic stress which is the cause and effect of copper toxicity. So the body starts retaining calcium to buffer the effects of the copper and that calcium slows you down.

***v-Copper toxicity***

Copper toxicity is another disturbing chemistry which affects liver functions. Excess of copper impairs mineral balance and create hormonal imbalance and a resistant obesity. Almost everything you eat has some copper in it. A lot of really popular foods like coffee, chocolate, avocado, soy, shellfish like shrimp and lobster, and certain beans and nuts like pecans are pretty high in copper. This isn't a problem with healthy liver, gall bladder and especially adrenal gland.

If adrenal function is strong, we just mobilize that copper and excrete it through the bile. Unfortunately, the way we live these days, most people are not able to get rid of the excess copper. Many people have impaired liver function, congested gallbladder or adrenal fatigue. If adrenal function becomes impaired, the copper builds up in the liver, brain, joints and lungs. When this happens, you see very specific problems, including mental, liver problems and poor detoxification of the body.
Vegetarian diets are very high in copper because the vegetable foods are a great source of this mineral. Since vegetarians don't eat meat, and possibly not even eggs, they are not getting enough zinc, which is the natural antagonist to copper. Zinc naturally balances copper and keeps it

from building up in the tissues. If you are not eating much in the way of meat and eggs, you will develop copper problems. Excess copper interferes with energy production at the cellular level. It impairs various energy pathways in the cell so it contributes to the very fatigue that tends to make you retain copper, leading to a vicious circle. Once this pattern gets going, it is totally self-reinforcing and very difficult to break, even by adding zinc-rich foods back into the diet.

***vi-Slow Oxidation***

The other thing that happens with high copper is slow oxidation, because high copper slows down both the adrenal and thyroid glands. Oxidation means to burn or mix with oxygen. Dr. George Watson, a researcher at UCLA, developed the concept of oxidation types. Those who burn food at a slower-than-ideal rate are slow oxidizers. If your thyroid and adrenal glands are very active you will be a fast oxidizer; if they are sluggish, you will be a slow oxidizer.

Stress from excess copper at first puts the body in a state of fast oxidation. Over time, however, the oxidation rate starts to decline and you go into the resistant stage. Now your body is in a constantly unstable condition of being overly stressed yet unable to fully respond. It is during that time that the copper starts to build up. You start to lose your ability to handle the metal. When exhaustion sets in, when your body can't handle it any longer, that is when the oxidation rate becomes slow. This is the time when body is in very resistant metabolic state and obesity.

Slow oxidizers tend to have high calcium levels and fast oxidizers tend to have high sodium and potassium. When you see someone's chart and they have high calcium, which means they are a slow oxidizer, along with very high sodium and potassium, which is the signature of fast oxidation, it means they are pumping themselves up enough to overcome the slow oxidation but the calcium brake is still on. The underlying condition is slow oxidation, and buildup of copper, but these individuals are revved up on stimulants.

People in slow oxidation are like people with low thyroid, because it is more or less the same thing. They have dry skin and hair; they sweat little and tend toward constipation, depression, fatigue, apathy, low blood sugar, adrenal insufficiency and low blood pressure. As with low thyroid, they tend to gain weight on the hips and have a low body temperature. Slow oxidizers tend to be withdrawn, introverted, and less expressive and may exhibit depression, despair and suicidal thoughts. As the slow oxidation becomes more extreme, more and more of these symptoms will develop.

***vii-Over exercise***

When you exercise too much, your body goes into a more extreme physical stress response. This can cause your cortical levels to remain high. Cortisol also known as "the stress hormone," is secreted by your adrenal glands and is involved in a variety of important physical functions, including:

- Metabolizing glucose
- Regulating your blood pressure
- Releasing insulin for blood sugar maintenance
- Your immune function
- The inflammatory response

However, when your cortisol level is chronically elevated which can happen if you exercise too much -- it stimulates your body to store fat and not build muscle. This may be the underlying problem if you engage in excessive amounts of exercise on a regular basis and find that you've hit a plateau where you cannot lose weight or build more muscle. One has to follow the rule of moderation and biochemical individuality.

***viii-Genetic factors***

Scientific studies into the causes of obesity show that the condition results from a complex combination of factors. One such factor which has come under increasing examination over the past ten years or so is genetics and, in particular, the genes involved in the regulation of leptin within the body. Leptin which takes its name from the Greek word leptos meaning thin, was discovered in 1994 and is associated with the Ob (lep) gene [Ob - obesity, lep - leptin] which is located on chromosome 7 in human beings. In somewhat simplified terms leptin is a protein hormone produced by fat cells which enters the blood stream and travels to the brain, where a high level of leptin in the blood tells the brain that you have sufficient energy reserves or that your energy reserves are too high and that the body needs to burn off some fat. In essence therefore leptin plays an important role in regulating both appetite and metabolism. In obese people levels of leptin found in the blood are normally very high and more than sufficient to suppress the appetite and increase the metabolism therefore obese are in a state of leptin resistance.

***ix-Ayurveda and adult obesity***

Inside the body, there are three doshas called tridoshas which govern the chemical and physiological activities. These three doshas are Vata (from ether and air), Pitta (from fire and an aspect of water), and Kapha (from water and earth).Individual constitution is acquired at birth and remains constant through life.

A balance among the tridosha is necessary for health. For example, the air principle kindles the bodily fire, but water is necessary to control fire, otherwise the bodily fire would burn the tissues. Vata moves Kapha and Pitta, since Kapha and Pitta are immobile. Together, the tridosha governs all metabolic activities; anabolism (Kapha), catabolism (Vata), and metabolism (Pitta). In childhood, anabolism and the Kapha elements are predominant, since this is the time of greatest physical growth. In adulthood, metabolism and the element of Pitta are most apparent, because at this stage the body is matured and stable. In old age, catabolism and Vata are most evident, as the body begins to deteriorate.

In Ayurveda underweight and overweight are signs that the vata, pitta, and kapha systems are out of balance. This can happen irrespective of how much or how little food you eat. Weight control problems happen when your food intake is not balanced by a proper digestion or metabolism. Overweight or obesity is mostly found in people with predominantly kapha type constitutions. This dosha is composed of water and earth. When it is imbalanced, the heavy characteristics of these elements become exaggerated.

However, obesity can be found in people with the other two doshas also. For example, people with pita dosha are generally of medium build. But they can suffer from poor digestion if their digestive fire is too low because they have burned themselves out. As a result, food isn't processed properly, and that, in turn, can result in weight gain or obesity. For people with vata dosha the problem generally is that of underweight rather than overweight. They cannot properly absorb nutrients. However, they can become overweight when imbalanced if they attempt to eat sweet, oily foods in an attempt to calm their vata imbalance. The Ayurveda approach to achieving your ideal weight is based on taking a realistic look at your body type and what it can be, and then nourishing it back to natural health. It is about getting to know your body and becoming in tune with its rhythms.

**Obesity and health risks**

Obesity can be an important risk factor for a number of health related complications including coronary heart disease, high blood pressure, brain stroke, diabetes, liver diseases, osteoarthritis, certain forms of cancer like cancer of the uterus, ovaries, colon, rectum and prostate. Though, the genetic factors responsible for causing obesity can't be controlled properly, the environmental factors, on the other hand can be effectively controlled with a change in lifestyle and eating habits..

## How to manage obesity

According to a study published in the March 2008 issue of the American Journal of Public Health, the desire to lose weight is a strong predictor of chronic disease. Stressing about weight can cause the body to release stress chemicals, which contribute to hypertension, heart disease, type 2 diabetes and hypercholesterolemia. Intense desire to lose weight leads to various crash diet plans. Crash diets don't work permanently because they don't change eating habits, and habits are where our lives, careers and bodies are made. Remember good habits are as addictive as bad habits. Instead of crash dieting treat your body as a sacred being given to you by God for a short period. That means feeding it well, giving it the exercise it needs, keeping it away from undue stress, harmful chemicals and appreciating it for what it provides. Then only you can expect an optimum holistic health to perform your role optimally in various roles. The positive attitude towards your inner leads to self-awareness and you find a lifelong friend, which is your own body.

Alyssa Ford writes in her magazine Experience Life "there are millions of diets out there. It can all be confusing as hell! If you listen to everything out there, you might end up eating nothing at all. I don't believe there is one right diet that fits for all people. We are all unique individuals with unique needs. Everybody's body is different. A diet that may work for someone else may not work for you. She writes don't try to follow someone else's diet. Instead feel into and find what most authentically works for you and your body type, rather than trying to fit your body into a preset plan. Your body has an innate intelligence. If you trust it and listen, it will guide you."

The state of consciousness you are in when you eat has an effect on your food that can either nourish or weaken your body. Food that is made with care, and love has a different energy, taste, vibration, feeling and impact in your body so love is the secret ingredient. Kute Blackson believes that if you are eating the "healthiest" food, but are in a state of anger, shame, guilt or self-hatred, then that would affect your body's chemistry negatively and the vibration of the food you ate. Yes, of course it's important to eat as many healthy organic foods as you can, but also to do so when you are in a state of gratitude and positivity. So often in our culture today, what motivates us to diet, or eat a certain way can be driven by fear of not looking a certain way by society's standard, or self-hatred of our own body. When you are driven by non-acceptance of yourself and body, no diet will bring you true peace, no food will really bring you true authentic nourishment.

Kute says that ultimately, we are all going to die no matter what you eat or don't eat. No matter how many vitamins you take, what type of special water you drink, or what kind of super foods you eat. The body will die. Your soul is eternal. So to get overly obsessed about diet is not healthy either. It's more important to have a healthy relationship with food so that you can feel at peace just as you are right now. I tend to believe that the more you love and accept yourself, the happier you feel, and in turn the healthier your body gets.

**SLP and obesity**

**Causes**

I categorize obesity into two types, size gain and weight gain. Size gain is due to water and wind retention and gives good results to dietary modification. Weight gain obesity is managed on long term basis and needs lifestyle modification. One strange phenomenon I have observed that my patient might lose between 6-10 inches and no weight loss even for a period of 6 months. Therefore I feel these two types are interdependent and at the same time independent of each other. Common factor is an unhealthy lifestyle and a weak body which is unable to burn the fat. All my obese patients are in a weak energy state or their metabolism is poor. According to Dr. Deepak Chopra human metabolism is an outcome of the collective functions of endocrine, immune and neurological systems. That is the reason that I never bother about counting calories, but have to give a food plan which is rich in proteins, complex carbohydrates, healthy fat, vitamins and minerals. As there are six body chemistries so I find six causes of obesity, which are:

1. Acidic body with hyper-liver; a resistant obesity is observed and majority of the people fix into this category. Their copper level is high and they are slow oxidizers. This is a chronic obesity and starts at a young age. As it is a metabolically resistant obesity and worsens after every calorie controlled crash diet plan. Each crash diet further overloads liver with toxins and compromises its multiple functions. Causes of this obesity are genetic, gestational, poor childhood brought up, environmental causes, young age emotional traumas, early age exposure to pharmaceutical drugs, mineral imbalance, and all other factors of an un-natural lifestyle. People of this obesity generally eat less and their food is not properly digested, absorbed, and eliminated. Grades of obesity vary with the grades of hyper-liver chemistry and worst obesity seen in acidic body with grade iii hyper-liver. Besides obesity this chemistry makes them suffer from lifestyle diseases from the age of as young as ten. They have early age tendency for disturb lipid profile, high blood pressure, dominant abdominal obesity, polycystic ovaries or impaired male reproductive health, fatty liver and forgetfulness. Multiple nutrient deficiencies lead to abnormal food cravings like sugary foods, colas, junk, clay, or even ice cubes chewing. Behavioral disorders, mood swings and depression is also observed. They look older to their physical age and suffer from hyperactive mind syndrome. Darkening of complexion and patches of hyper pigmentations are observed. Lethargy, fatigue and disinterest in exercise are other symptoms. As their body is having low oxygenation they suffer from headaches, dizziness, various fears, phobias and are claustrophobic as well.

2. Acidic body with hypo/sluggish liver: size gain is dominant and people with this chemistry are least prone to weight gain. Only weight gain is at a later age and is manageable easily. They have multiple allergies, especially upper respiratory and have multiple food allergies as well. They commonly suffer from stomach disorders, and frequent diarrhea which leads to nutritional deficiency. These deficiencies impair liver functions and slow down fat metabolism. Anxiety in their nature keeps them in a race mode and they pay least attention to their physical health. Un-natural lifestyle, environmental stress and their competitive nature disrupts the body rhythms. Obesity is of mild nature and responds to SLP very effectively.

3. Hyper-acidic body with hyper-liver: weight gain and size gain obesity is present. They have a monster appetite and they want to nibble after every 2-3 hours, otherwise suffer from low energy. They have a tendency for hypoglycemia and low blood pressure. Dysfunctional liver creates insulin resistance, and fluctuations in sugar levels. Physically they are very active and interested in doing strenuous exercises. Bouncing back of obesity and sagging of muscles is observed after they leave their exercise regimen. Their obesity is in the resistant category and they also suffer from various lifestyle diseases. Environmental factors, un-natural lifestyle and emotional traumas are root causes. Their management is better than type one.

4. Hyper-acidic body with hypo/sluggish liver; right organ pulse reflects a hyper acidic stomach and rest of the body symptoms are directly related to this state. Blood pulse describes acidity, wind and heat in the blood. Size gain is dominant and a panic mode is present in this chemistry. Nibbling is present with no interest in the food. Size gain is more as compare to weight gain. This obesity is mild and responds well to SLP.

5. Acidic body, hyper-liver and water retention. Most of the times three levels of pulses are found bilaterally and but the strength

and length of each pulse varies. This pulse tells about a serious derangement of the body chemistry. Both types of obesity are present and this explains dysfunctional status of stomach, Liver and kidney. This chemistry leads to a bloated body, circulatory imbalance, swelling on dependent parts, chronic disorders in a progressive state. Morbid obesity is part of this chemistry and difficult to reverse. SLP works holistically in the slow reversal of the lifestyle disease and obesity.

6. Acidic body, hypo-liver and water retention; size gain obesity is dominant. Gastritis, constipation, upper respiratory tract infections like tonsillitis, adenoids, sinusitis, shifting joint pains, weak cervical and lower back, and lower body obesity is observed. Foods with diuretic properties give excellent results and obesity is settled with SLP in 3-6 months and there are less chances of rebound obesity phenomenon.

**Resistant weight loss**

In routine clinical practice, I observe lot of people struggling for their weight loss but it is resistant to any crash diet. Common causes of resistant or recurrent obesity are processed low calorie foods, prolonged food intervals or starvation, repeated crash diets, poor dietary habits, emotional traumas, hyperactive mind, fatty liver, incorrect exercise and sleeplessness.

**SLP and Obesity management**

I absolutely agree with Alyssa and Kute that we should respect our body and its natural rhythm. Without proper nutrition, sleep and happiness, it is impossible to lose weight. Following is a list of all those components, which are part of a SLP personalized lifestyle modification program for obesity management.

I. 8-rules of Correct eating to create harmony in metabolism

**II.** Detoxification is recommended in spring and autumn season

**III.** About six hours of nocturnal sleep is induced

**IV.** Stress is managed to decrease cortisol hormone which blocks weight loss, I found stress the worst factor of resistant obesity

V. Body compatible exercises, only when body is ready to do

**VI.** Once you gain your holistic health only then follow crash diets for 5-7 days once a month

**VII.** Food supplements especially pre-biotic, probiotic, enzymes, antioxidants and essential fatty acids.

When weight management is done through a natural lifestyle modification, weight loss is gradual but permanent and there are no residual side effects. There is always reversal of a degenerative disease process and holistic health is achieved.

# CHAPTER NO: 11

## DIGESTIVE HARMONY: KEEPS YOUR MIND RELAXED

Human gut is a beautifully orchestrated system of integrated harmony, which is in harmony with nature as well. Lipski writes in her book 'Digestive Wellness'that, biological approach is a better solution than the medical therapy. The biological approach is being careful about your biochemical individuality. She writes one person's need for a specific nutrient can be thirty fold higher or lower than another person's. A healthy food can become a remedy only if it matches your biochemical individuality. But humanity is listening more to science and logic regarding their food choices, therefore suffering badly from various digestive ailments.

Jordan S. Rubin writes in the article "How to Restore Digestive Health" that chronic disease wreaks havoc on the American populace. One million Americans suffer from AIDS; eight million have cancer, and twelve million battle heart disease. However, there is one disorder that afflicts more individuals than the combined total of all of these other potentially deadly disorders, and, surprisingly, it is rarely mentioned. Thirty-eight million Americans are victims of digestive disorders, including Crohn's disease, ulcerative colitis, diverticulitis, celiac disease, and IBS, constipation, diarrhea, GERD, candida and food allergies.

### Grim Statistics of Digestive Disorders in America

I. Two of the top five most widely prescribed prescription drugs in this country are for digestive disorders. The other three drugs in the top five are prescribed for heart disease and arthritis.

II. Colorectal cancer, one of the most severe digestive or gastro-enterological diseases, is the second leading cause of cancer deaths.

III. More than 60 million Americans experience heartburn at least once a month, and about 25 million are daily sufferers, leading to gastro-esophageal reflux disease (GERD), which, if left untreated, can lead to more serious conditions.

IV. As many as 37 million episodes of diarrhea occur annually among America's 16.5 million children under five. This problem leads to three million physician visits each year and 163,000 hospital visits; it also accounts for 13 percent of all hospital stays for children in this age group.

V. Irritable Bowel Syndrome (IBS) alone affects almost 20 percent of the adult population in America

In my practice I see every second person suffering from indigestion, flatulence, and constipation. People take psyllium husk in routine to help their bowel movement. People are taking scientific foods which are highly processed to get rid of their digestive problems, but in fact it aggravates their stomach disorders. Frequent intake of stomach medicines and un-natural foods convert their minor digestive problems into bigger digestive issues like chronic gastric ulcer, ulcerative colitis, IBS, and multiple food allergies.

Wise men, poets and philosophers have long honored the process of digestion as the basis of good health, sound sleep and a happy attitude. "I am convinced digestion is the great secret of life," said the prolific and quotable Reverend Sydney Smith. Shakespeare believes "Now good digestion wait on appetite, and health on both!" Rudolf Steiner, the Austrian philosopher and mystic, placed the highest importance on complete and thorough digestion. He described digestion as the annihilation or breaking down of the outer world, which is food, into nothingness or chaos. A primary task of the human ego, according to Steiner, was the building up of that pregnant chaos into compounds that bear our own imprint.

## Special Characteristics of Digestive Tract

### *i-GALT*

Gut Activated Lymphatic System, 60% of the immune system is located in the GALT. A disordered gut can translate into a disordered immune response and can result into every autoimmune disorder. The small intestine is a major locus of immune system activity, it is loaded with intraepithelial lymphocytes (CD8 cells) as well as Peyer's patch lymphocytes (CD4 cells) that interact in complex ways with the commensal microflora.

### *ii-Intestinal flora*

A total of one hundred trillion bacteria live together in our digestive system, in either symbiotic or antagonistic relationships. Their total weight is about 4 pounds. There are 400 to 500 types of bacteria in our digestive systems, each of which has many types of strains. These bacteria manufacture substances that raise or lower our risk of disease and cancer, effects of drugs, immune competence, nutritional status, and rate of aging.

Leo Galland writes in his article "Three GI Ecosystem "

"The GI microbial world is comprised of 3 very different compartments: Gastric, Small Intestinal & Colonic. Each has a distinct biochemical and physiologic "climate." The Gastric ecosystem is characterized by a low pH environment that kills most external bacteria coming in with food. Gastric contents are emptied relatively rapidly (usually within 60-90 min), and there is a thick mucus barrier between the gastric mucosa and gastric contents. The high acidity is one of the body's major defense systems against exogenous pathogens. It is important to appreciate that a healthy human stomach produces roughly 2 liters of acidic gastric juice daily. Helicobacter pylori is a very common inhabitant of the human stomach. While in many people it is pathogenic, in others it is not. The Small Intestinal ecosystem is an entirely different world from the gastric compartment. It is characterized by great length (roughly 25 feet), immense surface area (approximately the size of a tennis court), and an alkaline pH owing to duodenal and pancreatic bicarbonate secretion. The colonic ecosystem is characterized by its slow motility (48 hours is typical for emptying), and its immense bacterial count. The colon has a pH in the range of 6-8. Many things can affect the complex ecology of the colon. Common disruptors include: antibiotics, unabsorbed bile acids, unabsorbed fructose from the small intestine, bacterial putrefaction, altered intestinal motility, a host of different drugs, and chronic stress."

Leo Galland writes "It is hard to remember that there was once a time when the medical community had to be convinced that Helicobacter pylori played a role in causing peptic ulcers. Over the last 3 decades, eradication of this organism has become almost a second-nature reflex on the part of most doctors. Recently, however, some researchers have begun to question the wisdom of reflexively killing off this organism, which is one of the most widely prevalent microbes living in the human GI tract. They point out that H. pylori is so ubiquitous in many populations that it is more or less "normal," and that in most people who carry it, it does not cause overt disease. Moreover, they note that gastric colonization with organism inhibits ghrelin, a very important signaling molecule that increases appetite."

Dr. Martin Blaser and his team of microbiologists at New York University have forwarded an argument that H. pylori could be playing an important role in preventing obesity, and that eradication of the organism may be contributing to the risk of obesity by increasing ghrelin output. Dr. Blaser and other H. pylori "defenders" also note that incidence of gastro esophageal reflux (GERD), asthma and obesity are inversely correlated with prevalence of H. pylori. There's no doubt that this organism can be pathogenic. It lives under the mucous layer, protected from stomach acid, and it provokes TH1 cells, and triggers gastric mucosal IL-8 secretion, which promotes inflammation. This organism produces ammonia, which raises stomach pH. It also damages acid-producing cells. On the other hand it can also induce hyperacidity by destroying somatostatin-producing antral mucosal cells. Dr. Leo suggests that lactobacillus obtained from fermented foods

&supplements, can inhibit the growth of H. pylori. He also suggests that garlic, cabbage, broccoli because of their thiosulfinate and sulforaphane respectively Inhibit growth of H. Pylori.

***iii-Second brain***

Indeed, the human digestive tract contains over one million nerve cells, about the same number found in the spinal cord. There are actually more nerve cells in the overall digestive system than in the peripheral nervous system. Furthermore, major neurotransmitters found in the brain-including serotonin, dopamine, glutamate, norepinephrine and nitric oxide-occur plentifully in the gut as well. Enkephalins-described as the body's natural opiates-also occur in the intestinal tract, as do benzodiazepines, psychoactive chemicals similar to mood-controlling drugs like Valium and Xanax.

Jordan Rubin describes the "brain-gut" connection very well in his book *The Maker's Diet*: "Early in our embryogenesis, a collection of tissue called the 'neural crest'appears and divides during fetal development. One part turns into the central nervous system, and the other migrates to become the enteric nervous system. Both 'thinking machines'form simultaneously and independently of one another until a later stage of development. "Then the two nervous systems link through a neural cable called the "vagus nerve," the longest of all cranial nerves. The vagus nerve "wanders" from the brain stem through the organs in the neck and thorax and finally terminates in the abdomen. This is your vital brain-gut connection.

"Serotonin in the gut is thought to initiate peristalsis, the rhythmic movement of food through the digestive tract. Drugs like Prozac actually divert serotonin from the intestinal tract to the brain, leading to digestive problems including constipation in many patients. The gut produces the same pain-alleviating chemicals as those in anti-anxiety drugs. Says Rubin, "If you overeat because you feel anxious, your body may be trying to use the extra food to produce more benzodiazepines.

We are not sure whether the gut synthesizes benzodiazepine from chemicals in our foods, from bacterial actions or from both. We do know that extreme pain appears to put the gut into overdrive in order to send benzodiazepine directly to the brain for immediate pain management."

***iv-Special anatomical structure***

The gastrointestinal (GI) tract is a long hollow tube stretching from the head to the end of the body, including the mouth, pharynx, esophagus, stomach, small intestine, and large intestine. The salivary glands, liver, gallbladder, and pancreas are also important parts of this far-reaching system. The main purpose of the GI tract is to break down carbohydrates, fats, and proteins into molecules small enough to be absorbed through cell membranes. In that way, it provides the cells with the necessary energy for life and health.

Digestion begins in the mouth when food is chewed and starch is broken down by ptyalin, an enzyme secreted in saliva. Food then enters the stomach, where it is reduced to tiny particles and further transformed by gastric juices. The solid portion remains in the stomach for one to six hours until it liquefies completely; liquid passes into the duodenum (small intestine), where numerous enzymes produced by the pancreas, along with bile from the liver, break it down further for absorption. When it finally arrives in the large intestine, all nutritional value has been spent, and the only remaining process is the removal of water before final elimination. Every section of the GI tract is prone to its own unique disorders--some merely annoying, others potentially fatal.

***v- Primary site of every disease***

According to Hippocrates, “All disease begins in the gut.” An underlying principle in Chinese medicine is that good digestion is the key to good health. Wrong intake of a healthy food converts it into an end product, which is highly injurious to the integrity of human health. The science of Ayurveda explains this process in a perfect way, and the Ayurveda approach of explaining digestion is very simple and effective. The food we eat is digested by agni or body fire which is present in our body. It is very much similar to the way we cook the food. The agni or body fire helps to digest the food which is consumed, much like the fire of a stove cooks the food kept on it. The agni is mainly situated in Jatara or in upper part of digestive system and is called as Jataragni. The agni is further categorized as bhootagni (which digests the 5 pancha mahabhoota factors present in food), dhatwagni (The agni present in tissues which help them to absorb required nutrients), and malagni (the agni which helps in formation of body wastes like stools, sweat and urine).

The jataragni controls bhootagni, dhatwagni and malagni. Through this it is evident that ayurveda approach of digestion explains cellular metabolism too. The factors which help agni to digest the food completely are: Thridoshas -Vata, Pitta and Kapha help agni to digest the food. If the process of digestion is compared to that of cooking rice, the stomach, like the vessel receives food. Vata provides the necessary conditions like the air blower, Pitta acts like the stove, providing optimum working conditions while Kapha provides the moisture needed much like the water in the vessel. When all these factors are normal and well balanced, an optimum condition is created to digest the food completely. When food is completely digested by all the agnis, the body tissues will be well nourished and one is blessed with attractive complexion, glow, longevity, strength, good health, growth, enthusiasm, vitality and overall healthy development of body and mind.

***vi-Stomach channel***

Acupuncture therapy considers balancing of 12 major meridians. Stomach, large intestine and small intestine are three hollow organs channels. These three digestive systems related channels traverse the whole body. Longest route is of stomach channel starting from the face and finishing at the base of the second toe. This channel or meridian has 45 points. The clinical uses of this channel are for stomach disorders, spleen and other abdominal organs disorders. Other disorders covered are of face area, chest, breast, and lower limbs. So you can have an idea about the diversity of stomach functions.

## Causes of digestive disorders

i. Artificial, processed, GMO, and chemical loaded foods
ii. Incompatible foods not suiting to a particular biochemical individuality
iii. Incompatible food combinations in a single meal
iv. Irregularity in eating habits especially food timings
v. Avoidance of favorite natural foods, which can never disrupt the digestive balance.
vi. Eating in hurry, absence of traditional eating rituals
vii. Myth of using carbonated drinks with foods to facilitate the digestion
viii. Improper gap between the meals
ix. Improper mastication of food
x. Repeated intake of antibiotics, pain killers, antidepressants, anticancer medicines, steroids or even synthetic vitamin supplements kill intestinal flora
xi. Multiple life related stress disorders
xii. Lack of six hours of night sleep, can cause IBS and constipation
xiii. Absence of collective family meals

## Ayurveda and digestive disorders

Common digestive problems such *as* gastric reflux (also known as heartburn and GERD) and irritable bowel syndrome (IBS) can cause symptoms such as gas, bloating, stomach pain, or abdominal cramps. The discomfort, and often embarrassment, that result from digestive disorders often limits a person's quality of life. Ayurveda treatments can bring relief from these symptoms for the millions who suffer with digestive disorders by restoring harmony to the body, mind, and spirit.

Lifestyle changes have long been recommended for digestive disorders with the goal of decreasing the inflammation of the digestive tract.

Ayurveda treatments are well suited for these diseases because they focus on creating balance with our bodies through nutrition and mental and spiritual tranquility. In Ayurvedic medicine, herbs, metals, massage, and other products and techniques are used with the intent of cleansing the body and restoring balance. This is believed to help treat illness and promote wellness. Ayurvedic practitioners expect patients to be active participants in their treatment, by making the necessary lifestyle changes. Ayurvedic Medicine recommends yoga as a form of exercise to build strength and health. To reduce stress and improve mental energy, Ayurveda suggests massage therapy, self-massage, yogic breathing techniques, and meditation. Regular practice of these arts will help you lead a healthy and harmonious life.

Ayurveda describes three types of toxins that may build up in the body. The most common type is *ama*, which is formed when the digestive tract is either weak or overloaded with the wrong foods. If *ama* is not cleared from the body, it will continue to build and can cause an imbalance of the *doshas*, or the natural forces at work in the body. When the causative factors of the imbalance are not addressed, the *ama* can react with *subdoshas* and create *amavisha*. *Amavisha* is the strongest toxin, and it can cause disease. The third type of toxin is environmental toxins, and requires you to eliminate your exposure to the contaminant. A temporary lapse in good dietary habits will create *ama*. Long-term eating habits that are not appropriate for a person's *dosha* will cause the development of *amavisha*. Digestive disorders are related to *amavisha*, indicated by their chronic nature.

The first treatment is detoxification and cleansing of the body. If this is not done, other methods of treatment will not be effective. Detoxification includes therapeutic use of laxatives, enemas, fasting, and cleansing of the sinuses. Diet is the most important aspect of Ayurvedic treatment. Certain tastes and foods can either calm or irritate the *doshas*. After an Ayurvedic practitioner determines a person's *dosha* profile, a specific diet will be recommended to correct *dosha* imbalances and to improve health. Meals should be taken in a calm manner with proper chewing and without overeating to ease the burden of digestion.

**SLP causes of digestive disorders**

i. Processed, scientific or industrial food usage
ii. Skipping of breakfast, or late breakfast
iii. Non- compatible foods in terms of body type and food type
iv. Intake of tea, coffee, juices, betal leaf and fizzy drinks with food
v. Short or very long intervals between the foods
vi. Incorrect intake of water
vii. Forceful or voluntary control of food portions
viii. Neglecting the importance of family rituals of food intake.
ix. Commonly observed chemistry is acidic body with hyper-liver and hyper-acidic body with hypo-liver state.

**SLP digestive wellness**

i. Select natural foods because these are rich in anti-oxidants, enzymes, prebiotics and probiotics.
ii. Cooking medium should be natural non-processed butter which is rich in vitamin D and it reduces intestinal inflammations. Other oils can be natural ghee or butter oil, cold pressed mustard oil and coconut oil. Cooking in olive oil is unhealthy if it is overheated. I have observed raised triglycerides, mood swings, digestive disorders and hormonal imbalances after regular Pakistani cooking in olive oil. Foods rich in omega 3 fatty acids should be part of our routine meal. Hydrogenated oils have high proportion of omega 6 fatty acids which cause gut inflammation.

iii. Don't take water, fizzy drinks, juices, milk or yogurt drinks with your meals. This combination weakens the stomach juice and cause abdominal obesity.

iv. Dining room should be a comfortable room. Do not read, watch T.V. or listen to telephone while taking food. Do not indulge in hot discussions and don’t talk unpleasant events on the table, remember gut is your second brain.

v. Follow SLP eight rules of correct eating for digestive wellness.

# CHAPTER NO: 12

# HOLISTIC HEART: THE SEAT OF WISDOM

By far, one of the most important systems in our entire body is cardiovascular system. Every year, millions of people around the world experience less than optimal cardiovascular health and this is by no means restricted just to the male population. According to the American Heart Association (AHA), many people across all age groups experience less than optimal cardiovascular health. It pretty much goes without saying how important it is to keep your entire cardiovascular system working as efficiently as possible to get holistic health. The heart is a powerhouse of emotional and intuitive intelligence... and it has way more influence over how we perceive and react to the world than the brain.

There are multiple factors affecting the holistic functioning of the heart. These factors are physical, emotional, and metaphysical leading to various cardiac ailments.

## 1-Physical causes of Heart Disease

### *I- Coronary artery blockade*

The current thinking about heart disease focuses only on the blood supply to the myocardial (heart) cells from the network of coronary arteries, that is, the arteries that supply blood to the heart itself. There are four main arteries, each supplying blood to a different region of the heart. Medical experts believe that when one or more of these arteries gets blocked with plaque, a condition starts called atherosclerosis. The inside of the artery becomes narrowed, the blood flow becomes compromised and, in times of myocardial stress (such as exercise or emotional trauma), the insufficient blood flow causes damage to the particular region of the heart fed by the blocked artery. This diminished blood flow first causes pain (angina) and then, if more severe, death to the heart tissue.

It should be mentioned that this theory about the cause of heart attacks has led to a massive industry devoted to its diagnosis and treatment. Angiograms (in which dye is injected into the vessels to see if they are blocked), bypasses, stents, angioplasties (like roto-rooters for blocked arteries), cholesterol- lowering drugs and low fat, low-cholesterol diets are all based one hundred percent on the acceptance of blocked arteries as the only Cause of acute coronary syndrome.

Interestingly, in the 1940s and 1950s, when the coronary blockage theory was first proposed, the majority of cardiologists did not accept it. They pointed out that while coronary arteries are not the only arteries to have plaque; the only tissue to suffer from decreased blood flow during a heart attack is that of the heart. In other words, no one has a spleen attack or a kidney attack, yet the arteries feeding these organs also get plaque buildup. In a 1998 paper by Mirakami, the author found that of those with an acute MI, 49 percent had a blockage, 30 percent had no coronary blockage, 14 percent had insufficient blockage to impair blood flow, and 7 percent had “another condition.”

In a 1972 paper, a researcher named Roberts showed that in acute MIs, only 50-60 percent had evidence of sufficient blockage to impair blood flow. And a 25-year autopsy study of patients who died from an acute MI, carried out by Spain and Bradess, found that only 25 percent had sufficient blockage to account for their MI, while a total of 75 percent had only mild to moderate blockage. These same authors reported on a surprising discovery: when a heart attack is fatal, the longer the time elapsed between the MI and death (and then subsequent autopsy), the more likely they were to find significant blockages. If death occurred one hour after onset of an MI, only 16 percent had sufficient blockages to account for their MI; if death occurred 24 hours after the onset of an MI, the number with sufficient blockages to account for the heart attack increased to 53 percent. Therefore the authors concluded that the arterial blockages are a consequence, not a cause, of myocardial infarction.

***II-Cholestrol link***

Health officials in the United States urge everyone over the age of 20 to have their cholesterol tested once every five years. Part of this test is your total cholesterol, or the sum of your blood's cholesterol content, including HDL, LDLs, and VLDLs. The American Heart Association recommends that your total cholesterol is less than 200 mg/dl, but what they do not tell you is that total cholesterol level is just about worthless in determining your risk for heart disease, unless it is above 330. Ron Rosedale, MD, who is widely considered to be one of the leading anti-aging doctors in the United States, does an excellent job of explaining this concept: "Notice please that LDL and HDL are lipoproteins -- fats combined with proteins. There is only one type of cholesterol and there is no such thing as "good" or "bad" cholesterol. Cholesterol is just cholesterol".

It combines with other fats and proteins to be carried through the bloodstream, since fat and our watery blood do not mix very well. Fatty substances therefore must be shuttled to and from our tissues and cells using proteins. LDL and HDL are forms of proteins and are far from being just cholesterol. In fact we now know there are many types of these fat and protein particles. LDL particles come in many sizes and large LDL particles are not a problem. Only the so-called small dense LDL particles can potentially be a problem, because they can squeeze through the lining of the arteries and if they oxidize, otherwise known as turning rancid, they can cause damage and inflammation.

Thus, there is "good LDL" and "bad LDL." Also, some HDL particles are better than others. Knowing just your total cholesterol tells you very little. Even knowing your LDL and HDL levels will not tell you very much. Dr. Rosedale points out, "cholesterol is a vital component of every cell membrane on Earth. In other words, there is no life on Earth that can live without cholesterol. We would not be here without it. No wonder lowering cholesterol too much increases one's risk of dying. Cholesterol is also a precursor to all of the steroid hormones. You cannot make estrogen, testosterone, cortisone, and a host of other vital hormones without cholesterol."

One large study conducted by Dutch researchers found that men with chronically low cholesterol levels showed a consistently higher risk of having depressive symptoms. This may be because cholesterol affects the metabolism of serotonin, a substance involved in the regulation of your mood. On a similar note, Canadian researchers found that those in the lowest quarter of total cholesterol concentration had more than six times the risk of committing suicide as did those in the highest quarter. Dozens of studies also support a connection between low or lowered cholesterol levels and violent behavior, through this same pathway: lowered cholesterol levels may lead to lowered brain serotonin activity, which may, in turn, lead to increased violence and aggression. And one meta-analysis of over 41,000 patient records found that people who take statin drugs to lower their cholesterol as much as possible may have a higher risk of cancer, other studies have linked low cholesterol to Parkinson's disease.

Sally Fallon, the president of the Weston A. Price Foundation, and Mary Enig, Ph.d, an expert in lipid biochemistry, have gone so far as to call high cholesterol "an invented disease, a "problem" that emerged when health professionals learned how to measure cholesterol levels in the blood. If your cholesterol is too low (less than 150mg) all kinds of nasty things can happen to your body. Remember, every single one of your cells needs cholesterol to thrive -- including those in your brain. Perhaps this is why low cholesterol wreaks havoc on your psyche. Weston A. Price Foundation has posted various studies on their website about the cholesterol- heart disease myth. "In Framingham, Massachusetts, the more saturated fat one ate, the more cholesterol one ate, the more calories one ate, the lower people's serum cholesterol. . . we found that the people who ate the most cholesterol, ate the most saturated fat, ate the most calories weighed the least and were the most physically active." --William Castelli, MD, Director, the Framingham Study

"The diet-heart hypothesis has been repeatedly shown to be wrong, and yet, for complicated reasons of pride, profit and prejudice, the hypothesis continues to be exploited by scientists, fund-raising enterprises, food companies and even governmental agencies. The public is being deceived by the greatest health scam of the century." --George Mann, ScD, MD, Former Co-Director, The Framingham Study "An analysis of cholesterol values in 1,700 patients with atherosclerotic disease revealed no definite correlation between serum cholesterol levels and the nature and extent of atherosclerotic disease."--Michael DeBakey, MD, Famous Heart Surgeon.

After twenty years of routine cardiology practice Dr. Stephen Sinatra, a cardiologist at Manchester Memorial hospital realized that high cholesterol was not the main cause of heart disease, led to an entirely new direction for his practice. He shifted from aggressive lipid lowering to strategies aimed at reducing systemic inflammation which he believes is the primary driver of heart disease. He has come to believe that the lipid-based explanation for CVD is, by and large, a fallacy--albeit a profitable one. He expresses his view eloquently and in thorough detail in a recent book called, The Great Cholesterol Myth (Fair Winds Press 2012), co-authored with nutritionist Jonny Bowden. Written for educated, health conscious consumers, the book is packed with references to hundreds of studies most of them in mainstream journals that give good reasons for questioning the lipid hypothesis and the statin-mania that it spawned. "The established view in conventional medicine is that cholesterol is the main marker for CVD. Nothing could be further from the truth,"

***Hazards of Cholesterol lowering drugs:***

Statin drugs work by inhibiting an enzyme in your liver that's needed to manufacture cholesterol. What is so concerning about this is that when you go tinkering around with the delicate workings of the human body, you land into high risk chemistry. For starters, statin drugs deplete your body of Coenzyme Q10 (CoQ10), which is beneficial to heart health and muscle function. Because doctors rarely inform people of this risk and advise them to take a CoQ10 supplement, this depletion leads to fatigue, muscle weakness, soreness, and eventually heart failure. Muscle pain and weakness, a condition called rhabdomyolysis, is actually the most common side effect of statin drugs, which is thought to occur because statins activate the atrogin-1 gene, which plays a key role in muscle atrophy. By the way, muscle pain and weakness may be an indication that your body tissues are actually breaking down -- a condition that can cause kidney damage. Other side effects are depression, dizziness, poly-neuropathy, memory impairment, liver disorders, immune suppression and even cancer. Many in the conventional clinical community seem to have overlooked the CARE (Cholesterol and Recurrent Events) study, published in 1999, which looked at 500 post-menopausal women randomized to placebo or pravachol therapy. The women taking the statin did have fewer CV events, but there was no difference in overall mortality, because the pravachol group also showed a statistically significant increase in breast cancer (Sacks FM, et al. N Engl J Med. 1996; 335: 1001-1009.)

***III-Transfats: the real killer fats***

Transfatty acids are a type of fat molecule produced by a process called "partial hydrogenation," which rearranges the hydrogen atoms in liquid unsaturated fatty acids to produce an unnatural fat, which like saturated fat is solid at room temperature. These Transfats have many serious side effects in the body:

i. Transfats raise Lp(a) (indicating they cause heart disease), while saturated fats lower Lp(a).
ii. Transfats interfere with immune function, while saturated fats enhance immune function.
iii. Transfats inhibit the body's use of omega-3 fatty acids and the production of long-chain omega-3 fatty acids, while saturated fats

enhance the body's use of omega-3 fatty acids and the production of the long-chain versions.

iv. Foods containing Transfats are associated with increased asthma; saturated fats are needed for the proper functioning of the lungs.

v. Transfats contribute to weight gain, while some types of saturated fats (the medium chain triglycerides) boost metabolism and help with weight loss.

vi. Transfats are associated with increased cancer and decreased fertility. Sources of saturated fat, such as butter and meat fats, contain many nutrients that fight against cancer and promote fertility.

Transfats are used in most processed foods, such as commercial cakes, pies, cookies, crackers, bread, chips, pretzels, snack foods, breaded foods and salad dressings. Most restaurants fry foods in oil blends containing transfats. Any food item cooked in "partially hydrogenated" oil contains transfats. Small amounts of transfats are found in deodorized vegetable oils (such as canola oil) as well. The only way to avoid transfats is to avoid processed foods. Instead, prepare your own foods using fresh, natural ingredients like natural non processed butter instead of margarine or spreads.

***IV-Inflammation and heart disease***

Inflammation is body's natural response to invaders, it perceives as threats. The process of inflammation constricts the blood vessels, thickens the blood, accumulation of chemicals and cells to repair the damage. When an artery is damaged a scar is formed in the artery called a plaque. This plaque, along with the thickening of your blood and constricting of your blood vessels that normally occur during the inflammatory process, can indeed increase your risk of high blood pressure and heart attacks. Now liver will be notified to make more cholesterol and release it into your bloodstream to repair the plaque. If due to unhealthy lifestyle vessel is damaged frequently a state of chronic inflammation develops. The test usually used to determine if you have chronic inflammation is a C-reactive protein (CRP) blood test. CRP level is used as a marker of inflammation in your arteries.

i. A CRP level under 1 milligrams per liter of blood means you have a low risk for cardiovascular disease

ii. 1 to 3 milligrams means your risk is intermediate

iii. More than 3 milligrams is high risk

***Chronic inflammation is actually caused by:***

- Oxidized cholesterol (cholesterol that has gone rancid, such as that from overcooked food)
- Eating lots of sugar and grains
- Eating foods cooked at high temperatures
- Eating trans fats
- A sedentary lifestyle
- Smoking
- Emotional stress

### *V-Nutritional deficiencies*

#### *a-Vitamin D deficiency*

There are only 30,000 genes in your body and vitamin D has been shown to influence over 2,000 of them. That is one of the primary reasons it influences so many diseases. A new study has linked a lack of sunshine, the body's most natural source of vitamin D, to the prevalence of cardiovascular disease. Factors that affect sunlight, and therefore vitamin D production, are tied to a patient's cardiovascular risks. In other words, the more sunlight you get, the better your cardiovascular health will be. There are a number of physiological mechanisms triggered by vitamin D production through sunlight exposure that act to fight heart disease. According to the study the mechanisms are:

i. An increase in the body's natural anti-inflammatory cytokines.

ii. The suppression of vascular calcification.

iii. The inhibition of vascular smooth muscle growth.

Other studies have also suggested a potential association between abnormal vitamin D levels and cardio-metabolic disorders including heart disease, diabetes, and metabolic syndrome. Johanna Parker, from University of Warwick (United Kingdom), and colleagues conducted a systematic literature review of studies examining vitamin D (25-hydroxy vitamin D [25OHD] as an indicator of vitamin D status) and cardio-metabolic disorders. The team reviewed 28 studies involving a total of 99,745 subjects across a variety of ethnic groups and including both men and women. The studies revealed a significant association between high levels of vitamin D and a decreased risk of developing cardiovascular disease (33% compared to low levels of vitamin D), type 2 diabetes (55% reduction) and metabolic syndrome (51% reduction). Writing that: "High levels of vitamin D among middle-age and elderly populations are associated with a substantial decrease in cardiovascular disease, type 2 diabetes and metabolic syndrome," the researchers say that: "If the relationship proves to be causal, interventions targeting vitamin D deficiency in adult populations could potentially slow the current epidemics of cardio-metabolic disorders."

***b-Vitamin B complex***

Scientific studies have proven that Folic acid and other B vitamins reduce the risk of coronary heart disease and stroke. These nutrients work by attacking homocysteine, an amino acid in the blood that attacks blood vessel walls and promotes cardiovascular disease. High blood levels of homocysteine, also known as hyperhomocysteinemia, pose a risk of cardiovascular disease. Beresford estimated that up to 50,000 coronary heart disease deaths could be prevented by increasing folic acid intake-by eating more fruit and vegetables. Another study, involving researchers from several U.S. universities and medical centers, examined the relationship between homocysteine, folic acid, and B6 in the narrowing of the carotid artery. This artery feeds blood to the head and neck, and its condition is indicative of coronary and cerebrovascular disease. Therefore for lowering homocysteine Levels we need;

i. Folic Acid - also known as Vitamin B9, folic acid can help the body produce the enzymes necessary to remove homocysteine from the blood.

ii. Vitamin B6 - along with folic acid and Vitamin B12, helps reduce homocysteine levels.

iii. Vitamin B12 - works with folic acid and Vitamin B6 to assist in homocysteine removal.

***c-Vitamin K2***

In1945, Dr. Weston Price described "a new vitamin-like activator" that played an influential role in the utilization of minerals, protection from tooth decay, growth and development, reproduction, protection against heart disease and the function of the brain. Using a chemical test, he determined that this compound which he called Activator X occurred in the butterfat, organs and fat of animals consuming rapidly growing green grass, and also in certain sea foods such as fish eggs. Dr. Price died before research by Russian scientists became known in the West. These scientists used the same chemical test to measure a compound similar to vitamin K. Vitamin $K_2$ is produced by animal tissues, including the mammary glands, from vitamin $K_1$, which occurs in rapidly growing green plants.

A growing body of published research confirms Dr. Price's discoveries, namely that vitamin $K_2$ is important for the utilization of minerals, protects against tooth decay, supports growth and development, is involved in normal reproduction, protects against calcification of the arteries leading to heart disease, and is a major component of the brain. Vitamin $K_2$ works synergistically with the two other "fat-soluble activators" that Price studied, vitamins A and D. Vitamins A and D signal to the cells to produce certain proteins and vitamin K then activates these proteins. Vitamin $K_2$'s ability to protect us from heart disease is much more clearly established. Research is in fact rapidly redefining heart disease largely as a deficiency of this vitamin. While it is most clearly established that vitamin $K_2$ deficiency causes calcification of the cardiovascular system, vitamin $K_2$ appears to protect against the inflammation and accumulation of lipids and white blood cells that characterize atherosclerosis as well.

The inverse association between heart disease and vitamin $K_2$ intake is more straightforward. In The Rotterdam Study, which prospectively followed just over 4,600 men aged 55 or older in the Netherlands, the highest intake of vitamin $K_2$ was associated with a 52 percent lower risk of severe aortic calcification, a 41 percent lower risk of coronary heart disease (CHD), a 51 percent lower risk of CHD mortality, and a 26 percent lower risk of total mortality. Even though the study population consumed ten times more $K_1$ than $K_2$, vitamin $K_1$ had no association with either the degree of aortic calcification or the risk of heart disease.[20]The profound effects of variations in such small amounts of dietary $K_2$ emphasize just how powerful this substance is in the prevention of degenerative disease.

***d-Minerals***

Potassium, Magnesium and Calcium are the minerals, collectively known as electrolytes, are involved in regulating blood pressure. The DASH diet, a well-studied diet that helps lower high blood pressure, focuses on foods rich in these three minerals. Based on dietary studies, these minerals can help keep blood pressure at healthy levels or help reduce the risk of certain cardiovascular diseases. It is not known whether taking supplements of these minerals will help reduce your risk of heart disease. The best approach is to get plenty of these minerals from the foods you eat. The benefits of magnesium in treating heart disease include the well-known decrease in ischemic heart disease and sudden death found in communities drinking hard water (magnesium containing), powerful prevention of platelet clumping (clot prevention) known to be caused by magnesium, strong blood vessel dilating properties of magnesium, and effective action to block dangerous heart rhythms in persons taking magnesium.

***e-CoQ$_{10}$ Deficiency***

Co Enzyme Q10 (Co Q10) is a nutritional supplement used around the world as a heart energizer. Researchers found that in most of the cases of heart problems, there was an associated deficiency of CoQ10. On the corollary, all the well-functioning hearts had an adequate amount of CoQ10 in the tissue. Furthermore, when supplemental CoQ10 was administered, the ailing hearts started showing signs of new life. Experts say that adequate levels of CoQ10 are necessary for a well-functioning system. When the levels of CoQ10 drops below optimum levels, disease takes over or already had done so. Coenzyme Q10 is an essential ingredient in the body's production of energy and in the normal metabolism of fat and energy. It participates in biochemical reactions in our bodies that provide energy. It is of extreme benefit to sufferers of angina. It prevents the accumulation of fatty acids within the heart muscle by improving the conversion of fatty acids and other compounds into energy. When a person is suffering from cardiomyopathy and other kinds of heart failure, the supplements of coenzyme Q10 are thought to help the remaining muscle cells do their jobs more efficiently.

Coenzyme Q10 is manufactured by the body and stored in your organs: liver, kidneys and heart. It is believed that, in our body, the vitamins such as niacin, vitamin B6, vitamin B12, vitamin C and folate assist our body to convert the amino acid tyrosine to coenzyme Q10. Heart tissue biopsies in patients with various heart diseases show a CoQ10 deficiency in fifty to seventy- five percent of cases. Furthermore, cardiovascular diseases, including angina, hypertension, mitral valve prolapse, and congestive heart failure, require increased tissue levels of CoQ10. A growing number of nutrition oriented doctors say that supplements of Co Q10 are absolutely essential for people with heart failure. Co Q10 was said to have several patients who used it to live longer, more active lives, has saved some people who would otherwise have died waiting for donor hearts and has even allowed some to take their names off the transplant list.

The filling phase of the heart requires more energy than the contraction phase, and is therefore more sensitive to $CoQ_{10}$ deficiency. Energy starvation of the heart due to $CoQ_{10}$ deficiency causes stiffening of the heart walls in the left ventricle and results in impaired filling of the heart, or diastolic dysfunction. Fatigue or lack of energy is a common symptom of diastolic dysfunction. The stiffened heart walls increase energy requirements of the heart thereby increasing $CoQ_{10}$ utilization and further depleting $CoQ_{10}$ reserves. A vicious cycle sets in. As diastolic dysfunction worsens, blood pressure and heart rate increase, the heart walls thicken, and pulmonary hypertension often develops. When diastolic dysfunction is sufficient to produce pulmonary congestion (that is, a damming up of blood into the lungs causing shortness of breath), congestive heart failure is said to be present. Estimates indicate that 15 percent of those under age 50 and 50 percent of those over age 70 have diastolic dysfunction, and more than half of those presenting with acute pulmonary congestion have diastolic heart failure. Systolic heart dysfunction caused by coronary artery disease and diastolic dysfunction due to $CoQ_{10}$ deficiency are both common in the older population.

***VI-Oxidative Stress***

Oxidative Stress (OS) is not a disease but a condition that can lead to a disease or accelerate it. OS occurs when the available supply of the body's antioxidants is insufficient to handle and neutralize free radicals of different types. The result is massive cell damage that can result in cellular mutations, tissue breakdown and immune compromise. Biochemical antioxidants not only scavenge free radicals, but also inhibit their formation inside the body. These include lipoic acid, and repair enzymes such as catalase, superoxide dismutase (SOD), glutathione peroxidase. Melatonin, a hormone produced by the pineal gland, is also a potent antioxidant. Cholesterol, produced by the liver, is another major biochemical antioxidant, which the body uses to repair damaged blood vessels. It is probably for this reason that serum cholesterol levels rise as people age.

With age comes more free radical activity and in response the body produces more cholesterol to help contain and control the damage. OS causes atherosclerosis and coronary thrombosis leading to various cardiac ailments. The increased oxidative stress resulting from coronary artery disease increases utilization of ubiquinol, the reduced form of $CoQ_{10}$, resulting in low levels of both total $CoQ_{10}$ and ubiquinol. Levels of ubiquinol in those with CAD have been found to be inversely proportional to triglyceride levels. Diabetes causes severe depression of $CoQ_{10}$ levels, and because development of CAD usually occurs slowly, diastolic heart failure is common in diabetic patients.

***VII-Milk pasteurization***

J.C. Annand, a British researcher, observed an increase in heart disease in districts that implemented pasteurization compared to those where milk was still sold unpasteurized. Pasteurization transforms the physical structure of the proteins in milk, such as casein, and alters the shape of the amino acid configuration into a foreign protein that your body is not equipped to handle. Pasteurization destroys vitamins, minerals and enzymes present in the real milk.

### *VIII-Myogenic Theory of heart disease*

The myogenic theory was developed by Quintiliano H. de Mesquita, a cardiologist and scientist from Brazil, deceased in October 2000. Dr. Mesquita has made around 30 pioneer contributions to medical science. This new theory is based in a complex biological mechanism where physical and psycho-emotional stresses are important players in triggering the acute myocardial infarction, through the weakening of an area of the heart muscle. Supported by Infarct Combat Project the myogenic theory opposes the classic postulation of the thrombogenic theory developed in the beginning of the last century by James Bryan Herrick. In thrombogenic theory the myocardial infarction is due to the occurrence of thrombosis in the coronary artery. Carlos Monteiro, an independent researcher and president of Infarct Combat Project, says the many flaws existing in the original thrombogenic theory etiology led to amendments on it. He also states that almost all medical solutions offered today through drugs or surgeries, in this sense, are palliative measures. These measures are without curing or reducing significantly, in absolute terms, the mortality from coronary heart disease. This is confirmed by many studies. Dr. Thomas Cowan, a well-known physician, writer and lecturer, from San Francisco, CA, knowing about the myogenic theory, invited Carlos Monteiro to write a report on Dr. Mesquita's decades-long studies. The article was published in Fourfold Healing Newsletter of November/December 2005, with an introduction by Dr. Cowan discussing this new explanation for heart disease. Dr. Thomas Cowan explains the Myogenic theory in his article "What Causes Heart Attacks"

***Briefly, the myogenic theory of MIs states that:***

1. The coronary obstruction theory does not adequately explain all the observed facts concerning MIs.
2. The major etiologic (cause and effect) factor in an MI is a destructive chemical process; specifically, in situations of stress on the myocardial (heart muscle) tissue, often as a result of small vessel disease, the myocardial tissue gets insufficient oxygen and nutrients. This leads to destructive lactic acidosis in the tissue

which, if unchecked, leads to death of the myocardial cells. This process is largely unrelated to coronary artery disease.

3. The regular use of cardiotonics, primarily low-dose whole digitalis extracts or an extract of another herb called g-strophanthin, prevents this lethal acidosis and therefore prevents and corrects the true cause of this syndrome. The result is substantially lower morbidity and mortality from heart disease.

The myogenic theory postulates that as a result of disease in the small vessels the capillaries and small arterioles which is a consequence of such factors as stress, diabetes, smoking and nutritional deficiencies, heart cells, which are very active metabolically, suffer from inadequate oxygen and nutrient supply. This oxygen and nutrient deficiency increases under stressful conditions. When this happens, the heart cells revert to their backup system, which is anaerobic fermentation for energy generation very similar to what happens in your leg muscles when you run too far or too hard. The anaerobic fermentation produces lactic acid which collects in the tissues. Because the heart, unlike your leg muscles, cannot rest, the acidosis progresses if untreated, leading to actual death of the myocardial cells.

As a result of this necrotic process, inflammatory debris collects in the tissues, and it is this debris that is the actual source of the coronary artery blockages seen in death from acute MI. As you would predict, the longer the time period between the MI and death, the greater the likelihood of blockage exactly as observed in the studies. The only conclusion one can draw from this is that the heart cells die first and only then does the artery become blocked with debris liberated at myocardial cell death, which is precisely the kind of debris that is found in these blockages. The myogenic theory points us to a very different kind of preventive treatment for heart disease, one that focuses on small vessel disease and the prevention of heart tissue acidosis. The theory also explains why stress, diabetes and smoking are such strong risk factors for MI, because these factors have all been shown to primarily affect small capillaries and small blood vessels, not the large coronary arteries.

It turns out that there are simple, inexpensive and very effective compounds that effectively prevent lactic acidosis in the heart tissues. These medicines have been known for centuries as cardiotonics and have been used for treating heart disease in every traditional medical system in the world. The two best known are digitalis (the common foxglove) and strophanthus, an African vine. These plants are the source of so-called cardiac glycosides: digoxin and digitoxin from digitalis, and ouabain from strophanthus. The function of these compounds is to regulate the rhythm and power of the cardiac contraction and to prevent or reverse lactic acid buildup in the cardiac tissue. This is why these plants have been used for centuries to treat congestive heart failure, rhythm disturbances and other disorders of heart function.

The amazing thing is that these compounds are exact chemical copies of hormones made by our adrenal glands. And our adrenal glands produce these cardiotonics out of cholesterol. Now we know why all the draconian dietary and pharmaceutical measures to lower cholesterol have not resulted in a decrease in the rates of MI, and why numerous studies have shown that as we age, those with the highest levels of cholesterol live the longest. When we lower cholesterol, we are depriving our bodies of the very substance they need to manufacture cardiotonics.

The myogenic theory also explains why stress can lead to heart attacks. In conditions of stress, our adrenal glands must work very hard to create numerous hormones that regulate the blood sugar and help the body heal. If the adrenal glands are weak or overloaded, production of cardiotonics goes on the back burner. The final irony is that the traditional Chinese doctors were correct. The kidneys (their way of referring to the adrenal glands) help the body deal with stress as well as make hormones (digoxin and ouabain) that keep our marvelous hearts healthy, strong and open to enjoy the full richness of life.

**2-Emotional causes of heart disease**

“If someone wishes for good health, one must first ask oneself if he is ready to do away with the reasons for his illness. Only then is it possible to help him.” Hippocrates

When illness or disease is indicated, the body is communicating to us that our way of thinking (although unconscious) is out of harmony with what is beneficial to our being. Illness indicates the need to change in our belief system and tells us that we have reached our physical and psychological limits. Illness is thus a gift whose purpose is to bring back the equilibrium in our being. The physical body does not create illness because the physical body can do nothing by itself. What maintains its life is our soul, our inner self. Metaphysics is a philosophy that methodically investigates the nature of first principles and problems of ultimate reality. Its link with the physical is critical to permanent healing and is by no means contraindicated in conjunction with conventional healing. On the contrary, it is medicine’s most valuable teammate.

The most frequent causes of illness are negative attitudes, guilt, the need for attention, or the need to escape an unpleasant situation. Fear, anger, bitterness, jealousy, and worry can cause 80% of diseases from heart disease and ulcers to cancer. Studies of psychiatric patients, community samples, and patients with known heart disease demonstrated that depressive disorders, stressful life events, and poor social support are associated with increased incidence of morbidity, and mortality of atherosclerotic heart disease. Considerable evidence suggests that depression is an independent risk factor in the patho-physiological progression of cardiovascular disease.

The heart is placed virtually at the center of the body. If you are centered, you are living from the heart in a balanced state of love and trust that is in sync with the natural flow of the universe. Your perspective is one of balance and you tend to listen to the mutterings of your own heart when faced with decisions. A heart disorder is the manifestation of the opposite mindset. If you are having heart trouble, you probably tend to take everything to heart, or to take things far too seriously. You are not allowing for the proper flow in your life, whether its the flow of ideas, of love or of your very lifeblood. You are fighting the current of life to the point of physical and emotional exhaustion. You tend to deny your own needs and fulfill other people's needs in order to be loved. You seek love through what you do for others. The main message associated with any heart condition is Love YOURSELF!

According to The Seven Spiritual Laws of Yoga, the heart chakra is governed by the Law of Giving and Receiving, which states that the universe operates through constant and dynamic exchange. Every act of giving is an act of receiving. When you welcome a gift into your life, you provide someone else the joyful experience of giving.

***Acupuncture and heart***

According to Acupuncture heart is a holistic organ which controls brain and mental functions along with its own functions. The clinical uses of heart channel are to treat diseases along the channel, heart disease, mental disorders (anxiety, schizophrenia, hysteria, insomnia, and epilepsy), all types of tremors, speech disorders and autonomic disturbances like increased sweating.

## 3-Metaphysical causes of a heart disease

According to biophysics, the central nervous system and fats of the body, store the information required to operate the body functions and maintain homeostasis. This information has to be passed to all the cells and tissues of the body, for ultimately these are what are being governed. Although physical anatomy reveals that efferent and afferent nerves form connections with organs, but they do not connect to every cell. Biophysics investigations have found that it is, in fact, the blood that provides a medium in which nervous system information can be transferred to every cell of the body.

Information stored in the CNS is transferred to the heart through the cardiac nerves. The heart, through a combination of pressure waves (pumping), electron activity, and photon activity, induces information into the red blood cells where it is temporarily stored. This information flows through the arterial system to the capillaries, where oxygen, nutrients and information are transferred to the cells. The cells respond by taking up the nourishing supply and returning carbon dioxide, metabolic by-products and information about how they are performing their required job. This information flows back through the blood to the brain and CNS. The information received by the brain from the cells is compared with the instructions that were sent out. If cells are not doing as requested or the body's requirements have changed, then new instructions will be sent out via the heart and blood. Biophysical role of heart is sensitive to a thought process, electromagnetic radiation by new machines, earth magnetic fields and polarity. Cardiac arrhythmias and early age cardiac diseases are an outcome of biophysical imbalances.

Chakra medicine which is part of quantum physics says that heart chakra corresponds to thymus gland. This gland plays a vital role in good immunity, a holistically weak heart leads to suppressed immunity and ultimately a disease.

**Religion and role of heart**

Quran repeatedlymentions about three human senses, ability to see, hear and ability of heart for higher mental functions. It relates the state of heart to differentiate between an enlightened and an ignorant human being. Quran says if these three abilities are blocked, a human being acquires animal instincts and can commit unethical deeds easily. If heart energy is blocked, mental and spiritual being is badly affected leading to a bad physical health.

## Blood and its circulation

Looking at live blood under a microscope is an incredible learning tool and begins an incredible journey whereby we come to understand that there are dynamic life processes going on every second in our bodies. It is an environment that is an ever changing canvas of life that holds forms that develop and grow and illustrates what some call "the fungus among us." Today, researchers who want to observe living blood use standard laboratory microscopes with high magnification that are specially set up to view the blood under "darkfield" or "phase contrast" conditions. Using this kind of microscope technology, German bacteriologist Guenther Enderlein (a student of Bechamp) observed tiny microorganism like elements which he called protits. He stated that these tiny elements flourished in the blood cells, in the plasma body fluids, and in the tissues, living in harmony with the body in a symbiotic or mutually beneficial relationship. He considered the protit as one of the body's smallest, organized, biological units. The most interesting thing about this microorganism is its ability to change and adapt to its environment. It was observed that when there was severe change or deterioration in the body's internal environment (mostly noted by changes in ph), these elements would pass through several different stages of cyclic development, advancing from harmless agents to disease producing (pathological) bacteria or fungi. His book 'The Life Cycle of Bacteria' (Bakterian Cyclogenie) presented his theory. From his research he was able to produce natural biological answers to many of the degenerative disease processes plaguing western civilization today.

Good health requires, above all else, strong and steady blood flow through clear blood vessels. Healthy blood circulation delivers fresh nutrients to your cells, and prevents accumulation of waste materials within your cells. Both of these actions are equally necessary for healthy cells. This basic health principle is at the heart of an alternative treatment for multiple sclerosis (MS), discovered by an Italian physician and researcher, Dr. Paolo Zamboni.Beyond protecting ourselves from heavy metal poisoning, to optimally protect our blood vessels, it's worthwhile to remember the following points:

1. Excessive intake of sugar and other refined carbohydrates is a primary cause of deterioration of blood vessel walls. The mechanisms involved are many, and include increased blood viscosity and hyperinsulinemia.

2. Cheap vegetable oils that are high in polyunsaturated fatty acids (safflower, sunflower, cottonseed, corn) tend to be rich sources of free radicals that damage blood vessel walls.

3. A buildup of homocysteine can induce blood vessel damage. To prevent homocysteine buildup, it's vital that you ensure adequate intake of vitamins B12, B6, and folate

4. Chronic anger and anxiety can damage blood vessel walls through hyper sympathetic activity.

5. Excessive intake of foods that are cooked at high temperatures increases your exposure to free radicals that can contribute to blood vessel damage.

Blood viscosity is a fundamental yet often overlooked parameter for circulatory health, and a robust predictor of cardiovascular diseases (read, Blood Viscosity: The Unifying Parameter in Cardiovascular Risk). In this review, we turn our attention from the arterial system to the brain in order to highlight the important connections between blood viscosity and age-related cognitive impairment or dementia. The relationship between blood viscosity and blood flow (or perfusion) makes intuitive sense, to be sure, and it has also been confirmed through empirical studies. Clinically, measurement of blood viscosity could be a useful surrogate measure of perfusion, and much better suited than perfusion studies for routine use in the general population. Simply put, elevated blood viscosity translates directly into reduced blood perfusion. When blood flow is sufficiently disturbed, hyper viscosity can present as organ dysfunction with or without sensation of pain. The pattern of exponential increases in blood viscosity after the age of 60, as reported by the research group at the National Institute of Aging, helps to define an at-risk population that may benefit from blood viscosity monitoring and treatment.

The availability of clinically practical instrumentation for blood viscosity measurement, such as is now available at Meridian Valley Laboratory, creates a new avenue for detecting and controlling age-related blood flow disturbances in mid-life and senior adults, especially those 60 years of age and greater. During the personalized lifestyle modification, I have noticed thick blood viscosity giving various symptoms. A viscous blood circulates slowly and affects distant body areas like head, face and lower limbs. Besides presenting complaints I use the tool of pulse diagnosis and NES scan to assess the blood circulation. Impaired circulation affects peripheral more as compare to central blood circulation to protect the vital organs. The signs and symptoms of poor peripheral circulation are numbness, swelling of limbs, cold extremities, headaches, dizziness, impaired memory and deteriorating vision.

**Hypertension**

Harold M. Schmeck writes in his article ' Wide effects of heart hormone are found' that the revolutionary discovery of a hormone made by the human heart is scarcely two years old, but it has already spawned a whole new field of research as scientists begin to understand the substance's natural role and investigate ways of using it to treat heart disease, high blood pressure and kidney failure. Specialists who study heart and kidney function are fascinated by what they have already learned about the hormone. It helps dispose of excess sodium in the blood and thus seems to play a role in regulating the amount of salt in the body. It appears to act as a counterbalance to other vital hormones in governing blood volume and pressure. It is present in large amounts in the blood of patients who suffer from congestive heart failure and certain kinds of abnormally fast, irregular heartbeats.

Dr. Laragh of New York Hospital-Cornell Medical Centre said he had never seen "a single subject so intensively studied." One reason for the intense interest, he said, is that the concept of the heart as a hormone-producing organ is revolutionary. "I think the astonishing thing about this hormone, that all studies are showing, is that within minutes of its secretion by the heart it reduces the blood volume," Dr. Laragh said. The effect of this reduction in circulating blood is to reduce sharply the workload on the heart.

In either case, scientists say, it might be possible to mobilize the hormone's actions for medical needs or to produce related substances that could be used as drugs. The wealth of new research by many scientists is aimed at applications and also at better understanding of the hormone's natural role. Conventional medical system is not aware of the etiology of high blood pressure. 'Essential hypertension 'is the type of high blood pressure which does not have any etiology, and 90% of hypertension patients fall into this category. My clinical experience has clearly taught me that high blood pressure is a condition and not a disease. It is always secondary to a chemical imbalance, and disrupted biorhythms. There are two major reasons for high blood pressure, which can be reversed very easily and blood pressure becomes normal. First it is hyper-liver chemistry and second is water retention leading to high blood volume. Hyper-liver produces free radicals resulting in sympathetic hyperactivity leading to hypertension. In other words toxin overload leads to high blood pressure. Water retention increases blood volume which increases cardiac output and peripheral resistance leading to high blood pressure.

Through SLP I have helped many hypertension patients in normalization of their blood pressure without medications. University of British Columbia researchers have found that drug therapy has little value in early stage hypertension. They collected data from 4 randomized placebo-controlled trials representing more than 8,900 people with mild hypertension, defined as systolic blood pressure 140-159 mm Hg or diastolic blood pressure 90-99 mm Hg. The "first line" drugs in question included thiazide or thiazide-like diuretics, beta blockers, and reserpine.

Some patients in some studies were taking 2 or more drugs. Studies were between 4-5 years' duration.
There were no meaningful differences in mortality, incidence of coronary heart disease, or total cardiovascular events between patients on active treatments and those on placebos. None of the drug classes showed any significant efficacy in reducing disease incidence or death.
The investigators did find a trend toward reduced risk of stroke (0.3% with anti-hypertensive vs. 0.7% with control, p = 0.078) in the largest of the 4 trials, but other than that there were no other measurable benefits (Cochrane Database System Rev. 2012 Aug 15;8:CD006742 ). There was, however, a significant side-effect burden associated with drug treatment. There was an aggregate 9% adverse response rate among the drug-treated patients, and five times more people on active treatment versus placebo dropped out of studies due to adverse events.

**SLP causes of cardiovascular disorders**

The above mentioned eight physical causes of the heart disease, especially the myogenic theory has explained the role of liver in generation of the heart disease. In all of my cardiac patients I have noticed that homeostasis of biorhythms is dysfunctional along with a dysfunctional liver. Acidic body with hyper-liver creates a toxin overload leading to oxidative stress. Hyper-liver produces more triglycerides and less cholesterol, therefore deficiency of biological antioxidant cholesterol. People with acidic body and hyper-liver are hypoxic as well, therefore increasing anaerobic myocardial metabolism leading to acidosis which leads to cell death. People with acidic body and sluggish liver suffer from multiple nutritional deficiencies leading to high homocystein and a weak cardiac muscle due to poor micro circulation. They have poor supply of nutrients, antioxidants and excess of free radicals which impairs cardiac health. Their low body temperature causes arrhythmias.

A chronic chemistry of acidic body with hypo-liver and water retention has a tendency for left ventricular hypertrophy and cardiomegaly which responds pretty good to a liver specific lifestyle modification. There is a tendency for diastolic heart failure. Patients of this chemistry have generalized water retention and increased blood volume putting extra load on heart. I can recall last year three of my patients who were having left ventricular hypertrophy have normalization of their heart size with SLP over a period of six months. SLP helps in diagnosing a pre-cardiac disease, management and prognosis of a cardiac disease through simple tools specifically pulse diagnosis and NES scan. SLP manages cardiac patients in an excellent manner and overall health improves. By adopting a natural personalized lifestyle modification quality and circulation of blood improves, water retention settles, peripheral resistance decreases and ultimately it relaxes heart muscle. As SLP leads to a uniform blood circulation therefore blood pressure is normalized automatically.

**SLP reverses cardiac ailments by:**

I. Improvement in blood quality in terms of nutrients, circulation, and viscosity
II. Removal of free radicals by antioxidant
III. Introducing healthy fats and vitamin D
IV. Immune enhancement, therefore decreasing inflammation tendencies
V. Decreasing subtle chemical stress, by deep breathing
VI. Improving sleep quality and duration
VII. Yoga balances chakras which create a harmony between endocrine glands, liver, circulation and heart

**SLP Treatment for cardiovascular ailments**

1. Eat according to the eight rules of diet correction
2. Be careful about the nocturnal sleep
3. Do conscious efforts to handle emotional blocks, on day to day basis
4. Remember fear, guilt and sadness are very unhealthy for cardiac health
5. While taking decisions trust the feeling of your heart, because heart is connected to intuitive mind.
6. Healthy exercise should be part of your routine. Exercise keeps your calf muscle healthy which is called 'second heart'. Sensible and body compatible exercise, controls lymphatic and blood circulation perfectly.
7. Watch your peripheral body temperature, cold feet effect heart rhythm
8. Breathing exercise and meditation are excellent remedies for cardiac health.
9. Follow your religious practices, because your heart gets energy from your belief system.

# CHAPTER NO: 13

# WATCH YOUR BREATH: RESPIRATORY DISORDERS

## Special characteristics of respiratory system

### *1-The breathing process*

When you breathe on a physical level, you pull in oxygen. Everyone knows our body needs oxygen to survive. We breathe to deliver oxygen to the brain, to oxygenate the blood in our body and so on. When you breathe deeply, you expel the carbon dioxide and natural buildup of water in your lungs therefore keeping the lungs dry and free from illness. We do this naturally, but when we're stressed or in situations of great fear, we have a tendency to alter our breathing. This alteration can cause a buildup of the fluids in the lungs and a person slowly develops bronchitis or even phenomena.

This physical requirement often causes us to forget about the "life force energy" that our spiritual body requires. Life force energy is also called Prana and Qi, and when we breathe, we pull in this energy along with the oxygen. It is an energy that helps our spiritual body connects to the world around us. It helps us balance, address issues and find higher states of awareness that can assist in our enlightenment. Qi is just as important to our spiritual body as oxygen is for our physical body. No modern Western idea corresponds exactly to the range of meanings of Qi because It does not refer to the oxygen breathed into the chest. Qi exists in the human body without form, color or substance. The ancient Chinese likened it to fire. Qi is the form of energy composing the chakras and currents in the subtle body are unknown to medical science. It is an all-pervasive "organic" energy. More recently, Russian parapsychologists have introduced the notion of bioplasma, which is explained as a radiant energy field interpenetrating physical organisms. Journal of the American Medical Association 246:1967, 1981 writes "The respiratory center of the brain, which receives chemical, reflex, somatic and cerebral inputs, is a good computer in automatically regulating the rate, depth and pattern of respiration under various situations. Therefore artificial regulation during physical exercise is not the best for health."

***2-The breathing principle***

George Catlin (July 26, 1796 –December 23, 1872) was an American painter, author and traveler who specialized in portraits of Native Americans in the Old West. Catlin appears to have written an eccentric book, which was in an 8th edition by 1882, titled "Shut Your Mouth". This is a serious essay suggesting that all manner of ills arise in people who were slack jawed, people who do not routinely keep their mouths closed. The author says that even too much talking is harmful because of the mouth being open for the purpose. "There is no person in society but who will find... improvement in health and enjoyment..." from keeping his or her mouth shut.[4]George Catlin made a critical observation regarding the hierarchy of physiological functions required for health. "Man can exist several days without food, but only for few minutes without the action of his lungs. Rest assured that the great secret to life is the breathing principle."

According to Dr. Raymond Silkman, "Airway capacity is the biggest and most important part of the well-being of a human being. It is important to stress the fact that breathing through the mouth and breathing through the nose have extremely disparate effects on the body. We are not designed to breathe through our mouths. The body is able to live by breathing through the mouth, but it suffers greatly for doing it." To summarize his excellent article, published in *Wise Traditions* Winter/Spring 2006, Dr Silkman compares an underdeveloped cranium to an “over-packed suitcase,” and discusses how the resultant problems can affect the entire body. Lack of oxygenation or nourishment to cranial tissues, -1organs and improper drainage of waste products through the lymphatic system, in turn cause nerve conduction issues, hormonal imbalances and negative effects on brain function and mental clarity. Salivary ph drops or becomes acidic in mouth breathing. A forward head posture can develop, which in turn causes spinal misalignments, fatigue and fibromyalgia.

Due to mouth breathing maxilla (upper jaw bone) also becomes underdeveloped, affecting the eyesight and facial aesthetics and further narrowing the nasal passages, which do not drain or function properly. Mouth breathing can further depress the development of the maxilla and this underdevelopment is the main cause of mouth breathing in the first place. With underdevelopment of the maxilla due to poor nutrition before conception and *in utero* obstruction of the nasal passages sets the stage for sleep apnea. Researchers in the famous Framingham heart study found that “force vital capacity,” the maximum volume of air that a person can exhale after a maximum inhalation, is the primary predictor for long term health and vitality. Framingham researchers William B. Kennel and Helen Hubert state: “This pulmonary function measurement appears to be an indicator of general health and vigor and literally a measure of living capacity.” According to Dr. Kennel, “Long before a person becomes terminally ill, vital capacity can predict life span.”

Some 80-90 percent of all of the body’s metabolic energy production is created by oxygen, with only 10-20 percent created from food and water. Furthermore, the respiratory system is responsible for eliminating 70 percent of the bodily metabolic waste. In 1924, Nobel Laureate Dr. Otto Warburg linked lack of oxygen with cancer. “Summarized in a few words, the prime cause of cancer is the replacement of the respiration of oxygen in normal body cells by a fermentation of sugar.”Dr. Price wrote “Life in all its fullness is Mother

Nature obeyed," Catlin formed a similar opinion: "Most habits against Nature, if not arrested, run into disease." "Air is an Elementary principal, created by the hand of God, who creates nothing but perfections.

We need to learn from the Native Americans and place more emphasis on optimizing "the breathing principle." Breathing is something we do thirty thousand times a day, and breathing improperly, even for the one-third of our lives spent asleep, may undermine our vitality and even shorten our lifespan. Catlin observed that the American Indians practiced calm nasal breathing both day and night. Spiritual seekers for centuries have claimed that mastering the breath unlocks the mysteries of the universe. But, according to respiratory physiology expert Roger Price, learning to breathe properly is a fundamental, "mainstream"issue, not one to be avoided because it is a "sacred"issue or an "alternative care"issue. Thus, the Breathing Principle is a subject worthy of study, beginning with Catlin's command, "Shut your mouth!"

In yoga practice, the Law of Giving and Receiving is alive in every breath you take. With each inhalation and exhalation, you exchange billions of atoms with the environment. In each yoga pose, the complementary pairs of muscles are contracting and relaxing, holding and releasing. When the life force is flowing freely through your body/mind, you are in natural alignment with the generosity and receptivity of the universe. There are specific yoga poses that enliven the flow of energy through the fourth chakra, including Badda Konasana or butterfly pose.

***3-Mal-respiration in sleep: sleep apnea***

George Catlin's comments on nightmares and the associated "night terrors" actually describes sleep apnea, no person on earth who has got up from a fit of the nightmare will dispute the fact that when consciousness came, he found his mouth and throat wide open, and parched with dryness. Every attack of the nightmare, I proclaim, is the beginning of death. Though the spasm lasts for few minutes but death would have been the consequence how awful to be so near death, and so often. It is very evident that the back of the head should never be allowed, in sleep, to fall to a level with the spine; but should be supported by a small pillow, to elevate it a little, without raising the shoulders or bending the back, which should always be kept straight. When you lay your head upon a pillow, advance it a little forward, so as to imagine yourself in a gallery of a theater looking into the pit." He continues: "Lying on the back is thought by many to be an unhealthy practice; and a long habit of sleeping in a different position from infancy to old age may even make it so; but the general custom of the Savage Races, of sleeping in this position from infancy to old age, affords very conclusive proof, that if commenced in early life it is the healthiest for a general posture that can be adopted."

Both Dr. Price and George Catlin wondered why tuberculosis claimed so many lives in modern man. In Catlin's day, the disease was called "consumption." Catlin lost his wife and one of his children to pneumonia, and in his book he ponders the cause of respiratory illness, linking it to mouth breathing:" I am compelled to believe that a great proportion of the diseases prematurely fatal to human life, as well as mental and physical deformities, and the destruction of the teeth, are caused by the abuse of the lungs, in the Mal-respiration of sleep." The statistics on sleep apnea in the US show eighteen to twenty million Americans approximately one in fifteen people have diagnosed sleep apnea. Undiagnosed sleep apnea affects perhaps another seventeen million people.

Recent studies have shown that Sleep Disordered Breathing is associated with Type II diabetes now epidemic of diabetes in this country. Up to 50 percent of people afflicted with diabetes have sleep apnea! Still more studies link sleep apnea with diabetes, obesity and GERD.[14] Furthermore, people who suffer from sleep apnea are up to four times more likely to have a stroke and three times more likely to have a heart attack. Drowsy driving leads to at least one hundred thousand car crashes and over fifteen hundred deaths each year, according to the National Highway Safety Administration.

## Respiratory disorders

### Causes

#### *1-Acid reflux and asthma*

Interestingly, 41.1 percent of non-smokers who have a chronic cough and 60 percent of those who have asthma also have acid reflux. Asthma in children and adults is increasing at exponential rates. In 1995, almost fourteen million people were diagnosed with asthma while today that number has jumped to over thirty-four million. Acid reflux may cause people to breathe tiny drops of hydrochloric acid into their lungs, which can irritate the delicate pulmonary lining and cause spasms in the airways, triggering an asthma attack. Second, frequent episodes of acid reflux may cause digestive acid to damage the esophageal lining and expose some of the nerves that are connected to the lungs. Irritation of the nerve endings may initiate a constriction of airways, thereby causing an asthma attack. Additionally, the acid can cause inflammation of the throat and larynx.

Surprisingly, asthma medications that dilate the bronchial tubes can trigger acid reflux symptoms, as they may cause the stomach cardiac sphincter to relax, allowing acid to escape up through the esophagus. Regrettably, the conventional treatments for asthma merely address the symptom of narrowed breathing passages. Seven million people suffer from ear infections every year. Acid reflux may cause persistent ear infections as refluxed liquid enters the upper throat and damage the lining of the adenoids causing them to swell. The swollen adenoids can block the passages from the sinuses and Eustachian tubes, and fluid can build in the sinuses and middle ear.

### *2-Environmental Toxins*

Survival in the modern world is becoming more and more difficult because of the presence of the huge variety of environmental toxins. Environmental toxins are responsible for various respiratory disorders as well. Pesticides and industrial poisons are now proven as a cause of SARS--Severe Acute Respiratory Syndrome. They also accumulate mercury--one of the most toxic substances on the planet in our biosphere, in the oceans, in fish, and in our own bodies.

Electromagnetic pollution, irradiation, ultra-pasteurization, fluorescent lights and toxic additives like MSG and aspartame are other pollutants. These toxins are responsible for the rising rates of acute and degenerative disease along with multiple respiratory allergies. Pesticides work by interfering with vitamin A pathways. Therefore, adequate vitamin A is a key to surviving in the modern world. Household chemicals have fumes produced by mixing ammonia and bleach. When bleach and ammonia are combined, they create a gas called chloramines. When inhaled, this gas releases ammonia, hydrochloric acid, and oxygen free radicals in the lungs. Small amounts of chloramines may cause mild irritation, but it can corrode the tissues of the lung and damage the cells.

### *3-Drugs used in medical practice*

There are hundreds of drugs routinely prescribed against a variety of disorders that apparently can cause all kinds of lung diseases and damage, according to a recent report. This damage can happen within a very short time or after several years. The effects are mostly unpredictable and some are irreversible. According to a French researcher, so far 310 therapeutic substances have been identified as having such effects, and each year 20 to 30 new substances are being added to the list. "This means the number is really much greater if you consider that each active principle in a preparation is usually marketed in several different forms," said French lung expert Philippe Camus of the University Medical Centre of Dijon. There are no less 50 different lung diseases and syndromes (ranging from simple coughs and breathlessness to pleurisies and even acute respiratory failures) that seem to be either caused or aggravated by drugs.

At the head of this list are a number of antihypertensive beta-blockers, angiotensin-converting enzyme (ACE) inhibitors used to treat congestive heart failure or hypertension. Some antibiotics, anti-rheumatics (including methotrexate and several non-steroidal anti-inflammatories), or ergot derivatives which are used to improve the brain functions of elderly are also responsible for respiratory disorders. A recent British study even showed that a commonly used analgesic, acetaminophen (paracetamol), was not entirely free of blame either. Conducted on more than 1,500 patients, the study concluded that people who take acetaminophen (e.g., Tylenol) every week have an 80% greater risk of suffering from asthma than people who never take any, while those who consume it daily are over twice as likely to have asthma.

An Oslo University team presented a recent study linking the use of busulphan and cyclophosphamide with a temporary reduction in the pulmonary function. A Spanish team reported similar results concerning the same medicines, prescribed during the preparation of a bone marrow transplant and against breast cancer. A team from Cairo University announced results in showing that pneumonitis due to methotrexate is not unusual (over 8%) among Egyptians treated for rheumatoid arthritis. Professor Camus and colleagues reported new cases of serious pulmonary complications found in patients suffering from bladder cancer, who had been given injections of BCG and mitomycin directly in the bladder. One patient even died of it, after an attack of accelerated interstitial pneumonia.

***4-Nutritional factors***

Common nutritional factors for respiratory disorders and allergies are pasteurized milk, fizzy drinks and fruit juices. Resistance to tuberculosis increased in children fed raw milk instead of pasteurized, to the point that in five years only one case of pulmonary TB had developed, whereas in the previous five years, when children had been given pasteurized milk, 14 cases of pulmonary TB had developed. *The Lancet*, page 1142, May 8, 1938Raw organic milk strengthens the immune system with the seeding and feeding of diverse beneficial essential bacteria. Vegetable juice is a great alternative to fruit drinks because it does not have all the sugar. Cod liver oil usually dramatically improves the immune response. Fermented foods also increase the beneficial bacteria in the gut to fight infections.

A new study about fruits and vegetables suggests that a high consumption of antioxidants such as vitamin C, vitamin E, and selenium and beta carotene improves lung function. And it appears that such antioxidants may improve lung function in both smokers and nonsmokers, according to the report presented April 21 at the Experimental Biology '98 meeting in San Francisco. Indeed, intake of the antioxidants may help protect against chronic obstructive pulmonary disease (COPD) -- such as asthma, bronchitis and emphysema. The most important message is that diets rich in fruits and vegetables have been repeatedly shown to lower the risk of coronary heart disease and cancer, but very few studies have considered whether such diets may protect lung function or decrease risks of COPD. This study does show that consuming more antioxidant is associated with better lung function. The difference between those two groups and their lung function is approximately equivalent to the difference between a group of nonsmokers and a group of smokers who have smoked a pack a day for 10 years.

***5-Oxidative stress***

Oxidative Stress (OS) is not a disease but a condition that can lead to or accelerate a disease process. Asthma, emphysema, chronic pulmonary diseases are respiratory system manifestations of OS.

***6-Surgical interventions***

Surgical removal of tonsils or adenoids is another contributory factor for future respiratory disorders. A study of 300 patients found there was little difference in reduction of symptoms between the 150 children who had tonsillectomies and those that did not. In fact, during the 18 months following the procedures, there was no difference in the groups. Experts say this research backs the trend of declining tonsillectomies in the United States, which dropped from more than 1 million annually in the 1970s to 250,000 that are now performed each year.

## SLP and respiratory disorders

In the last 26 years of my clinical practice, I rarely have seen a patient of respiratory disease without having a digestive disorder. Upper respiratory disorders like flu or sinusitis are related to reflux or chronic indigestion. People with body chemistry like acidic body with sluggish liver, hyper-acidic body with sluggish liver and acidic body with hypo-liver and water retention suffer from hay fever, sinusitis, adenoids, chronic tonsillitis or changing season flu. People with acidic body with hyper-liver, hyper-acidic body with hyper-liver and acidic body with hyper-liver and with water retention suffer from asthma, chronic allergic coughs, pneumonias, fibrosis or other chronic lung disorders. SLP will help you in recovering from the respiratory disorders if you follow below mentioned rules.

I. Follow eight rules of correct eating.

II. Watch your breathing pattern, convert your shallow breathing into deep breathing

III. Learn about the breathing exercises of yoga and practice them every day.

IV. Improve sleep by correct time, duration and posture. Have 6-8 hours of night sleep and try to sleep on right with slightly elevated head.

V. Allocate about 30 minutes in routine to your hobby or passion to combat everyday stress, which further leads to shallow breathing.

VI. Take a supplement of vitamin A, C and E to strengthen the bronchial linings. Cod liver oil capsules are an excellent food supplement. Daily supplements of vitamins C and E help counteract the negative effects of ozone on lung function in athletes. Previous studies have found that even low levels of ozone, an air pollutant, can have significant effects on lung function, evident as little as one hour after exposure. These effects have previously been studied in athletes exercising indoors, under laboratory conditions.

**VII.** Exercise in a closed space should be avoided. Routine morning walk is highly recommended for good lung health.

## CHAPTER NO: 14

## SHARPEN YOUR REFLEXES: NEUROLOGICAL DISORDERS

Human brain is extremely complex organ to understand. This organ, despite weighing just 3 pounds (1.36 kg), contains over 100 billion neurons, or signaling units. These neurons are responsible for receiving messages and making sense out of them. "Neuroscientist now knows, the brain is an organ of mind-boggling plasticity like the rest of your body, dynamic, not fixed for life. Larry Squire, professor of neuroscience at the University of California at San Diego and past president of the national Society for Neuroscience, has said, "If you could use a video camera to watch the brain respond to experiences, I have no doubt you would see it growing, retracting, reshaping."

Neurodegenerative diseases pose some of modern medicine's most difficult challenges. Our aging population face epidemic proportions of those ailments. The diseases also invade the most inaccessible areas of the brain, making it extremely difficult to track the illnesses and determine the mechanisms behind them the essential starting points for designing direct treatments or cures. Nevertheless, researchers have given themselves a head start by applying such tools as agonists and antagonists, antibodies and other cell labeling reagents, microscopy, and imaging analysis systems to gain insights into the ways in which the nervous system functions and malfunctions. "The road ahead is really exciting," declares Weiping Jiang, assistant director of R&D Systems.

Understanding neurological diseases "is clearly the Holy Grail within science at the moment," adds Keith Watling, director of cell signaling and neuroscience for Sigma-Aldrich. Neurological conditions can be misunderstood for a variety of reasons. They have no explanation for the disease because medical science is not interested in curing anything, as Dr. Alan Greenberg reminds us when he says, “Despite the investment of hundreds of billions of dollars of research, not even a single degenerative disease has been cured in the last hundred years.” Some of the symptoms are off-putting or upsetting to observers, which creates a stigma of the condition and isolates the person suffering from it. Persons experiencing some of these symptoms may have a hard time identifying that there is indeed a disorder causing the odd effects in the body.

**Causes of Neurological disorders**

***I-Neurotoxin exposure***

Dr. Russell Blaylock, neurosurgeon speaking of the recent explosion in neurodegenerative disease says, “Things that used to be rare, we're seeing all the time now".Dr. Blaylock states clearly that the epidemic is here because we have such a large combination of toxins converging, and simultaneously attacking the cells of our bodies. “For instance, we know that cellular neurodegenerative diseases are connected to mercury, aluminum, pesticides and herbicides, and they produce brain damage through an excitotoxic mechanism. The food chemicals like MSG and aspartame tremendously accelerate this toxicity. That's why we're seeing this explosion in neurodegenerative diseases". Blaylock states that Alzheimer, autism, ADD and parkinsonism are increasing so enormously because we are exposed to carcinogenic toxins and excitotoxins.

Excessive levels of toxic elements, such as lead, cadmium, mercury, and aluminum have an "unbalancing" effect on the levels of essential trace element in the body's cells. In 1998 Julie Varner and two colleagues published research on the effects of aluminum-fluoride and sodium-fluoride on the nervous system of rats. They concluded, "Chronic administration of aluminum-fluoride and sodium-fluoride in the drinking water of rats resulted in distinct morphological alterations of the brain, including the effects on neurons and cerebro-vasculature. Therefore fluoride in dental products and drinking water is responsible for multiple degenerative neurological disorders. The presence of MSG, aspartame, mercury and aluminum in vaccines, dental amalgam, in the air, water and foods will bring on symptoms of tremors, forgetfulness, and disorientation. The integrity and function of the blood brain barrier BBB is critical for overall brain function. The common causes of generalized changes in BBB permeability include organic solvents, enzymes, mercury, heavy metals and free radicals.

Individuals newly diagnosed with Parkinson's disease were more than twice as likely to have been exposed to insecticides in their home, compared to those without the disease.[26] In September 2000; *The Lancet* reported that farmers and gardeners regularly exposed to pesticides may have more than five times the risk of developing mild cognitive dysfunction. Children exposed prenatally and during infancy to common environmental toxins like dioxin and polychlorinated biphenyls (PCBs) can suffer behavioral, learning, and memory problems because these chemicals may be disrupting the normal action of thyroid hormone.[21]Combinations of insecticides, weed killers, and artificial fertilizers, even at low level shave measurable detrimental effects on thyroid, other hormones and brain as well.

The mercury-autism connection has surfaced to the public's attention with the publication of "Deadly Immunity," by Robert F. Kennedy, Jr. in the July issue of Rolling Stone magazine. Kennedy describes about a meeting of Center for Disease Control and Prevention, held June 2000 at which CDC epidemiologist Tom Verstraeten presented evidence to industry and government officials that thimerosal, the mercury-based preservative in vaccines, was responsible for the epidemic of autism in America's children. More than 500,000 children suffer from autism, with 40,000 new cases diagnosed every year

.

The disease was unknown until 1943, when it was identified and diagnosed among eleven children born after thimerosal was first added to baby vaccines in 1931. "You couldn't' even construct a study that shows thimerosal is safe," says Dr. Boyd Haley, one of the world's authorities on mercury toxicity and head of the chemistry department at the University of Kentucky."It's just too darn toxic. If you inject thimerosal into an animal, its brain will sicken. If you apply it to living tissue, the cells die. If you put it in a Petri dish, the culture dies. Knowing these things, it would be shocking if one could inject it into an infant without causing damage." The introduction of thimerosal into vaccines coincided with an increase in the number of vaccines given to children. Infants who receive all their vaccines, plus boosters, by the age of six months are exposed to levels of ethylmercury, injected directly into the bloodstream, 187 times greater than the EPAs limit for daily exposure to methylmercury, a related neurotoxin.

### *II-Minerals deficiency*

#### *a-Magnesium deficiency*

Magnesium has been seen to attenuate increased blood-brain barrier permeability during insulin-induced hypoglycemia in animal studies. Magnesium has its important role at the BBB and researchers think that this metal protects brain tissue against the effects of cerebral ischemia, brain injury and stroke through its actions as a calcium antagonist and inhibitor of excitatory amino acids. Magnesium is essential in regulating central nervous system excitability thus magnesium-deficiency may cause aggressive behavior, depression, or suicide.

Dr. Lewis B. Barnett, head of the Hereford Clinic and Deaf Smith Research Foundation in Hereford, Texas, reported that children of all ages, stricken with epilepsy who failed to respond or responded only slightly to modern anti-seizure drugs and therapy, when placed on high doses of magnesium, experienced “stunning improvement”. In the same study, all participants were shown to have marked magnesium deficiency. "Within a matter of weeks the blood magnesium level returned to normal, and in every case, except one, there was definite clinical improvement" reported Dr. Barnett after providing oral doses of magnesium and a normal diet to the 28 children in the study. The lower the magnesium levels the more severe was the seizure activity.

The Department of Family Medicine, Pomeranian Medical Academy, states that dietetic factors can play a significant role in the origin of ADHD and that magnesium deficiency can result in disruptive behaviors. Even a mild deficiency of magnesium can cause sensitiveness to noise, nervousness, irritability, mental depression, confusion, twitching, trembling, apprehension, and insomnia. Magnesium depletion, particularly in the hippocampus, appears to represent an important pathogenic factor in Alzheimer's disease. It is associated with high aluminum incorporation into brain neurons. Richest natural sources of magnesium are whole grains, brown rice, lentils, nuts, seeds, fish, banana, avocado, dark leafy vegetables and dark chocolate.

***b-Zinc deficiency***

Relatively high levels of zinc are found in the brain, especially the hippocampus. Zinc plays an important role in the transmission of the nerve impulse between brain cells. Deficiency of zinc during pregnancy and lactation has been shown to be related to many congenital abnormalities of the nervous system in offspring. In children, "insufficient levels of zinc have been associated with lowered learning ability, apathy, lethargy, and mental retardation." The USDA references a study of 372 Chinese school children with very low levels of zinc in their bodies. The children who received zinc supplements had the most improved performance--especially in perception, memory, reasoning, and psychomotor skills such as eye-hand coordination.

Three earlier studies with adults also showed that changes in zinc intake affected cognitive function. New research has identified a specific contingent of neurons, called "zinc-containing" neurons, which are found almost exclusively in the forebrain, where in mammals they have evolved into a "complex and elaborate associational network that interconnects most of the cerebral cortices and limbic structures." This suggests the importance of zinc in the normal and pathological processes of the cerebral cortex. Furthermore, age-related tissue zinc deficiency may contribute to brain cell death in Alzheimer's dementia. The natural sources of zinc are beef, lamb, chicken, sea food, wheat germ, mushrooms, nuts, seeds, spinach and cocoa powder.

***c-Copper, Zinc Imbalance***

Copper is an essential trace mineral, but it is needed only in minute amounts. It works in a paired relationship with zinc, sometimes in complement and sometimes opposing. Copper is present in foods like veal liver, nuts, seeds, oyster, cocoa and is also absorbed from the environment. When zinc is present in abundance, and when there is enough quality protein available to bind it, excess of copper can be readily excreted trough the bile. When the diet is lacking in zinc, protein, and fats, use of high-copper foods, and environmental copper, primarily ingested through our water, promote buildup of copper in our tissues.

The late Carl C. Pfeiffer of the Brain-Bio Center in Princeton, New Jersey, has provided us with the most comprehensive overview of nutritional problems associated with copper and zinc in his classic study *Mental and Elemental Nutrients*. He writes that the "deficiency of zinc accentuates copper excess." Disruption of the copper-zinc ratio is an overlooked contributor to intractable fatigue that follows excessive reliance on a plant-based diet. The result is toxic accumulation of copper in tissues and critical depletion of zinc through excretion.

In heavily plant-based diets in particular, zinc is sharply reduced relative to copper, protein is curtailed, and fat is provided scantily at best. The excess copper that builds up in tissues is in unbound, inorganic form, highly immobile and creates a low-level toxicity that interferes with many body systems. Particularly affected are the liver and digestion, which are already affected by increasing deficiency of zinc. The copper-zinc ratio in grains is disturbed by refining. This ratio tends to be low in plant foods anyway, and is shifted further in favor of copper by the refining process. There are numerous other factors contributing to this imbalance, but most devastatingly zinc is lost from our bodies every day when we are under stress. The more stress, the higher the losses, and yet zinc is needed in large amounts by our stress-resisting adrenal glands. When we are zinc-deficient our innate coping resources can start to unravel, and the grind of everyday stress can seem overwhelming.

***d-Chromium deficiency***

Chromium helps regulate blood glucose. Larry Christen says that people with major depression often have disturbances in processing glucose and consequently have exaggerated glucose responses, twice that of normal people. Although the brain is only 2% of body weight, it can consume 20-30% of the body's entire energy. Brain does not store sugar therefore it needs smooth supply of sugar for its optimum functioning.

***e-Selenium, a brain booster***

The trace mineral selenium has a huge impact on brain function. Nerve cells must have selenium to produce glutathione, one of brain's most important antioxidants. Selenium deprived brains also show disturbances in the activity of neurotransmitters serotonin, dopamine, and adrenaline signifying brain damage and dysfunction, according to a recent research.

***III-Role of other nutritional factors***

"The ability of a meal's composition to affect the production of brain chemicals distinguishes the brain from all other organs. The crucial compounds that regulate other organs are largely independent of whatever was in the last meal we ate but not the brain." Richard Wurtman, MIT.

***a-Good and bad fats***

Hydrogenated vegetable oils like corn, safflower, and sunflower oils have very high levels of omega 6 fatty acids, which is a bad fat. Healthy fats are omega 3 fatty acids found in sea food, nuts, lean meat and greens. Excess of bad fats and shortages of good fats can eventually lead to brain cell dysfunction and death. Brain destructive fat is omega 6 fatty acid and, "One of the most fearful potential consequences of omega 6 dominance in brain cells is persistent inflammation of brain tissue. Such inflammation can injure cerebral blood vessels, set up processes that kill brain cells, wrap nerve cell membranes disrupting normal functioning, interfere with neuronal message transmission, and promote strokes."

Chronic low level inflammation can lead to Alzheimer's and probably all degenerative brain diseases. Brain images of the prefrontal cortex of schizophrenics show that the fats in cellular membranes are being broken down or destroyed at a rapid speed. Therefore Dr. Peet theorizes that in schizophrenics' neuronal membranes are distorted and the neurotransmitters, including dopamine, and receptors are unable to transmit messages properly. Dr. Peet also thinks that schizophrenics are defective in metabolizing arachidonic acid, which is also important in facilitating messages. Eating extra omega 3 fatty acids relieves symptoms of schizophrenia and attention deficit disorder.

***b-Role of blood sugar***

A major secret of superior brain functioning is to eat in ways that give your brain cells steady access to desirable levels of blood sugar. Deficiency of blood sugar can cause the brain to slow down and malfunction and, high level of sugar can be extremely detrimental. For optimal brain function, blood sugar level should be normal; fluctuations in blood glucose have bad effects on mood and cognition.

Dr. Lester Packer, a biochemist says “we can’t live without oxygen, or glucose, but both can also be extremely toxic.”

How well we understand and manage those two critical elements greatly influences the functioning of our cells, including our nerve cells, and our vulnerability to aging and disease affecting our brain. “High levels of blood sugar or glucose create high blood levels of insulin. These twin devils can be hazardous to your brain, blood vessels, and the rest of your body.” Researchers say that high insulin can be detrimental to synaptic activity in the brain, interfering with message transmission between brain cells. Memory disturbances due to ineffectual insulin inside brain cells might be a kind of diabetes or pre-diabetes of the brain. Low glycemic index foods and avoidance of mixing simple and complex carbohydrates prevent fluctuation in the blood sugar level and therefore prevent a sugar shock to vital systems.

***c-Food antioxidants***

Scientists have recognized that many mental problems from conception to death stem from many rampaging free radicals and insufficient availability of antioxidants. “Your brain is particularly vulnerable to free radical damage for two reasons. First it is a hotbed of activity; it never stops working. Brain cells need a constant flow of blood and oxygen to produce energy, which increases the production of free radicals. Second the brain is composed of 50% fat, which makes it vulnerable to lipid peroxidation.”Said Dr. Lester Packer, University of California, Berkeley. Antioxidants can save you from your susceptibility to genetic diseases, including brain diseases and disorders, by stopping the expression or activation of the disease prone genes. Fruits and vegetables are loaded with antioxidants in the form of vitamins, carotenoids and polyphenols, therefore should be part of routine food plan.

***IV-Gut and brain disorders***

British neurologist Dr. Natasha Campbell discovered that patients of autism, learning disabilities, psychiatric illness and other mental problems always suffer from digestive problems which are often of a severe nature. Through her research, she has determined a distinct correlation between unhealthy intestinal flora, poor digestion and toxicity from chemicals created by undigested foods, which can severely affect brain chemistry. She coins this relationship the Gut and Psychology Syndrome, or GAPS. But if a child manifests problems such as autism or ADD/ADHD at an early age, then the causes are familial and generational, explains Campbell-McBride.

Undigested carbohydrates, poor digestion and candida overgrowth result in the production of the chemicals ethanol(alcohol) and acetaldehyde(carcinogen), which can have profound consequences on brain chemistry. Many other toxins and bacteria fostered by poor digestion are routinely found in stool samples of patients with GAPS, many of which produce neurotoxins that can result in autistic behavior. When candida produces ethanol in the small intestine, a person will seem drunk after a meal of carbohydrates, even though he has consumed no alcohol. In fact, eventually a person will actually crave the foods that produce alcohol in the small intestine. This is one reason why multitudes of children and adults have an insatiable appetite for high-carbohydrate junk food and why a multi-billion dollar processed food industry continues to thrive. We all know that alcohol is extremely toxic, especially to a developing fetus or a child. The following are some of the wide-ranging effects of a prolonged presence of alcohol in gut from an overgrowth of Candida in the body:

i. Damage and inflammation to the gut lining and resulting mal-absorption
ii. Nutrient deficiencies
iii. Stress to the immune system
iv. Liver damage
v. Accumulation of toxins

vi. Un metabolized neurotransmitters and hormones that can cause abnormal behavior
vii. Brain damage that can lead to lack of self-control
viii. Impaired coordination, aggression
ix. Loss of memory and stupor; peripheral nerve damage
x. Muscle tissue damage and weakness
xi. Metabolic alteration of proteins, carbohydrates and lipids
xii. Pancreatic degeneration

Thus, poor digestion can set up conditions in which it is difficult to think and enjoy life. As our diet causes mood problems and interferes with mental clarity, we become chemically dependent or addict to the very foods that are making us sick.

***V-Soy and brain degeneration***

In a major ongoing study involving 3,734 elderly Japanese-American men, those who ate the most tofu during midlife had up to 2.4 times the risk of later developing Alzheimer's disease. As part of the three-decade long Honolulu-Asia Aging Study, 27 foods and drinks were correlated with participants'health. Men who consumed tofu at least twice weekly had more cognitive impairment than those who rarely or never ate the soybean curd.[1, 2] Higher midlife tofu consumption was also associated with low brain weight. Brain atrophy was assessed in 574 men using MRI results and in 290 men using autopsy information. Shrinkage occurs naturally with age, but for the men who had consumed more tofu, White said "their brains seemed to be showing an exaggeration of the usual patterns we see in aging."

Tofu and other soybean foods contain isoflavones, three-ringed molecules bearing a structural resemblance to mammalian steroidal hormones. White and his fellow researchers speculate that soy's estrogen-like compounds (phytoestrogens) might compete with the body's natural estrogens for estrogen receptors in brain cells. While soybeans are relatively high in protein compared to other legumes, they are a poor source of protein because other proteins found in soybeans act as potent enzyme inhibitors. These "anti-nutrients" block the action of trypsin and other enzymes needed for protein digestion. Trypsin inhibitors are large, tightly folded proteins that are not completely deactivated during ordinary cooking and can reduce protein digestion.

Therefore, soy consumption may lead to chronic deficiencies in amino acid uptake. Soy's ability to interfere with enzymes and amino acids may have direct consequence for the brain. As White and his colleagues suggest, "isoflavones in tofu and other soy foods might exert their influence through interference with tyrosine kinase-dependent mechanisms required for optimal hippocampal function, structure and plasticity." High amounts of protein tyrosine kinases are found in the hippocampus, a brain region involved with learning and memory. One of soy's primary isoflavones, genistein, has been shown to inhibit tyrosine kinase in the hippocampus, where it blocked "long-term potentiation," a mechanism of memory formation.

The brain uses the amino acids tyrosine or phenylalanine to synthesize the key neurotransmitters dopamine and norepinephrine, brain chemicals that promote alertness and activity. Dopamine is crucial to fine muscle coordination. People whose hands tremble from Parkinson's disease have a diminished ability to synthesize dopamine. An increased incidence of depression and other mood disorders are associated with low levels of dopamine and norepinephrine. Also, the current scientific consensus on attention-deficit disorder points to a dopamine imbalance. Soy has been shown to affect tyrosine hydroxylase activity in animals, causing the utilization rate of dopamine to be "profoundly disturbed."
When soy lecithin supplements were given throughout perinatal development, they reduced activity in the cerebral cortex and "altered synaptic characteristics in a manner consistent with disturbances in neural function." Researchers at Sweden's Karolinska Institute and at the

National Institutes of Health are finding a connection between tyrosine hydroxylase activity, thyroid hormone receptors, and depleted dopamine levels in the brain--particularly in the substantia nigra, a region associated with the movement difficulties characteristic of Parkinson's disease.

***VI-Magnetic fields and brain disorder***

In several studies, the association between the magnetic fields, suicide, and depression has been further explored. A 1990 study cited by Charles Poole and associates found a normal suicide rate among electric utility workers. But soon after, a study by David Savitz et al. of the University of North Carolina found significantly more signs of depression among electrical workers than controls. In a survey by Poole's group, people living very near a transmission line right-of-way were nearly three times as likely to be depressed as people living far away. In contrast, a study by S. McMahan et al. compared women who lived right next to a power line to ones who lived only a block away. There were no significant differences in depression. But then, in a 1989 study by Stephen Perry et al., depressed patients had stronger power-line magnetic fields outside their homes than healthy controls. Earlier Perry and a colleague similarly found that people hospitalized for depression were significantly more likely than their healthy apartment-block neighbors to have lived near the main electrical supply cable. Even geomagnetic storms were implicated as a trigger of depression in a study by R. W. Kay.

Electromagnetic fields have been suggested to contribute to the risk of depression by causing pineal dysfunction. The Pineal Gland is a magneto sensitive organ, what means that it is sensitive to electromagnetic fields (EMF). It is sensitive to electromagnetic waves from computer monitors, cellular phones, microwave ovens, high voltage lines, etc.. Electromagnetic fields suppress the activity of the Pineal Gland and reduce melatonin production. EMF also affects serotonin. Using two available nationwide data sets, the authors identified from the Finnish Twin Cohort Study 12,063 persons who had answered the 21-item Beck Depression Inventory of self-rated depressive symptoms in 1990. The personal 20-year histories of exposure (i.e., distance and calculated annual average magnetic fields) before 1990 to overhead 110- to 400-kv power lines were obtained from the Finnish Transmission Line Cohort Study. However, the risk of severe depression was increased 4.7-folds among subjects living within 100 m of a high-voltage power line.

***VII-Liver and brain health***

As liver is the main chemical manufacturing factory of the body, so it is the root cause of every brain disorder. A hyperactive liver initiates a chemical imbalance which leads to toxin overload, magnesium, zinc deficiencies, and blood sugar fluctuations. As we already know these are the important causative factors for neurodegenerative disorders. Liver dysfunction is a contributory factor in gut dysfunction leading to multiple chemical imbalances due to alcohol production. Chemical imbalances further creates load on liver functions and body enters into a vicious cycle of mental symptoms and neurodegenerative diseases. I have seen patients with acidic body and hyper-liver suffering from memory loss, fogginess of mind, apprehensions, body jerks, epilepsy, claustrophobia and headaches. Hyper-liver state creates an imbalance between copper and zinc resulting in a hyper-active mind, which is a pre-depression state.

## The quantum link between brain and mind

Consciousness defines our existence and reality, but the mechanism by which the brain generates thoughts and feelings remains unknown. Most explanations portray the brain as a computer, with nerve cells ("neurons") and their synaptic connections acting as simple switches. However computation alone cannot explain why we have feelings and awareness, and an "inner life." We also don't know if our conscious perceptions accurately portray the external world. At its base, the universe follows the seemingly bizarre and paradoxical laws of quantum mechanics, with particles being in multiple places simultaneously, connected over distance, and with time not existing. But the “classical” world we perceive is definite, with a flow of time. The boundary or edge (quantum state reduction, or 'collapse of the wave function") between the quantum and classical worlds somehow involves consciousness. Mind transfers electrical impulses, which at later stage are converted into chemical information.

When a perception of any kind takes place, an electrical impulse is sent from the senses to appropriate neurons in the brain. This impulse is carried along the axon out to the dendrites. Between each of the billions of dendrite connections within our brains there are little gaps. These gaps, called synapses, are microscopic in size. Communication takes place between these synapses through the use of neurotransmitters. Quantum physics has determined that wave patterns are the essential building blocks of the brain's electrochemical neurotransmitters. It is at the synapse that quantum wave patterns are transformed into neurotransmitters. Through this neuronal synaptic firing the translated wave frequencies are made coherent. These coherent frequencies are then transferred from dendrite to dendrite to the appropriate areas of the brain.

Psychologist William Greenough conducted studies on rats in isolation as well as in stimulating environments. Upon examining their brains he discovered that the rats in the stimulated environment revealed, "that neurons grew larger dendrites with more synapses in response to complex experience." It could be concluded, therefore, that a stimulated brain is able to process more information because it is richer in synaptic connectivity. Many diseases of brain function, such as epilepsy and schizophrenia, are caused by problems in how neurons communicate with each other. A University of Houston (UH) researcher and his team are analyzing these commands and connections in an attempt to prevent those diseases. Robert A. Welch Professor in UH's biology and biochemistry department, describes his team's findings in a paper titled "Liver X receptor β and thyroid hormone receptor α in brain cortical layering," appearing in the current online issue of the journal Proceedings of the National Academy of Sciences, one of the world's most-cited multidisciplinary scientific serials.

"The brain works like a computer," said Gustafsson, who also is director of the Center for Nuclear Receptors and Cell Signaling at UH. "We know something about the hard wire, but so far we know nothing about 'wireless connections.' Our work is about how and when the components of the 'computer' are assembled and how the connections between the components are made." "Like a computer, such connections determine how fast we think and how good our memories are, but also whether we will develop diseases like epilepsy or schizophrenia," he said. "Since the commands to the neurons come from hormones and environmental pollutants, it is essential that we understand how the commands are given and received if we are going to prevent those diseases, which appear to be due to the incorrect positioning of neurons."

Liver X and thyroid hormone receptors, which were studied for this paper, have been found to be essential to the developing cortex in mouse embryos and thereby sometimes regulate the same genes. The first part of the paper explains the importance of the liver X receptor, or LXR, which has been shown to be an important factor in brain development and, very likely, in neurological diseases. LXR plays key roles in cholesterol regulation and the central nervous system, regulating brain cholesterol levels, as well as in maintenance of motor neurons in the spinal cord. Gustafsson said the LXR belongs to a gene family called nuclear receptors that is akin to a "military division." If the LXR "commander" is taken away, the neurons under its command do not move. The second part of the paper says another "commander," called a thyroid hormone receptor, can later wake up the neurons that have stopped on the way and make them move again so that the formation of the cortex is restored.

The science of biophysics works on the concept of information exchange. The nervous system and endocrine system are perhaps the closest in their physiology to a purely information based systems, and they control most of our body activity. The presence of the physical, chemical anatomy provides a conduit for these virtual energy transfers and the subtle energies provide the instructions for the physical to perform its work. The meaning behind the nerve impulses is derived from interpretation of the information they are carrying.

During the prenatal period, the growing nervous system produces low frequency sounds. Soon after birth, it begins to demonstrate complex electrochemical signal and patterns, including brain waves. These are an expression of its myriad and intricate functions, as it monitors and responds to outer and inner phenomena. Brain waves are natural sounds and patterns, whose fields vary over the course of the day, or depending on the kinds of tasks one is performing. These brain waves frequencies also contribute to the energy field that sets up the rest of the nervous system. This is the overlapping point between mind and brain, so both of them are interdependent and at the same time independent as well.

Candace B.Pert, a famous neuroscientist from USA, was the first person to make the laboratory discovery of how emotions and health are linked at the molecular level. She has shown in her pioneering work that our internal chemicals neuropeptides and receptors are actual biological underpinnings of our awareness manifesting as our emotions, beliefs, and expectations. She has shown that our mind is non-local and present in every cell of our body. "Our biochemical messengers through neuropeptides act with intelligence (soul) by communicating information and orchestrating vast, complex information. Mind, body, spirit and emotions are unified with a system of intelligence that Dr. Deepak calls the Field of Intelligence but I call this the Energy of God. He has explained that what we see is an image of our mobile brain which moves throughout our entire body. It is located in each and every cell in our body and not just in our head. It is a cybernating gigantic loop directing and admitting information, simultaneously and intelligently guiding what we call life. These neurotransmitters carry all the basic messengers, positive or negative in our life".

## The Feel-Good Foods

The foods that protect us against depression and neurological disorders are the same foods that traditional cultures valued for good health. They provide vitamins A and D, calcium and arachidonic acid in abundance. So the feel-good foods are:

1-Cod liver oil (vitamins A and D)
2- Butter from grass-fed animals (arachidonic acid, vit. A and D)
3- Egg yolks from grass-fed chickens (arachidonic acid, vit.A & D)
4- Fats from grass-fed animals (arachidonic acid, vitamins A & D) 5- Organ meats from grass-fed animals (arachidonic acid, vitamins A and D)
6- Bone broths (calcium)
7- Raw whole milk from grass-fed animals (calcium, arachidonic -acid, vitamins A and D)
8- Fish eggs (vitamins A and D)
9- Small whole fish (calcium, vitamins A and D)
10- Shell fish (vitamins A and D)

## SLP Hyperactive Mind Syndrome

It is an important clinical experience which I see in everyday practice. It is a subtle phenomenon, therefore the individual carrying it, is not aware of this state. Hyperactive mind is a racing mind, and it makes the individual to think on four five projects simultaneously. People with hyperactive mind don't have rejuvenating sleep and they sleep with an alert mind. They are aware of all activities in their surroundings and they wake up with a fatigued body. It is a state where mind is set in a hyperactive mode and, there is an uncontrolled trail of thoughts. Person loses control on the self; body is set in an auto-mode. People with hyper mind wake up in the morning with headaches, puffy eyes and a swollen face. I have found the hyperactive mind a pre-state to all psychological and neurological disorders. In this state the mental aging is more than biological aging and mind is many years older to the chronological age.

This hyper activity of mind produces lot of free radicals, consumes excess of sugar, oxygen, and creates mineral imbalance. Therefore it becomes a root cause of multiple physical and mental diseases. Best tools to relieve this state are to adopt a natural and healthy lifestyle and activate your built-in passion or hobby. You need to allocate about half an hour to your favorite hobby every day, because at this time your thought process slows down and stillness of mind happens. Follow eight rules of diet correction regularly, SLP can switch off this mental state within two weeks by giving internal chemical homeostasis and by speeding up the detoxification process.

***Causes of a hyperactive mind are:***

1-genetically determined acidic body with hyper-liver

2- Multiple emotional traumas since childhood

3- Competitive, creative, perfectionist and ambitious personality

4- Lack of contentment, high expectations, and weak family bonds

5- Erratic dietary pattern, lot of processed foods, less night sleep

6- Disbelief, poor religious connections

***SLP Prevention/ reversal of a neurological disorders***

1-Avoid processed foods and shift to natural whole foods

2- Take nuts, seeds and fish in surplus quantity

3- Learn and practice detoxification techniques to get rid of toxins.

4- Incorporate open air exercise, walk and yoga.

5-Practice breathing exercises

6-Learn your individual mind stillness technique

7- FollowSLP eight rules of diet correction to balance biorhythms and heal liver

8- Use afood supplement rich in omega 3 fatty acids, minerals and vitamins

## CHAPTER NO: 15

## MAXIMIZE YOUR MOVEMENTS: JOINT DISORDERS

Dr. Susan E. Brown writes in her book "Better Bones, Better Body" that "when we think about our physical selves, we often consider them as a jumble of single parts: eyes, mouth, arms, legs and so on. But the truth is, we are composed of *trillions* of parts, all of which must perform together seamlessly to keep us in working order. This "interconnectedness" is the key to understanding how poor health in one part of your body can quickly undermine the integrity and wellness of other areas and so it is with the bones. Bones may seem to be "dead" and inert, but in fact, they are living tissue, charged with many important jobs that the rest of the body relies on, including mineral storage for use in chemical processes throughout the organ systems. Our bones are transforming all the time, breaking down and then building back up. Our bodies are in tune with this type of natural process, which occurs even on a cellular level. Without this constant coordination between our internal systems, we simply couldn't function and our physical condition would almost immediately become dire."

"From the time we are born, our bones are growing and acquiring strength and density, until about the age of 30, when we generally achieve "peak bone mass." You might assume that it's all downhill from there, and that systematic loss of bone mass is inevitable. While it is true that the bones tend to thin and become less substantial as we get older, it is possible and natural to retain enough bone mass and strength to withstand the stresses and strains of daily life. This information alone confirms that, with just a little help, our bones have the capability of lasting us a lifetime."

Bones play many roles in the body. They provide structure, protect organs, anchor muscles, and store calcium. Adequate calcium consumption and weight bearing physical activity build strong bones, optimizes bone mass, and may reduce the risk of osteoporosis later in life. Peak bone mass refers to the genetic potential for bone density. By the age of 30, the average woman has acquired most of her skeletal mass. A large decline in bone mass occurs in older adults, increasing the risk of osteoporosis. For women this occurs around the time of menopause. It is important for young girls to reach their peak bone mass in order to maintain bone health throughout life. A person with high bone mass as a young adult will be more likely to have a higher bone mass later in life. Inadequate calcium consumption and less physical activity could result in a failure to achieve peak bone mass in adulthood.

Osteoporosis or "porous bone" is a disease of the skeletal system characterized by low bone mass and deterioration of bone. Osteoporosis is a very common problem, affecting one in three women and one in five men over the age of 50. It's characterized by increasing your risk of fractures, most often your hips, spine and wrists. Interestingly, nearly 75 percent of all hip fractures occur in women, and hip fractures worldwide rose 25 percent in just ten years, between 1990 and 2000. Osteoporosis is a major health risk for nearly 30 million Americans, in large part because many are clueless about how to prevent it. As a result, osteoporosis has become yet another boon for the pharmaceutical industry.

**Calcium and bone health**

Dr. Susan writes "years ago, in the first edition of my book, Better Bones, Better Body, I noted that high calcium intakes did not seem to prevent fractures. Cross-cultural data, in fact, suggested that countries with the highest calcium intake actually had the highest rates of osteoporotic hip fractures. Recently, sophisticated meta-analysis of the major published studies on the topic confirm my early breakthrough observation and go beyond it to suggest possible risks of high, imbalanced calcium intakes. High calcium intakes do not prevent fractures, and may actually increase risk of hip fracture among some." Dr. Thompson wrote an entire book 'The Calcium Lie' about many food myths regarding bone health. Talking about the source of calcium he thinks that unprocessed salts are one of the best sources of these ionic trace minerals responsible for catalyzing many important functions in your body.

He wrote that bone is composed of at least a dozen minerals, and if you focus exclusively on calcium supplementation you are likely going to worsen your bone density, and will actually increase your risk of osteoporosis. Dr. Thompson believes that the overconsumption of calcium in the goal of preventing osteoporosis creates other mineral deficiencies and imbalances that will also increase your risk of heart disease, kidney stones, gallstones, osteoarthritis, hypothyroidism, obesity and type 2 diabetes. He believes almost everyone needs trace minerals, not just calcium, because you simply cannot get all the nutrients you need through food grown in mineral depleted soils. By encouraging our children to drink lots of calcium-rich milk, we are actually putting them on a path leading to hardening of their arteries later in life, increased risk of heart disease, hypothyroidism, and obesity.

In January 2008, the Reuters news service reported on a study published in the British Medical Journal which found that calcium supplements may boost the risk of heart attacks in older women. In a study of 122,000 women called The Nurses'Health Study, which analyzed the risk factors for major chronic diseases, one of the most surprising conclusions related to osteoporosis. The study found that women with the highest calcium consumption from dairy products actually had substantially more fractures than women who drank less milk. Hair Tissue Mineral Analysis (HTMA) is the most effective way to determine mineral imbalances and calcium excess in the body. In treating 1,000 patients in his private practice Dr. Robert Thompson, co-author of The Calcium Lie, has seen evidence that 95% of us are mineral-deficient and more than 90% of us have too much calcium in our bodies. These alarming figures are supported by the HTMA reports prepared by Dr. David Watts over the past 20 years. Without enough minerals in the right proportions, your body can't make enough of the hydroxyapatite crystals that make up bone matrix and build bone strength. Without adequate minerals, bones are weakened, more prone to injury, and unable to supply our body with minerals needed for other functions.

In 2002, The National Osteoporosis Foundation (NOF) reported that 44 million Americans had compromised bone density (either osteoporosis or osteopenia, low bone density that often leads to fractures). The organization projected that these figures will skyrocket within the next few years –increasing to 52 million Americans by the year 2010, and to 61 million Americans by the year 2020. Excess calcium actually makes bones weaker because it exaggerates our mineral imbalances and deficiencies. Calcium excess causes other minerals to be lost or excreted in the urine. Osteoporosis should be a concern not just of women, but men as well. Also, this concern should not be limited only to older individuals. It is estimated that 55% of all people over the age of 50 have some form of bone deterioration, and 20% of those sufferers are men. Today, 2 million men have been diagnosed with osteoporosis and 12 million are at risk.

**Role of vitamin D in bone health**

Insufficient vitamin D leads to less calcium absorption, elevated blood concentrations of parathyroid hormone, and increased rates of bone thinning, which may eventually lead to bone fracture. In line with this are several studies that have found that older people who experience a hip fracture have lower serum concentrations of 25-hydroxyvitamin D than do those without a fracture. Milk is often thought to decrease osteoporotic bone loss and fracture risk since it is a primary source of calcium and vitamin D. However, while milk, and other dairy food, intake has been found beneficial in women under the age of 30 years, there has been no clear benefit documented for women over the age of 50 years. Recently, data from a study of 10,000 Americans supported once again that vitamin D is more important to bone health than is calcium. Data from the U.S. National Health and Nutrition Examination Survey (NHANES III) published in early 2009, found that calcium intakes of 566 mg per day among women and 626 mg per day among men are likely adequate for those not burdened with low vitamin D levels. Among men, calcium intake was not associated with bone density at any level of vitamin D studied.

It is known that calcium, at low or moderate doses, is largely dependent on the action of 125-dihydroxyvitamin D for active transport. Sufficient amounts of vitamin D are important in the prevention of postmenopausal bone loss. For instance, one 18-year study, which examined calcium and vitamin D intakes, milk consumption, and use of calcium supplements among postmenopausal women, found that those with higher vitamin D intakes, either from food alone or from food plus supplements, had a significantly lower risk of hip fracture. However, calcium intake did not appear to be associated with fracture risk. Some 25 percent to 50 percent of the elderly have vitamin D deficiency, which can lead to loss of muscle strength and an increased likelihood of falling that, in turn, increases the risk of hip fracture. It is clear that vitamin D is associated with stronger bones.

Sunlight exposure is a major source of vitamin D, however older adults may not spend enough time in the sun to get adequate amounts of vitamin D. Also, sunscreens, of which usage has increased, significantly reduce skin production of vitamin D. Another problem with obtaining vitamin D from sunlight is that synthesis of vitamin D is absent during the winter months in higher latitudes where nearly all of the United States is located. This is where cod liver oil, which contains vitamin D, comes in. However, you need to be careful with cod liver oil, as you can easily overdose on it. Too much vitamin D is harmful and will actually worsen your bone density. Common causes of vitamin D deficiency are mal-absorption of foods and low calcium levels.

### Vitamin K2

Vitamin K2 serves as the biological "glue" that helps plug the calcium into your bone matrix and is crucial for preventing osteoporosis. Supplement with vitamin K2 if you are not getting enough from food alone. Fermented foods such as natto, typically have the highest concentration of vitamin K. It is a fermented soybean food, contains nattokinase, a powerful beneficial enzyme rich in vitamin K2 and comes loaded with a healthy bacteria called bacillus subtilus that may also serve as a probiotic. Levels of vitamin K found in natto (K2) have been shown to far exceed those amounts found in dark green vegetables (K1). In fact, vitamin K2 concentration after the consumption of natto has been shown to be about 10 times higher than that of vitamin K1 after eating spinach. While natto is the most potent natural source of vitamin K2, the nutrient is also readily available in fermented dairy products, especially cheese. Most cheeses are rich in vitamin K2... particularly, curd cheese. And even though it's not as high in vitamin K2 as natto, curd cheese may be more palatable on a day-to-day basis for many people. Raw curd cheese made from grass fed cows would be best. But when compared to natto in equal portions, Japanese food natto contains over 27 times more vitamin K2 than curd cheese.

### How to make bones strong

#### *i-Selection of natural foods*

If you eat a diet full of processed foods, it will produce biochemical and metabolic conditions in your body that will decrease your bone density, so avoiding processed foods is the first step in the right direction. High quality nutrient dense, organic, locally-grown food is ideal. Raw dairy, organ meat, organic eggs, seafood, and meat are nutrient dense foods which are rich in proteins, minerals, vitamins and are good for bone health.

***ii-Fruits& vegetables***

Fruits and vegetables are also a good source of calcium & magnesium. Even though some have a poor Cal/Mag ratio, the vast majority are at least 2 to 1 ratio. The best are avocados at

1: 2 pineapple and raspberry are about 1:1.5 cauliflower, peas and mangoes are almost 1:1 tomato, asparagus and many green leafy veggies are about 1.5 :1 blackberries & broccoli are about 2:1. One food in particular worth mentioning are onions, which are high in gamma-glutamyl peptides that have been shown to increase bone density.

***iii-Foods with high ORAC value***

Foods with high ORAC (oxygen radical absorbency capacity) value which include prunes (with highest ORAC 5770/100g), blue berries (2234/100g ) and raisins (2830/100g) play an important role in maintaining good bone health. High ORAC value dry fruits are part of SLP Pre-breakfast, and I always get good response in bone and joint disorders, with raisins. Professor Bahram Arjmandi and colleagues presented hot-breaking research findings on theirone-year human trial testing the potential of prunes to reverse bone loss in postmenopausal women. Dr. Arjmandi is studying 144 osteopenic postmenopausal women, simply giving them 100 grams of dried prunes daily (10-12 prunes each day) and looking for changes in bone mineral density. The findings includea significant increase in ulna and spine bone mineral density in the women who ate the prunes. As Dr. Arjmandi and colleagues write, "The findings of this one-year study confirm our earlier observation that dried plum has the ability to reverse bone loss."

### *iv-Essential fatty acids*

For strong bones we need to balance omega 3 and omega 6 fatty acids ratio in our routine food. Omega 6 in excess causes bone inflammation therefore avoid oils like corn oil, safflower and soy oils, because they contain excess of omega 6.

### *v-Minerals*

Important bone forming minerals are phosphorus, magnesium, chromium, silica, zinc, manganese, copper, boron, potassium and strontium.

### *vi-Vitamins*

Vitamins required are vitamin D, vitamin A, C, B6, B9, B12, K1 and vitamin K2. Fats and proteins are two essential components as well. Remember, none of these nutrients does its work in isolation you need some of each and every one, so they can all work together to keep your bones standing strong all your life long.

### *vii-Bone broth: a super bone tonic*

Because of the rich bone matrix, broth made from bones is a great remedy, a tonic for the sick, a digestive aid, and a healing elixir. And unlike bitter medicines, broth can be incorporated into delicious soups, stews and sauces. Bone broth is an excellent source of gelatin, calcium and other minerals. Recent scientific studies are proving that gelatin can contribute to the building of strong cartilage and bones. In fact, the evidence goes back more than a century and not only established gelatin's value to cartilage and bones but also to the skin, liver, digestive tract, immune system, heart and muscles.

Early research has also indicated that gelatin helps the liver. This is plausible in that the liver uses the amino acid glycine present in gelatin for detoxification, and its ability to detoxify is limited by the amount of glycine available. Back in 1935, Reuben Ottenberg, MD wrote in the *Journal of the American Medical Association*: "It has been suggested that the administration of extra amounts of proteins containing an abundance of glycine will help the work in the liver. This seems particularly plausible since the recent work of Quick, who has shown that the ability of the liver to perform this protective synthesis is limited by the amount of glycine available." A 1907 Italian study established that gelatin injections increased the calcium in the circulating blood, which in turn was shown to stimulate bone building.

A 1999 German study also proved the role of gelatin and their study was inspired by reports of the positive influence of gelatin on degenerative diseases of the musculoskeletal system and curiosity about the "therapeutic mechanism and the absorption dynamics." Mice fed radioactive gelatin hydrolysate were compared to control mice administered radioactive proline. They found that 95 percent of the gelatin was absorbed within the first 12 hours, and the labeled gelatin found in the tissues was similar to that of labeled proline with one exception--the absorption and accumulation of gelatin in the cartilage was twice as high.

This suggested a salutary effect of gelatin on cartilage metabolism that would not occur with the ingestion of proline alone. They concluded, "These results demonstrate intestinal absorption and cartilage tissue accumulation of gelatin hydrolysate and suggest a potential mechanism for previously observed clinical benefits of orally administered gelatin." The amino acids in gelatin, like all amino acids, can only be properly utilized when the diet contains sufficient fat-soluble activators--vitamins A and D--found exclusively in animal fats. So don't hesitate to put cream in your broth-based soups and sauces, and include other sources of vitamins A and D in your diet, such as butter, egg yolks and cod liver oil.

***viii-A body compatible food***

William Wolcott the founder of the Health excel system of Metabolic Typing and author of 'The Metabolic Typing'wrote that there is no one diet that is right for everyone, and that there are no "good foods" or "bad foods" except those relative to each person's biochemical individuality. Similarly, although everyone needs to obtain all available nutrients in his or her daily diet, taking therapeutic doses of a nutrient such as calcium, for example, is another matter altogether. His opinion is there are two kinds of calcium deficiency: an actual quantitative deficiency and a relative deficiency of utilization due to bio-unavailability. In order for calcium to be utilized, two factors are necessary, calcium, and calcium's synergistic nutrients (calcium requires other specific nutrients in order to be utilized). "The missing factor in all bone studies is a true understanding of the fundamental homeostatic control systems (FHC), such as autonomic, endocrine and seven others, and their relationship to minerals, particularly calcium, potassium and magnesium, and the FHC connection to such problems as causal as well as remedial."

Out of six SLP body chemistries three body types with hyper-liver suffer more from bone and joint pains and have an early onset of osteoporosis. These individuals have hyperactive mind, digestive disorders, mal-absorption of foods, toxin overload and poor quality of sleep. They are calcium and vitamin D deficient and have normal or high tissue calcium levels. SLP body types with sluggish or hypo-liver have swollen joints and infective type of arthritis with low level of calcium and multiple mineral deficiencies due to poor metabolism, weak immunity, and various digestive disorders. They are cold intolerant and their joints get worst during winters. They crave for sugary foods, are anxious and have a tendency for frequent attacks of infections especially upper respiratory tract. Therefore we need a well-connected biorhythms systems for the optimal calcium absorption and healthy bone formation.

***viii-Exercise***

Studies show that correct exercise is just as important to your bone health as eating a calcium-rich diet. Strength building exercises like weight training is especially helpful for adult males. Females need regular walk, swimming, and mild exercises for their bone health.

## Osteoporosis and its mismanagement

### *Hazards of osteoporosis treating drugs*

There are a variety of drugs on the market to combat bone loss, but the first line of therapy typically includes oral bisphosphonate drugs, these medicines have multiple side effects and less healing affects. Their side effects are:

***i-Cancer risk***

Oral bisphosphonate osteoporosis drugs could be associated with an approximately twofold increased risk of esophageal cancer. A new study showed that long-term users of the drugs had nearly double the risk for the rare but deadly cancer. Concerns about a link between bisphosphonates and esophageal cancer first reached the public a year and a half ago, when an FDA report cited 23 cases of the cancer in Fosamax users in the U.S., and another 31 cases in Europe and Japan.

***ii- Hypocalcemia (blood calcium levels are too low)***

***iv-Serious eye inflammation and possible blindness***

***v-Severe musculoskeletal pain***

***vi-Stomach ulcers***

Particularly when taken together with anti-inflammatory drugs. In one study, 8 percent of participants taking Fosamax and 12 percent of those receiving the anti-inflammatory Naprosyn developed stomach ulcers. But when the two drugs were taken in combination, the rate of stomach ulcers rose to a whopping 38 percent.

***vii-Liver damage***

Although the mechanism is still unknown, researchers believe drugs like Fosamax may inhibit the synthesis of cholesterol in your liver, which may alter liver function. Regardless of the mechanism, if you're taking Fosamax or related bisphosphonate drugs you need to beware of the possibility of liver dysfunction, and your doctor should monitor you properly.

***viii-Kidney failure***

***ix-Atrial* fibrillation**

Women who have used Fosamax are nearly twice as likely to develop atrial fibrillation, which is the most common kind of chronically irregular heartbeat. One study published in the Archives of Internal Medicine found that Fosamax was associated with an 86 percent higher risk of atrial fibrillation compared to those who had never used the drug. Atrial fibrillation can cause palpitations, fainting, fatigue, or congestive heart failure. It can also lead to embolic strokes.

***x-Thigh bone fractures***

The FDA asked Merck (the maker of Fosamax) to "add information about the report of femur fractures" to the medication's package insert back in 2008, according to an ABC News report. According to a recent report by a US panel of experts reviewing the evidence of increased risk of unusual femur fractures, 94 percent of patients who had experienced a femur break had been on bisphosphonate drugs.

## Gout: new concepts

The understanding of gout gets into some of the most interesting questions about the history of medicine and the understanding of physiology and its relationship to human disease. It is also interesting because there are many misconceptions that abound about gout, among both laymen and medical professionals. Gout is one of the oldest and probably most painful diseases known to mankind. The newer theories about gout recognize the fact that the disease is not simply a result of high-protein intake. For example, we have discovered that uric acid levels are high in those patients with syndrome X, otherwise known as insulin resistance. This means that excessive carbohydrate consumption, particularly of refined flour and sugar, can also raise the uric acid levels and precipitate gout. This fact also explains the frequent finding of obesity in those suffering from gout.

Another overlooked factor is the fact that traditional peoples always balanced protein intake with plentiful fat intake as well as gelatinous soup broths. Thus, gout is better understood as a situation of excessive protein intake compared to the fats and gelatin intake, two factors which balance the protein intake. This is why people with historically high protein intake who also eat lots of fats and soup broths, with no refined carbohydrates, rarely if ever suffer from gout. Finally, the specific nutrient that seems to prevent the buildup of uric acid is vitamin A, a fat-soluble vitamin that is particularly associated with the kidney. In fact, gout can be seen as a problem of the kidneys not being able to excrete enough of the uric acid to prevent the buildup, rather than simply a matter of excessive protein intake.

**Pain management**

Pain management also called pain medicine s that branch of medicine employing an interdisciplinary approach to the relief of pain and improvement in the quality of life of those living with pain. The typical pain management team includes medical practitioners, clinical psychologist, physiotherapist, occupational therapist, and nurse practitioners. Acute pain resolves with the efforts of one practitioner; however, the management of chronic pain frequently requires the coordinated efforts of the treatment team. An integrated biopsychosocial approach is more appropriate for patients with chronic pain. Multimodal therapy involving nerve blocks and non- pharmacologic techniques like acupuncture, physical therapy, rehabilitation and psychological training of patients is needed to treat chronic pains.

***SLP and Pain management***

Pain is the crying of the body parts to complain about the serious abuses going on in other body systems. Joint pain is the result of ischemia, inflammation, toxins and wind or water retention in the joints, resulting in nerve irritation leading to various types of pains. Therefore for pain management we need to harmonize our body with its built-in nature. Chronic headaches, cervical spondylitis, lumbago, acute and chronic arthritis respond well to SLP. Smooth muscle pains like stomach cramps, intestinal colic, uterine cramps and even unstable angina responds to SLP lifestyle modification.

**SLP causes of joint disorders**

I have learnt that bone and joint disorder is always secondary to multiple biorhythm imbalances. The imbalances are:

I. Shift in body ph: an acidic blood ph extracts calcium from bones leading to joint disorders. The nature and intensity of joint pains vary with the level of shift in the ph. An acidic ph gives pain which increases on movement, an alkaline body chemistry produces bone and joint pains which increase at rest.

II. Poor thermoregulation: cold extremities indicate poor circulation to the periphery resulting in ischemic pains and aggravation of arthritis. Burning extremities indicate more blood in the peripheral circulation which cause swollen joints and difficulty in movement. There is also lymphatic and venous congestion leading to pains which get better on lying down position.

III. Poor detoxification: accumulation of cell debris, free radicals, environmental toxins, end products of medicines and processed foods accumulate in various tissues and cause muscle and joint pains. These toxins irritate nerve endings which result in chronic pains and swollen joints.

IV. Water intoxication, leads to accumulation of water in joint spaces. Joints are badly swollen, pain aggravates at night and relieves with hot foods.

**SLP and joint disorders**

I. Follow eight rules of diet correction
II. Avoid over usage of pain killers
III. Bone broth is a pain reliever
IV. Be regular about an exercise or walk in your routine
V. Handle your stress on daily basis
VI. Yoga is super for flexibility of muscles and joints

For gout I write a food plan which has meat, eggs, fish, non-processed butter or ghee and lentils. People are supposed to take these foods in a moderate quantity and with a dietary discipline. Within 2-4 weeks their symptoms start settling and uric acid comes to a normal value within 12 weeks.

# CHAPTER NO: 16

## HORMONES: INFORMATION CARRIERS

In physiology, the endocrine system is a system of glands, each of which secretes a type of hormone into the bloodstream to regulate the body. It derives from the Greek words endo meaning inside, within, and crinis to secrete. The endocrine system is an information signal system like the nervous system. Hormones are substances (chemical mediators) released from endocrine tissue into the bloodstream that attach to target tissue and allow communication among cells. Hormones regulate many functions of an organism, including mood, growth, development and metabolism. The endocrine system is made up of a series of ductless glands that produce chemicals called hormones. A number of glands that signal each other in sequence are usually referred to as an axis, for example, the hypothalamic-pituitary-adrenal axis. Features of endocrine glands are, in general, their ductless nature, their vascularity, and usually the presence of intracellular vacuoles or granules storing their hormones. In contrast, exocrine glands, such as salivary glands, sweat glands, and glands within the gastrointestinal tract, tend to be much less vascular and have ducts or a hollow lumen.

### Functions

As the body's chemical messengers, hormones transfer information and instructions from one set of cells to another. Although many different hormones circulate throughout the bloodstream, each one affects only the cells that are genetically programmed to receive and respond to its message. Hormone levels can be influenced by factors such as stress, infection, and changes in the balance of fluid and minerals in blood. The glands release the hormones into the blood stream and are transported to the various cells and body parts. When the hormones reach the target site, they bind to the receptor cells with a lock and key mechanism. The hormone may be present within the nucleus or on the surface of the cells. Once bound to the receptor, the hormones transmit a signal that triggers an action by the site. Hormones control the organs function and affect the growth and development of the organs. It is due to the hormones that the sexual characteristics of the organs develop and act accordingly. They also determine the use and storage of energy in the body, regulate the fluid, salt and sugar levels in the blood. Minute amount of hormones trigger large reactions within the body. All hormones are proteins, but all proteins are not hormones. Steroids are not derived from proteins, but from the fatty substances from cholesterol.

**Bio-feedback**

The body has a well-controlled feedback system that manages the on/off button of the endocrine gland. When the chemical level or the nutrient level in the body is abnormally high or low, the endocrine glands secrete the hormones. Once the levels of the body fluids are normal the hormones secretions are shut down. When the glands receive information to secrete hormones, it is a positive feedback mechanism. When the glands receive information to stop the secretions of the hormones, it is known as negative feedback. The main function of the endocrine system is to maintain a stable environment within the body or homeostasis. The major function of the endocrine system is promoting the structural changes of the body. For example, the permanent changes occurring in the body over the period of time like height, development of sexual organs, etc. is a part of the structural changes.

**Types of endocrine glands**

There are 8 major glands that help in the endocrine system functions. These major endocrine glands are as follows:

1. Hypothalamus
2. Pituitary gland
3. Parathyroid gland
4. Thyroid gland
5. Adrenal glands
6. Pancreas
7. Ovaries (in female body)
8. Testes (in male body)

In addition to the specialized endocrine organs mentioned above, many other organs that are part of other body systems, such as the kidney, liver, heart and gonads, have secondary endocrine functions. For example the kidney secretes endocrine hormones such as *erythropoietin* and *renin*.

Endocrine organs are richly supplied with blood vessels, and as organs they are relatively soft tissues. They are intended to be efficient at absorbing molecules, and for these reasons they are more susceptible to environmental toxicities than many other tissues in the body. When people have long term, chronic endocrine problems, the possibility of environmental toxicity must be considered. Science had believed for centuries that the nervous system was the supreme coordinator of bodily functioning, despite the many marvels of coordination and balance which nervous workings couldn't explain. As the chemical secrets of the endocrines have been revealed, it has become more and more apparent that the endocrine system and the involuntary nervous system work together most intimately.

Take the alarm reaction. “Stress" has come to the body. A "message" is transmitted to the cores of the adrenals by the nerves. The cores secrete a chemical into the blood stream. This chemical steps up the action of the heart and narrows the blood vessels so the blood will be pushed through them with more force. It also relaxes and enlarges airways so the lungs can take in more air, more quickly. When this chemical reaches the pituitary, it secretes chemicals which cause the adrenal casings, the thyroid, the parathyroid and even sex glands (which are not exclusively sexual in function) to secrete their hormones. All these chemicals complete the instantaneous preparation of "body" and "mind" to deal with stress. The end results are the seemingly superhuman feats of muscular strength and of quick thinking which we all know the human being can and does perform when he has to.

**Hormonal disorders:**

**Thyroid dysfunctions**

The thyroid gland, located at the base of the neck, makes the hormone T4 (thyroxine). T4 converts to T3 (triiodothryronine) and RT3 (reverse T3). It is T3 that turns on the ATP-making machinery inside each living cell, while the RT3 slows it down. Production of these thyroid hormones is controlled by TSH (thyroidstimulating hormone), which is released by the pituitary gland in the brain. The pituitary takes its orders from the hypothalamus (also part of the brain). The pituitary gland is situated at the base of the brain (above the roof of the mouth). It sends out instructions to many glands, including the thyroid gland, telling them how much hormone to produce. One such hormone is TSH (Thyroid Stimulating Hormone) which signals to the thyroid gland to make thyroid hormone. The pituitary gland determines how much TSH to secrete (that is, how much thyroid hormone to tell the thyroid gland to make) based on (a) how much thyroid hormone is available; (b) how much thyroid hormone the body needs; and (c) how much thyroid hormone the body (actually the adrenals) can tolerate.

Thus a high TSH level is the pituitary gland way of saying that it has a high need for thyroid hormone or that the body can tolerate more thyroid energy than it is getting, and it is meant to generate more thyroid hormone production. Conversely, a low TSH reflects either a low need or desire for thyroid hormone or a low tolerance for the thyroid hormone, and it is meant to reduce thyroid hormone production. An optimal value of TSH means the thyroid hormone levels match the body's energy needs and/or ability to utilize the energy. Thyroid hormones (T4, T3, and RT3), once released into the bloodstream, exist either as protein-bound or in a free form. Protein acts as a sponge or reservoir to which hormones bind and then can be freed. Hormone in free form is available to interact with a cell's receptor site to produce its hormonal effect. It is only the free form hormone that is biologically available or active. When the hormone is bound to a protein it is restrained from interacting with a cell's receptor site. Moreover, the symptoms of an unhealthy thyroid are very much similar to the symptoms of other diseases.

I. An under active thyroid leads to continuous weight gain despite being on a strict diet.
II. Hyperthyroidism will also make your immune system weak, making you vulnerable to colds and other common illnesses.
III. A disorder in thyroid will cause skin to look dull and dry, hair dry; and weak nails
IV. A thyroid disorder can slow down metabolism, so one is exhausted from completing even the simplest of tasks.
V. Inadequate thyroid hormones also affect your mental alertness and mood, thus making you easily irritated and depressed.

***Management of a dysfunctional thyroid***

Most doctors treat thyroid dysfunction by prescribing a synthetic thyroid replacement hormone, and although this artificial hormone will increase thyroid hormone in the body, it can sometimes have little to no effect on energy levels or feelings of wellness.

***i-Role of foods***

According to The National Center for Toxicological Research, soy products contain properties that cause the thyroid gland to malfunction, which can contribute to thyroid diseases. To help the thyroid regain its functioning, it is important to avoid all soy, including whole soy beans, which are also called edamame beans, soy flours, soy butter, soy milk, and soy proteins. It is also advisable to eliminate soy sauce from the diet, which can sometimes be overlooked as a source of soy. As referred to in The Colorado Thyroid Disease Prevalence Study, adding coconut oil into the diet can improve thyroid gland functioning and can encourage proper distribution and production of thyroid hormone throughout the body. For thyroid support, it is important to use extra virgin coconut oil, which is taken from the initial pressing of the raw coconut. Other dietary factors that contribute to healthy thyroid function include adequate protein and iodine, trace elements such as iron, zinc and selenium (needed to prevent anemia and for key enzymes to make hormonal conversions); B vitamins, including $B_{12}$, vitamin C, and, above all, adequate vitamin A from animal sources.[11]

Foods that depress thyroid activity are broccoli, cabbage, brussel sprouts, cauliflower, kale, spinach, turnips, soy, beans, and mustard greens. These foods should be included in the diet for hyperthyroid conditions and avoided for hypothyroid conditions. An easy way to supplement iodine without adding salt to food is to take a kelp supplement. Kelp is seaweed that is naturally high in iodine and about 225 mcg per day should be enough to repair problems caused by hypothyroidism. Seaweed, seafood, yogurt, meat and potatoes are few foods that naturally produce iodine when eaten. Bladder wrack is another form of seaweed that can be added to the diet or taken as a supplement. It is high in iodine but also contains potassium, calcium, iron and zinc. Bladder wrack is believed to naturally increase the metabolism by accelerating the functions of the thyroid. The University of Maryland Medical Center (UMMC) recommends taking 600 mg of bladder wrack three times per day to maintain thyroid health when diagnosed with an under active thyroid.

*ii-Herbs which help thyroid*

In addition to the herbal supplement kelp, the thyroid needs ample amounts of vitamins A, B, C and E to work properly. Herbs containing these vitamins include raspberry leaf, chamomile, chickweed, alfalfa, yellow dock and sage.

*iii-Role of minerals*

Sometimes when a person has hypothyroidism, it is because he has low levels of selenium. Selenium helps to regulate the functions of the thyroid. Copper helps the thyroid to control metabolism levels and can be found in sheep sorrel. Zinc encourages the thyroid to properly use hormones in the body and is found in alfalfa and chamomile. Calcium and magnesium help many metabolic processes function correctly. Calcium and magnesium must be present together in sufficient quantities, or the body can't use either. The optimal ratio is 3 parts calcium to 1 part magnesium. Never supplement calcium without also supplementing magnesium, because if you do so, the body will actually use its stored Mg to try and process the supplemented Ca, the end result of which is that the body actually depletes its stored calcium reserves because the Mg holding it in place was taken away trying to process the supplemented Calcium.

*iv-SLP and a dysfunctional thyroid*

My clinical observation is that a dysfunctional thyroid is always secondary to a dysfunctional liver, therefore one has to take care of liver health by creating a harmony in biorhythms.

## Metabolic syndrome

Metabolic syndrome is also known as metabolic syndrome X, syndrome X, insulin resistance syndrome, reaven's syndrome, and CHAOS (Australia). The term "metabolic syndrome" dates back to at least the late 1950s, but came into common usage in the late 1970s to describe various associations of risk factors with diabetes that had been noted as early as the 1920s. Different definitions of metabolic syndrome are;

***IDF: international Diabetes Federation*** consensus definition of the metabolic syndrome (2006) is Central obesity and any two of the following:

I. Raised triglycerides: > 150 mg/dL (1.7 mmol/L), or specific treatment for this lipid abnormality.
II. Reduced HDL cholesterol: < 40 mg/dL (1.03 mmol/L) in males, < 50 mg/dL (1.29 mmol/L) in females, or specific treatment for this lipid abnormality
III. Raised blood pressure: systolic BP > 130 or diastolic BP >85 mm Hg, or treatment of previously diagnosed hypertension.
IV. Raised fasting plasma glucose :(FPG)>100 mg/dL (5.6 mmol/L), or previously diagnosed type 2 diabetes. If FPG >5.6 mmol/L or 100 mg/dL, OGTT is strongly recommended but is not necessary to define presence of the Syndrome.

***WHO:*** The WHO criteria (1999) require presence of diabetes mellitus, impaired glucose tolerance, impaired fasting glucose or insulin resistance, and two of the following:

I. Blood pressure: ≥140/90 mmHg
II. Disturb lipid levels
III. Central obesity: waist: hip ratio > 0.90 (male); > 0.85 (female), or body mass index > 30 kg/m$^2$
IV. Micro albuminuria: urinary albumin excretion ratio ≥20 μg/min or albumin: creatinine ratio ≥30 mg/g

***EGIR:*** The European Group for the study of Insulin Resistance (1999) requires insulin resistance defined as the top 25% of the fasting insulin values among non- diabetic individuals and two or more of the following:

I. central obesity: waist circumference ≥94 cm (male), ≥80 cm (female)
II. dyslipidemia: TG ≥2.0 mmol/L and/or HDL-C < 1.0 mmol/L or treated for dyslipidemia
III. hypertension: blood pressure ≥140/90 mmHg or antihypertensive medication
IV. fasting plasma glucose ≥6.1 mmol/L

***NCEP:***The US National Cholesterol Education Program Adult Treatment Panel III (2001) requires at least three of the following*:*

I. central obesity: waist circumference ≥102 cm or 40 inches (male), ≥88 cm or 36 inches(female)
II. dyslipidemia: TG ≥1.7 mmol/L (150 mg/dl)
III. dyslipidemia: HDL-C < 40 mg/dL (male), < 50 mg/dL (female)
IV. blood pressure ≥130/85 mmHg
V. fasting plasma glucose ≥6.1 mmol/L (110 mg/dl)

***Pathophysiology***

It is common for there to be a development of visceral fat after which the adipocytes (fat cell) of the visceral fat increase plasma levels of TNFα and alter levels of a number of other substances (e.g. adiponectin, resistin, PAI-1). TNFα has been shown not only to cause the production of inflammatory cytokinesis but possibly to trigger cell signaling by interaction with a TNFα receptor that may lead to insulin resistance.

***Risk Factors***

***i-Stress***

Recent research indicates that prolonged stress can be an underlying cause of metabolic syndrome by upsetting the hormonal balance of the hypothalamic-pituitary-adrenal axis (HPA-axis). A dysfunctional HPA-axis causes high cortisol levels to circulate which results in raising glucose and insulin levels which cause insulin-mediated effects on adipose tissue, ultimately promoting visceral adiposity, insulin resistance, dyslipidemia and hypertension with direct effects on the bone, causing "low turnover" osteoporosis.

***ii-Overweight and obesity***

Central obesity is a key feature of the syndrome, reflecting the fact that the syndrome's prevalence is driven by the strong relationship between waist circumference and increasing adiposity. However, despite the importance of obesity, patients that are of normal weight may also be insulin resistant and have the syndrome.

***iii-Sedentary lifestyle***

Physical inactivity is a predictor of cardiovascular disease CVD events and related mortality. Many components of the metabolic syndrome are associated with a sedentary lifestyle, including increased adipose tissue (predominantly central); reduced HDL cholesterol and a trend toward increased triglycerides, blood pressure, and raised fasting glucose levels. Compared with individuals who watched television or videos or used their computer for less than one hour daily, those that carried out these behaviors for greater than four hours daily have a twofold increased risk of the metabolic syndrome.

***iv-Ageing***

The metabolic syndrome affects 44% of the U.S. population older than age 50. A greater percentage of women older than age 50 have the syndrome than men. The age dependency of the syndrome's prevalence is seen in most populations around the world.

***V-Diabetes mellitus***

It is estimated that the large majority (75%) of patients with type 2 diabetes have the metabolic syndrome. The presence of the metabolic syndrome in these populations is associated with a higher prevalence of CVD than found in patients with type 2 diabetes without the syndrome.

***Vi-Coronary heart disease***

The approximate prevalence of the metabolic syndrome in patients with coronary heart disease is 50%, with a prevalence of 37% in patients with premature coronary artery disease particularly in women.

***Vii-Schizophrenia***

Patients with schizophrenia may have a predisposition to metabolic syndrome that is exacerbated by their generally sedentary lifestyle, poor dietary habits, possible limited access to care, and antipsychotic-induced adverse effects. It has been found that 32% of persons with schizophrenia meet criteria for metabolic syndrome; the prevalence is higher in women than in men.

***Viii-Joint diseases***

There are new findings regarding the morbidity associated with rheumatic diseases. Both psoriasis and psoriatic arthritis have been found to be associated with metabolic syndrome.

## Signs and symptoms of metabolic syndrome

1. Fasting hyperglycemia, impaired glucose tolerance or insulin resistance
2. High blood pressure
3. Central obesity (also known as visceral, male-pattern or apple-shaped adiposity), overweight with fat deposits mainly around the waist;
4. Decreased HDL cholesterol;
5. Elevated triglycerides
6. High Uric acid
7. Fatty liver progressing to non- alcoholic fatty liver disease
8. Polycystic ovarian syndrome in women
9. Acanthosis nigricans

***Prevention***

Various strategies have been proposed to prevent the development of metabolic syndrome. These include increased physical activity, such as walking 30 minutes every day and a healthy, reduced calorie diet. There are many studies that support the value of a healthy lifestyle as above. However, one study stated that these measures are effective in only a minority of people, primarily due to a lack of compliance with lifestyle and diet changes. The International Obesity Taskforce states that interventions on a sociopolitical level are required to reduce development of the metabolic syndrome in populations.

A 2007 study of 2,375 male subjects over 20 years suggested that daily intake of a pint (~473 ml) of milk or equivalent dairy products more than halved the risk of metabolic syndrome. A 2003 study indicated that cardiovascular exercise was therapeutic in approximately 31% of cases. The most probable benefit was to triglyceride levels, with 43% showing improvement; but fasting plasma glucose and insulin resistance of 91% of test subjects did not improve. Many other studies have supported the value of increased physical activity and restricted caloric intake (exercise and diet) to treat metabolic syndrome. Restricting the overall dietary carbohydrate intake is more effective in reducing the most common symptoms of metabolic syndrome than the more commonly prescribed reduction in dietary fat intake.

**SLP and metabolic syndrome**

It is a common disorder; every fourth patient coming to me has a raised cholesterol, low HDL, high uric acid, raised or borderline fasting sugar and central obesity. Ultrasound findings confirm various levels of fatty liver. Unfortunately it is seen at a young age of as early as 21 years. Causes observed are:

I. Erratic dietary pattern
II. Dependence purely on processed foods
III. Followed multiple crash diet plans to lose weight on their own
IV. Lot of incorrect scientific foods, prescribed by doctors or dietitians
V. Wrong type, time and duration of gym. exercises
VI. Sensitive nature and multiple environmental stresses
VII. Poor quality of nocturnal sleep
VIII. Free usage of allopathic medicines / antidepressants
IX. On pulse analysis acidic body with hyper-liver chemistry is found.

## Polycystic ovary syndrome (PCOS)

It affects about 5% to 10% of reproductive age women in the United States and is considered the most common endocrine abnormality among them. According to the latest consensus, the diagnosis can be established when 2 of the following criteria are present: oligo-ovulation, an ovulation, clinical or laboratory hyperandrogenism, and polycystic ovaries on ultrasound (enlarged ovary, echo dense stroma, > 10 "cysts" 2 -10 mm). PCOS is a rather heterogeneous syndrome. Although some patients are thin, about 50% are obese; some patients are clinically hyper-androgenic, whereas others have a normal phenotype; some women have insulin resistance and others have normal glucose metabolism.

The presenting symptoms can vary as well. Most women are evaluated for infertility resulting from the irregular cycles, but other presenting symptoms include irregular bleeding, obesity, and cosmetic problems. Therapy has to be tailored to the patient's needs. In recent years, it has become evident that beyond a reproductive or cosmetic problem, PCOS represents a metabolic risk. Many women with PCOS have hypertension, impaired glucose tolerance, lipid abnormalities, obesity, or any combination of these. Even those patients who are seen for infertility "only" need to be screened for these metabolic risk factors, and they require counseling regarding this risk and its management.

Any hormone problem that interferes with normal ovulation results in what is known as a "polycystic" ovary, which, regardless of the cause, will produce increased amounts of androgen. Conversely, increased androgen production interferes with normal ovulation. Evidence has also pointed to obesity as part of the androgen excess syndrome; overweight women produce increased androgens even if they have no underlying abnormality in the adrenal gland. It is not known for certain whether obesity is a cause or an effect or simply a part of PCOS. Moreover, increased insulin found in women with PCOS stimulates ovarian androgen production; increased androgen production contributes to insulin resistance. Yet increased androgen production also leads to an increased body weight (obesity), which in turn contributes to insulin resistance.

Women with PCOS who are not overweight also frequently have insulin resistance. PCOS is an inherited, autosomal dominant trait, meaning if a woman has PCOS, it should be looked for in her mother, sisters and daughters. And, since it is autosomal dominant, male relatives can also carry the gene and can transfer the problem to their daughters. Having PCOS puts women at an increased risk of developing diabetes, coronary artery syndrome, lipid disorders (such as elevated cholesterol and high blood pressure) and possibly breast cancer. It was realized early on that weight control improves many aspects of PCOS. The cycles become more regular, androgen levels are reduced, lipid and glucose metabolism improves, and spontaneous pregnancy may follow. It was also realized that obese patients do not have to reach the normal body mass index; a weight reduction of even a few percent has clinical benefits. This is because visceral fat is metabolically more active, and weight loss of a few percent is associated with significant loss of visceral fat. On the basis of these observations, weight management by dieting and exercise is now recommended to all overweight/obese women with PCOS.

Studies have shown that lifestyle changes (in this case, intensive exercise with a goal of ≥150 min/week of activity) resulting in weight loss reduced the risk of type 2 diabetes. The same studies found lifestyle changes to be superior to metformin. Thus, all women with PCOS should be encouraged to follow a healthy diet and to engage in regular exercise. Their chance to achieve a pregnancy will improve and the risks during pregnancy will be reduced. A healthier lifestyle will also reduce their long-term risks for diabetes, hypertension, dyslipidemia, and cardiovascular disease. It is important for all primary care providers to identify patients who may have PCOS. These patients need to undergo the appropriate screening tests and should be counseled about diet and exercise. Pharmacologic intervention could be combined with this approach as appropriate, but the above-mentioned studies suggest that lifestyle modification is the first-line treatment.

***Methods of Preventing PCOS Development***

I. Weight management

II. Drugs (such as the anti-diabetic drug Metformin)

III. Suppress ovarian function with oral contraceptives or other drugs

IV. Making an early diagnosis

***SLP management of PCOS***

*I.* Follow eight rules of diet correction

*II.* Avoid or less industrial foods to avoid xenoestrogens, especially broiler chicken and transfat laden foods.

*III.* Devote about 30 minutes to your hobby to overcome stress

*IV.* Include sports in your routine

*V.* Watch less movies, detach yourself from the fantasy world. Indulgence into watching too much mature media stuff leads to hormonal hyperactivity.

*VI.* Yoga helps in massaging the pelvic organs, therefore helps PCOS

*VII.* Supplements of cod liver oil and primrose oil should be used

## Male hormonal problems

Men unhealthy lifestyle adversely affects their fertility. Common problems observed are early onset of baldness and premature andropause (male menopause) as well. Common causes of male hormonal issues are:

***i-Emotional stress.***

Stress may interfere with certain hormones needed to produce sperm. Sperm count may be affected if you experience excessive or prolonged emotional stress. A problem with fertility itself can sometimes become long term and discouraging, producing more stress. Infertility can affect social relationships and sexual functioning.

***ii-Malnutrition/incorrect eating.***

Deficiencies in nutrients such as vitamin C, selenium, zinc and folate may contribute to infertility. Excess of processed foods impair male fertility.

***iii-Obesity.***

Increased body mass may be associated with fertility problems in men.

***iv-Cancer and its treatment.***

Both radiation and chemotherapy treatment for cancer can impair sperm production, sometimes severely. The closer radiation treatment is to the testicles, the higher the risk of infertility. Removal of one or both testicles due to cancer also may affect male fertility.

***v-Alcohol and drugs.***

Alcohol or drug dependency can be associated with poor health and reduced fertility. The use of certain drugs also can contribute to infertility. Anabolic steroids, for example, which are taken to stimulate muscle strength and growth, can cause the testicles to shrink and sperm production to decrease.

***vi-Medical conditions.***

A severe injury or major surgery can affect male fertility. Certain diseases or conditions, such as diabetes, thyroid disease, Cushing's syndrome, or anemia may be associated with infertility.

***vii-Age.***

A gradual decline in fertility is common in men older than 35.

***vii-Environmental exposure.***

Overexposure to certain environmental elements such as heat, toxins and chemicals can reduce sperm count either directly by affecting testicular function or indirectly by altering the male hormonal system. Specific causes include:

***a-Pesticides and other chemicals.***

Herbicides and insecticides may cause female hormone-like effects in the male body and may be associated with reduced sperm production and testicular cancer. Lead exposure may also cause infertility.

***b-Drug abuse.***

Use of cocaine or marijuana may temporarily reduce the number and quality of sperm.

***c-Tobacco smoking.***

Men who smoke may have a lower sperm count than those who don't smoke.

**Premature puberty**

A report was presented at the annual Pediatric Academic Society meeting describing how a preschool-age girl and her kindergarten-age brother began growing pubic hair. This was not an isolated case; in 2004, there was similar cluster of five children, and previous clusters in outbreaks occurring along the lines of disease epidemics or environmental poisonings. In 1979, there was an outbreak of breast enlargement among hundreds of Italian schoolchildren, most likely caused by estrogen contamination of beef and poultry. Most commonly, these outbreaks traced to accidental drug exposures. But some physicians worry that children are at higher risk of early puberty due to the increasing availability of classes of drugs, cosmetics and environmental contaminants called endocrine disruptors.

In the case of the two children described in the report, their testosterone level was about 100 times the normal amount. The cause was traced to a concentrated testosterone skin cream being used by their father. The children absorbed the testosterone through normal skin contact with their father. Sex hormones like testosterone are particularly potent because they are easily absorbed through the skin and resist degradation. Other known triggers of early puberty have included a shampoo that contained estrogen and placental extract, shampoos containing lavender and tea tree oils, and industrial pollutants. It's about time medical "experts" are finally recognizing the growing number of health problems resulting from contact with toxic chemicals.It is shocking, but nevertheless, increasingly common for five and six year old children to go through precocious puberty. The signs of which include:

For girls before age 8:

I. Breasts

II. Armpit or pubic hair

III. First menstruation

For boys before age 9:

I. Enlarged testicles and penis

II. Armpit or pubic hair

III. Facial hair

**Love hormone**

In his beautiful book, The Scientification of Love,French obstetrician Michel Odent explains how Oxytocin, a hormone released by the pituitary gland stimulates the release of chemical messengers in the heart. Oxytocin, which is essential during birth, stimulating contractions, and during lactation, stimulating the 'milk ejection reflex', is also involved in other 'loving behaviors.' "It is noticeable that whatever the facet of love we consider, oxytocin is involved," says Odent. "During intercourse both partners--female and male--release oxytocin." One study even shows that the simple act of sharing a meal with other people increases our levels of this 'love hormone.'

The oxytocin is part of a complex hormonal balance. A sudden release of Oxytocin creates an urge toward loving that can be directed in different ways depending on the presence of other hormones, which is why there are different types of love. For example, with a high level of prolactin, a well-known mothering hormone, the urge to love is directed toward babies. While Oxytocin is an altruistic hormone and prolactin a mothering hormone, endorphins represent our 'reward system.' "Each time we mammals do something that benefits the survival of the species, we are rewarded by the secretion of these morphine-like substances," says Odent. During birth there is also an increase in the level of endorphins in the fetus so that in the moments following birth both mother and baby are under the effects of opiates. The role of these hormones is to encourage dependency, which ensures a strong attachment between mother and infant. In situations of failed bonding between mother and baby there will be a deficiency of the appropriate hormones, which could leave a child susceptible to substance abuse in later life as the system continually attempts to right itself.

## Hormone disrupters

An analysis published in the journal, Chemical Research in Toxicology found 31 potential estrogen-mimicking food additives during their research. Chemicals with estrogen like effects known as xeno-estrogens, have been linked to a range of human health problems, including reduced sperm counts and increased risk of breast cancer. Other important hormone disrupters are:

1. Bovine growth hormone commonly added to commercial dairy
2. Soy products which are loaded with hormone like substances
3. Bisphenol A, commonly used in many plastics
4. Phthalates also commonly used in plastics
5. Perfluorooctanoic acid (PFOA) -- better known as Teflon
6. The propyl gallate, a preservative used to prevent fats and oils from spoiling
7. 4-hexylresorcinol, which is used to prevent discoloration in shrimp and other shellfish.

### *Prevention from hormone disrupters*

The disruption of your hormone system, and all of the consequences resulting from it, is a typical way that environmental toxins negatively impact your body. No surprise, Congress told the EPA to develop a comprehensive screening program within three years a decade ago. The agency never got around to it, however, due to efforts to squash it by representatives from the chemical industry serving on a program committee. Here are some measures you can take to protect you and your children from common toxic substances which will cause them to go into puberty more than a decade before they were designed to:

1. Store your foods in a glass container, whenever possible, as it is the most inert container you can use.

2. Only use natural cleaning products in your home.

3. Buy and eat, as much as possible, organic foods, especially milk which is frequently contaminated with bovine growth hormone.

4. Avoid processed foods.

5. Switch to natural brands of toiletries, including shampoo, toothpaste, antiperspirants and cosmetics.

## Diabetes Mellitus

### *Factors causing diabetes*

The main cause of diabetes is the western diet--based on refined carbohydrates that rush sugar into the bloodstream, trans fatty acids that interfere with insulin receptors in the cells, and difficult-to-digest foods like pasteurized milk and modern soy foods that put a strain on the pancreas--but another cause of chronic high blood sugar levels, one that is often overlooked, is stress. Under stress, the adrenal glands produce adrenaline, an important stimulus for the production of glucagon, which raises blood sugar levels and allows the body to react with a "fight or flight" response. Chronic stress--the stress on the adult in the workplace, the stress on the student under pressure to perform, the stress on the child expected to conform to rigid guidelines or who has been sexually or emotionally abused, even the stress of a spiritual or religious outlook that assumes a clockwork universe or a vengeful god--results in constant outpourings of adrenaline resulting in overstimulation of glucagon to keep blood sugar levels high. The body then responds with increased production of insulin to bring blood sugar levels down.

Polyneuronal Extopy (PNE), more commonly known as panic disorder, is a common symptom of a condition in which high levels of insulin accompany normal blood sugar levels. The condition derives from the vicious circle of constant stress causing increased release of sugar into the bloodstream, kept in check by increased outpourings of insulin, leading to chronic anxiety even under conditions that normally should not produce stress. Over time, especially when the diet is poor, the beta-cells of the pancreas become exhausted and can no longer produce large amounts of insulin. The result is full blown diabetes, characterized by chronically high blood sugar levels--as though the body has balanced a kind of bitterness in the exterior world with excess sweetness in the blood.

***Sugar regulation***

One of the most finely tuned mechanisms of the human body is the regulation of sugar levels in the bloodstream. While levels of cholesterol and triglycerides can vary widely, the levels of glucose in the blood must be maintained within a narrow range for the body to function at optimum levels--or even to function at all. The regulation of blood sugar levels is carried out by two hormones, insulin and glucagon. The principal role of insulin is to rapidly remove glucose from the blood and transport it into the muscles, liver and adipose tissue, thus lowering the blood sugar level and feeding the cells. (Note: the red blood cells and the cells in the brain, kidney and intestinal tract do not require insulin for glucose uptake.) Insulin promotes the storage of glucose as glycogen in the liver and adipose tissues. Glucagon has the opposite effect to insulin. In response to low levels of blood sugar, its task is to increase glucose concentration. Glucagon acts primarily on the liver and adipose tissue (but not on the skeletal muscle) to stimulate the production of glucose from glycogen and raise the blood sugar levels to normal.

Insulin is produced by the so-called beta-cells while glucagon is produced by the alpha-cells, both of which are found in the islets of

Langerhans in the pancreas. The ratio of insulin to glucagon in the blood determines whether glucose is used for energy or stored. If insulin is high compared to glucagon, carbohydrates will be created and/or stored after a meal; if insulin is low compared to glucagon, glucose will be added to the bloodstream rather than stored. Thus the type-II diabetic, who produces plenty of insulin that stays in the bloodstream rather than interacts with the cell membrane, will tend to gain weight easily, whereas the type-I diabetic, whose insulin production is low or non-existent, will not gain weight no matter how much he eats.

Originally, doctors thought that diabetes was simply a disease of insulin deficiency, a disease in which the pancreas was unable to produce enough insulin to meet the body's demands, and that it could be successfully managed. Over time, researchers have produced better delivery systems for insulin, and ways to produce more purified and effective types of insulin--from porcine insulin to human insulin produced through genetic engineering. The medical profession has learned that giving insulin orally was unsuccessful, that subcutaneous injections were better, and that delivering it through a pump was best. Yet with all the improvements that have been made since 1920, diabetes remains one of the leading causes of death and disability in the western world.

Today, doctors realize that diabetes is a much more complicated condition than one of simple insulin deficiency. They have also discovered that there are two types of diabetes. Type I diabetes, which is also called insulin-dependent or childhood diabetes, usually develops before the age of 30, and involves a malfunction of the pancreas. Type I diabetes is thought of as autoimmune disease in which some trigger causes the body's immune system to attack its own insulin-producing cells, the beta-cells in the islets of Langerhans in the pancreas. In time, the pancreas loses its ability to produce insulin, blood sugar rises, and serious adverse consequences, including death, can occur if the person is not supplied with insulin. As yet, there is no consensus as to what the autoimmune trigger for Type I diabetes might be. Some evidence points to early feeding of pasteurized cow's milk, soy products and grains, or the use of vaccines, as likely triggers. Type I diabetes is often very difficult to control and, if not successfully controlled, can lead to the early onset of many of the complications listed above. Type II diabetes, which is much more common than Type I diabetes, has a different etiology. It is the form of diabetes that is literally crying out for a new perspective from the one currently offered by the medical profession.

The control of the blood sugar is one of the most fundamental requirements for a healthy life. Blood sugar levels can become abnormal in one of two ways: they can become too low, which we define as a blood sugar less than 80 and call hypoglycemia; or they can become too high, defined as a blood sugar over 110, which is called hyperglycemia. While neither hypoglycemia, nor hyperglycemia is good for your health, they appear to call forth very different reactions in the human being. For example, if your blood sugar drops below 40, you will become disoriented, confused, and if the situation persists, slip into a coma and die. This situation is a true medical emergency. When blood sugar is between 40-60mg, you feels shaky, jittery, anxious, sweaty, confused and irritable. When blood sugar is between 60-80mg these same symptoms occur, but they are less severe.

The body reacts to the emergency situation of low blood sugar in many ways. When blood sugar even begins to drop below 80, the body produces a number of hormones, principally adrenaline and glucagon. The main effect of adrenaline is to make more sugar available to the cells. It is the production of adrenaline that accounts for the familiar shaky, jittery feeling that many have experienced during these hypoglycemic episodes. Glucagon helps raise blood sugar levels by increasing fat breakdown and stimulates the conversion of fat into sugar. There may be at least 10 more hormonal or biochemical reactions that occur during the early stages of hypoglycemia. One is the release of growth hormone, which has also been found to increase blood sugar in times of stress. As you can see, the body is well prepared to ward off this potential emergency. It has multiple overlapping mechanisms to prevent a precipitous fall in blood sugar, and many of these reactions produce clear symptoms that provoke us into action. Severe hypoglycemia is clearly a situation our adaptive physiology has learned to avoid.

The situation is very different with respect to hyperglycemia. These people are at strong risk for all the major complications of diabetes including coronary artery disease and neurological disease, yet they feel nothing, their bodies give them little warning. Some have conjectured that the body has a hard time dealing with hyperglycemia because the condition that causes it namely overeating is a relatively new phenomenon in human history because of modern foods. On the other hand, hypoglycemia induced by lack of food has been a frequent occurrence to which the body has adapted with a variety of mechanisms. Compared to dozens of hormones that are produced when our blood sugar drops too low, the body has only two mechanisms to deal with blood sugar that goes too high.

One is exercise any muscular activity drives the sugar from the blood into the muscle cells where it is used as fuel. The second is the production of insulin. Insulin production is the body's way of saying that the sugar level is too high, that the body is overfed with sugar. Insulin helps remove sugar from the blood into the cells where it is stored as fat. Understanding this basic physiology leads to some interesting conclusions. One is that controlling the level of insulin produced is the key to controlling obesity. For without insulin there can be no weight gain. The second conclusion we can draw is that the cause of type II diabetes is actually quite simple. Type II diabetes occurs when for many years the consumption of foods that raise the blood sugar chronically exceeds the amount of sugar needed by the muscles for exercise. This forces the body to gradually make more and more insulin in order to bring this sugar level down. Eventually, the body cannot make enough insulin to lower the sugar level, the sugar level remains chronically high and the patient is diagnosed with diabetes.

### *Complications of diabetes*

Complications of diabetes include heart disease and circulation problems; kidney disease; degeneration of the retina leading to blindness; neuropathy resulting in numbness, tingling, pain and burning in the extremities; foot ulcers leading to gangrene; and high risk of infection.

### *Insulin resistance*

Along the way a curious thing happens called insulin resistance. This means that as the blood sugars are chronically elevated, and the insulin levels are rising, the cells build a shield or wall around themselves to slow down this influx of excess sugar. Insulin resistance is a protective or adaptive response, it is the best the body can do to protect the cells from too much glucose. But as time goes on the sugar in the blood increases, more insulin is made by the pancreas to deal with this elevated sugar and the cells resist this sugar influx by becoming insulin resistant, in a sense by shutting the gates. This leads to the curious situation in which blood sugar levels are high but cellular sugar levels are low. The body perceives this as low blood sugar. The patient has low energy and feels hungry so he eats more, and the vicious cycle is under way.

Having a chronically elevated insulin level is detrimental for many other reasons. Not only do high insulin levels cause obesity (insulin tells your body to store fat), but they also signal that fluid should be retained, leading to edema and hypertension. Chronic high insulin provokes plaque development inside the arteries and also suppresses growth hormone needed for the regeneration of the tissues and many other physiological responses. During the 1980s, researchers began to ask whether obesity, coronary artery disease, hypertension and other common medical problems that occur together are really separate diseases, or manifestations of one common physiological defect. The evidence now points to one defect and that is hyperinsulinemia, or excessive insulin levels in the blood. Hyperinsulinemia is the physiological event that links virtually all of our degenerative diseases. It is the biochemical corollary or marker of the events described in heart disease.

***Diabetes is a modern age disease***

The problem of diabetes can be summarized by saying that the western diet has changed our eating habits and we are eating like marathon runners, when in fact most of us simply sit on the couch. When we regulate the carbohydrate intake to match our exercise level, type II diabetes cannot develop. Type I diabetes responds equally well to a high-fat, low carbohydrate diet. In fact, before insulin was available, the only way to treat type I diabetes was a high-fat diet from which carbohydrate foods were completely excluded because the body does not need insulin to assimilate proteins and fats.

Unless eaten to great excess, fats do not contribute to diabetes--with one exception. Transfatty acids in partially hydrogenated vegetable oils can cause insulin resistance. When these man-made fats get built into the cell membrane, they interfere with the insulin receptors. In theory, this means that one could develop insulin resistance without eating lots of carbohydrates. But in practice, partially hydrogenated vegetable oils are always used in the very high-carbohydrate foods--French fries, cookies, crackers, donuts and margarine on bread or potatoes--that flood the bloodstream with sugar. Transfatty acids in modern processed foods present a double problem for which the human species has developed no defenses.

***Diabetes and lifestyle modification***

Studies of indigenous peoples by Weston Price and many others reveal the wisdom of native diets and life-style. For not only did so-called primitive peoples follow the "perfect" anti-diabetes life-style program, but their diets incorporated specific foods only recently discovered to play an important role in the prevention and treatment of this disease. In general, indigenous peoples had a low carbohydrate intake coupled with a lot of physical activity. In fact, those peoples especially prone to diabetes today, such as northern Native Americans and Inuits, consumed virtually no carbohydrate foods. In warmer climates, where tubers and fruits were more abundant, these foods were usually fermented and consumed with adequate protein and fat. It is only in the change to Western habits that their so-called "genetic" tendency to diabetes manifests.

There are three other nutritional factors in indigenous diets that are helpful for diabetics. First, the diets were rich in trace minerals. Modern science has shown us that trace mineral deficiencies--particularly deficiencies in zinc, vanadium and chromium--inhibit insulin production and absorption. Without vanadium, sugar in the blood cannot be driven into the cells and chromium is necessary for carbohydrate metabolism and the proper functioning of the insulin receptors. Zinc is a co-factor in the production of insulin. Traditional foods were grown in mineral-rich soil, contained mineral-rich bone broth and salt, and included mineral-rich water or beverages made with such water. In the modern diet, the best sources of zinc are red meats and shell fish, particularly oysters. Extra virgin unfiltered olive oil supplies vanadium, and chromium is found in nutritional yeast, molasses and organ meats like liver.

Second, indigenous peoples ate a portion of their animal foods, such as fish, milk or meat, uncooked--either raw or fermented. This strategy conserves vitamin B6, which is easily destroyed by heat. Vitamin B6 is essential for carbohydrate metabolism; it is often the rate-limiting vitamin of the B vitamin complex because it is one of the most difficult to obtain in the diet. Indigenous peoples intuitively understood the need to eat a portion of their animal foods completely raw. Third, traditional peoples consumed foods rich in fat-soluble vitamins, including butterfat from grass-fed animals, organ meats, shellfish, and fish liver oils. High levels of vitamin A are absolutely essential for the diabetic because diabetics are unable to convert the carotenes in plant foods into true vitamin A. Vitamin A and vitamin D also protect against the complications of diabetes, such as retina and kidney problems. And vitamin D is necessary for the production of insulin.

Putting all these rules together, we find that a nutrient-dense traditional diet fits all the requirements for the prevention and treatment of diabetes. The diet should include sufficient trace minerals from organic and biodynamic foods, Celtic sea salt, bone broths, shellfish, red meat, organ meats, unfiltered olive oil and nutritional yeast. High levels of vitamins A and D are essential, as are raw animal foods to provide vitamin B6.Please note that in this approach there are no restrictions on total food intake, nor do we pay attention to the so-called glycemic index of various carbohydrate foods. Fats consumed with any carbohydrate food will lower the glycemic index. Worrying about glycemic indices adds nothing to the therapy and only increases time spent calculating food values rather than enjoying its goodness.

One should eat abundantly from good fats and proteins--only carbohydrate foods need to be restricted. Treatment of diabetes may thus entail a strong emotional or spiritual component; a good diet will go a long way to lower insulin requirements and heal the insulin-production mechanism, but removing the origins of stress is an important factor for long-term recovery. A change in job or life-style, therapy and a reassessment of any philosophical assumptions that breed fear rather than love may all be necessary to bring harmony to the body's finely tuned mechanism for keeping blood sugar levels in balance.

(Adapted from The Fourfold Path to Healing by Tom Cowan, MD, with Sally Fallon and Jaimen McMillan)

***Nutrition for Diabetics***

Vitamin A: Plentiful vitamin A is crucial to the successful treatment of diabetes. The diabetic pancreas is deficient not only in its ability to produce insulin, but also in the production of a variety of key enzymes, including the enzymes the body needs to convert carotenes into vitamin A. Therefore, the diabetic must take in more pre-formed vitamin A than the non-diabetic. Vitamin A is key to the prevention of the side effects of diabetes, including retina problems, kidney problems, neuropathy, infection and slowness to heal. The diabetic should take cod liver oil to provide a minimum dose of 20,000 IU vitamin A per day, in addition to vitamin A-rich foods like liver, egg yolks, seafood and cream and butter from pasture-fed animals.

Vitamin D: Vitamin D is needed for the production of insulin. A dose of cod liver oil that provides 20,000 IU vitamin A will provide 2,000 IU vitamin D. Several recent studies have shown that babies who receive cod liver oil during infancy, and whose mothers take cod liver oil during pregnancy, have much lower rates of diabetes. Other sources include lard, shellfish (especially shrimp), organ meats, egg yolks, cream and butter from pasture-fed animals.

Fatty Acids: The diabetic lacks the enzymes needed to make special long-chain, super-unsaturated fatty acids from essential fatty acids. Cod liver oil provides EPA and DHA from the omega-3 family. Gamma-linolenic acid (GLA) from the omega-6 family is provided by evening primrose oil, black currant oil or borage oil. Four capsules per day providing about 200 mg GLA is recommended.

Vitamin B1: A recent study found that diabetic rats given vitamin B1 (thiamine) had a 70-80 percent reduction in the development of kidney damage. Good sources include nutritional yeast, nuts, vegetables, and liver.

Vitamin B6: Plentiful supplies of vitamin B6 are critical for the health of the diabetic. B6 helps prevent carpal tunnel syndrome, to which the diabetic is prone. The best sources of B6 are raw animal foods such as raw whole milk, raw cheeses, raw fish and raw meat.

Alpha-Lipoic Acid: Also known as thoitic acid, alpha-lipoic acid is a vitamin-like enzyme cofactor necessary for converting glucose into ATP (chemical energy). Produced naturally in the body, it is also found in potatoes, carrots, yams, sweet potatoes, beets and red meat. As the diabetic needs to limit consumption of starchy vegetables, the best sources would be red meats and small amounts of pickled beets.

Chromium: A key mineral for diabetics, chromium is necessary for carbohydrate metabolism and proper functioning of the insulin receptors. Sources include nutritional yeast, molasses and organ meats like liver.

Vanadium: Without vanadium, sugar in the blood cannot be driven into the cells. An excellent source is unfiltered extra virgin olive oil.

Zinc: Zinc is a co-factor in the production of insulin. The best sources of zinc are red meats and shell fish, particularly oysters.

Thus, supplements for the diabetic should include cod liver oil; evening primrose, borage or black currant oil; and nutritional yeast. The diet should be rich in animal foods including raw butter, cream, whole milk and cheese from pastured animals; raw meat and fish; beef and lamb; seafood, especially shellfish; unrefined salt for trace minerals; bone broths for minerals; unfiltered olive oil; molasses, egg yolks; and a variety of fresh and fermented vegetables, especially beets.

This article appeared in Wise Traditions in Food, Farming and the Healing Arts, the quarterly magazine of the Weston A. Price Foundation, Winter 2003.

**SLP and diabetes management**

I have found many lifestyle factors responsible for the initiation of diabetes. Type II diabetes has following unhealthy lifestyle factors which take about 10-15 years to set-in a fully developed disease.

- A chronic self-neglect at physical, mental and spiritual levels
- Poor eating habits, in terms of type, quantity and time of food intake.
- Over ambitious nature and obsessed with perfection
- Sleep disorder, especially less night sleep
- Sensitive nature with lot of emotional issues
- Less/hyper physical activity, with poor nourishment
- Confused personality and weak faith

For type I diabetes, besides genes the role of intrauterine life traumas to the fetus should be in mind. Intrauterine life traumas for type I diabetes, could be nutritional, emotional, physical and mental. A malnourished, divorced or single parent, and working mother has high chances of giving birth to a type I diabetes prone child.

Diabetes especially the fasting blood sugar starts responding to a carefully organized nutrient dense SLP food plan only after two weeks. I found the levels of fasting blood sugar and Hba1c are the real indicators of sugar control. My food plans for diabetics are composed of whole wheat roti, brown rice, raw dairy, eggs, meat, organ meat, gram, chick peas, potato with skin, fish, nuts, figs, and yogurt. All above mentioned foods are rich source of minerals and vitamins required for the good control of diabetes. You have to strictly follow the SLP 8-rules of diet correction to have your meals. Remember healthy foods taken at a wrong time and incompatible food combinations cannot control high sugar levels.

## CHAPTER NO: 17

## A HOLISTIC FEMALE: INTEGRATED GYNAECOLOGY

Dr. Joan Borysenko, in her book 'A woman's Book of Life'describes the biology, psychology and spirituality of a feminine life. In her ground-breaking study of the feminine life cycle, she writes that a female's physical, emotional and spiritual lives are, in fact, perfectly interconnected. She writes that the medical community excludes women from studies because they are too complicated. Women change every seven days during the time that they menstruate: physically, emotionally, and intuitively. In her opinion "On top of that, they change in seven year cycles throughout life. So science has always focused on men, and simply applied the data to women. But it doesn't work very well".

She further says that "from the very beginning, brain development in men and women is different, though nature and nurture both play a part. Whether you're male or female, if you grow up in an abusive home, you will develop right brain dominance; it will specialize to read the emotions on faces, as you learn to intuit safe or unsafe situations. However, even in healthy homes, women's right brains specialize in this fashion while male right brains specialize to see things three dimensionally, for spatial orientation. From an early age, little girls are tuned to detecting what's occurring with others. They maintain this capacity throughout their life, although they begin to silence their relationship wisdom somewhere around puberty."

## Special Characteristics of a female

In the early 1950s a researcher by the name of Jost discovered that the normal course of human development is female. He removed the fetal gonads (testis) from the gestating male rabbit embryos and the resultant bunnies were normal females. He wrote that "in the absence of gonads female development ensued. Therefore the development in mammals is in the female direction unless acted upon by some product made or regulated by the Y-chromosome."If we look at some of most basic interactions between egg and sperm, mature eggs are different from any other cell in the body, engaging in incorporative and nurturing behavior. The ovum actively takes the sperm inside and supports the replication of its genetic material. Furthermore, eggs can repair sperm that are defective, including those with chemically induced mutations in the genetic code. While both egg and sperm have mitochondria, the egg is an enormous cell, while the sperm is little more than a nucleus with a tail that allows it to swim off in search of the egg. The few mitochondria that the sperm contains power its heroic journey and are unceremoniously cast off when the egg incorporates the sperm's nucleus.

The prodigious cytoplasm of the egg however is rich in mitochondria who's DNA helps direct nuclear genes and actively contributes to the development of the embryo. Cytoplasmic genes derived from the mitochondrial DNA are thus contributed solely by the egg."The fact that mitochondrial DNA comes only from the maternal line. The mitochondrial DNA in our cells today is very similar to what it was at the dawn of creation since it has not been contaminated by the messy genetic mixing that occurs when males and females pool their genes since the sperm's mitochondria are lost when the egg incorporates the sperm. So in tracing the origins of mitochondrial DNA, biologists have also been able to trace our matrilineal family tree back to an African Eve, sometimes called Mitochondrial Eve.Without Eve's clever mitochondria, their ability to mend broken sperm and initiate embryogenesis, the entire human race would vanish."

Children up to the age of about seven are similarly developed physically, as childhood progresses and we begin to develop language skills the left hemisphere myelinates. This probably correlates with the development of the linear, rational thinking that emerges in middle childhood, after the age of seven. However primary process skills are more easily accessed by women than by men because of the fact that the right hemispheric pathways through which women become especially attuned to reading emotions, and developing the skills of self-in-relation, are also involved in intuitive perception.

**FSH &LH: hormones of wisdom**

The greatest sadness in medical science is the medicalization of menopause. It's considered a disease, like our ovaries are failing. Dr. Susan Love says "ovaries don't change; they just change careers - like so many of us do in mid-life. No longer in the business of manufacturing eggs, they now produce male hormones as well as our female ones. We make 20 times more testosterone in mid-life than we did in our younger years. During the child bearing years, our pituitary gland secretes a couple of hormones - FSH and LH - that affect ovulation. Now, in menopause, instead of making less FSH and LH - because you don't need to make any eggs anymore - there's a 1,300-fold increase of these hormones! Conventional medicine says the pituitary continues to produce FSH and LH in the hopes of goosing our ovaries into coughing up one last egg! The body never makes a 1,300-fold excess of anything out of a mistake. There's a reason for it".

Many pioneering doctor researchers, such as Christiane Northrup and Mona Lisa Schultz are beginning to wonder whether FSH and LH are not the neurotransmitters of intuition and wisdom. Empirical studies suggest that while psychic dreams, insights and intuitions occur only during menstruation. Intuition use to increase during childbearing years, peri-menopause and menopause states as well. Studies show that women who have a positive view of menopause have far fewer negative symptoms than women who fear it. That's the mind-body connection at work. Therefore, the idea that we may need hormonal replacement therapy needs to be looked at very carefully. Certainly, hormonal fluctuations can be difficult, and many women need support. But we have options. 95% of women who chose natural therapies to treat the symptoms of menopause report satisfaction with alternative medicine.

Dr. Christine Northrup has written a book "Women's Bodies, Women's Wisdom"that proposed complementary or alternative therapies for women's diseases. In particular, Dr. Northrup promotes a body-mind connection to gynecological dysfunction and claims that many female problems can be linked to sexual abuse and trauma. The female reproductive cycle is governed by two hormones-estrogen and progesterone. For a period of about two weeks, from the end of menses until ovulation, the ovaries secrete relatively large quantities of estrogen. Estrogen stimulates new growth, more blood vessels and more nutritive supply to the endometrium, the lining of the uterus, thus preparing the womb for the implantation of the egg should fertilization take place. During the second phase, estrogen production decreases while progesterone, the other female hormone, increases.

Progesterone causes a decrease in the blood supply to the endometrium so that, if no fertilization occurs, the endometrial is expelled during menstruation, ten to fourteen days later. The secretion of these hormones is cyclical and governed by complex factors, including other hormones from the thyroid, adrenal and pituitary glands. Thus, the entire endocrine system is involved and requires nourishment in order for the menses to occur with regularity and ease.In order to produce estrogen and progesterone as required for the reproductive cycle, the body needs adequate amounts of cholesterol, because all the sex hormones are made from this vital substance. Remember cholesterol is the mother of all hormones. For this reason alone vegetarian diets for women are unwise as vegetarian diets will lower cholesterol. Furthermore, in order to avoid animal fats, vegetarians are likely to consume large amounts of Trans fatty acids found in "cholesterol-free" margarine, spreads and vegetable shortenings. There is considerable evidence that transfatty acids interfere with reproduction, possibly because they disrupt the action of the P450 cytochrome enzyme systems needed for the conversion of progesterone into the various types of estrogens.

The thyroid gland is intimately involved in the female reproductive cycle. As early as 1899, physicians were successfully treating menstrual and fertility problems with natural thyroid supplements. Adequate thyroid function is particularly critical for women during their childbearing years. Children born to mothers with low thyroid function score lower in intelligence test.In his pioneering studies of isolated primitive peoples, Dr. Weston Price discovered that the diets of healthy population groups contained much higher levels of the fat-soluble vitamins A and D than the American population of his day. In fact, foods rich in these factors, such as butterfat from cows eating rapidly growing green grass, liver and other organ meats, cod liver oil, fish, shellfish and fish eggs, were considered important for reproductive health and great effort was expended to provide these foods to prospective parents, pregnant and nursing women and growing children. Sadly, these are the very foods that women tend to avoid as they are seduced by the false promises of vegetarianism and dieting.

**Endometriosis**

Endometriosis occurs when the endometrium does not slough off normally at menstruation. It is usually accompanied by menorrhagia (heavy bleeding), severe menstrual cramps, and pain with defecation, intercourse and even ovulation. In severe cases the endometrial or lining of the uterus migrates to other sites such as the intestines and the bladder. The islands of the endometrial cause pain when they go through the cycle of menses and bleed as if they were normal uterine tissue. Cysts and fibroid tumors are common side effects. It is thought that endometriosis and related disorders are associated with a disruption in the estrogen-progesterone cycle, resulting in high levels of estrogen and low levels of progesterone. In monkeys, exposure to dioxin, which is an estrogen-like compound, resulted in moderate to severe endometriosis.

Orthodox treatment includes estrogen-blocking drugs, such as Danocrine, and laser treatment of the endometrium. Unfortunately Danocrine can provoke many side effects, including weight gain, fatigue, dizziness, headaches, acne, increased facial hair, pelvic and back pain, breast problems, cramps, hot flashes, depression, rashes and allergies. When laser treatment is not successful, the only remaining surgical option is hysterectomy. In fact, the leading cause of hysterectomy is excessive bleeding, often associated with endometriosis. Most popular books on endometriosis warn patients not to eat animal foods such as butter, liver and eggs because these contain arachidonic acid, a long-chain fatty acid which serves as the substrate for localized tissue hormones-called prostaglandins-that provoke inflammation.

Actually endometriosis is not really an inflammation of the type that occurs after an injury; and arachidonic acid also serves as the substrate for prostaglandins that counteract inflammation. The irony-actually the tragedy-of this advice is that animal foods like butter, liver and eggs are excellent sources of vitamin A. And endometriosis and excessive bleeding respond very well to vitamin A therapy. In South Africa, vitamin

A has been used as standard practice for the treatment of menorrhagia (excessive bleeding) since 1977 with a 92 percent cure rate. The liver is exquisitely designed to store vitamin A so that this vital nutrient is available in times of scarcity. Many conditions prevent the conversion of beta-carotenes into true vitamin A, including low thyroid function; and even individuals who convert beta-carotene easily cannot obtain optimum amounts from plant foods. Finally, both synthetic vitamin A and synthetic beta-carotenes can be toxic. Yet books on women's health usually recommend supplements containing the synthetic forms.

Calcium, phosphorus, magnesium, zinc, potassium, iron and good quality protein are all recommended for endometriosis and related conditions. Yet the body cannot absorb these minerals and protein without adequate amounts of natural, animal sources of vitamin A and D in the diet. Iron deficiency is a critical problem for women suffering from heavy bleeding but iron cannot be absorbed without adequate vitamin A.[30] Many women have reported that bleeding worsened when iron was given without supplementation with vitamin A.

## Breast Cancer

Breast cancer was a rare disease in 1900. Today it occurs in epidemic proportions-by some estimates one in every eight women will contract breast cancer, many of them during their childbearing years. The following nutrients are considered protective against this terrible disease: vitamin C, carotenes, vitamin A, vitamin D, vitamin CoQ10, conjugated linoleic acid (CLA), sphingomyelin and butyric acid.Of these, only the first two (vitamin C and carotenes) are found in plant foods. The rest are provided exclusively from animal foods, particularly butter and fats from animals allowed to graze.

The animal-based nutrients promote breast health in many ways. In particular, they support both thyroid and adrenal function. Low cortisol salivary levels are associated with decreased survival in breast cancer patients. Corticoid steroid hormones are secreted by the adrenal glands and help the body deal with stress. Like the various sex hormones, they are made from cholesterol. For patients with benign breast disease, treatment with 150,000 IU vitamin A resulted in notable pain reduction in nine of 12 participants.Breast cancer has a strong association with low levels of vitamin D and lack of sunlight.Although women with breast cancer often develop a deep fear of dietary fats, a study by Walter Willet of Harvard found no correlation with fat intake and breast cancer. In other words, women on low fat diets had just as much breast cancer as women on high-fat diets.

*Trans*fatty acids from partially hydrogenated vegetable oils have been positively associated with cancers of organs rich in fat tissues, such as the breast and prostate glands. These altered fats are found in almost all processed foods, particularly foods consumed by vegetarians who want to avoid "cholesterol and saturated fat." Processed liquid vegetable oils high in omega-6 fatty acids have also been associated with increased rates of breast cancer. The diets of healthy traditional peoples, including Americans at the turn of the century, did not contain these factory-produced oils. Conjugated linoleic acid has been shown to be very protective against breast cancer. It is found in butterfat, beef fat and lamb fat of grass-fed animals.

The biggest scam promoted in the guise of women's health is, quite possibly, the promotion of soy foods, rich in plant-based estrogens such as genistein, for the prevention and treatment of breast cancer. Women are not being told that an exhaustive report by the UK Ministry of Agriculture, Forestry and Fisheries found that the phytoestrogens in soy offer no protective effect. In fact, in 1997, researchers found that dietary genistein stimulated breast cells to enter the cell cycle, a condition that presages malignancy. The soy blocks absorption of calcium, zinc and magnesium. Soy also produces goiter because it depresses thyroid function.

### *Mammography*

American radiologists, with the encouragement of the National Cancer Institute and the American Cancer Society, have spent the last ten years convincing women that they should get a mammogram after the age of forty. Weston A. Price Foundation has been urging our female readers not to get mammograms at any age. Their reasoning has been that early treatment with surgery, radiation, and chemotherapy does not prolong life and may actually shorten it. Breast cancer therapy is a failure, but no one wants to own up to it. Some years ago a British surgeon blasted American doctors as "immoral" for screening women under 50 for breast cancer. On a visit to the Long Island Jewish Hospital Medical Center Dr. Baum said the screening was "opportunistic" and did more harm than good. "Over 99 percent of premenopausal women will have no benefit from screening. Even for women over 50, there has been only a one percent biopsy rate as a result of screening in the United Kingdom. The density of the breast in younger women makes mammography a highly unreliable procedure." (Medical Tribune, 3/26/92). A yet unpublished Canadian study even suggests, the rumor goes, that younger women are more likely to die if they expose themselves to mammograms instead of just relying on physical breast exams.

### *Mammography dangers*

The dangers of new technologies apply to testing methods, as well as surgical procedures and drugs. Ironically, we are now beginning to see examples of tests for cancer actually increasing the incidence of cancer. Women are constantly reassured that mammography is safe "because the amount of radiation is very small." But this reassurance completely overlooks a serious problem with mammography. Sometimes it's not an "overlook" but a complete disregard for the danger involved when the procedure is not performed carefully. Although widely used for early cancer-detection screening, remarkably little attention has been paid to the techniques of breast compression used in the mammography procedure. It is generally accepted that a cancer should be handled as carefully as possible, with very gentle palpation, in order to avoid accidental spread of the disease. As long ago as 1928, Dr. D.T. Quigley warned of the dangers of rough treatment of breast cancers. Although the principle of gentle handling of cancer is widely accepted, when it comes to testing for the disease, all logic seems to go out the window and the handling of tissues, such as the female breast, gets very rough indeed.

Techniques used are designed for maximum detection of cancerous tissue without regard to the possible disastrous consequences. One survey found that the mammographers used "as much compression as the patient could tolerate" and had no idea how much compression they were actually using. As the guidelines state, for proper mammography, "adequacy of the compression device is crucial to good quality mammography." In other words, squeeze the hell out of the breast for clear pictures and just forget about the Hippocratic admonition to do the patient no harm. The recommended force to be used in order to compress the breast tissue enough for a proper mammogram is 300 Newton. That's the equivalent of stacking 50 one-pound bags of sugar on the breast.

As so often happens in clinical medicine, the practice of the art is often not consistent with the findings of science. One animal study found that the number of metastases will increase by 80 percent if the tumor is manipulated. A human study reported in the British Medical Journal confirms these ominous findings. They discovered there were 29 percent more deaths from breast cancer in women who had had mammography. A report from the National Cancer Institute of Canada was interesting in that it completely missed the point on why cancer seems to be higher in women who take their doctor's advice and get mammograms. They reported, as in the above study, that women who have regular mammograms are more likely to die of breast cancer than women who avoid this test. But the investigators didn't blame the mammography procedure itself for the bad results they found and instead blamed "modern treatment." Professor Anthony Miller, Toronto University Medical School, who was director of the study, said, "You may find the cancer earlier but the women are still going to die. Modern treatment does not work for these early cancers." While we agree completely with Dr. Miller's assessment of modern cancer therapy, it is unfortunate that their study was blind to the danger of the mammography procedure itself.

According to updated guidelines set forth by the U.S. Preventive Services Task Force, women in their 40's should not get routine mammograms for early detection of breast cancer. The group's previous recommendation was for routine screenings every year or two for women age 40 and older. They now recommend that before having a mammogram, women ages 40 to 49 should talk to their doctors about the risks and benefits of the test, and then decide if they want to be screened. While roughly 15 percent of women in their 40's detect breast cancer through mammography, many other women experience false positives, anxiety, and unnecessary biopsies as a result of the test, according to data.

**Infertility**

An estimated 25 percent of American couples cannot conceive children. The fault may lie with either the male or the female. In both sexes, influences on the development of the sexual organs during infancy and childhood can determine the ability to conceive later in life. A father's poor eating habits could make his future children sick, suggests new research on mice involving the University of Texas. The study, recently published in the journal 'Cell', found that male mice that ate a low-protein diet passed on to their offspring cellular changes in their livers that affect fat and cholesterol metabolism. This passing on of traits linked to an environmental factor such as diet, using sperm as the vehicle, is one of the theories championed by researchers in the relatively new field of epigenetic. The field challenges long-held tenets that genetic information is passed on to offspring exclusively through

DNA, and that if environment has an impact, it would take many generations to modify traits.

Unfortunately, damage to the reproductive organs from lack of nutrients or exposure to environmental estrogens during early life is frequently irreversible. Even when the reproductive system has developed normally, nutritional deficiencies can inhibit conception. Much of the heartbreak of infertility can be traced to the substandard diet of teenage girls, diets usually high in sugar and transfatty acids and low in the all-important fat-soluble activators. The fad of vegetarianism, so prevalent today in American high schools and universities, puts young women at great risk for infertility problems.The fat-soluble vitamins play a critical role in fertility. Vitamin A is essential to the proper development of the follicle of the ovary, the structure that develops monthly to extrude an egg from the ovary and produce hormones that foster its successful implantation in the uterus.

Low levels of vitamin D are also associated with infertility.Any woman trying to get pregnant, either in the traditional way or with the aid of the various methods offered at fertility clinics, can benefit from the kind of diet that Weston Price recommended, one high in nutrient-dense animal foods from grass-fed animals. That often means overcoming a fear of cholesterol and saturated fats as these are contained in the very foods that nature uses to ensure successful reproduction. Actually, cholesterol is a woman's best friend. At a workshop held in 1992 at the National Heart, Lung and Blood Institute, researchers looked at every study that had been published about the risk of having high or low cholesterol and came to the same conclusion: mortality was higher for women with low blood cholesterol than for women with high cholesterol.

**A Pre-conception diet**

The traditional cultures universally had special preconception nutrition; their preconception nutrition consisted of the richest, most nutrient-dense foods they could get! They ate eggs, cream, butter, raw milk, fish (and fish eggs), organ meats, shellfish, and other rich (animal!) foods.

They often started these diets as soon as a young woman began planning marriage. Others began feeding special foods six months before the woman hoped to get pregnant. The fat found in dairy products is ideal because dairy products are very nutrient-dense foods. Eggs are also excellent food for pregnant women. Dr. Thomas Brewer, who devoted most of his life to researching pregnancy nutrition, as well as midwives and doctors around the world encourage pregnant women to eat two eggs a day. Eggs provide plenty of iron and will help you build your stores pre-pregnancy. Fish eggs have long been used in traditional cultures to promote fertility. If you can find high-quality cod liver oil to take in the preconception period take a teaspoon a day.

Consuming dairy products gives you an excellent nutritional package, including vitamin B6. B6 is vital to your health and having abundant B6 will prevent morning sickness. Drink fresh milk and enjoy robust cheeses as you try to conceive. Weston A. Price carried out extensive research on the nutritional habits of traditional cultures throughout the world. He found that the cultures that had strong, healthy babies all had special preconception nutrition programs. They fed women planning to conceive and pregnant women diets rich in seafood and high quality dairy products. Eating organic organ meats is an excellent way to get plenty of vitamins and minerals through your preconception nutrition. Choose organic liver and other organic organ meats. Also enjoy tasty fermented foods such as sauerkraut and kim chee. These foods enhance digestion and nutrient absorption. Find varieties that are traditionally prepared and are lacto-fermented. Fermented dairy products such as kefir and yogurt are excellent choices. Also enjoy plenty of fresh, leafy greens for their unsurpassed nutritional value. Choosing sprouted grain breads ensures that your breads will be easy to digest.

What you drink is also important. Drink plenty of fresh water every day. Limit sodas, colas, and caffeinated drinks. Enjoy fresh cold water, and juices with pulp (in moderation). You can also sip warm broths and soups. Your partner should be following the same dietary guidelines and enjoying the same excellent nutritional standards that you are. It will enhance his fertility and his health. Fish and high quality dairy, as well as leafy greens, whole grains, fresh meats, and fermented foods will make him healthier, more robust, and improve his fertility. If conception is more than seven months away, you can do a cleansing fast. In the six months leading up to conception, however, you need to be eating nutrient dense foods. You can also begin taking a vitamin and mineral supplement.

***Chinese concept of pre-conception diet / infertility***

Western medicine is based on the idea of man as machine. In the 17th century, Descartes, a French mathematician and philosopher, compared a healthy man to a well-made clock, composed of parts that can break down and be replaced or fixed. Attempts to better understand this complex machine resulted in focused studies of increasingly smaller parts of the machine. This led to specialization and fragmentation. Chinese medicine, on the other hand, still focuses on the whole body, including the spirit, as an entity. "In the TCM concept, a person is seen as an interaction between their body, mind and spirit," says Hirsh. "It's a very ancient and balanced approach to total wellness, and it tries to find the underlying cause of disease, rather than just treat the symptoms."

In the case of TCM, thinking about fertility begins long before infertility becomes an issue. Eugene Zhang, L.Ac., of Traditional Acupuncture and Chinese Integrative Medicine in Fairfax, Va., says it's important to maintain a healthy lifestyle for maximum fecundity. "When we speak of lifestyle, there are a lot of things involved, but in general we look at diet, sleep and work," says Zhang. "All of those tie together. If you're in a high-stress life it can complicate efforts to conceive, so we use acupuncture and herbs to assist in relaxation and to maximize the body's natural abilities." Living a healthy life is sound advice for anyone who is thinking of attempting pregnancy because, as Hirsh points out, being at optimum health is best not only for maximum fertility, but for a healthy pregnancy and the ability to bounce back more quickly after the pregnancy.

"I tell young couples that when you get engaged is when you should start cleaning it up so you and your mate can have healthy children," says Hirsh. Traditional Chinese Medicine (TCM) dates back approximately 5,000 years and has been used to treat infertility and miscarriage as early as 200 A.D. Using a combination of acupuncture, herbs, massage, diet, and exercise. TCM treats the root causes of a condition, balances disharmonies, and alleviates a patient's symptoms. The World Health Organization (WHO) has recently acknowledged the ability of TCM to facilitate healing in many diseases, and nearly one quarter of the world's population still turns to TCM for their primary health care. According to TCM, the inability to conceive does not necessarily imply infertility; it simply means an imbalance in one's optimum reproductive health. Traditional Chinese practitioners believe reproductive imbalance is caused by one or more of the following syndromes:

1. A "deficiency" syndrome prevents the hormonal system from properly influencing the sexual and reproductive functions. This is said to be a weakness of the "kidney and liver."
2. A "stagnancy" syndrome prevents the sexual and reproductive organs from functioning despite normal hormone levels and normal ability to respond to hormones. This is said to involve a stagnancy of "qi and blood," which restricts circulation to the tissues involved.
3. A "heat" syndrome, which causes the affected organs to function abnormally. This type of syndrome can produce abnormal semen quality in males, while gynecologic infections can cause female infertility by blocking the passages, changing the mucous membrane conditions, or influencing the local temperature.

Practitioners believe TCM can increase fertility in women by:

I. Establishing a regular menstrual cycle

II. Rebalancing hormonal functions, decreasing elevated levels of FSH and encouraging ovulation

III. Increasing endometrial lining

IV. Increasing and regulating beneficial cervical fluid

V. Unblocking fallopian tubes

VI. Decreasing stress levels

VII. Strengthening the immune system

VIII. Increasing the libido

TCM can increase fertility in men by:

I. Improving sperm motility

II. Improving semen volume

III. Improve sperm quality (morphology)

IV. Decreasing stress

V. Increasing the libido

After a TCM practitioner diagnoses a pattern of disharmony, treatments for fertility generally involve weekly acupuncture appointments and daily consumption of an herbal formula. Diet modifications, exercise, and massage may also be recommended.

**Important fertility tips to boost ovarian health**

Follow the wisdom of ancient tribes who use to organize a pre-conception diet about six months prior to their daughter's wedding. Chinese nation has got the same wisdom and they follow almost the same culture. Here are the most important things you need to do in order to ensure your body is ovulating and making healthy eggs:

I. Sleep in the complete dark, even a little light shining into your eyes can affect ovulation patterns.

II. Healthy foods that support ovulation, rich in B vitamins like B6 and B12, magnesium, calcium, zinc and CoQ10.

III. Make sure your thyroid gland is working at its optimum. Take foods that contain iodine like kelp and sea vegetables.

IV. Take fertility vitamins daily to prevent mineral deficiency that affects poor ovarian response.

V. A state of stress can delay or suppress ovulation, therefore learn to handle stress.

**Menopause**

Natalie Angier, author of *Women:* An Intimate Biography, points out that the condition of menopause is unique to humans. In all other species, the female is fecund throughout her life, able to give birth until the time of death; but human females enjoy a long period in later life in which they are freed from the role of child-bearer. Actually, menopause occurs in human females for a very practical reason. Human mothers in foraging societies can care for one infant, but because human children develop slowly, they are not able to provide food for themselves and their children when a second child is born. Assistance comes from grandmothers and aunts who no longer bear children and are thus freed up to aid in the nourishment of the younger generation. Humans differ from other animals in the complexity of their nervous systems, complexity that requires many years to develop. If human females did not experience the cessation of fertility that allows them to assist in providing for growing children, the human race could not exist. Yet modern medicine treats menopause as a disease requiring treatment with powerful drugs.

The drugs used to "treat" menopause are estrogens, derived from mares' urine (as in Premarin); plant foods (such as soy); or even "natural" estrogens extracted from human urine. They are prescribed to millions of women with the promise of prolonged youth, protection against osteoporosis, relief from vaginal dryness and freedom from hot flashes. According to the popular press, "Estrogen helps keep skin thicker and less wrinkled by slowing the breakdown of collagen."[49] But the search for the fountain of youth through Hormone Replacement Therapy (HRT) carries considerable risk.

According to the patient insert that comes with Wayerst Laboratories drug Premarin, side effects include nausea and vomiting, breast tenderness or enlargement, enlargement of benign tumors of the uterus, retention of excess fluid that may worsen certain conditions such as asthma, epilepsy, migraine, heart disease or kidney disease, and "a spotty darkening of the skin, particularly on the face." More serious side effects include cancer of the uterus and breast, gallbladder disease and abnormal blood clotting, according to the insert. When these dangers are cited in magazines and newspapers, the most common response is the claim that HRT reduces the risk of heart disease, so much so that this reduction more than compensates for the "slight increase in risk" for breast or uterine cancer. But a 1998 study reported 24 percent more deaths from heart disease in a group of women taking HRT than those taking a placebo. These results were not statistically significant but they do suggest that HRT is not protective against heart disease.

To counteract the effects of estrogen therapy, some practitioners are recommending progesterone as an antidote-either in synthetic form or as a "natural" ingredient of various rub-on creams. Because the "natural" progesterones come from plant sources, they are assumed to be safe. But these "natural" progesterones must undergo several synthetic chemical conversions. The soybean product is derived from a sterol compound called stigmasterol, which is then synthesized to progesterone. The yam product is derived from diogenine. Whether rubbed on or taken by mouth, progesterones, like estrogens, can interfere with the body's natural cycle of hormone production. The long-term effects are largely unknown and it is easy to overdose. The amount of progesterone in a cream may vary greatly from one product to another and there is no way of telling how much reaches the bloodstream.

Not to be outdone in the hormone-meddling activities foisted on the American woman, some clinicians now recommend the addition of androgens-male hormones-to the estrogen cocktail. They cite evidence that these male hormones may improve a woman's energy and mood, reduce breast pain, energize waning libido and protect against osteoporosis, citing "a direct, positive correlation between post-menopausal circulating levels of androgens and protection from vertebral crush fractures."[52]The truth is that every woman in the world experiences a decline in the level of female hormones and a rise in the level of male hormones at menopause. This is nature's way of equipping the female sex for her new role as forager, worker and sage. Like the male youth of eighteen, she experiences hot bloodedness, signalized by hot flashes, as she prepares for a lustier life than the cloistered one she led as a mother of small children.

For the vast majority of women, production of sex hormones is best left to the body's exquisitely tuned endocrine system. Any woman will stay young for a long time if she eats properly and launches herself into a project worthy of her enthusiasm and love. That means, of course, that women must make wise dietary choices so that the endocrine system is properly fed. It means avoiding processed foods and consuming only foods that are dense with nutrients. Hormone Replacement Therapy is a tender trap that keeps potential heroines from enjoying the adventures that await them outside their castle walls.

## Wise Choices, Healthy Bodies

In primitive societies, women's roles and women's diets were dictated by the tribal culture and did not require the individual woman to exercise her decision-making powers. By contrast, modern society gives us unlimited freedom. Every trip to the grocery store, every visit to the refrigerator presents the opportunity for wise or foolish choices about our diet. The modern woman has been told that she can do everything-work full time, raise a family, provide meals, keep a household that runs smoothly and peacefully and remain appealing and young. Nature tells us something different, by conferring on women the gift of menopause, nature informs us that mothers of small children need help. They cannot do it all, not in primitive societies, much less in the modern age. The pressures for young women to be both wage-earner and mother can place enormous stress on our bodies at just the stage when our strength is needed for the production and care of healthy children and that stress often leads to disease.

## SLP and a holistic female

My 27 years of clinical experience has made me learn in-depth about a holistic female. I think her hormonal composition gives her wisdom, tolerance, capacity to do long term planning, intuition and an endless patience. In my society I see lot of adult females going through various emotional traumas but still coping with life with no serious ailment and regret. Their immune system seems to be stronger than a man's immunity. In my opinion the strongest emotion of a mother's love makes her stand like a rock against the hardships of a married life. Men even can't imagine the level of patience, physical tolerance, wisdom and intuition their female partner carries. Social and cultural upbringing of a male has given him an impression that he is superior to a female. Because of this social superiority myth and his built-in nature of physical superiority makes him believe it to be true. This myth makes him behave accordingly, and during the marital life he keeps on proving his supremacy on his partner. As a result the emotional harmony in their relationship is lost, they start compromising with each other and they live like two strangers.

Very rarely, I have seen a man who completely understands the holistic nature of his wife. In contrast the female partner knows more about her husband and always tries to make him comfortable at a later age she even nurture him like a mother. This is an amazing God gifted ability to a woman, but her weak point is that she is too sensitive and emotional. If this weakness dominates she can get serious degenerative ailments at an early age. I believe a woman is dominated by various emotions from the age of 14- 44 years and this corresponds roughly with the child bearing period. This is also the time of maximum emotional traumas from husband and in-laws. In a female from age forty onwards, the male hormone starts increasing, this change corresponds with her husband's andropause (male menopause, when the male hormones gradually start decreasing). Now the same woman has to take care of her aging partner, her children, grandchildren and other financial and social responsibilities.

Due to her hormonal composition at this stage she is balanced in termsof emotional, logical, and intuitional aspects of her being. Psychosocial studies have proven that a widow copes with the life problems in a better way than a widower.When a female patient comes to me I work primarily on their emotional rejuvenation along with their physical health. After following 2-3 months of SLP, they tell me that their emotional traumas are no more going deep and seem to bounce back. Once they are emotionally rejuvenated, only then reversal of their degenerative disease starts. I don't know exactly which component of the food heals emotional traumas, but few of them also mentioned about an inner voice or connection which has started guiding them. Through a personalized lifestyle modification I simply try to connect nature with nature through nature, human body's auto pilot activates on its own for the safe landing of an individual body into a holistic being.

Following benefits in women have been noticed after following SLP:

I. Hormonal balance

II. Healing of chronic pelvic inflammatory disease

III. Reversal of polycystic ovaries

IV. Improved chances fertility

V. Smooth pregnancy without or less severe hypertension, edema, vomiting, gestational diabetes and show a controlled weight gain

VI. Betterment of skin health

VII. Restoration of female body curves and measurements

VIII. Menopausal issues are well handled

IX. Manage or revertchronic female degenerative disorders

X. Graceful aging with less dependence on artificial anti-aging tools

XI. Delayed mental aging

XII. Activation of subconscious mind or intuition

# CHAPTER NO: 18

## LET THE FLOWER BLOSSOM: CHILDREN ISSUES

A recent review of the literature on grandmothers' roles in non-western societies (Aubel, 2005) revealed that grandmothers, in virtually all cultures and communities, have considerable knowledge and experience related to all aspects of maternal and child development, and that they have a strong commitment to promoting the well-being of children, their mothers, and families. Societies around the world acknowledge that grandmothers play an influential role in the socialization and care of children as they grow and develop. They also help in the education and supervision of their daughters and daughters-in-law. The study concluded that while certain harmful practices are promoted by grandmothers in various cultures, given the wide-ranging role they play and their influence and intrinsic commitment to promoting the well-being of women and children, they should be viewed as key actors in development programs. The rationale for involving grandmothers in community programs is also supported by the policies of UNICEF, the World Bank and WHO related to the health and well-being of women and children.

Imagine a child rose according to the nutritional wisdom of our ancestors living in traditional set up. This child grows up free of the common ailments and diseases that we currently take for granted. This child's strong, white teeth grow in straight and free of tooth decay. This child's face is broad and well formed. This child is attentive and engaged, and can learn easily and readily because of optimal brain development. This child is energetic by day and sleeps soundly at night. This child is sturdy but not overweight. This child has a strong immune system, does not experience childhood illnesses or allergies, and has a stable, cheerful and optimistic disposition.

Dr. Price research has found a direct relationship between the dental caries and malnourishment. While dentists do correlate cavities to nutrition, their focus tends to be on sugar or acid-generating foods. The typical solution for decay is to fill the cavities, encourage the child to increase their level of dental hygiene while decreasing their consumption of sweets. According to Price, when given enough specific nutrients, the body will re-mineralize the tooth naturally so that no decay arises. The body can also repair damage that has already occurred. Otherwise we are faced with choosing amongst a short list of dental materials to put in our children's mouths, all of which are toxic to a certain degree.If the child is fed on a diet which is not traditional, there are various problems which are, narrow nasal Passages, constricted ear canal, constricted glands in the head, reduced surface area in the lungs, digestive disorders, bone problems and a narrow or flattened pelvis. Yet, depending on how early a child is nourished adequately, many of these conditions can be reversed or improved.

While it is never too late to institute changes, the earlier the better the most ideal period being before a child is even conceived. Almost all of American children have thin faces and have braces to straighten their teeth. Increasing numbers have poor eyesight as well. They are plagued with allergies, asthma, and even diseases that were formally associated with adults, like cancer and arthritis. Seven million of them are diagnosed with learning disabilities. According to the Mayo Clinic, up to 20% of known pregnancies now result in miscarriage. They suspect the actual number is much higher because many miscarriages occur very early in pregnancy, before a woman even knows she's pregnant. There are 250,000 birth defects reported each year.

## Factors affecting the growth and development

***i-Proximity and touch***

Human brains have evolved from earlier mammals. The first portion of our brain that evolved on top of its reptilian heritage is the limbic system, the seat of emotion. It is this portion of the brain that permits mothers and their babies to bond. Mothers and babies are hardwired for the experience of togetherness. The habits of breastfeeding and co-sleeping practiced by the majority of mothers in non-industrialized cultures, and more and more in our own, facilitate two of the main components needed for optimal mother/child bonding: proximity and touch."The easiest and quickest way to induce depression and alienation in an infant or child is not to touch it, hold it, or carry it on your body." -- James W. Prescott.

Research in neuroscience has shown that touch is necessary for human development and that a lack of touch damages not only individuals, but our whole society. Human touch and love is essential to the health of a baby. A lack of stimulus and touch causes the stress hormone, cortisol to be released which creates a toxic brain environment and can damage certain brain structures. According to James W. Prescott, PhD, of the Institute of Humanistic Science, and former research scientist at the National Institute of Child Health and Human Development, sensory deprivation results in behavioral abnormalities such as depression, impulse poor control, violence, substance abuse, and in impaired immunological functioning in mother deprived infants. For over a million years babies have enjoyed almost constant in-arms contact with their mothers or other caregivers, usually members of an extended family, receiving constant touch for the first year or so of life. "In nature's nativity scene, mother's arms have always been baby's bed, breakfast, transportation, even entertainment, and, for most of the world's babies, they still are." says developmental psychologist, Sharon Heller in, The Vital Touch: How Intimate Contact with Your Baby Leads to Happier, Healthier Development.

To babies, touch is equal to love and fully loved babies develop healthy brains. During the critical period of development following birth the infant brain is undergoing a massive growth of neural connections. Synaptic connections in the cortex continue to proliferate for about two years, when they peak. During this period one of the most crucial things to survival and healthy development is touch. All mammal mothers seem to know this instinctively, and, if allowed to bond successfully with their babies they will provide continuous loving touch. Touch deprivation in infant monkeys is so traumatic that their whole system goes haywire, with an increase of stress hormones, increased heart rate, weakimmune system and sleep disturbances.

Anthropologist, Ashley Montagu concluded that given our upright position and large brains, human infants are born prematurely while our heads can still fit through the birth canal, and that brain development must therefore extend into postnatal life. He believed the human gestation period to actually be eighteen months long, nine in the womb and another nine outside it, and that touch is absolutely vital to this time of "extero-gestation." Newborns are born expecting to be held, handled, cuddled, rubbed, kissed, and maybe even licked. All mammals lick their newborns vigorously, off and on, during the first hours and days after birth in order to activate their sensory nerve endings, which are involved in motor movements, spatial, and visual orientation. These nerve endings cannot be activated until after birth due to the insulation of the watery womb environment and the coating of vernix casseus on the baby's skin. Dr. Janov's says that you can kiss a brain into maturity, he believes that very early touch is central to developing a healthy brain. "Irrespective of the neuro juices involved, it is clear that lack of love changes the chemicals in the brain and can eventually change the structure of that brain."

***ii-Poor Nutrition; well –fed but malnourished***

There are key nutrients needed for brain development, we can infer that without them, full development may be delayed, interrupted or never realized. These key nutrients are vitamins A and D, choline, DHA, zinc, tryptophan and cholesterol. Most of them are found in the cod liver oil, the liver, butter, and egg yolks from grass-fed animals, while some are found in the seafood and the meat of grass-fed animals. Dr. Price discovered that there were no processed foods in any of the diets of the tribal healthy people he studied.There were animal foods in every diet, and the food was all nutrient dense, meaning it contained high levels of vitamins and minerals. Nutrient dense foods are seafood, organ meats, raw dairy, eggs and meat. If a mother can't breast feed the baby, goat milk can be started. After 6-8 months raw cow's milk is safe to be given. Avoid all processed weaning cereals and formula milk. Ideal weaning foods are egg yolks, yogurt, fish, liver, bone broth, fruits with pulp and vegetables like potatoes and peas.

### *iii-Infant Massage*

Infant massage has been used by some cultures for hundreds of years and is now becoming popular in the United States. Touch is one of the first senses to develop and is vital to an infant's development. Not only does massage promote bonding, it offers many health benefits. Infant massage may strengthen the immune system, promote weight gain in premature infants, improve muscle tone and coordination, increase circulation and oxygenation, enhance motor skills and neurological development, promote sleep, and relieve colic. Massage around their mouth, especially to help comfort them when they are teething. To help expel gas, massage your infant's tummy in clockwise circles (you can also gently push their knees to their tummy and hold them there for 10 seconds). Infant massage also benefits the parent because it can reduce tension, anxiety, increase self-esteem and confidence in the parenting role.

### *iv-Childhood traumas*

The Adverse Childhood Experiences (ACE) Study is an ongoing research project which is perhaps the largest scientific research study of its kind. Its purpose it to analyze the relationship between multiple categories of childhood trauma, health and behavioral outcomes later in life.

ACE is examining the effects of:

I. Recurrent physical abuse

II. Recurrent emotional abuse

III. Contact sexual abuse

IV. An alcohol and/or drug abuser in the household

V. An incarcerated household member

VI. Someone who is chronically depressed, mentally ill, suicidal or institutionalized.

VII. Mother is treated violently

VIII. One or no parents

IX. Emotional or physical neglect

The ACE study, published in the American Journal of Preventive Medicine found that both the prevalence and risk increased for severe obesity, physical inactivity, depressed mood, and suicide attempts as the number of childhood exposures to trauma increased. They also found a strong relationship between the number of childhood traumas and the number of health risk factors for leading causes of death in adults. In particular, they found a significant relationship between the number of childhood trauma exposures and the following disease conditions:

I. ischemic heart disease

II. cancer

III. chronic bronchitis or emphysema

IV. history of hepatitis or jaundice

V. skeletal fractures

**VI.** poor self-rated health

**Breast feeding**

Breast milk is nature's perfect food for babies, it contains special substances that give the growing baby immunity to infection and disease. Breastfeeding bonds a mother to her baby, stimulates important hormonal activities in her body, helps her lose weight after pregnancy and protects her against future breast cancer. Mother's milk contains long-chain polyunsaturated fatty acids (LCP) that the baby needs for the development of its nervous system. These special fats accumulate in the brain and retina, if they are absent in the infant diet, the child is likely to suffer from learning disabilities and reduced visual acuity.The most important LCP's are arachidonic acid (AA) of the omega-6 family, docosahexaenoic acid (DHA) of the omega-3 family.

What is less well known is that the levels of LCPs in human breast milk greatly depend on the mother's diet. An important 1997 study compared the fatty acid composition of breast milk of mothers in two Chinese provinces with that of Canadian mothers.Mothers in the traditional province of Chongqing had higher levels of milk fat than those from westernized Hong Kong, and higher levels of AA, due to a special period of feeding for the first four weeks after the birth of the baby during which Chongqing mothers consume up to ten eggs per day and large amounts of chicken and pork. The diet of Hong Kong mothers was much lower in fat and calories, but because of high fish consumption, their levels of DHA were as high as those of Chongqing mothers. But breast milk levels of AA and DHA in both provinces were much higher than those of Canadian mothers.

The dietary change is reflected in the milk composition like the content of erucic acid (a long-chain monounsaturated fatty acid) increased in the milk of Chongqing mothers during the later weeks of lactation, reflecting a dietary switch from animal fats to rape seed oil. Levels of omega-6 linoleic acid were high in the milk of Hong Kong mothers, reflecting their use of high-omega-6 vegetable oils derived from corn and soy.Ideal breast milk contains high levels of both saturated fats and LCPs. This can be accomplished by consuming high levels of animal fats plus eggs, cod liver oil and oily fish throughout the lactation period. Saturated fats in mother's milk stimulate the immune system and work synergistically with LCPs to maintain them in the tissues where they belong. Levels of fat in a mother's milk will decrease with each baby unless she takes special care to consume high levels of nutrient-dense fats between pregnancies and during each lactation.

Numerous studies support the benefits of breastfeeding. For example, breastfed babies tend to be more robust, intelligent and free of allergies and other complaints like intestinal difficulties.Other studies have shown that breastfed infants have reduced rates of respiratory illnesses and ear infections.Some researchers believe breastfed infants have greater academic potential than formula-fed infants, which is thought to be due to the fatty acid DHA found in mother's milk and not in most US formulas.However, other studies show the opposite. In 2001, a study found breastfed children had more asthma than bottle-fed.A Swedish study found that breastfed infants were just as likely to develop childhood ear infectionsand childhood cancer as formula-fed babies. This proves that quality of breast milk is dependent on the mother's diet which should be nutrient dense.

"The typical modern diet is filled with products based on sugar, white flour, additives and commercial fats and oils, which do not nourish and build. The proper nutrients are necessary to create breast milk that will provide all a growing baby needs. These include good quality proteins from foods such as grass-fed meats and organ meats, good quality fats from butter, coconut oil, olive oil, cod liver oil and egg yolks, as well as complex carbohydrate-rich foods like vegetables, whole grains and legumes--think whole food, natural and seasonal, with a big emphasis on healthy fat.Ideally, breastfeeding should be maintained for a year, with a goal of six months for working mothers. The first year of life requires a full spectrum of nutrients, including fats, protein, cholesterol, carbohydrates, vitamins and minerals. Once breast milk is no longer the sole source of these nutrients, add foods which are nutrient dense to baby's feed".

There are other benefits to breast feeding, Joseph Chilton Pearce in his 1992 work, Evolution's End, describes the dual role of the heart cell, saying that it not only contracts and expands rhythmically to pump blood, it communicates with its fellow cells. "If you isolate a cell from the heart, keep it alive and examine it through a microscope, you will see it lose its synchronous rhythm and begin to fibrillate until it dies. If you put another isolated heart cell on that microscopic slide it will also fibrillate. If you move the two cells within certain proximity, however, they synchronize and beat in unison." Perhaps this is why most mothers instinctively place their babies to their left breast, keeping those hearts in proximity. The heart produces the hormone, ANF that dramatically affects every major system of the body. "All evidence indicates that the mother's developed heart stimulates the newborn heart, thereby activating a dialogue between the infant's brain-mind and heart," says Pearce who believes this heart to heart communication activates intelligences in the mother also.

"On holding her infant in the left-breast position with its corresponding heart contact, a major block of dormant intelligences is activated in the mother, causing precise shifts of brain function and permanent behavior changes." In this beautiful dynamic the infant's system is activated by being held closely; and this proximity also stimulates a new intelligence in the mother, which helps her to respond, and nurture her infant. Another key to understanding how a mother's love shapes the emerging capacities of her infant is what doctors Thomas Lewis, Fari Amini, and Richard Lannon, authors of A General Theory of Love, call limbic regulation; a mutually synchronizing hormonal exchange between mother and child which serves to regulate vital rhythms. Human physiology, they say, does not direct all of its own functions; it is interdependent. It must be steadied by the physical presence of another to maintain both physical and emotional health. "Limbic regulation mandates interdependence for social mammals of all ages," says Lewis,

"But young mammals are in special need of its guidance: their neural systems are not only immature but also growing and changing.

One of the physiologic processes that limbic regulation directs, in other words, is the development of the brain itself--and that means attachment determines the ultimate nature of a child's mind." A baby's physiology is maximally open-loop: without limbic regulation, vital rhythms collapse posing great danger, even death. The regulatory information required by infants can alter hormone levels, cardiovascular function, sleep rhythms, immune function, and more. Lewis, et al contend that the steady piston of mother's heart along with the regularity of her breathing coordinate the ebb and flow of an infant's young internal rhythms. They believe sleep to be an intricate brain rhythm that the neurologically immature infant must first borrow from parents. "Although it sounds outlandish to some American ears, exposure to parents can keep a sleeping baby alive."

***Harmful effects of artificial baby milk formula***

For starters, just one bottle of formula alters the ph of the baby's intestinal tract. In one study (Chieri, 1997), a researcher experimented with formula of different ph levels. In every single case, all of the formulas failed to induce a prevalence of colonization with bifida bacteria at one month of age in the intestinal tract. The intestinal tract needs to maintain a low ph to help prevent the growth of pathogens in the gut. This kind of ph is only consistent with babies receiving human milk.

I. Fewer instances of diarrheal illnesses are the most readily acknowledged benefit of exclusive breastfeeding in terms of both rateand severity. One study indicates that babies fed a combination of formula and breast milk are roughly 4% more at risk for death due to diarrheal illnesses. The babies that are exclusively formula fed are about 14% more at risk for death from diarrheal illnesses (Victoria, 1989).

II. Formula fed babies are more likely to have ear infections (Teele, 1989; Paradise, 1994).

III. Formula fed infants are more at risk for rotavirus.(Holberg, 1991).

IV. Formula fed infants are more likely to develop insulin dependent diabetes (AAP, 1994; Pettitt, 1997).

V. Formula fed infants are having a higher incidence of childhood cancer and lymphoma. The longer a child is breastfed, the greater the risk reduction (Davis,1988 Schwartzbaum, 1991; Shie, 1995).

VI. Formula fed babies do not receive the same ingredients that breastfed babies receive that promote brain growth and development. DHA and arachidonic acid, which are essential for brain growth and central nervous system development, are not found in formula. Researchers are questioning if the absence of those ingredients in formula contributes to the fact that children breastfed as babies have higher IQ's (more than ten points higher on average) than children formula fed as infants (Lucas, 1992; Rogan && Gladen, 1978, 1993)

VII. Soy formulas have been proven to be just as antigenic as cow's milk formulas and are not recommended by the American Academy of Pediatrics (1998). Soy formulas also have a greater incidence of wheezing, rhinitis, and ear infections. There is no cholesterol in soy, and there are high levels of manganese, aluminum, and plant steroids (phytoestrogens--which may influence sexual function). Soy fed infants has a phytoestrogen circulation that is 13,000-22,000 times higher than maternal plasma estrogen concentrations (Setchell, 1997).

VIII. If you are considering travel to other countries, you should know that exclusive breastfeeding provides complete protection against cholera because it is a water-borne illness.

## Children health issues

I will discuss only those disorders which are the outcome of a chemical imbalance, an un-healthy lifestyle of their parents.

### *1-ADHD*

Attention Deficit Hyperactivity Disorder (ADHD) strikes against 7-year-old children at an average but could also occur in infancy and even in adulthood. Largely replacing the term Attention Deficit Disorder or ADD, this condition does not only affect self-esteem, but also take its toll on a child's schooling and relationship with others.

ADHD has the following symptoms

- **i.** Frequent fidgeting
- **ii.** Restlessness
- **iii.** Excessive talking
- **iv.** Blurting out words and answers at inappropriate times
- **v.** A combination of other traits pointing to ADHD

A U.S. government survey claims that 1 in 10 U.S. children now have ADHD. This is a sizable increase from a few years earlier. ADHD (attention deficit hyperactivity disorder) makes it hard for children to pay attention and control impulsive behavior. About two-thirds of the children diagnosed with ADHD are on some form of prescription medication. According to AP medical writer Mike Stobbe: "In the latest survey, 9.5 percent said a doctor or health care provider had told them their child had ADHD, the diagnosis is in many ways a matter of opinion. There's no blood test or brain-imaging exam for the condition. Sometimes reading disabilities or other problems in the classroom cause a teacher or others to mistakenly think a child has ADHD." Researchers suggested growing awareness and better screening may be responsible for the rising numbers, but there are a number of food additives that experts think may worsen ADHD as well. They include:

i. Blue #1 and #2 food coloring

ii. Green #3

iii. Orange B

iv. Red #3 and #40

v. Yellow #5 and #6

vi. Sodium benzoate

***Management of ADHD***

Dietary interventions additional calcium or magnesium, for example can effectively alleviate the symptoms of ADHD. Eliminating grains, sugars, and sodas from diet prove to be extremely useful. There is so much hard work and patience required in dealing with ADHD, but proper guidelines in diet, lifestyle, and attitude can ease you and your child throughout the process.

***2-Autism***

A pair of studies on autism rates show that somewhere around one percent of all U.S. children currently have an autism spectrum disorder (ASD). The rate is even higher in children 6 to 11 years old and especially among boys. Among all children aged 2 to 17, one in 100 currently have an ASD, which is considerably higher than the previously estimated rate of one in 150. There was a 100 percent increase in parent-reported ASD rates compared to 2003. One possible explanation for some of the increase is the expansion of the ASD classification within the public schools to include not only full-blown autism, but also milder forms of ASD such as Pervasive Developmental Disorder and Asperger's

Syndrome. But it is difficult to believe that this accounts for the entire increase.

One possible answer is the Hepatitis B vaccine, which also contained 25 micrograms of mercury containing thimerosal. Only 8 percent of infant children received the Hep. B vaccine in 1992, when that birth cohort showed an ASD rate of 60 per 10,000. By 1994, the number of children receiving Hep. B vaccine had reached just 27 percent -- and the cohort showed an ASD rate of 66 per 10,000. The Hepatitis B coverage rate rose to 82 percent by 1996, when that cohort's ASD rate exploded to around 100 per 10,000, or one in 100. A similar British study puts the overall U.K. rate at one in 83. These numbers sadly support the surprising findings earlier this year, when the journal Epidemiologypublished a study showing a sevenfold increase in autism cases in California, between the years of 1990 to 2006. In 1990, 6.2 of every 10,000 children born in California were diagnosed with autism by the age of 5, by 2001 it had risen to 42.5 in 10,000.Many researchers are now advocating for a shift in autism research to focus on environmental factors such as pesticides, viruses and chemicals in household products rather than genetics. The toxins that are at the top of this list are:

i-Mercury and other metals, such as aluminum. The major route of exposure here is from vaccines, and also from eating contaminated seafood. According to Lee Grossman, President and CEO of Autism Society of America (ASA): "A person with an autism spectrum disorder has a number of underlying and seemingly unnoticed immunological, inflammatory or mitochondrial issues happening, and there could be any number of factors that trigger this, and it is certainly plausible that vaccines are one of those triggers."According to the CDC's national immunization survey 8 percent of infants received the Hep. B vaccine in 1992. At the time the ASD rate was 67 in 10,000. Four years later, at which time 82 percent of infants received the Hep. B vaccine, the ASD rate rose to about 100 in 10,000.

Recent studies have shown that the Hepatitis B vaccine can damage myelin in those with certain genetic factors. For example, one recent study found that children who received the vaccine were 50 percent more likely to develop "central nervous system inflammatory demyelination"than children who did not receive the vaccine. GlaxoSmithKline's Engerix B brand of the vaccine was shown to be the worst of the bunch, increasing the risk of demyelination by 74 percent. It also nearly tripled the risk of developing multiple sclerosis in genetically susceptible people.

ii-Viruses and microbes, such as mold. Children with autism not only have overwhelmed detoxification pathways and often heavy metal toxicity, but, according to Dr. Klinghardt, they also have a silent, daily toxin production in their body caused by toxic microbes.

iii-Electromagnetic Fields (EMF). These come not only from cell phones, cordless phones, but also from electrical outlets and WiFi. Dr. Klinghardt considers EMF "synergistically causal," partly because it potentiates the production of toxic microbes and endotoxins.

iv-Another major contributor to autism that has recently been appreciated is vitamin D deficiency in pregnant women. The vitamin D receptor appears in a wide variety of brain tissue early in the fetal development, and activated vitamin D receptors increase nerve growth in your brain. I believe one of the most important changes that could radically reduce autism is to make certain that all pregnant women normalize their vitamin D levels to 50-60 ng/ml.We already know that children are now born toxic due to the increasing toxin load of their mothers. We know that the childhood vaccination schedule has gone from requiring 10 vaccinations in 1976, to now including 36 injections before your child reaches 12 months of age.

***3-Behavioral disorders***

Child violence is a new epidemic the main vector of this epidemic disease, is chronic malnutrition. If it is true that body chemistry plays a definitive role in causing abnormal behavior, then it is largely a waste of time to treat violent criminals by incarcerating them and neglecting the critical factor of their diet. Constant parental guidance was available fifty years ago, with the mother at home cooking good wholesome meals and providing onthespot emotional support. Ever higher taxes have forced both parents to work outside the home, purchase factory foods and allow unsupervised television programming that breeds rampant materialism. The desire for modern day gadgets, fashionable clothes and joining gangs as a substitutes for the caring intimacy no longer provided by their family, all these contribute to our sick society.

But the major culprit is bad food, several important researchers have firmly established the link between malnutrition and childhood violence. Department of Psychology, University of Southern California has conducted studies on"The effect of childhood malnutrition on externalizing behavior"and found that that poor nutrition contributes to the development of child behavior problems. More randomized, controlled trials that manipulate nutritional intake and evaluate behavior in children are needed to evaluate the etiological role of nutrition in externalizing behavior in order to inform intervention and prevention efforts.

***4-Allergies to food or environment***

"Conventional drugs used for treating asthma, particularly steroids, can impair immune function and lead to more serious health problems. Doctors tell you that steroids (cortisone, prednisone) only cause side effects after many years. But new research shows that permanent damage is immediate and devastating. Studies show that steroids cause permanent, debilitating effects after a single dosage. "Steroids are probably the sleaziest of modern day medications" says John Mills, former professor of medicine at the University of California, San

Francisco and chief of infectious diseases at San Francisco General Hospital.Children are up to three times more likely to develop conditions like asthma and hay fever due to chemicals found in some wall paints and cleansers.

Researchers from Karlstad University in Sweden found youngsters had up to 180 per cent greater risk of developing allergies if they were exposed to chemicals known as PGEs (platinum group elements) in their bedrooms. Study leader Professor Carl-Gustaf Bornehag, said " the study shows for the first time that the concentration of PGEs, propylene glycol and glycol ethers, in bedroom air was linked to an increased risk of developing asthma, rhinitis and eczema in children, the increase in risk varied between 50 and 180 per cent. It was also found that a higher concentration of PGEs in indoor air was associated with children administered antibodies (IgE) against allergens such as cats, dogs, pollen. The study also revealed that the use of water-based paint in the dwelling, as well as water-based cleansers, was linked to a higher concentration of PGEs in bedroom air.The chemicals can also be found in some plastic toys and packaging".

As your child grows, he or she will be exposed to all different kinds of foods, additives and preservatives, some of which may cause allergic responses.In addition to the “standard” physical responses, such as belly aches, hives, there may be unexpected changes in your child’s behavior.

Behavioral changes are normal as children grow, however, if the child suddenly and uncharacteristically begins to act out, talk back, use vulgar language or have serious emotional issues such as aggression, anger or depression, it simply might be an unusual form of allergy or sensitivity. This is especially true if a child has many relatives with known allergies and sensitivities. Such reactions can often be linked to certain foods. Exposures to food allergens could be due to the food itself or a chemical used in processing. These can cause a child to suddenly act, behave, speak, walk, talk, write and breathe in different and often inappropriate ways. The cause of these changes can be missed for years by doctors, teachers, and parents alike.

## A Healthy child

Imagine a child rose according to the nutritional wisdom of our ancestors. This child grows up free of the common ailments and diseases that we currently take for granted. This child's strong, white teeth grow in straight and free of tooth decay. This child's face is broad, well-formed and glows with health. This child is attentive and engaged, and can learn easily and readily because of optimal brain development. This child is energetic by day and sleeps soundly at night. This child is sturdy but not overweight. This child has a strong immune system, does not experience childhood illnesses or allergies, and has a stable, cheerful and optimistic disposition.

## SLP Management of Child's health disorders

Fortunately I have got good results of SLP in child's health disorders and my young patients are my favorite clients. While communicating with them, I feel the purity and innocence of nature in them. SLP has shown reversal of a disease process in digestive disorders, allergies, asthma, behavioral disorders, learning disabilities and in bed wetting. I am little careful in claiming the reversal in the ADHD and autism but they are managed well because of the slowing of the disease process and intensity of their symptoms weaken too. In my opinion these two disorders will take about two years for their reversal and I don't have follow ups for these children longer than six months. In order to have a healthy and happily growing child we have to consider following:

1. Focus on pre-conception diet
2. Parents should follow a natural lifestyle before planning for a baby
3. Child's upbringing should be in a joint family setup on traditional principles
4. Baby should be fed on breast milk or raw goat or cow's milk
5. Weaning should be based on natural and nutrient dense foods
6. Start introducing the SLP eight rules of correct eating from about 1-2 years of age
7. Bowel movement should be watched carefully.
8. Child should not be exposed to drinks, juices, biscuits, and junk snack, before the age of two years.
9. Avoid exposing the child to multi colored plastic toys and stuffed toys.
10. Baby is highly vulnerable to the toxicity of electromagnetic devices. Therefore don't expose them to cell phones, laptops, video games, or even televisions before seven years of age
11. Encourage outdoor activities and sports
12. Story telling develops their imagination, which they later relate with practical life
13. Child should spend some time with grandparents for their healthy growth and development.
14. Yoga is another natural immune boosting method. Children can be started on a regular yoga practice, including pranayama and simple creative visualizations once they turn 7 years of age.

**How to manage baby food**

There are three concepts to keep in mind. First, make your little one a "whole foods baby"! Avoid processed and refined foods as much as possible, including many brands of baby food; they are usually devoid of nutrients and have added "undesirables." It is always best to make your own baby food from organic, whole foods you can freeze it in one-serving sizes for later use. Number 2 is go slowly and be observant;

every baby will have an individual response to different foods. Introduce new foods one at a time and continue to feed that same food for at least four days to rule out the possibility of a negative reaction. Signs of intolerance include redness around the mouth, abdominal bloating, gas and distention, irritability, fussiness, over-activity and awaking throughout the night, constipation and diarrhea, frequent regurgitation of foods, nasal and/or chest congestion, and red, chapped or inflamed eczema-like skin rash.

Finally, respect the tiny, still-developing digestive system of your infant, babies have limited enzyme production, which is necessary for the digestion of foods. In fact, it takes up to 28 months, just around the time when molar teeth are fully developed, for carbohydrate enzymes namely amylaseto fully kick into gear. Foods like cereals, grains and breads are very challenging for little ones to digest. Thus, these foods should be some of the last to be introduced. Foods introduced too early can cause digestive troubles and increase the likelihood of allergies. The baby's immature digestive system allows large particles of food to be absorbed. If these particles reach the bloodstream, the immune system mounts a response that leads to an allergic reaction. Six months is the typical age when solids should be introduced, however, there are a few exceptions.

Babies do produce functional enzymes like pepsin and proteolytic enzymes and digestive juices (hydrochloric acid in the stomach) that work on proteins and fats. This makes perfect sense since the milk from a healthy mother has 50-60 percent of its energy as fat, which is critical for growth, energy and development. In addition, the cholesterol in human milk supplies an infant with close to six times the amount most adults consume from food. In some cultures, a new mother is encouraged to eat six to ten eggs a day and almost ten ounces of chicken and pork for at least a month after birth. This fat-rich diet ensures her breast milk will contain adequate healthy fats. Thus, a baby's earliest solid foods should be mostly animal foods since his digestive system, although immature, is better equipped to supply enzymes for digestion of fats and proteins rather than carbohydrates. This explains why current research is pointing to meat (including nutrient-dense organ meat) as being a nourishing early weaning food. Now have an idea about the various food intake by different age group babies

4-6 Months
Minimal solid foods are tolerated by baby
Egg yolk--if tolerated, preferably from pastured chickens, lightly boiled and salted
Banana--mashed
Cod liver oil-- 1/4 teaspoon high vitamin or 1/2 teaspoon regular, given with an eye dropper

6-8 months
Organic liver--grated and added to egg yolk
Pureed meats--lamb, turkey, beef, chicken, liver and fish
Soup broth--(chicken, beef, lamb, fish) added to pureed meats and vegetables, or offered as a drink
Fermented foods--small amounts of yoghurt,
Raw mashed fruits--banana, melon, mangoes, papaya, avocado
Cooked, pureed fruits--organic apricot, peaches, pears, apples, cherries, berries
Cooked vegetables--zucchini, squash, sweet potato, carrots, beets, with butter or coconut oil

8-12 months
Continue to add variety and increase thickness and lumpiness of the foods already given from 4-8 months
Creamed vegetable soups
Homemade stews--all ingredients cut small or mashed
Dairy--cottage cheese, mild harder raw cheese, cream, custards
Finger foods--when baby can grab and adequately chew, such as lightly steamed veggie sticks, mild cheese, avocado chunks, pieces of banana

Cod liver oil--increase to 1/2 or 1 teaspoon

Over 1 Year
Grains and legumes--properly soaked and cooked
Leafy green vegetables--cooked, with butter
Raw salad vegetables--cucumbers, tomatoes, etc.
Citrus fruit--fresh, organic
Whole egg--cooked

Foods to avoid
Up to 6 months: Certain foods, such as spinach, celery, lettuce, radishes, beets, turnips and collard greens, may contain excessive nitrate, which can be converted into nitrite (an undesirable substance) in the stomach. Leafy green vegetables are best avoided until 1 year. When cooking vegetables that may contain these substances, do not use the water when they were cooked in to pure.
Up to 9 months: Citrus and tomato, which are common allergens.
Up to 1 year: Egg whites should also be avoided up to one year due to their high allergenic potential. Always avoid commercial dairy products (especially ultra-pasteurized), modern soy foods, margarines and shortening, fruit juices, reduced-fat or low-fat foods, extruded grains and all processed foods.

This article appeared in Wise Traditions in Food, Farming and the Healing Arts, the quarterly magazine of the Weston A. Price Foundation, Summer 2005.

## CHAPTER NO: 19

## CANCER: IT IS A MAN MADE DISEASE

A study of ancient bodies has determined that cancer is a man-made disease, one fueled by the excesses. Tumors turn out to be extremely rare until very recent times, when pollution and poor diet became issues. Researchers analyzed potential references to the disease in classical literature, and also searched for signs in the fossil record and in mummified bodies. But despite examining tissue from hundreds of Egyptian mummies, they confirmed only one case of cancer. According to the Daily Mail: "dismissing the argument that the ancient Egyptians didn't live long enough to develop cancer, the researchers pointed out that other age-related disease such as hardening of the arteries and brittle bones did occur. Fossil evidence of cancer is also sparse, with scientific literature providing a few dozen, mostly disputed, examples in animal fossil". According to the latest statistics compiled by the American Heart Association, cancer surpasses heart disease as the top killer among Americans between the ages of 45 to 74. Cancer rates for various types of cancer are on the rise, and environmental/lifestyle factors are increasingly being pinpointed as the culprits, such as:

- Pesticide and other chemical exposures
- Pharmaceutical drugs
- Processed foods (plus the chemicals in the packaging)
- Wireless technology , and medical diagnostic radiation exposure
- Obesity, stress, and poor sleeping habits
- Lack of sunshine and use of sunscreens

This not an all-inclusive list, of course, but as the research into the health of our ancient ancestors shows, cancer is not a naturaldisease, and genetics are not a primary factor. Cancer is, by and large, the tragic result of humans veering too far off course –avoiding health-sustaining diets and activities, while embracing a highly unnatural lifestyle and continually dousing your insides and outsides with excess chemicals. According to Professor Rosalie David, co-author of the recently published study stated: “There is nothing in the natural environment that can cause cancer. So it has to be a man-made disease, down to pollution and changes to our diet and lifestyle."

Cancer is a toxicity issue, thereforeyou must stop taking in more toxicity by avoiding electricity in cooking (microwaves, electric ranges) andyou have to make sure that the body is able to eliminate the toxicity that’s already there. This is not as simple as having a daily bowel movement, although some people don’t manage even that. It means making sure the organs are working together optimally and particularlythe liver and gall bladderfunctions are important because they eliminate toxins. Virtually everyone has some kind of energy blockage that needs to be fixed. In addition to toxicity,nutritional deficiencies must be addressed. Virtually everyone has nutritional deficiencies now, because of the poor quality of the soil in which conventional produce is grown and because most people don’t eat enough produce anyway. But even organic produce doesn’t have everything we need. Herbs are a good way to remedy these deficiencies, herbs are foods, so the body assimilates them better than chemically synthesized vitamin or mineral pills. Herbs also have trace elements that promote their action, which synthetic products don’t.

The good news is, medical science is finally starting to catch up with common sense, and studies are emerging showing the powerful potential of food and lifestyle to both prevent and treat cancer but widespread adoption of many of these recommendations will take many decades at best. Remember the words of German philosopher Arthur Schopenhauer who, 200 years ago, said all truth goes through three stages. First it is ridiculed, then it is violently opposed and finally it is widely accepted as self-evident. In the last 30 years of the 20th century the global cancer burden has doubled, and it will likely double again between 2000 and 2020 and nearly triple by 2030. Projected mortality estimates for 2030 range from just over 13 million, to 17 million people dying from the disease.There is a lot that can be done right now to significantly impact your cancer risk. Even the conservative American Cancer Society states that one-third of cancer deaths are linked to poor diet, physical inactivity, and carrying excess weight. So making healthy lifestyle changes is one of the most important ways to protect yourself from cancer.

## Various Cancer prevention strategies

### *i-Whole food as a medicine*

Science is trying to alter its course to investigate the power of optimal nutrition to improve health and prevent chronic disease from occurring in the first place. To anyone who is well-versed in alternative medicine, this is simply common sense. But many are still in denial about the power each individual wields over their own health. Preventing disease and even treating disease can be as simple as modifying your diet and lifestyle essentially, altering the environment of your body, to provide the best, most health promoting growth medium possible for all your cells. Part of the explanation for why food can have such a powerful influence on serious diseases such as cancer is due to its influence on a biological process called 'angiogenesis' the process your body uses to build blood vessels. Cancerous cell like all other cells in human body, cannot thrive without the oxygen and nutrients supplied by your capillaries. Excessive angiogenesis (too many blood vessels) promote diseases such as cancer.

Most of us actually carry around microscopic cancer cell clusters in our bodies all the time. The reason why we all don't develop cancer is because as long as your body has the ability to balance angiogenesis properly, it will prevent blood vessels from forming to feed these microscopic tumors. Trouble will only arise if, and when, the cancer cells manage to get their own blood supply, at which point they can transform from harmless to deadly. As our ancestors intuitively understood, Nature has loaded a large number of foods and herbs with naturally occurring inhibitors of angiogenesis, rendering them natural "anti-cancer medicines." Simply by consuming these anti-angiogenetic foods you can naturally boost your body's defense system and prevent blood vessels from forming and feeding the microscopic tumors that exist in your body at any given time. A number of different foods found to have particularly powerful anti-angiogenetic influence, such as broccoli and turmeric.

***ii-Burzynski's nutritional typing***

The Burzynski team uses individualized meal plans in their treatment. Each patient consults with a qualified nutritional expert, and the diet is customized to the patient based on the genomic analysis. In addition, they also use SNPs analysis, or Single Nucleotide Polymorphisms analysis, which determines how various nutrients and medications are metabolized in your body. "Nutrition is very important," Dr. Burzynski says. "One of the things, is to control inflammation, that's one of thingsmust do before you get cancer, and also when you have cancer.Keeping your body with the proper nutrients is essential. We don't want to feed the cancer. Things that promote cancer, we try to eliminate. We try to eliminate a lot of sugar. That for the most part will fuel the cancer growth".

“We want to eliminate glutamine. Glutamine is an amino acid. It's great if you want to be a bodybuilder or if you don't have cancer, but if you do have cancer, for the most part, we encourage our patients to stay away from glutamine because that unfortunately is going to be one of the essential ingredients to cancer growth."Certainly, the diet depends on the context of the medications they are using for the patient. Certain dietary ingredients are going to support the medications which we prescribe. Some others may neutralize it.“We have to take under consideration which medication we prescribe. And then make sure that the patient is not taking supplements or dietary ingredients that can fight these medications. This is also established for every patient."

***iii- Follow the 24 hours rhythm of your body clock by***

I. Turn off computers and electronic gadgets once the sun sets, and avoid watching TV late at night. Again, the blue light emitted from TV's and computer screens mimic the blue light found in daytime sunlight, which can alter your melatonin production.

II. Sleep in total darkness! If there is even the tiniest bit of light in your room it can disrupt your circadian rhythm and your pineal gland's production of the hormones melatonin and serotonin. Sleep when it's dark outside and get up when the sun comes up. At minimum, strive to sleep between 10 p.m. and 6 a.m.

III. Avoid working the night shift. It's been linked to significantly lower levels of serotonin, which may cause sleep problems, anger, depression and anxiety.

***iv- Connect to biorhythms***

As we have already learnt that everything in nature has a rhythm, and that includes your body. The ebb and flow of the ocean's tide, the rising and setting of the sun, and the transition from one season to another all happen with comforting regularity. Your body, too, strives to keep its 24-hour cycle, or circadian rhythm, steady and even. This is why most of us naturally feel like waking when the sun comes up, and sleeping when it's dark. Researchers have also shown how your circadian rhythm is involved in everything from sleep, to weight gain, mood disorders, and a variety of diseases. Unfortunately, modern life throws multiple wrenches into the works, as it were, mainly by artificially extending 'daytime.'

Glowing Gadgets Disrupt Your Circadian Rhythm and today there are any number of glowing gadgets tricking your brain into thinking it's still day time, well past sundown.There's growing concern among experts that the proliferation of glowing gadgets like computers may fool your brain into thinking that it's still daytime after the sun has gone down. Exposure during the night can disturb sleep patterns and exacerbate insomnia. But the problem has grown worse thanks to the popularity of Apple's new slate computer, the iPad. Many consumers use an iPad to read at night, and unlike paper books or e-book readers like the Amazon Kindle, which does not emit its own light, the iPad's screen shines light directly into your eyes from a relatively close distance.According to CNN:"That makes the iPad and laptops more likely to disrupt sleep patterns than, say, a television sitting across the bedroom or a lamp that illuminates a paper book, both of which shoot far less light straight into the eye, researchers said."

This extended exposure to artificial light can disrupt your sleep cycle and make minor insomnia worse. The reason is when light receptors in your eyes are triggered, they signal your brain to 'stay awake.' To do that, your brain stops secreting melatonin, which is both a hormone and a potent antioxidant against cancer. Normally, your brain starts secreting melatonin around 9 or 10 pm, which makes you sleepy. These regularly occurring secretions thus help regulate your sleep cycle. However, if you regularly trick your brain into altering this cycle, sleep disturbances are not far behind. It can even create a state of permanent "jet lag." The trouble with many of the electronic gadgets available today is the type of light they emit. Computer screens and most light bulbs emit blue light, to which your eyes are particularly sensitive simply because it's the type of light most common outdoors during daytime hours. As a result, they can disrupt your melatonin production.

The CNN article details one man's personal experiment to test the veracity of the claim that night time light exposure will disrupt your sleep."J.D. Moyer decided recently to conduct a little experiment with artificial light and his sleep cycle. The sleep-deprived Oakland, California, resident had read that strong light -- whether it's beaming down from the sun or up from the screens of personal electronics can reset a person's internal sleep clock.So, for one month, whenever the sun set, he turned off all the gadgets and lights in his house from the bulb hidden in his refrigerator to his laptop computer”. It worked for him and instead of falling asleep at midnight, Moyer's head was hitting the pillow as early as 9 p.m. He felt so well-rested during the test, he said, and that friends remarked on his unexpected morning perkiness."I had the experience, a number of times, and just feeling kind of unreasonably happy for no reason. And it was the sleep," he said. "Sure, you can get by with six or seven hours, but sleeping eight or nine hours -- it's a different state of mind."

Your circadian rhythm has evolved over many centuries to align your physiology with your environment. However, it is operating under the assumption that you're still behaving as your ancestors have for generations: sleeping at night and being awake during the day. If you push these limits by staying up late at night, depriving yourself of sleep, or even eating at strange hours (such as at 2 a.m.), you are sending conflicting signals to your body. As a result, your body doesn't know whether it should be producing chemicals to tell you to go to sleep, or gear up for the beginning of your day. But maintaining this natural circadian rhythm affects far more than just your sleep pattern. Your body actually has many internal clocks in your brain, lungs, liver, heart and even your skeletal muscles and they all work to keep your body running smoothly by controlling temperature and the release of hormones.

Your body temperature and hormone production also vary with your personal internal clock. This, in turn, influences such things as: the easiest time to detect disease in your body, times when you'll be less sensitive to pain and times when you'll be more productive at work. Disrupting your natural rhythm can also make you more vulnerable to disease. For example, reduced melatonin levels, due to prolonged exposure to light, is known to increase your risk of cancer. It also activates your stress response and weakens your immune system, which is why irregular sleep cycles can lead to stress, constipation, stomach ulcers, depression, heart disease, and many other illnesses.

### Cancer Treatments: Chemo or Natural?

Contrary to 'conventional wisdom,' chemotherapy is rarely the best option for cancer treatment as it usually doesn't cure cancer or extend life, and it rarely improves the quality of life. Dr. Ralph Moss, who is the author of eight books on cancer treatment, has reviewed thousands of studies as part of the research for his books and he has not found one single good study showing that chemo cures cancer or extends life.What chemo does do, however, is expose your body to toxins that kill all cells that multiply and divide rapidly. This includes not only cancer cells, but also other rapidly multiplying and dividing cells, such as bone marrow, reproductive system cells and hair follicles. These are powerful drugs that present an assault on your system one that your body must then overcome along with the cancer. And the effects do not end right after the treatment. One UCLA study found that chemotherapy can actually change the blood flow and metabolism of your brain in ways that can linger for 10 years or more after treatment.

The role of epigenetics in health and disease is becoming ever clearer, and I firmly believe this field of study will eventually transform the current medical paradigm. The conventional belief has been that genes controlled their own expression and were therefore the direct cause of certain diseases. This laid the groundwork for the idea that your genes predetermined your health but genes are in fact not self-regulating.Having "bad genes," does not at all mean you're doomed to suffer some inevitable fate. Genes are merely blueprints, and these blueprints are activated and controlled by something else entirely, namely their environment. This environmental informationwhich includes diet, toxic exposures, thoughts and emotions. They can create more than 30,000 different variations from each blueprint, allowing for an astounding amount of leeway in modifying the expression or "read-out" of each gene!

**Dr. Mercola's Natural Cancer Prevention Strategies**

Dr. Mercola says, 'I believe you can virtually eliminate your risk of cancer and other chronic disease, and radically improve your chances of recovering from cancer if you currently have it, by following some relatively simple risk reduction strategies—all of which help promote a healthful biological environment in which your cells can thrive and combat disease naturally". Dr. Mercola's top 12 cancer prevention strategies include:

1. Reduce or eliminate processed food, fructose and grain intake

2. Normalize vitamin D levels by getting plenty of sunlight exposure and consider careful supplementation when this is not possible. If you take oral vitamin D and have cancer, it would be prudent to monitor your vitamin D blood levels regularly.

3. Control fasting insulin and leptin levels (Improved insulin and leptin control is the natural outcome of reducing or eliminating fructose, grains, and processed foods from your diet.)

4. Normalize ratio of omega-3 to omega-6 by taking a high-quality krill oil or fish oil and reducing your intake of most processed vegetable oils.

5. Get regular exercise, one of the primary reasons exercise works is that it drives your insulin levels down. Controlling insulin levels is one of the most powerful ways to reduce your cancer risks. If you have limited time Peak 8 is your best bet but ideally you should have a good strength training program

6. Get regular, good sleep

7. Eat according to your nutritional type. The potent anti-cancer effects of this principle are sorely underappreciated. However, some cancer specialists are now using nutritional typing as an integral part of their cancer treatments.

8. Reduce your exposure to environment toxins like pesticides, household chemical cleaners, synthetic air freshness, and air pollution.

9. Limit your exposure and provide protection for yourself from EMF produced by cell phone towers, base stations, cell phones and WiFi stations. On May 31, 2011, the International Agency for Research on Cancer (IARC), an arm of the World Health Organization (WHO), declared that cell phones are "possibly carcinogenic to humans".

10. Avoid frying or charbroiling your food, instead boil, poach or steam your foods.

11. Have a tool to permanently reprogram the neurological short-circuiting that can activate cancer genes. Even the CDC states that 85 percent of disease is caused by emotions. It is likely that this factor

may be more important than all the other physical ones listed here, so make sure this is addressed. Energy psychology seems to be one of the best approaches and my particular favorite tool, as you may know, is the Emotional Freedom Technique, German New Medicine is another powerful tool.

12. Eat at least one third of your food raw.

**Researches about natural cancer treatments**

Cancer research has uncovered many links between what people eat and their risk of then getting certain cancers. Many researchers have provided information about studies done by the National Cancer Institute. In one study using 35,000 male subjects, the Institute looked at the ability of selenium to prevent cancer. The investigators found that a low intake of selenium can cause a great increase in a male's risk for getting prostate cancer. Another breakthrough study was performed at the Northern California Cancer Center in Fremont, California. The data compiled by those California researchers has indicated that exposure to the sun can help to prevent prostate cancer as well, which is something considerably new in the cancer research field. Further studies have shown that a generous amount of Vitamin D, such as what one gets from sunlight, will cut a man's chances in half for getting prostate cancer.

As physicians and researchers begin to make greater use of the new drugs for treating cancer, it becomes obvious that medicine needs to pay closer attention to holistic cancer cures in addition to these traditional treatment methods. Holistic cures take into consideration all of the parts of the body, not just the specific body part that has the cancer, but the mind and spirit is as well. The case of one woman in California illustrates the need for a holistic approach to cure cancer. The woman has been receiving chemotherapy for a lung cancer. She has learned that the drug that is helping to fight her cancer has also created changes in her blood and her blood is getting thicker.As a result, she must avoid eating foods with Vitamin K, a vitamin that helps to thicken blood. The woman continues to sacrifice by not eating certain foods that she loves such as dark green vegetables. If one can understand that this particular woman is affected by what she eats, researchers and physicians should be aware that what humans eat may have more of a relevant link to cancer than they first thought was the case.

**SLP Causes of Cancer**

During my practice I got a chance to observe few hundred cancer patients, with past or current history of suffering from cancer. I have learnt one can't get cancer without the presence of a dysfunctional liver, disrupted biorhythms, or a weak mental / spiritual connection. I have found few common lifestyle factors in their life, which are;

1. Intake of processed or chemical laden foods in routine
2. Erratic eating pattern regarding quantity, selection and timing of foods
3. Wrong type of food selected for their biochemistry
4. Incompatible food combinations, even if the foods are natural
5. Wrong intake of water
6. Over dosage of synthetic or food supplèments
7. Sleep deprivation, in terms of amount, quality and time
8. Wrong exercise, in terms of body compatibility, time of doing exercise and duration of exercise

**9.** History of multiple emotional traumas since childhood

**10.** Multiple types of stresses like social, financial or overwork

**11.** Constant exposure to environmental pollutants, drugs, alcohol, chemical or electromagnetic

**12.** Lack of religious practices, poor faith, insecurity, fears and guilt

**SLP management of Cancer**

***Prevention***

I. Take natural foods according to eight rules of diet correction in order to harmonize your circadian rhythms and to keep liver healthy

II. Have 6-8 hours of night sleep to give sufficient time for liver and immune system rejuvenation

III. Defuse your stress daily by allocating little time to your hobby

IV. Only a body compatible exercise should be done, with correct duration and time of doing it

V. Take supplements like probiotics, omega 3,6 fatty acids, enzymes and antioxidants in routine.

***Treatment***

*I.* Follow above mentioned five preventive rules in your life

*II.* Get treatment done with Rife frequencies, Bob-Becker Protocol, which includes ozone therapy, blood electrification, magnetic pulsar therapy and colloidal silver to stop the proliferation of cancer cells and a gradual reversal of cancer depending upon the stage of disease

*III.* Ionic detoxification to facilitate cleansing of body

IV. Family support in the form of collective ritual practices, laughter therapy, and strong family bonding activities are required.

V. Chakra balancing is required

*VI.* Spiritual therapy according to your faith

I would like to share here, that I am a cancer survivor myself, which initiated due to a strong emotional trauma in my life. It was an advanced disease which, reversed only with natural foods, herbs, family support and a strong spiritual help. I have not taken a single Allopathic tablet to manage my ailment and did not take a single day off from my routine clinical practice during my ailment. My laboratory reports took one year to get cancer free.

# CHAPTER NO: 20

# OTHER LIFESTYLE DEPENDENT HOLISTIC HEALTH ISSUES

## 1-Vitamin D deficiency

Much has been written about the benefits of vitamin D and deficiency related dysfunctions. We doctors are mainly blaming less sunlight exposure, which is not the only reason for its deficiency. Problem with conventional medical system is that when it cannot find the correct root cause, it always blames a "difficult to cure root cause" which is humanly non-accessible.

***Scientific facts about vitamin D***

Vitamin D is a group of fat-soluble secosteroids responsible for intestinal absorption of calcium and phosphate. In humans, vitamin D is unique because it can be ingested as cholecalciferol (vitamin D3) or ergocalciferol (vitamin D2) and because the body can also synthesize it (from cholesterol) when sun exposure is adequate (hence its nickname, the "sunshine vitamin"). Vitamin D is carried in the blood stream to the liver, where it is converted into the pro-hormone calcidiol which is also known as calcifediol (INN), 25-hydroxycholecalciferol, or 25-hydroxyvitamin D abbreviated 25(OH)D; and which is the specific vitamin D metabolite that is measured in serum to determine a person's vitamin D status.Circulating calcidiol may then be converted into calcitriol, the biologically active form of vitamin D, either in the kidneys or by monocyte-macrophages in the immune system. When synthesized by monocyte-macrophages, calcitriol acts locally as a cytokine, defending the body against microbial invaders.

Following the final converting step in the kidney, calcitriol (the physiologically active form of vitamin D) is released into the circulation. By binding to vitamin D-binding protein (VDBP), a carrier protein in the plasma, calcitriol is transported to various target organs.[87] Calcitriol circulates as a hormone in the blood, regulating the concentration of calcium and phosphate in the bloodstream and promoting the healthy growth and remodeling of bone. Calcidiol is also converted to calcitriol outside of the kidneys for other purposes, such as the proliferation, differentiation and apoptosis of cells; calcitriol also affects neuromuscular function and inflammation. Vitamin D3 (Cholecalciferol) is produced photo chemically in the skin from 7-dehydrocholesterol, which is produced in relatively large amount in the skin of most vertebrate animals, including humans.

The vitamin D receptor VDRs belongs to the nuclear receptor super family of steroid/thyroid hormone receptors, and VDRs are expressed by cells in most organs, including the brain, heart, skin, gonads, prostate, and breast. VDR activation in the intestine, bone, kidney, and parathyroid gland cells leads to the maintenance of calcium and phosphorus levels in the blood (with the assistance of parathyroid hormone and calcitonin) and to the maintenance of bone content.[64] There are only 30,000 genes in your body and vitamin D has been shown to influence over 2,000 of them. That's one of the primary reasons it influences so many diseases.

***SLP causes of vitamin D deficiency***

I will try to relate the sources of vitamin D, role of body organs and body systems contributing in the metabolism and absorption of vitamin D, and an unhealthy lifestyle. The vitamin D deficiency is not a simple phenomenon to understand, and probably it took many decades to develop this deficiency, globally. First look at the factors required for proper metabolism of vitamin D in the human body:

- Proper and sufficient exposure to sunlight
- Foods rich in cholesterol required to produce more vitamin D
- Intake of healthy proteins to produce sufficient vitamin D binding proteins (VDBP), broiler chicken based meals make us protein deficient.

- Healthy skin and availability of right type and amount of cholesterol in skin layers, application of sun blocks and various skin lotions impair the absorptive capacity of skin for vitamin D
- Organs / system required for absorption and bioavailability of vitamin D are: skin, parathyroid gland, monocytes-macrophages in immune system, liver to produce calcidiol, kidney to produce calcitriol, proper circulation of blood for availability of vitamin D to the target body areas

***Unhealthy lifestyle factors responsible for vitamin D deficiency***

- Low fat, fat free and transfats laden foods have invaded our routine diet and cause deficiency of fat soluble vitamin D. Vitamin D rich natural foods like raw butter, ghee, whole milk, organ meats and egg yolks are avoided under the instruction of a medical doctor.
- According to the rules of biological clock we are supposed to follow specific meal timings for the optimum absorption of various nutrients especially vitamin D which has got the involvement of multiple systems for its absorption. Maximum absorption of vitamin D is from an early breakfast which is rich in, fats and proteins. However people prefer to eat dead foods for the breakfast in the form of packaged cereals, bran or white flour products or foods with naked calories with no focus on timings
- In a routine meal, chemically incompatible foods are combined to produce unhealthy metabolites which are liver and kidney toxic, therefore disturbing their metabolic functions. A dysfunctional liver will impair vitamin D conversion into calcidiol, resulting in low serum levels of vitamin D in Laboratory tests. Therefore a dysfunctional liver is the root cause of commonly observed low levels of vitamin D. Low calcidiol will affect the production of calcitriol from kidney and immune cells. Calcitriol works on target organs therefore its deficiency will be affecting multiple biological functions of a human body and resulting in various signs and symptoms.
- Repetition of same food groups, natural or artificial for weeks or months result in overloading of one type of nutrient/metabolite which impair liver and kidney functions. So keep on switching between various natural food groups to facilitate proper detoxification of liver and kidneys, which will result in optimum absorption of various nutrients.

- Less outdoor activity has dropped the blood oxygen level, therefore putting extra load on our lungs. Another factor which has affected the health of our lungs is the breathing pattern. Lifestyle stress has forced humans to adopt shallow breathing patterns and which has affected lung immunity. Acupuncture says that lungs look after the health of our skin. If lung function is impaired, skin absorption of vitamin D will be impaired indirectly.
- Our second brain resides in our gut, stress filled lifestyle and artificial foods have badly affected the gut environment and biological flora resulting in poor absorption of vitamin D.
- Another unhealthy important lifestyle factor is less nocturnal sleep. Sleep deprivation is giving less rejuvenation time to liver, kidney, gut and endocrine glands, therefore impairing nutrient absorption especially vitamin D.

***How to manage vitamin D deficiency***

Vitamin D deficiency is a result of an unhealthy lifestyle resulting in multiple chemical imbalances and dysfunction of various organs, therefore modify your lifestyle holistically to make the vitamin D levels normal.

- Modify your dietary habits by following 8-rules of diet correction
- Learn to recognize and manage your stress on every day basis.
- Do some outdoor activity to get sufficient oxygen and sunlight and learn how to breathe properly.
- Take natural foods and fermented foods in routine to take care of your gut, which will facilitate the absorption of vitamin A and D
- Do follow short detox programs at every change of weather

**2- Allergies**

Allergy symptoms range from making you miserable to putting you at risk for life-threatening reactions.According to the leading experts in allergy, an allergic reaction begins in the immune system. Our immune system protects us from invading organisms that can cause illness. If you have an allergy, your immune system mistakes an otherwise harmless substance as an invader. This substance is called an allergen. The immune system overreacts to the allergen by producing Immunoglobulin E (IgE) antibodies. These antibodies travel to cells that release histamine and other chemicals, causing an allergic reaction.An allergic reaction typically triggers symptoms in the nose, lungs, throat, sinuses, ears, lining of the stomach or on the skin. For some people, allergies can also trigger symptoms of asthma. In the most serious cases, a life-threatening reaction called anaphylaxis can occur.

A number of different allergens are responsible for allergic reactions. The most common include:

•Pollen

•Dust

•Food

•Insect stings

•Animal dander

•Mold

•Medications

•Latex

A variety of tests exist to diagnose allergic conditions. If done they should be ordered and interpreted in light of a person's history of exposure as many positive test results do not mean a clinically significant allergen. Tests include placing possible allergens on the skin and looking for a reaction such as swelling and blood tests to look for an allergen-specific IgE. Medical treatments for allergies include avoiding known allergens, steroids that modify the immune system in general, and medications such as antihistamines and decongestants which reduce symptoms. Many of these medications are taken by mouth, although epinephrine, which is used to treat anaphylactic reactions, is injected.

Immunotherapy uses injected allergens to desensitize the body's response.

## SLP allergy management

### *Adult allergy*

The causes of adult allergy are:

- The mismanaged childhood health disorders, which were medically treated
- Chronic stomach and liver disorders
- Processed foods / scientific foods
- Wrong usage of water and fluids
- Irregular eating pattern and irregular bowel habit
- Various toxins
- Sensitive and introvert nature
- Poor quality and less night sleep
- Excess tea, coffee, cigarette, drugs, or alcohol

Adult allergy management:
Allergy is controlled gradually over a period of 3-6 months depending upon its intensity and duration, once it is reversed and the person is careful about his lifestyle it will never revert. An allergy affected person has to follow below mentioned program.

- a personalized lifestyle based food plan, considering his body type or biochemical individuality
- a 6-8 hours of sound nocturnal sleep
- get Ionic detox done which helps by decreasing toxin load on liver and kidney
- start taking probiotics, enzymes, and cod liver oil in routine
- Discontinue strenuous mechanical exercises and focus more on yoga and breathing exercises at least for 12 weeks

### *Child allergy*

The causes of a child's allergy are:

- Poor pre-conception health of the couple

- Mismanaged pregnancy in terms of foods, eating habits, stress, loads of synthetic supplements, excess weight gain, PET, or any emotional trauma.
- Exposure of mother to general anesthesia or various medicines during delivery
- Less or no breast feeding
- Presence of formula milk or packaged baby foods
- Baby vaccinations
- Soother, teething rings or toys
- Pampers, synthetic clothes

***Child allergy management***

All child allergies have deep roots which were dependent on the chemistry of his/her parents during conception, therefore it has to be managed at an early age to prevent serious future allergy complications.

- Parents have to follow a holistically healthy lifestyle before they plan a baby. SLP adult and pregnancy food plans are holistic and prevent incoming infant allergies and other health issues as well
- Baby should be on mother's milk, if not available, then on formula milk for few months, after six months baby can be gradually shifted to diluted buffalo milk
- Child allergy is always associated with stomach disorder, homeopathy is helpful in managing baby's indigestion
- Start the day with first feed of few ounces of warm honey water for 4-6 weeks, it helps settling the stomach acidity and allergy
- Six months onwards 1-2 table spoon of sweet green tea, or mint tea after the food will heal the gut lining and less toxins will be produced
- SLP toddler and child food plan given in previous chapter should be introduced gradually with an accuracy about food intervals

## 3-Water retention

It is a common presentation and quite bothersome for a person. General causes of water retention are excess of water intake, regular intake of cold or chilled water, intake of chilled drinks or juices, and intake of excess of alkaline foods. Alkaline foods have high water content and can lead to water retention. Chemical salt available in the market is an important factor causing water retention. Other general causes are water intake while eating food, irregular eating pattern, lack of night sleep, prolonged stress and intake of various medicines esp. hormones or steroids. Water retention is part of the premenstrual syndrome. During this time, hormonal fluctuations can cause havoc in a woman's body.

In some women the monthly rise in estrogen raises the hormone aldosterone. Aldosterone, in turn, causes the kidneys to retain fluids and the woman to suddenly gain a few water-filled pounds. While PMS is the major cause of water retention in women, water retention for both men and women can also be related to kidney problems. Heart, liver, or thyroid malfunctions can also play a role in water retention. Thanks to the effects of gravity, retained water tends to accumulate in the feet, ankles, and legs, although no area of the body is immune. Other water prone areas are chin and eye esp. upper lids.

***Symptoms of water retention***

These symptoms vary from person to person depending upon age, gender, presence of some other disease, duration of water retention and degree of water retention. I have seen two worst cases of water retention, one was on sixty glasses of water and other with forty glasses of water daily. First one died due to heart and kidney failure, fate of the second one is unknown. Common symptoms are:

- Swollen, bloated or puffy body
- Difficulty in losing weight
- Disproportionate body especially lower one
- Lose and toneless skin

- Saggy muscles
- Tendency for muscle and joint pains
- Mental and physical fatigue especially early morning
- Drowsiness
- Dizziness or loss of balance control
- Uncontrolled blood pressure
- Tendency for left ventricular hypertrophy
- Hormonal imbalances
- Mood swings
- Various allergies (flu, asthma, eczema, arthritis etc)
- Depressive and pessimistic personality

***SLP Treatment***

- Be careful about food intake and dietary habits
- Water intake should be carefully regulated
- Temperature of water and drinks should be close to the body temperature
- For resistant water retention, take lemonade without salt or sugar instead of plain water
- For relieving water retention peanuts, raisins, black tea, coffee, dark chocolate, cinnamon or cloves can be used for few days. These foods taken at pre-breakfast, snack or meal time will work as a diuretic.

## 4- Detoxification

Conventional medicine defines the process of detoxification as a set of interventions aimed at managing acute intoxication and withdrawal. It denotes a clearing of toxins from the body of the patient who is acutely intoxicated and/or dependent on substances of abuse. Detoxification seeks to minimize the physical harm caused by the abuse of substances. In holistic therapeutic system the practice of detoxifying the body to rid it of unhealthy toxins has been around for centuries. Hippocrates recommended fasting to improve health, and many religious groups have historically used fasting as a way of purifying the spirit. The body has its own extraordinary internal detoxification system. Three important organs doing detoxification are liver, colon and kidneys.

The Liveracts like a filter in preventing toxic substances contained in foods from passing into your blood stream.The colon has bacteria that produce both healthy and unhealthy chemicals. You want to keep your colon flowing regularly since its main role is to flush out toxic chemicals before they can do you any harm. The kidneys are constantly filtering your blood and getting rid of toxins in the form of urine.Today the marketplace is cluttered with detox diets that promise to help you lose weight, boost your energy levels and more. However, many popular detox diets, especially those that involve extreme low-calorie fasting, can rob the body of important nutrients and place the body in starvation mode, which actually slows your metabolism. Other downsides of many detox diets include: dehydration, fatigue, dizziness, nausea and even colon damage.

***SLP Detox***

- Follow 8-rules of correct eating, which does detoxification in first two weeks, later because of improved functions of liver, colon and kidneys, there is less accumulation of toxins. SLP helps to detox by regulating bowel movement, maintaining blood / tissue ph and by regulating core blood temperature. Detoxification is evident because of better blood and lymph circulation as well.
- Besides giving SLP food plans, yoga, and breathing exercises are recommended to counter subtle stress, which is a root cause of toxin overload.
- Probiotics, enzyme preparations, omega 3,6, fatty acids are prescribed.
- Juice fast of 3-10 days is recommended
- Religious fast twice a week is also a good detox

**5- Holistic aging versus Degenerative aging**

Aging is the process of becoming older, a process that is genetically determined and environmentally modulated. Science cannot predict the duration of a human life. Genetics too, fail because a centenarian may not have a centenarian parent. According to Dr Chopra: "Aging is much more of a choice than people ever dream" and for that, it is essential to reinterpret the concept of body and realize the "changeless I" inside of us, which the ancient sages in India simply called the Self (Soham). He considers three distinct ways to measure someone's age: "Chronological Age –how old you are by the calendar; Biological Age how old your body is in terms of critical life signs and cellular processes, i.e., how time has affected your organs and tissues compared to other people of your chronological age; and Psychological Age how old you feel you are."

My professional experience has taught me that a person lives in three different age groups at one time. A man of chronological age 50, would have biological age of 55 and mental age of 60 years. Out of three aging processes, mental is the worst one because it accelerates the physical aging. Therefore a young man with advanced mental aging will develop speedy biological aging and will suffer from degenerative diseases at an early age. When you age holistically, mental aging is slower than the biological aging and longevity is the outcome. I believe aging is an outcome of various external and internal environmental factors, which are interdependent and independent as well. For example; food is an external factor but controls internal environment, and at the same time unhealthy internal chemistry leads to abnormal food cravings. Centenarians go through a holistic aging process and have few common healthy lifestyle factors. In order to delay degenerative aging, we have to follow a nature oriented lifestyle with a special focus on mind. But in routine life, if we are health conscious we try to nourish our body with a healthy lifestyle but we always forget to nourish our mind and therefore suffer from mental aging. Every human being is born with a built-in passion for a hobby which is an anti-dote to mental stress. For holistic aging we have to allocate little time for our hobby, which will slow mental aging, therefore delay degenerative aging.

### *Signs of Holistic aging*

If you are between the age group of 40-60, you can use the following check list to assess your type of aging:

- Not suffering from degenerative diseases like cardiac, diabetes, obesity, hypertension, musculoskeletal disorder, liver disease, kidney disorders, COPD, metabolic disorders or cancer
- Not conscious of their age, and do not try to hide their age
- Not suffering from recurrent attacks of infection
- Least dependence on allopathic medicines
- Enjoys sound, and natural sleep
- Delayed physical signs of aging like wrinkling of facial, hand and feet skin, healthy shiny hair and delayed graying.
- Pleasant by temperament, youth enjoys their company and they wanted to follow their foot steps
- Depressive episodes are temporarily and they don't allow stress chemicals to infiltrate into the cell environment
- Good self-critic, open to criticism, always in a learning mode and have many mentors
- Never wanted to live in the past and try to avail present opportunities to its optimum
- Can laugh easily and find happy moments in stressful situations also
- Nature is at priority in terms of food, exercise, stress, relationships, and even in vacations
- Life plans are short term and they don't waste energy in long term planning
- Believe in intuition and gut feeling therefore well aligned with mind and spirit. Blessed with wisdom and have good connection with mind and spirit which delay their mental aging
- Leaves this world peacefully, with less pain and complications

- Miraculous phenomenon of spontaneous remission is seen in terminal stages of cancer, only in those individual who are aging holistically

***Signs of Degenerative aging***

- Show signs of weak immune system with medicine dependence
- Have a complex about their actual age
- Unhappy or dissatisfied with everything in life with lots of expectations from others
- Attention seekers
- Anti-nature and prefers short cuts regarding food, rest, exercise and even stress management
- Always in a race mode with a poor planning
- Irritable, short tempered, suffer from various complexes and critical about other people
- Confused in terms of belief, faith and conviction
- Stress induced facial skin wrinkling at an early age
- Lives in the past and fond of repeating past success stories
- Never carry charisma and people try to avoid their company
- Never attain enlightenment and speedy mental aging ultimately brings them to the mental level of a child
- Are dependent on food, drug, cigarette, or alcohol for stress relieve
- Death is due to multiple complications and terminal part of life is mostly debilitating

***SLP anti-aging tips are:***

- Self-awareness is an anti-aging key
- After having self-awareness, love and pamper yourself, allocate little time for your holistic self-grooming

- Try to follow a nature dependent, traditional lifestyle
- Food intake should be regulated on SLP 8- rules of correct eating
- Sound night sleep is a potent anti-aging tool
- Be honest with yourself and practice honesty, which will develop your charisma
- Try to incorporate your passion into your profession, so that it becomes a source of fulfillment
- Be clear in your faith, disbelieve leads to rapid physical aging

**6-The Dashboard of a human car**

A dashboard is a control panel placed in front of the driver of an automobile, housing instrumentation and controls for operation of the vehicle. Gauges such as a speedometer, tachometer(revolution counter), odometer (shows distance travelled) and fuel gauge, and indicators such as gearshift position, seat belt warning light, parking-brake-engagement. The human body also has a dash board but its gauges are spread all over the body. While driving a car we keep an eye on the dashboard to avoid accidents and malfunctioning of the engine. Same benefits we can get if we keep a check on the human body's dashboard. Speedometer and odometers are reflected in the nostrils, chest movement and breathing pattern. But the difference is that we keep an eye on a car's dash board but we never have a look at our gauges conveying very important life information and ultimately a person comes across a fatal ending.

It is an inherently well-known fact that each emotion can manifest quite differently in the body. Anger can cause elevated heart rate and flushed cheeks, fear can upset your stomach, and happiness may cause you to feel warm all over. A new study performed by researchers at Aalto University and the University of Tampere, both in Finland, topographically mapped where various emotions appear in the body, and found that each common emotion had a distinct topographical map, and also that these patterns were consistent across very different cultures. The study was performed online, with over 700 volunteers from Finland, Sweden and Taiwan. The researchers incited different emotional reactions in the volunteers, and then asked them to add color to a map of the human body, which they were provided with, to indicate where each specific emotion affected them physically in some way.

The most common emotions happiness, sadness, anger, etc. were found to have a strong physical presence. The observation that these topographical emotion maps remained much the same between the Finnish, Swedish and Taiwanese participants highlights the biological roots of these emotions, which seem to run much deeper than cultural conditioning. Lauri Nummenmaa, an assistant professor at Aalto University, says, "Emotions adjust not only our mental, but also our bodily states. This way they prepare us to react swiftly to the dangers, but also to the opportunities, such as pleasurable social interactions present in the environment. Awareness of the corresponding bodily changes may subsequently trigger the conscious emotional sensations, such as the feeling of happiness...The findings have major implications for our understanding of the functions of emotions and their bodily basis."

You can judge fuel or energy reserves from the facial expressions, skin color, and face wrinkles, according to Chinese face reading various body organs are reflected on the face. Forehead lines reflect the status of your gut, pigmentation on face indicates stress, grief, hormonal imbalance and a dysfunctional liver. Glow of facial skin is an indicator of optimum holistic health and slow aging of internal organs like liver, heart, kidney and brain. Eyes are windows through which you can assess the state of mind and soul. Sunken eyes indicate hyperactive liver and presence of chronic degenerative disorder in the body. Puffy upper lids show water retention, swollen lower eye border shows stomach dysfunction. Twitching of right eye shows abnormal alkaline body chemistry and left eye twitching shows stress, acidic ph and hyper liver. Chronic redness in eyes shows dysfunctional liver and overheating of the body. Drowsy, shrunken and drooped eyes indicate low B.P., low body temperature, low sugar and poor circulation to the head and neck area.

Dull eyes again indicate low vitality, healthy eyes are sparkling and wide open. Frequent blinking of eyes tell about the stress in the body. Well-formed nostrils indicate proper oxygenation of blood. Deformed or distended nostrils indicate blocked sinus and improper breathing leading to oxygen deficiency in the body. Color of lips tells quality of blood, vertical lines on the lips indicate suppressed immunity and gut disorders. Double chin indicates water retention. Rounded jaw line indicates obesity and saggy facial muscles. Heavy upper body indicates acidic ph of body tissues and heavy lower half of the body indicates hormonal imbalance, water retention, chronic stress, and wrong exercises. Cracked heel indicates a stomach disorder and poor immunity, deep cracks indicate serious immunity disorders.

Humans are blessed with an early disease warning sensors, giving various signals but we never listen to our body. Every disease has an incubation period which varies for acute and chronic diseases. During this period the battle between the pathogen and immune system is going on. The debris of this war are reflected on skin and various internal systems. The fast pace lifestyle and outer world commitments have totally disconnected us from the preventive health aspect of our holistic being.

## 7- Teens and holistic health

Whatever I have written here is the result of my 25 years of independent research, clinical experience and observation with children of all age group. A retrospective study was conducted during 12weeks of a weekly interactive workshop done on a group of 30 teenage boys and girls. The objective was to learn more closely about adolescence problems. Summary of that program was, none of the teens were happy with their parents and their life standards. They wanted to achieve quickly something in their life with a poor clarity about that something. Following is a guideline to learn about your teenager and how to handle their problems.

***How to identify teen's holistic health issues:***

Following signs and symptoms will give you an idea:

1. spends less time with the family or wants to be alc
2. spends more time with friends and in outings
3. likes junk food more than home cooked food
4. education grades starts declining

5. bullying others or is being bullied easily
6. can't sleep at night
7. always lethargic or fatigued
8. Has started losing weight or putting on weight in a disproportionate manner
9. unhappy with parents or other siblings
10. irritable and shows mood swings
11. suffers from a hyperactive mind syndrome HMS, it is a state of body which develops as a result of multiple mineral deficiencies and resulting imbalances, especially of calcium, magnesium, copper and zinc. Other important causative factor is that their blood oxygenation level is poor. In order to compensate for these deficiencies their mind is set in a race mode to get extra supply of nutrients and oxygen. This is a wakeful state and thought process is hyper-activated and mind starts wandering beyond the capacity of that teen, mostly at night. A child with hyperactive mind is always unhappy with the present life, lives in future or in the fantasy world, is restless and can't sleep at night. There are certain signs and symptoms which you can observe in a teen with
12. a hyper-active mind like poor immunity reflected in the form of frequent allergies, asthma, eczema, stomach disorders, young age high blood pressure, obesity, early mental maturity and suffers from fears and phobias. Some of the adolescence think their parents are conservative and do not carry sufficient wisdom therefore they do not talk to them. They try to involve themselves into bigger issues of the family, society or even the country but do not focusing on the age relevant issues

***Causes of HMS***

1. Maternal factors during pregnancy and post delivery
2. Formula milk fed babies
3. Poor infant care
4. Fed on processed or artificial foods in first two years of their life
5. Early age educational stress

6. Lot of expectations from the child regarding academic performance
7. Parental conflicts in presence of the child
8. Open discussion of family problems in front of the child
9. Over exposure to technology in the form of video games, cell phones, laptops and i-pads
10. Over exposure to TV and less outdoor activities

***HMS prevention and management***

1. Focus on pre-conception and conception diet
2. Focus on the child's food during the first year of life
3. Do not forget the role of touch, hugging and story telling
4. Parents should never discuss their issues in front of the child
5. Till the age of five years do not put your child in the stress of becoming the best student
6. Be their best friend and listen patiently to their everyday story, do not correct them. Develop their confidence and guide them accordingly
7. Ensure that the whole family takes dinner together and involve children in productive discussions.
8. Try to find their innate passion or hobby, it should be encouraged and groom it, this is their best inherent tool to switch off HMS
9. Encourage them to do sports, yoga or relaxing techniques
10. Try to strengthen their mind and spirit by telling them true spiritual stories

## 8-JET LAG AND FREQUENT FLYING DISORDERS

Jet lag is the result of biorhythm disruptions and a dysfunctional liver. Biorhythms are responsible for the harmony between the internal and external environment. Biorhythms are the set of sensors, which sense change in outside air, temperature, pressure, humidity, and food in relation to a human. Whenever they sense changes in above mentioned factors, the functions of liver are modified to align the internal environment with the external environment. Liver has to do many chemical changes to cope with the huge amount of external stress on the body. Liver has to do this readjustment to keep human body in a safe survival mode. Biological clock and pineal gland are important biorhythms which are connected to sun light or day/night rhythm. The jet lag is medically referred to as "*desynchronosis*, which is a physiological condition which results from alterations to the body's circadian rhythm.

***SLP causes***

Jet lag is a chrono-biologicalrelated problem, similar to issues often induced by shift work. When traveling across a number of time zones, the body clock will be out of synchronization with the destination time, as it experiences daylight and darkness contrary to the rhythms to which it has grown accustomed. The body's natural pattern is upset, as the rhythms that dictate times for eating, sleeping, hormone regulation and body temperature variations no longer correspond to the environment nor to each other in some cases. Other important external factors are the plane environment with artificial air pressure, artificial air composition, controlled temperature, high noise, and lot of artificial and processed foods served during the flight.

My opinion is processed foods served in wrong combinations at improper timings are a major factor in prolonging the physiological effects of jet lag or a frequent flyer disorders. I have got a chance to seeabout 10-15 young commercial pilots with bad holistic health. I have observed an early onset of aging in them. Pilots or crew members suffer more from mental aging because of their high stress job. If a person suffers from a speedy mental aging, the other two aging phenomenon like chronological or biological automatically set at an advanced pace, that is why most of them sufferfrom chronic degenerative disorders at an early age.

I have personally experienced the effects of jet lag on my body physiology by repeatedly checking my pulse while traveling to various international west/ east destinations. I observed that after about 2-3 hours of take off my liver pulse has become prominent, which indicated a stressed liver. Liver is the master biorhythm regulator but both are interdependent too, disruption of body clock sleep rhythm, subtle stress and abnormal food timings lead to a hyper-liver state which is responsible for multiple chemical adjustments to withstand this condition. If your basic health is good, then your liver will cope effectively with this massive shift in the biorhythms. If you have sub health or dysfunctional liver and you travel frequently then you have to be very careful.

***Symptoms***

The symptoms of jet lag can be quite varied, depending on the frequency of flying, flight time, and time of the day when journey starts. Other personal factors are medical status, personality, immune status and planning before traveling. An individual with sound medical health, calm mind and good planning abilities is going to suffer less and will not have residual jet lag effects. In a healthy person there are no Jet lag symptoms, otherwise symptoms can last for 3-10 days. Jet lag symptoms may include headaches, fatigue, irregular sleep patterns, insomnia, lower limbs swellings, numbness, disorientation, grogginess, depression, bloating, loss of appetite, diarrhea or constipation.

***SLP Management of jet lag***

It is possible to avoid or minimize the effects of jet lag by following some basic steps before, during, and after the flight.

Before the flight: It is recommended to visit the doctor to plan a coping strategy for medical conditions that require monitoring, including when to take medications or any other necessary detail.5-7 days prior to flight, become careful about your dietary intake, and try to follow SLP eight rules of correct eating. These rules will align your biorhythms and will try to bring liver in an optimum functional state. Focus on 6-8 hours night sleep, so that you don't carry any sleep debt. You can also start antioxidants, omega three fatty acids and probiotics two weeks prior to traveling.

During the flight: To avoid dehydration passengers are discouraged from taking alcoholic beverages and caffeine as caffeine disrupts sleeping schedules. It is recommended to drink plenty of water to help counteract the effects of the dry atmosphere inside the plane. Eat small portions of food and avoid heavy meal, satisfy your hunger by taking fruits, desserts, salads, nuts or dry fruits. Be careful regarding your food combinations i.e. strictly avoid taking drinks, juices, fruits, tea, coffee and desserts during or right after your meals. If you want to take these sugary foods take them 15-30 minutes before your next meal. This simple precaution will reduce the intensity of jet lag surely by 50%. Vitamin C rich fruits, juices or dairy products will facilitate liver in handling the chemistry of jet lag. Avoid using I pad, laptops or video games, watching movies or using cell phones during flight, their bright light will further disrupt your biorhythms. Listening to good music, doing recommended exercises, meditation, breathing exercises also help in decreasing flight related disorders on short and long term basis as well.

Upon arrival: Now your priority should be to focus on sleep and to cover your sleep debt by taking physical rest. By getting extra sleep you will be out of jet lag within few hours. Another helpful way to minimize jet lag is to adapt to the local time and eat accordingly. Also, exposure to sunlight is helpful, do follow SLP eight rules of diet correction upon arrival as well. Soups, fish, nuts, and dairy intake will help in quick recovery.

### *Suggestions for airline administration*

Airline administration should take the responsibility of their in- flight staff and should support them in managing holistic health. Below mentioned few important steps can improve the health of pilot, crew members and those, who fly frequently.

- An Integrated physician should certify the holistic health of pilot and crew members, when selected for these jobs.
- Their holistic checkup should be done quarterly.
- A family interaction will be required to assess the personality of that person in the home environment.
- Their lifestyle should be nature oriented.
- Airline staff food and foods served during flight should be natural and prepared in a healthy cooking manner.
- Fish, nuts, berries, milk, cheese and yogurt should form major portion of their personal and passengerfood plan.
- Yoga, breathing exercise, stretching should be part of a routine inter-continental flight and for these activities little space should be allocated in plane. 10-15 minutes of these exercises for the crew and for the frequently flying passengers during flight will reduce the effects of jet lag.

## 9-An observational comparative lifestyle study

In 2013 I got a chance to travel to USA, UK, and Thailand from 17th June to 14September 2013. This trip was of academic interest besides holidays. In June I got a chance to do a lifestyle modification certification course from Harvard University. Later I had a brief tour of best USA universities like MIT, Berkeley, Stanford, UCLA, and few more in California State. The enlightening aura of these prestigious institutes have energized my mind and soul. During this twelve weeks period I compared the lifestyles of various cultures and countries. My definition of Lifestyle is composed of, a person's dietary habits, the amount of nocturnal sleep, stress management, exercise and behavior. Below is an account of that observational study which encompasses comparison of above mentioned factors and few more lifestyle factors as well.

***American Lifestyle***

I found that Americans have worst eating habits, they eat mostly processed foods and are very casual about their eating habits especially breakfast. They take ice cold water and juices with meals which I have learnt is a strong disease causing factor. They take coffee with food especially with their breakfast, which spoils the nutrients of their food, so their food combinations are lethal. Alcohol intake, drugs and smoking is a common practice, which reflects their poorly managed stress. Their fast pace lifestyle has led to a disturb family life and conjoint or nuclear family life concept is rare. They think that doing exercise is as an important healthcare tool, this myth is further adding to their chronic diseases. The nocturnal sleep quality is average. They allocate little time for collective religious, traditional or culture promoting activities. In shopping areas you do not find local products, mostly you find "made in China" products. Americans are very casual about what they wear. A natural lifestyle and an unhealthy eating habits have made their skin look bad, it is pigmented, tone less and we can see early age wrinkling. American have high obesity incidence, and teen age obesity is quite common. They are the leaders in various researches, modern founder of holistic sciences, and work on many humanitarian projects.

***British lifestyle***

I found British people dietary habits slightly better than Americans. English breakfast composition is quite healthy and they prefer to take tea instead of coffee, though most of them are not into breakfast habit. They are not fond of ice cold water and take less drinks with foods.

Alcohol intake, and smoking is a common practice. Stress level is high, people appreciate nuclear family concept but number of single mothers is high. People are health conscious and lot of alternative therapists are licensed to practice. I have not observed collective promotion of religion, culture and tradition activities. I got a chance to watch a Shakespeare play 'Romeo and Juliet'organized by drama society of Cambridge University. British people are conscious about their routine dresses and careful about formal dress as well. Their poor nutrition and tanning craze has made their skin pigmented, saggy and can see early onset of face wrinkles. The incidence of obesity is comparatively low. I found very few international conferences as compare to USA.

***Thai lifestyle***

I observed that Thai people are careful about what they eat, and their staple diet is rice, noodle, soup or sea food. They do take traditional breakfast and they are not fond of English breakfast. They are less dependent on tea, coffee, cigarette or alcohol and prefer to take herbal teas during the day. They appeared less stressful and as a nation follow a simple lifestyle. The concept of a nuclear and a conjoint family prevails in their society. They prefer to wear their traditional dress and promote their Thai silk. They follow Buddhism, and you can see the statue of Lord Buddha on all hill tops. Government promotes Thai culture by organizing high budget plays, I got a chance to watch stage show Siam Nirmit which was good. Thai are very loyal to their queen and she is known as mother of the nation. Their labor class is hard working and honest, one of my family member lost I pad in the Thai airline and it was found scratch less after two weeks. Traditional holistic sciences are common and people prefer this treatment. I have observed less obesity and their skin health is good.

***Pakistani lifestyle***

I found Pakistanis are very careless about what they eat, and their eating habits have gone worst during last 15-20 years. Breakfast intake is not their preference and normally opt for processed and packaged foods. Generally natural foods are at preference, but doctors have confused the nation. During the day intake of tea, biscuits, coffee is a common practice and dependence on cigarette, alcohol and drug is increasing by the day. Due to a bad political system general public stress level is high, which is leading to multiple malpractices in every segment of society. People now are more into an in natural lifestyle but Pakistanis still carry a nuclear and conjoint family concept. They prefer to wear traditional and western dresses both, and Pakistani cotton is very popular in local and international market. It is a resilient nation, labor class is very hard working and creative but due to poverty moral values are getting compromised. Conventional medical system dominates and health standards are getting bad. Moderate obesity prevails and general skin condition is good. Despite security threats multiple international cultural, literary, sports, scientific and medical conferences and exhibitions are being organized, an indicator that Pakistanis as a nation are getting stronger.

# BIBLIOGRAPHY

## CHAPTER: 1


1. www.crescentlife.com
2. http://en.wikipedia.org/wiki/Holistic_science
3. http://en.wikipedia.org/wiki/Holism
4. http://en.wikipedia.org/wiki/Alternative_medicine
5. http://en.wikipedia.org/wiki/Institute_of_Medicine
6. http://en.wikipedia.org/wiki/National_Center_for_Complementary_and_Alternative_Medicine
7. http://en.wikipedia.org/wiki/Quantum_biology
8. David Peters, Editorial , journal of holistic healthcare
9. Michael Wayne(2005), Quantum Integrated Medicine Page 43, 61, 63, 117, 129
10. Revd Dr Jeremy Swayne(Dec.2008),JHH, Medicine and the healing
11. Deepak Chopra (1990), Quantum Healing
12. Live Science July 22, 2009
13. PLoS One July 16, 2009; 4(7): e6256 [Free Full-Text Article]
14. http//articles.mercola.com/sites
15. Mirka Knaster(1996), Discovering The Body's WisdomPage 9, 46, 47, 48, 49,
16. Dr. Roger J.Williams(1981), Nutrition Against Disease
17. Jeffrey S. Bland, Ph.D,HealthComm International, Inc Gig Harbor, WA
18. Integrative Medicine • Vol. 6, No. 3 • Jun/Jul 2007 *Neustadt and Pieczenik—Patient-Handout*
19. The Death Of Allopathic Nutrition, Address made to The Society for Orthomolecular Health-Medicine (OHM), March 1, 1998


## CHAPTER: 2

1. http://en.wikipedia.org/wiki/Circadian_rhythm
2. http://en.wikipedia.org/wiki/Biorhythm
3. http://www.holistichealthtopics.com/HMG/body.html
4. Michael Smolensky and Lynne Lamberg(2000), The Body Clock Guide to better health
5. Weston A. Price(2006), Nutrition and Physical Degeneration
6. Mol Cell Endocrinol. 2006 May22 De Leersnyder H,
7. mercola.com
8. Verne Verona, Nature's cancer fighting foods
9. enzinearticles.com
10. biomedix.com
11. http://en.wikipedia.org/wiki/Thermoregulation
12. *RawFoodExplained.com*
13. The Importance Of Body Temperature by Dr. Herbert M. Shelton
14. Los Angeles Times October 9,2006
15. CBC. CaNews
16. Katie Singer The Garden of Fertility
17. Westonapricefoundation.org
18. Top 10 Health Benefits of a Good Night's Sleep, By Mark Stibich, Ph.D., About.com


**CHAPTER: 3**


1. Elizabeth Lipski(1996), Digestive Wellness

2. www.healingedge.net
3. ChineseMedicineBlog.net, Traditional Chinese Medicine and Acupuncture Health information by West TCM, Vancouver/Langley Canada
4. My Personal Journey of Healing, julia Chang www.sensiblehealth.com
5. Practice of Natural Therapeutics by Henry Lindlahar, M.D
6. By Helmholtz Association of German Research Centres 9 sep2008
7. Rachel Nowak (April 2002),Liver's sieving declines with age
8. *From the Centre for Hepatology, Department of Medicine, Royal Free Campus, Royal Free and University College Medical School, London,*
9. Scientists find link between ageing livers and heart disease, ABC Online, Tuesday, May 7, 2002
10. YALE Bulletin& Calender, Discovery may yield new therapies for liver disease July 21, 2000
11. Robert Ziegler, Evolutionary Patterns of Living Systems
12. Naturism: Naked Beneath Your Clothing by John Veltheim
13. NAKATANI K(Osaka City Univ., Osaka, Jpn) KANEDA K(Osaka City Univ., Osaka, Jpn)
14. http://www.healthy.net/scr/article.aspx?Id=733 (3.1.13)
15.


**CHAPTER: 4**


1. Dr. Shigekazu HIGUCHI `Living Environments and Human Biological Rhythms'Sunday, 25th August, 2002
2. American Journal Of Clinical Nutrition August 2006
3. http://ezinearticles.com/?Benefits-Of-A-Healthy-Lifestyle
4. http://www.schoolforchampions.com/health/lifestyle_elderly.htm

**CHAPTER: 5**


1. en.wikipedia.org/wiki/Natural_food
2. en.wiktionary.org/wiki/natural_food
3. en.wikipedia.org/wiki/Whole_foods
4. http://en.wikipedia.org/wiki/Organic_food
5. http://en.wikipedia.org/wiki/Seasonal_food
6. Patrick Holford(1999), The Optimum Bible, The Crossing Press
7. Phyllis A. Balch, James A. Balch(2000), Prescription for Nutritional Healing
8. Paul Pitchford(2002), Healing with Whole Foods, North Atlantic Books Berkeley, California
9. Deepak Chopra(1993), Ageless body, Timeless Mind, Harmony Books, New York
10. http://en.wikipedia.org/wiki/Intuitive_eating
11. http://altmedicine.about.com/cs/healthessentials/a/Intuitive.htm
12. Your Body Works Like a Clock? Published by CHAN LEE PENG October 3, 2007, Category: Human Biology
13. http://biology.about.com/library/organs/blpathodigest.htm
14. http://www.faqs.org/nutrition/A-Ap/Appetite.html
15. http://www.faqs.org/nutrition /Ca-De/Cravings.html
16. Obesity (2009) 17 11, 2100–2102. doi:10.1038/oby.2009.264
17. John M. de Castro[2], The Time of Day of Food Intake Influences Overall Intake in Humans[1] , *Department of Psychology, University of Texas at El Paso, El Paso, TX 79968- 0553*
18. By Michelle Gelok, CBC News, Health isn't just what you eat, but when
19. http://foodpsychology.cornell.edu/new_findings/comfort_food.htm
20. http://www.ajcn.org/cgi/content/abstract/90/3/707S
21. http://jones.kaist.ac.kr/content/gene-involved-food-preferences-larval-drosophila- melanogaster

22. http://www.parentingscience.com/prenatal-learning-about-food.html

23. http://biology.about.com/library/organs/blpathodigest2.htm

24. Circadian rhythms in human salivary flow rate and composition by C. Dawes http://www.ncbi.nlm.nih.gov/pmc/articles/PMC1331668/

25. http://www.rawfoodexplained.com/digestive-physiology-and-food-combining/the-crux-of-food-combining.html

26. http://www.natural-remedies-only.com/food-combining.html

27. Connie Bennett,with Stephen T. Sinatra, Sugar Shock, by Berkley Books

28. http://www.authorviews.com/authors/bennett/obd.htmhttp://www.pakmed.net/academic/ayu06.htm

29. http://www.ehow.com/about_5232775_allergy-rotation-diet plan.html

*30.* Think You're Drinking Enough Water? By Leroy R. Perry, Jr. Condensed from *PARADE* http://www.naturodoc.com/library/nutrition/water.htm

31. Recommended Water Intake A Myth by Kate Melville http://www.scienceagogo.com/news/20020711213420data_trunc_sys.shtml

32. http://www.liaoning Proper Way to Drink Water?

33. http://www.mapi.com/en/articles/skinincjuly00.html

34. http://en.wikipedia.org/wiki/water_therapy

35. http://en.wikipedia.org/wiki/Hydrotherapy

36. Theresa Vernon , Metal and the mind, http://www.westonaprice.org/Metals-and-the-Mind.html

37. Nature Neuroscience May 2008; 11(5):572-8

38. http://articles.mercola.com/sites/articles/archive/2008/05/27/why-traumas-can-haunt-and-sabotage-your-health-for-years.aspx

39. http://en.wikipedia.org/wiki/Medical_sign

40. http://sportsmedicine.about.com/cs/overtraining/

41. Genetics and Molecular Medicine,

42.http://www.ama-assn.org/ama/pub/physician-resources/medical-science/genetics-molecular-medicine/family-history.shtml

43. http://www.bodymap.com/bodymap.html , visited on 3rd April 2010

44. Nature vs. Nurture, Kimberly Powell, Are We Really Born That Way

45.http://www.integratedmedicine.eu/pulse_analysis.html

46.http://en.wikipedia.org/wiki/Pulse_diagnosis

*47.* http://www.thenaturalguide.com/supplements.htm

*48.* http://www.responsibletechnology.org/gmo-basics/gmos-in-food

49. http://drbenkim.com/drink-too-much-water-dangerous.html

**CHAPTER: 6**

http://www.neshealth.com/en-gb/homepage.aspx

http://www.neshealth.com/en-gb/about-us.aspx

**CHAPTER: 7**

**1.** Theresa Vernon, Lac Metals and the Mind

**CHAPTER: 9**

1. en.wikipedia.org/wiki/Lifestyle_diseases

50.http://naturalhealthperspective.com/home/civilization.html

51.http://wiki.answers.com/Q/Top_10_list_of_lifestyle_diseases

52.http://www.associatedcontent.com/article/2010684/lifestyle_causes_of_male_infertility.html?cat=52

53.http://www.copperwiki.org/index.php/Lifestyle_Diseases

54.http://www.diseasescausedbyfungi.com/4737/lifestyle-diseases-list/

55.http://www.medscape.com/viewarticle/522390

56.http://www.mayoclinic.com/health/heart-disease-prevention/WO00041/NSECTIONGROUP=2

57.http://womenshealth.about.com/cs/cancerprevention/a/cancerprevent.htm

58.http://www.ncbi.nlm.nih.gov/pubmed/12570328

59.http://www.westonaprice.org/images/pdfs/Trifold-Butter2009.pdf

60.http://www.westonaprice.org/images/pdfs/trifold-realmilk2010.pdf

61.http://en.wikipedia.org/wiki/Orthomolecular_medicine

62.http://library.thinkquest.org/24206/orthomolecular-medicine.html

63.http://www.naturalscience.org/fileadmin/portabledocuments/fact_sheet_no_01.pdf

64.http://www.health-science-spirit.com/electropollution.html

**65.**http://articles.mercola.com/sites/articles/archive/2010/05/18/microwave-hazards.aspx

66.http://redandhoney.com/2013/02/is-your-mattress-toxic-hidden-dangers-in-your-sleeping-environment/#sthash.WVuSck0Y.dpuf

67.http://www.myessentia.com/learn/glues-toxic-components

68. **www.enn.com/pollution/article/33754**

69. http://www.cbn.com/CBNnews/108278.aspx

70. 5-http://www.cbc.ca/news/technology/disposable-diapers-are-they-dangerous-1.888074

71. 6-http://www.westonaprice.org/childrens-health/cloth-diapers-made-simple?

**CHAPTER: 10**

1. http://www.buzzle.com/articles/risk-factors-of-obesity.html
2. http://www.foodnavigator-usa.com/Financial-Industry/Study-finds-obesity-lifestyle-links

3. http://www.onepakistan.com/lifestyle/articles/health/3088-Childhood-obesity-easier-prevent-than-treat.html
4. http://www.westonaprice.org/msg-updates/298-obesity-epidemic-and-msg.html
5. http://www.calciumlie.net/
6. .http://www.westonaprice.org/mentalemotional-health/1573-metals-and-the-mind.html
7. **http://experiencelife.com/article/body-positive/**


**CHAPTER: 11**


1. The Long Hollow Tube: A Primer on the Digestive System, by Sally Fallon and Mary G. Enig, PhD
2. Digestive Wellness by Elizabeth Lipski, 1996
3. How To Restore Digestive Health, Written by Written by Jordan S. Rubin, NMD, CNC
4. http://www.altmd.com/Articles/Ayurveda-for-Digestive Disorders
5. http://www.healthsquare.com/fgpd/fg4ch05p2.htm
6. http://www.medicinenet.com/gastroesophageal_reflux_disease_gerd/article.htm
7. http://www.holisticprimarycare.net/topics/topics-a-g/digestive-health


**CHAPTER: 12**


1. http://www.ehow.com/about_5568242_psychological-associated-coronary-artery-disease.html
2. http://psy.psychiatryonline.org/cgi/content/full/41/4/372
3. http://www.lifepositive.com/Mind/Emotions/Metaphysical_causes_of_disease_and_how_to_deal_with_them32004.asp
4. http://www.westonaprice.org/brochures.html

5. http://www.westonaprice.org/modern-diseases/miscellaneous/597-oxidative-stress.html
6. http://www.lifepositive.com/body/body-holistic/heart/heart.asp
7. By Ralph E. Holsworth, DO, and Jonathan V. Wright, MD - Vol. 13, No. 2. Summer, 2012,

**CHAPTER: 13**

1. http://www.westonaprice.org/nutrition-greats/599-francis pottenger.html
2. http://www.realmilk.com/abstractsmilk.html
3. http://www.westonaprice.org/modern-diseases/digestivedisorders/1956-acid-reflux-a-red-flag.html
4. http://www.westonaprice.org/notes-from-yesteryear/1735-100-years-before-weston-price.htmlhttp://www.westonaprice.org/environmental-toxins.html
5. http://articles.mercola.com/sites/articles/archive/2000/09/24/drugs-lungs.aspx
6. The New EnglandJournal of Medicine 1999;341:848-849.
7. American Journal of Epidemiology 1999;149:306-314.
8. First World Congress on Lung Health and Respiratory Diseases Florence, Italy, August-September 2000
9. http://www.paganspath.com/meta/tbreathg.htm

**CHAPTER: 14**


1. http://www.eurekalert.org/pub_releases/2010-06/uoh-rau062410.php
2. http://www.sciencemag.org/products/adv_20051104.dtl
3. http://www.thenhf.com/articles_394.htm
4. http://www.enchantedmind.com/html/science/quantum_brain.html
5. http://www.westonaprice.org/book-reviews/thumbs-up/965-gut-and-psychology-syndrome.html
6. http://www.westonaprice.org/soy-alert/673-soy-and-the-brain.html
7. http://www.westonaprice.org/environmental-toxins/249-fluoride-worse-than-we-thought.html
8. http://www.westonaprice.org/modern-diseases/digestive-disorders/1956-acid-reflux-a-red-flag.html
9. http://www.westonaprice.org/modern-diseases/metabolic-disorders/591-copper-zinc-imbalance.html
10. Jean Carper (2000) Your Miracle Brain
11. Am J Epidemiol 1997;146:1037-45. depression; electromagnetic fields; epidemiology
12. http://www.westonaprice.org/mentalemotional-health/1571-pursuit-of-happiness.html


**CHAPTER: 15**


1. http://www.westonaprice.org/food-features/513-why-broth-is-beautiful.html
2. http://www.betterbones.com/blog/post/High-calcium-intake-does-not-prevent-bone-fractures.aspx
3. http://www.betterbones.com/blog/post/Natural-treatment-for-osteoporosis.aspx
4. http://www.betterbones.com/bonenutrition/20keybonenutrients.aspx
5. Dr. Susan E. Brown, PhD, *Better Bones Basics*

6. http://articles.mercola.com/sites/articles/archive/2004/02/28/vitamin-d-part-twenty.aspx
7. http://articles.mercola.com/sites/articles/archive/2008/06/28/do-arthritis-drugs-cause-cancer.aspx
8. http://articles.mercola.com/sites/articles/archive/2008/09/25/arthritis-drugs-cause-fatal-fungal-infections.aspx
9. http://www.rense.com/general70/worrisome.htm
10. American Journal Clinical Nutrition February, 2003;77:495-503
11. Do You Really Need Calcium to Build Strong Bones? Posted By Dr. Mercola | June 07 2003
12. Jean Carper (2000) Your Miracle Brain,pg152
13. WebMD September 2, 2010
14. USA Today September 4, 2008
15. New York Times June 5, 2008
16. http://www.nof.org/aboutosteoporosis/positivethoughts/thinkingfeeliggood
17. http://www.nof.org/aboutosteoporosis/prevention/healthyliving

**CHAPTER: 16**

1. Joan Borysenko, A Woman's Book of Life
2. Wise Traditions in Food, Farming and the Healing Arts, the quarterly magazine of the WAPFWinter 2000.
3. Natural Health for Fertility.com
4. http://www.preconception.com/articles/preconception/chinese-medicine-and-fertility-1227/

5. http://www.naturalbirthandbabycare.com/preconception-nutrition.html
6. http://www.parentingweekly.com/preconception/preconception_information/traditional_chinese_medicine_fertility.htm
7. http://www.getting-pregnant.com/preconception-nutrition.html

**CHAPTER: 17**

1. http://en.wikipedia.org/wiki/Endocrine_system
2. http://www.buzzle.com/articles/endocrine-system-function.html
3. http://en.wikipedia.org/wiki/Metabolic_syndrome
4. http://www.managingpcos.org.au/content/view/38/65/
5. Modern Diseases - Metabolic Disorders written by Bruce Rind, Friday, 19 June 2009
6. http://hypothyroidismdiet.net/
7. http://www.ehow.com/way_5479278_natural-thyroid-cures.html
8. Natural Thyroid Cures | eHow.com http://www.ehow.com/way_5479278_natural-thyroid-cures.html#ixzz1BH
9. http://www.infertilityphysician.com/androgen/pcos.html
10. New York Times October 17, 2006
11. Spartanburg Herald-Journal October 17, 2006

**CHAPTER: 18**

1. http://www.globalaging.org/armedconflict/countryreports/general/ik.htm
2. http://list.email.info.westonaprice.org/childrens-health/337-child-violence-is-malnutrition-the-cause.html
3. http://www.mercola.com/downloads/bonus/adhd-signs-treatment/report.aspx
4. http://articles.mercola.com/sites/articles/archive/2003/04/09/child-care.aspx

5. http://articles.mercola.com/sites/articles/archive/2008/01/17/scientific-proof-that-your-childhood-traumas-are-a-major-factor-in-your-all-your-illnesses.aspx
6. www.grandmotherproject.org.
7. Mothering March/April 2003
8. American Journal of Preventive Medicine May 1998; 14(4): 245-258
9. The Adverse Childhood Experiences (ACE) Study
10. http://www.askdrsears.com/html/4/t042500.asp#T042506
11. http://www.brighthub.com/health/alternative-medicine/articles/60541.aspx
12. http://www.brighthub.com/health/alternative-medicine/articles/29004.aspx
13. http://raisingchildren.net.au/articles/autism_spectrum_disorder_causes.html/context/1037
14. Huffington Post August 11, 2009
15. http://www.shirleys-wellness-cafe.com/asthma.htm
16. http://www.healthyfutures.com/allergysensitivitysolutions/parentchild/childfoodallergies
17.
18. : http://www.dailymail.co.uk/health/article-1322132/Bedroom-chemicals-raise-childs-allergy-risk-180.html#ixzz1BsLoKrtQ
19. http://www.angelfire.com/md2/moodyfamily/formula.html
20. http://www.westonaprice.org/childrens-health/successful-breastfeeding-and-successful-alternatives

**CHAPTER: 19**

1. Daily Mail October 15, 2010
2. Nature Reviews Cancer October 2010; 10: 728-733
3. Cancer September 1977; 40(3): 1358-1362
4. http://articles.mercola.com/sites/articles/archive/2010/12/03/cancer-not-found-in-ancient-mummies-appears-to-be-recent-disease.aspx

5. http://articles.mercola.com/sites/articles/archive/2011/05/21/drs-stanislaw-and-gregory-burzynski-on-cancer.aspx
6. http://articles.mercola.com/sites/articles/archive/2011/01/10/trouble-sleeping-caused-by-glowing-gadgets.aspx
7. http://www.goodhealthinfo.net/cancer/holistic_approach_cancer.htm
8. http://alternative.holplus.com/Alternative/Holistic Medicine/193518950.html

CHAPTER 20

1. http://www.healthy-holistic-living.com/vitamin-d-deficiency.html#ixzz2D0mH5Gz
2. http://www.healthy-holistic-living.com/benefits-of-vitamin-d.html#ixzz2D0nG1vXf
3. http://www.healthy-holistic-living.com/benefits-of-vitamin-d.html#ixzz2D0nnY1Af
4. http://en.wikipedia.org/wiki/Vitamin_D
5. http://hinduism.about.com/od/books/fr/agelessbody.htm
6. http://hinduism.about.com/od/bookextracts/a/longivity.htm
7. http://www.doctoroz.com/videos/48-hour-weekend-cleanse
8. http://www.mayoclinic.org/diseases-conditions/allergies/basics/definition/con-20034030
9. http://www.webmd.com/parenting/teen-abuse-cough-medicine-9/behavior-problems
10. http://sofs.hubpages.com/hub/Its-hard-on-teens
11. http://www.westonaprice.org/childrens-health/child-violence-is-malnutrition-the-cause
12. http://www.realmilk.com/

# Index

C



D



E

S

T



U



V



W



Y



Z

**BACK PAGE**

Shagufta Liver Program

**About the author**

An international and nationally Integrated Family Physician and Correct Eating activist. She does healing by prescribing a personalized lifestyle modification program by balancing biorhythms and rejuvenating liver. She offers individualized nutritional healing programs for clients throughout the country and abroad. The beauty of her nutrition program is that client food preference is the basis and there is no check on the calorie and quantity of food intake. She regularly updates herself from various Integrated Medicine and Lifestyle Medicine CME programs especially from Harvard University USA. She is a famous blogger, and a frequent speaker at various educational institutions, public seminars, health clubs, various television shows and lives in Lahore, Pakistan.

www.picchls.com

Made in United States
North Haven, CT
28 July 2025

71080020R00280